R. Gupta's®
POPULAR MASTER GUIDE

Supreme Court of India

Jr. Court Attendant
Chamber Attendant (R)

Recruitment Exam

- Specialised Study Material Prepared by Experts
- Numerous Solved Multiple Choice Questions

2019 EDITION

Ramesh Publishing House, New Delhi

Published by
O.P. Gupta *for* Ramesh Publishing House

Admin. Office
12-H, New Daryaganj Road, Opp. Officers' Mess,
New Delhi-110002 ☏ 23261567, 23275224, 23275124

E-mail: info@rameshpublishinghouse.com
Website: www.rameshpublishinghouse.com

Showroom
● Balaji Market, Nai Sarak, Delhi-6 ☏ 23253720, 23282525
● 4457, Nai Sarak, Delhi-6, ☏ 23918938

Book Code: R-1963

ISBN: 978-93-87918-02-3

HSN Code: 49011010

METHOD OF SELECTION

Selection shall be on the basis of Written Test based on Objective Type Question paper in bilingual (English and Hindi), as per details given below. The duration of Written Test will be 1½ hours.

Part	Subject	No. of Questions
A	General Intelligence & Reasoning	25
B.	Numerical Aptitude	25
C.	General English	25
D.	General Awareness	25

- There will be separate Written tests for the posts of Junior Court Attendant and Chamber Attendant(R).

- The candidates will be shortlisted for appearing in the Written Test on the basis of their qualifications, specialized knowledge and experience in the field of Driving/Cooking/Electrician/Carpentry, House-keeping work, watch & ward, security and caretaking work etc.

- The candidates who get shortlisted on the basis of their performance in the Written Test will be required to appear in a skill test in the field of Driving/Cooking/Electrician/Carpentry etc., to adjudge their proficiency in such a particular field, as the case may be. The Skill Test will be only qualifying in nature.

CONTENTS

Model Paper (Solved) 1-8

● **GENERAL INTELLIGENCE & REASONING** 1-68

● **NUMERICAL APTITUDE** 1-40

● **GENERAL ENGLISH**..1-48

● **GENERAL AWARENESS**..1-40

Supreme Court of India
Jr. Court Attendant & Chamber Attendant (R)
Recruitment Exam

General Awareness

1. With which field is the Oscar Award Associated?
   A. Literature   B. Music
   C. Movie   D. Sports

2. Which state is bounded by Bangladesh on three sides?
   A. Mizoram   B. Meghalaya
   C. Tripura   D. West Bengal

3. As per census 2011, total population of India is:
   A. 115.01 Crore   B. 125.05 Crore
   C. 121.08 Crore   D. 130.06 Crore

4. Which one of the following peaks is the highest?
   A. Everest   B. Nanda Devi
   C. Kanchenjunga   D. Nanga Parbat

5. Who invented revolver:
   A. E.G. Otis   B. Frank Whittle
   C. Samuel Colt   D. Charles Goodyear

6. 'Pedogenesis' refers to:
   A. the process of continuous erosion
   B. the process of production in plants
   C. the process of soil formation
   D. the process of reproduction in animals

7. The ozone layer in the atmosphere:
   A. causes rainfall
   B. creates pollution
   C. protects life on earth from ultraviolet radiation
   D. produces oxygen in the atmosphere

8. McMahon line is the line that divides:
   A. India and China
   B. India and Myanmar
   C. India and Nepal
   D. India and Bangladesh

9. Which is the longest river of the world?
   A. Nile   B. Ganga
   C. Amazon   D. Mississipi

10. Which of the following rivers does *not* form a delta?
    A. Kaveri   B. Godavari
    C. Krishna   D. Narmada

11. In India the 26th January is:
    A. Independence Day
    B. Revolution Day
    C. Republic Day
    D. Parliament Day

12. Area-wise which is the biggest state of India?
    A. Rajasthan
    B. Uttar Pradesh
    C. Madhya Pradesh
    D. Maharashtra

13. Who is the author of the famous book "Republic"?
    A. Plato   B. Aristotle
    C. Rousseau   D. Hobbes

14. Where is the headquarters of United Nations located?
    A. Washington   B. Geneva
    C. New York   D. Paris

15. The Sardar Sarovar Project is built on the river:

A. Tapti B. Godavari
C. Narmada D. Krishna

16. The Supreme Commander of the Indian armed forces is:
A. Prime Minister B. President
C. Home Minister D. Defence Minister

17. Who gave the slogan 'Jai Hind' to India?
A. L.B. Shastri B. S.C. Bose
C. M.K. Gandhi D. J.L. Nehru

18. The members of the Rajya Sabha are elected for
A. whole life B. six years
C. five years D. two years

19. Who called Gandhiji as "Mahatma"?
A. Jawahar Lal Nehru
B. G.D. Birla
C. Rabindra Nath Tagore
D. Gopal Krishna Gokhale

20. With which sport is Aagha Khan Cup associated?

A. Football B. Table Tennis
C. Volly ball D. Hockey

21. Jallianwala Bagh massacre took place in the city:
A. Meerut B. Agra
C. Amritsar D. Lahore

22. The first railway line in India was started in the year:
A. 1853 B. 1850
C. 1840 D. 1890

23. The battle field of Plassey is situated in:
A. Bihar B. Andhra Pradesh
C. Odisha D. West Bengal

24. Which of the following is the oldest Veda?
A. Samveda B. Yajurveda
C. Rigveda D. Atharaveda

25. The Universal donor group of blood is:
A. O B. A
C. B D. AB

General Intelligence & Reasoning

26. If the letters in ACE are coded as 135 and in BAD are coded as 214, then how can BED be coded?
A. 215 B. 254
C. 245 D. 345

27. If in a code language AND is written as BOE and RENT is written as SFOU, then how is DEAF written in that code?
A. EFBG B. FEBG
C. EGBF D. PQRS

Directions (Qs. 28 and 29): *Find the missing numbers/letters from the given responses.*

28. 5, 9, 13, 17, ..., 25.
A. 27 B. 23
C. 21 D. 19

29. BMO, CNP, DOQ, ...
A. FAT B. EPR
C. EOR D. BNS

30. Which one of the given responses would be meaningful order of the following?
1. Adult 2. Child

3. Infant 4. Boy
A. 2, 3, 1, 4 B. 3, 2, 4, 1
C. 1, 2, 3, 4 D. 3, 4, 2, 1

31. Which one of the given responses would be meaningful order of the following words?
1. Wall 2. Clay
3. House 4. Room
5. Bricks
A. 5, 2, 1, 4, 3 B. 2, 5, 4, 1, 3
C. 2, 5, 1, 4, 3 D. 1, 2, 3, 4, 5

Directions (Qs. 32 and 33): *Find the odd word/ letters/number from the given responses.*

32. A. refuse – accept B. give – take
C. cold – cool D. reward – punishment

33. A. 20 B. 64
C. 27 D. 125

Directions (Qs. 34 - 37): *Select the related letters/ word/number from the given alternatives.*

34. ABC : 123 : : BCD : ?
A. 456 B. 234
C. 345 D. 243

35. Physician : Treatment : : Judge : ?
A. Judgement   B. Lawyer
C. Court   D. Management

36. 12 : 15 : : 24 : ?
A. 36   B. 34
C. 30   D. 18

37. Long : length : : broad : ?
A. Breadth   B. Bread
C. Breed   D. Spread

38. Find the missing number.
594, 198, 66, _____
A. 33   B. 22
C. 44   D. 11

39. F is the brother of A and A is the daughter of B. How is F related to B?
A. Brother-in-law   B. Son
C. Uncle   D. Son-in-law

40. Arun travels 10 km towards North. From there he travels 7 km towards South. Explain his final position from the starting point A.
A. He is 3 km South of A
B. He is 4 km North of A
C. He is 3 km North of A
D. He is 1 km South of A

41. A word given in capital letters is followed by four answer words. Out of these, only one cannot be formed by using the letters of the given word. Find out the word.
INTERNATIONAL
A. NOTE   B. ALONE
C. LATER   D. RADIO

42. Keep the odd one out. (Identify that one which does not belong to the group)
A. Seek   B. Sang
C. Went   D. Came

43. Keep the odd one out.
A. Maharashtra   B. Chennai
C. Kerala   D. Punjab

Directions (Qs. 44 - 46): *Study the information given below and answer the given questions.*

In a certain code—

"facing problems with health" is coded as "mip hit ngi snk"

"health problem on rise" is coded as "hit sa rtv mip"

"rise with every challenge" is coded as "snk rtv lne riy"

"facing challenge each day" is coded as "ngi riy ncp hus"

44. What does the code "lne" stand for?
A. Facing   B. With
C. Every   D. Rise

45. What does the code "riy rtv snk" stand for?
A. Rise above challenge
B. Rise health challenge
C. Day rise challenge
D. With rise challenge

46. Which of the following is the code for "facing"?
A. ncp   B. rtv
C. ngi   D. snk

47. In a class, Sneha is 4th from the bottom. Harsha is 10th from the top. In between them there are 6 students with various ranks. How many students are there in the class?
A. 25   B. 20
C. 30   D. 28

48. Identify the one which does not belong to the group:
A. Mend   B. Rectify
C. Trouble   D. Repair

49. Identify the one which does not belong to the group:
A. Syndicate Bank   B. Corporation Bank
C. South Indian Bank   D. Canara Bank

50. Five students are sitting in a row. P is sitting between M and R. M is sitting next to B who is sitting on the extreme left and Q is sitting next to R. Who are sitting adjacent to M?
A. B and P   B. P and Q
C. P and R   D. R and Q

Numerical Aptitude

51. A man makes his upward journey at 16 kmp and downward journey at 24 kmp. What is his average speed in kmp?
A. 19.5   B. 19.2
C. 19.4   D. 20

52. A number is increased by 10% and then decreased by 10%. Then the number
A. Does not change
B. Increases by 1%
C. Decreases by 1%
D. None of these

53. A shop-keeper wants to sell his goods at cost price, but uses a weight of 800 gm instead of a kilogram weight. Thus he makes a gain of
A. 2%   B. 8%
C. 20%   D. 25%

54. At what rate per cent per annum of simple interest will a certain sum of money become double in 5 years?
A. 20%   B. 25%
C. 30%   D. 10%

55. In selling an article of ₹ 55 there is a gain of 10%. The gain by selling that for ₹ 58 is
A. 13%   B. 6%
C. 16%   D. 3%

56. By how much is the area of a square of side 6 cm increased when its side is increased by 2 cm?
A. 4 sq.cm   B. 16 sq.cm
C. 20 sq.cm   D. 28 sq.cm

57. If $x = 5$, $y = -2$, what is the value of $(2x^2 - 3y^2)$?
A. 62   B. 38
C. 50   D. 60

58. How many of the following numbers are divisible by 9?

1231, 2367, 6462, 5354, 7020, 1341
A. 3   B. 4
C. 5   D. 2

59. The difference between the place values of 7 and 3 in the number 527435 is
A. 5   B. 4
C. 45   D. 6970

60. The three angles of a triangle are $(5x + 6)°$, $(3x - 3)°$ and $(x - 3)°$. Then $x = $?
A. 30°   B. 40°
C. 20°   D. 10°

61. 40 men can dig a trench 32 metres long in 16 days. How many days will 60 men take to dig a trench 12 metres long?
A. 4   B. 16
C. 8   D. 20

62. $\dfrac{1}{4} + \dfrac{3}{8} + ? = \dfrac{13}{16}$

A. $\dfrac{5}{8}$ B. $\dfrac{3}{16}$

C. $\dfrac{2}{8}$ D. $\dfrac{5}{16}$

63. $\dfrac{4}{11}$ of $4\dfrac{1}{8}$ of ₹ 50 = ?

A. 75   B. 30
C. 40   D. 25

64. $\sqrt{\dfrac{49}{?}} = \dfrac{7}{15}$

A. 30   B. 25
C. 225   D. 105

65. Find the multiplier which will cause a number to increase it by 17%.
A. 17.7   B. 1.17
C. 117   D. 0.117

66. $\left(\sqrt{8} - \sqrt{3}\right)\left(\sqrt{8} + \sqrt{3}\right) = $?
A. 5   B. 15
C. 25   D. None of these

67. 15 = 75% of ?
A. 10.25   B. 22.5
C. 25   D. 20

68. A trader sells 10 chairs and 2 tables for ₹ 7,000 to a customer and to another customer he sells 10 chairs and 3 tables at the same price for ₹ 8,000. Find the cost of a chair.

   A. ₹ 600   B. ₹ 500
   C. ₹ 400   D. ₹ 300

69. Mr. Singh invested ₹ 19,000 in a 5% stock at 95 and sold it when its price has fallen to 90. Thus he lost

   A. ₹ 1,000   B. ₹ 100
   C. ₹ 500   D. ₹ 900

70. Mr. Naveen invested ₹ 19,000 in a 6% stock at 95. Find the annual dividend he gets.

   A. ₹ 600   B. ₹ 1,000
   C. ₹ 1,200   D. ₹ 1,500

71. The difference between the simple interest and compound interest on ₹ 100 at 10% for 2 years is

   A. ₹ 10   B. ₹ 1
   C. ₹ 5   D. ₹ 15

72. The area of a square is 64 sq.cm. Find its perimeter.

   A. 16 cm   B. 8 cm
   C. 32 cm   D. 10 sq.cm

73. A train is running at a speed of 72 km per hour. Find the distance it covers in 10 minutes.

   A. 7.2 km   B. 10 km
   C. 20 km   D. 12 km

74. $100° = ?$

   A. 100   B. 10
   C. 1   D. 0

75. Area of circle having radius 7 cm is

   A. 124 sq.cm
   B. 154 sq.cm
   C. 22 sq.cm
   D. 19 sq.cm

General English

Directions (Qs. 76 - 78): *First read the passage and then answer the questions based on it.*

PASSAGE

I was very fond of the old soldier in our little town. He had only one leg, having lost the other somewhere in Assam in 1942. He used to tell me about his adventures. He told me that he had run away from home to join the army. He had experienced his first battle in the Libyan desert. Out of his dozens of war stories, the one I liked best was the one of his escape from a Japanese prison-of-war camp in Burma. He told me again and again how he walked two hundred miles in two weeks. On the way he was bitten on the toe by a poisonous snake and he had to cut off part of the toe in order to survive. But by the time he got to an Indian Camp the wound had turned septic and the leg had to be amputated. He is, however, quite contented with his lot.

76. The author was very fond of the old soldier because

   A. He had lost one of his legs in war
   B. He used to tell the author about his adventures
   C. He was contented with his lot
   D. He had been to many countries

77. Why did the old soldier repeatedly tell that he walked two hundred miles?

   A. He ran away from home to join the army
   B. He had to cross the Libyan desert
   C. He had to escape from a prison-of-war camp
   D. He was a strong soldier

78. The story of the old soldier that the author liked most was that about

   A. his running away from home to join the army
   B. his first battle in the Libyan desert
   C. the loss of his leg in Assam
   D. his escape from a Japanese prison-of-war camp

Directions (Qs. 79 and 80): *In the following items, each passage consists of six sentences. The first sentence (S_1) and the final sentence (S_6) are given in the beginning. The middle four sentences in each have been removed and jumbled up. These are labelled P, Q, R and S. You are required to find out the proper sequence of the four sentences and choose your answer accordingly.*

79. S_1 : When Galileo was young, people believed that the earth was the centre of the universe.

S_6 : But time has proved that Galileo's view was right.

P : But Galileo began to argue that it was not so.

Q : This belief was supported by the state and the Church.

R : He said that the earth and other planets moved round the sun.

S : He was imprisoned for voicing this unorthodox view.

The proper sequence should be

A. PQRS	B. QPRS
C. QPSR	D. PSRQ

80. S_1 : No daily paper has ever found its way into this village.

S_6 : They carry this with them to the trading centres in the plains and cities.

P : These travellers come from distant places.

Q : On their return journey they have news from the hills.

R : The only news the inhabitants get is from travellers.

S : On their way into the hills they bring news from distant plains and cities of India.

The proper sequence should be

A. PQSR	B. QSPR
C. RPSQ	D. RQPS

Directions (Qs. 81 - 83): *In the following problems, some parts of the sentence have been jumbled up. You are required to rearrange these parts which are underlined and labelled P, Q, R and S to produce the correct sentence. Choose the proper sequence.*

81. The dog (P)/ with its customary fondness (Q)/ before the master (R)/ wagged its tail. (S)

The correct sequence should be

A. PSRQ	B. PQRS
C. PRSQ	D. QRSP

82. This is the book (P)/ about (Q)/ which (R)/ I told you. (S)

The correct sequence should be

A. PRSQ	B. PSQR
C. SPQR	D. PQRS

83. The fire before any serious damage was done (P)/ by volunteers (Q)/ was controlled (R)/ in the godown. (S)

The correct sequence should be

A. RSPQ	B. SRPQ
C. RQPS	D. QRSP

Directions (Qs. 84 - 86): *Each of the following 3 items consists of a word in capital letters, followed by four words or group of words. Select the word or group of words that is most similar in meaning to the word in capital letters.*

84. HOMESICK

A. Broomstick

B. House warming

C. Longing for home

D. Comfortable

85. MEDITATE

A. mediate	B. contemplate
C. celebrate	D. manage

86. PRIMITIVE

A. modern

B. prime

C. periodical

D. unsophisticated

Directions (Qs. 87 - 89): *Each of the following 3 items consists of a word in captital letters, followed by four words or group of words. Select the word or group of words that is most opposite in meaning to the word in capital letters.*

87. INSTANTLY
   A. repeatedly
   B. slowly
   C. immediately
   D. awkwardly

88. REMIND
   A. memorize   B. think
   C. forget   D. defeat

89. JUSTIFIABLE
   A. unreasonable
   B. virtual
   C. irresponsible
   D. understandable

Directions (Qs. 90 - 92): *In these questions, which of the phrases A., (B), (C) and (D) given below each sentence should replace the phrase printed in CAPITAL LETTERS to make the sentence grammatically correct?*

90. ONE OF THE FUNCTION OF a teacher is to spot cases of maladjustment.
   A. Most of the functions of
   B. One of the functions of
   C. Some of the functions
   D. One of the functions by

91. FINISHING HIS BREAKFAST, he started working on the problem that had been awaiting disposal for a longtime.
   A. His breakfast finished
   B. His breakfast having finished
   C. Having finished his breakfast
   D. Finished his breakfast

92. In our friends' circle, it is customary for each of the members TO BUY THEIR OWN TICKETS.
   A. Buying their own tickets
   B. Are buying their own tickets
   C. To buy his own ticket
   D. No correction required

Directions (Qs. 93 - 95): *Pickout the most effective word/words from the given words to fill in the blank to make the sentence meaningfully complete.*

93. The government is planning to set .... family welfare centers for slums in cities.
   A. another   B. for
   C. out   D. up

94. Each business activity .... employment to the people who would otherwise be unemployed.
   A. provides   B. takes
   C. given   D. sends

95. It is too difficult .... solve.
   A. for   B. to
   C. shall   D. can

Directions (Qs. 96 - 98): *Read each sentence to find out whether there is any grammatical error or idiomatic error in it. The error will be in one part of the sentence. The number of that part is the answer.*

96. After a complaint was filed, (A)/ police teams was given the photograph (B)/ of the accused from the CCTV footage (C)/ recorded at the hotel. (D)

97. Training have a (A)/ positive effect on (B)/ development of various (C)/ skills and abilities. (D)

98. The economic disparity (A)/have grown rapidly in (B)/ the era of globalization (C)/ and free market forces. (D)

Directions (Qs. 99 and 100): *Point out the correct spelling.*

99. A. genwin   B. genvine
    C. genuine   D. jenuine

100. A. goverment   B. government
     C. govarnment   D. gournament

ANSWERS

1	2	3	4	5	6	7	8	9	10
C	C	C	A	C	C	C	A	A	D

11	12	13	14	15	16	17	18	19	20
C	A	A	C	C	B	B	B	C	D

21	22	23	24	25	26	27	28	29	30
C	A	D	C	A	B	A	C	B	B

31	32	33	34	35	36	37	38	39	40
C	C	A	B	A	C	A	B	B	C

41	42	43	44	45	46	47	48	49	50
D	A	B	C	D	C	B	C	C	A

51	52	53	54	55	56	57	58	59	60
B	C	D	A	C	D	B	B	D	C

61	62	63	64	65	66	67	68	69	70
A	B	A	C	B	A	D	B	A	C

71	72	73	74	75	76	77	78	79	80
B	C	D	C	B	B	D	D	B	C

81	82	83	84	85	86	87	88	89	90
A	D	B	C	B	D	B	C	A	B

91	92	93	94	95	96	97	98	99	100
C	C	D	A	B	B	A	B	C	B

GENERAL INTELLIGENCE & REASONING

1. LETTER SERIES

In letter series, the letters follow a definite order. The given series of letters can be in natural order or in reverse order or combination of both. The letters may be skipped or repeated or consecutive. The given series may be single or may even comprise of two different series merged at alternate positions. While attempting questions on letter series one should note the pattern of alphabet series.

Alphabets in natural series are :

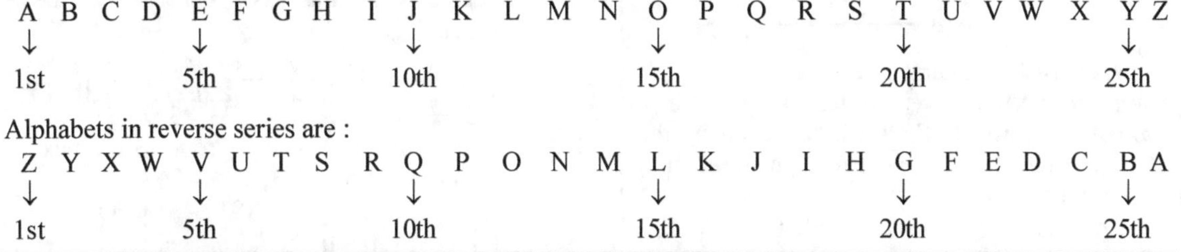

Note : On reaching Z, the series restarts from A and on reaching A, it restarts from Z.

EXERCISE

Directions : In each of the following series determine the order of the letters. Then from the given options select the one which will complete the given series.

1. B Y C X D W E ?
  (a) S   (b) T
  (c) U   (d) V

2. B A F E J I P O ? U
  (a) V   (b) T
  (c) S   (d) Q

3. B A D C ? H G J I
  (a) EF   (b) FE
  (c) FG   (d) DF

4. ADG, XVT, BEH, WUS, ?
  (a) VTR   (b) CFI
  (c) DFJ   (d) STU

5. GMSY, IOUA, KQWC, ?
  (a) MSYE   (b) NSYE
  (c) MTYE   (d) MSYF

6. ADG, GJM, ?, SVY
  (a) MPS   (b) MQR
  (c) MQS   (d) SPM

7. XYZ, UVW, ?, OPQ
  (a) RST   (b) STU
  (c) QRS   (d) TUV

8. JOBS, KMEO, LKHK, ?, NGNC
  (a) MJLH   (b) LIKG
  (c) MIKG   (d) MNGM

9. AZ, GT, MN, ?, YB
  (a) KF   (b) TS
  (c) RX   (d) SH

10. BMY, DNW, FOU, ?
  (a) HPT   (b) HPS
  (c) HQS   (d) GPS

11. AZ, CX, EV, ?
  (a) HU   (b) GS
  (c) GT   (d) HT

12. DMP, FLN, HKL, JJJ, ?
  (a) MIH   (b) III
  (c) LIH   (d) MII

13. ECA, JHF, OMK, ?, YWU
  (a) TRP   (b) LNP
  (c) QPN   (d) RPT

14. ABP, CDQ, EFR, ?
   (*a*) GHS   (*b*) HGS
   (*c*) GHR   (*d*) GHT

15. BEH, KNQ, TWZ, ?
   (*a*) IJL   (*b*) BDF
   (*c*) CFI   (*d*) ADG

EXPLANATORY ANSWERS

1. (*d*) : There are two alternate series.

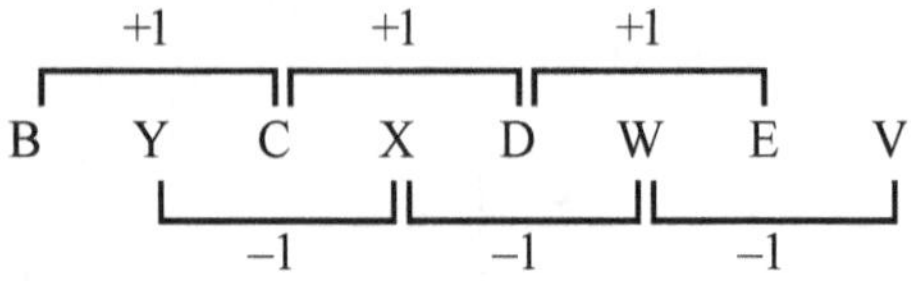

Series I : BCDE (natural order)
Series II : YXWV (reverse order)

2. (*a*) : Each vowel (AEIOU) is preceded by the letter that comes next to it in the natural alphabetical series.

3. (*b*) : The letters in natural series are divided into sections of two letters each. The letters in each section are written backward.

BA DC FE HG JI

4. (*b*) : There are two alternate series.

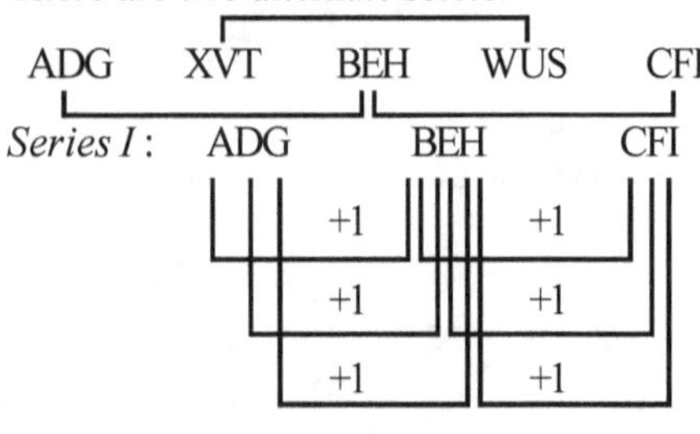

Series I :   ADG   BEH   CFI

Series II :   XVT   WUS

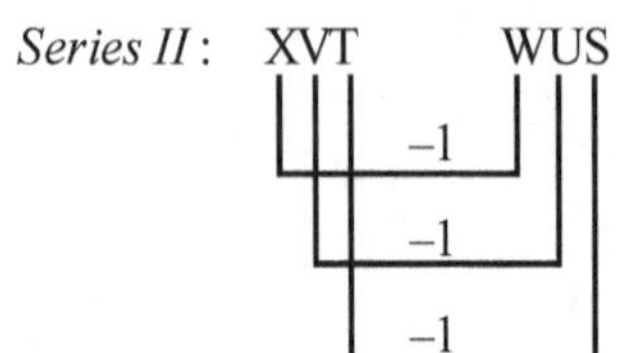

5. (*a*) : The series is formed by moving each letter two steps forward from one group to the next.

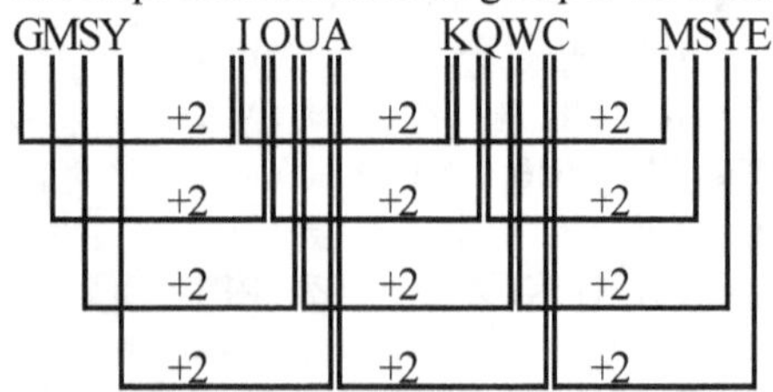

(The series restarts from A on reaching Z)

6. (*a*) : In each group of three letters the alphabet is in the succession of +3. The next group begins with the last alphabet of the previous group.

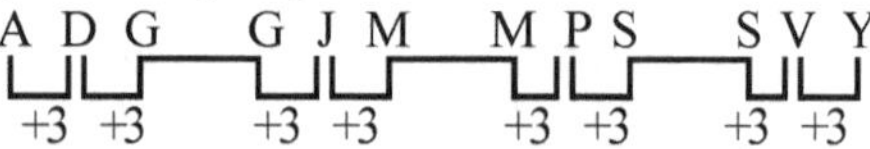

7. (*a*) : The alphabet from one group to the next are in recession of –3, *i.e.,*

XYZ   UVW   RST   OPQ

8. (*c*) : The alphabets in each group follow the pattern +1, –2, +3 and –4 respectively from one group to the next group.

JOBS KMEO LKHK MIKG NGNC

9. (*d*) : The letters in one group correspond to the letters in the next group in the manner +6, –6 respectively, *i.e.,*

AZ   GT   MN   SH   YB

10. (*b*) : The letters in one group correspond to the letters in the next group in the manner +2, +1, -2 respectively, *i.e.,*

BMY   DNW   FOU   HPS

11. (*c*) : The letters in each group correspond to the letters in the next group in the manner +2, –2 respectively, *i.e.,*

AZ   CX   EV   GT
+2   +2   +2
–2   –2   –2

12. (*c*) : The alphabets in each group correspond to the alphabets in the next group in the manner +2, –1, –2 respectively, *i.e.,*

DMP   FLN   HKL   JJJ   LIH
+2   +2   +2   +2
–1   –1   –1   –1
–2   –2   –2   –2

13. (*a*) : The alphabets in each group are moved five steps forward, *i.e.,*

ECA   JHF   OMK   TRP   YWU
+5   +5   +5   +5
+5   +5   +5   +5
+5   +5   +5   +5

14. (*a*) : The letters in one group correspond to the letters in the next group in the manner +2, +2, +1 respectively, *i.e.,*

ABP   CDQ   EFR   GHS
+2   +2   +2
+2   +2   +2
+1   +1   +1

15. (*c*) : All the letters in each group are moved nine steps forward.

BEH   KNQ   TWZ   CFI
+9   +9   +9
+9   +9   +9
+9   +9   +9

2. WRONG LETTER SERIES

In this type of series, the candidates are not required to find the letter or group of letters which will complete the given series but, they have to identify the letter or number which is wrong or misfit in the given series.

SOLVED EXAMPLE

1. Which of the following letters in the given series is wrong?

   J M P T V Y

   (*a*) J   (*b*) P   (*c*) T   (*d*) Y

   Ans. (*c*) : The letters in this series are moved three steps forward, *i.e.,*

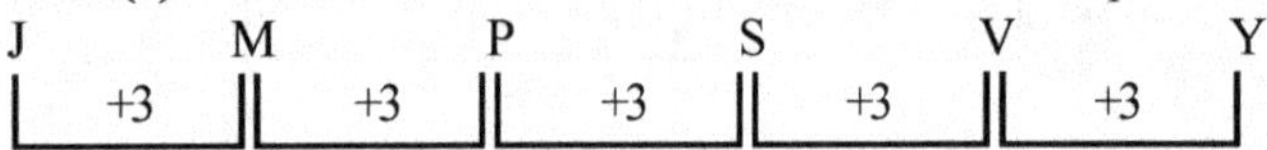

   Letter 'T' should have been 'S'.

EXERCISE

Directions : *Which letter(s) in each of the following series is wrong or is misfit in the series?*

1. AEHOU
   - (*a*) U
   - (*b*) O
   - (*c*) H
   - (*d*) E
2. CHMSWB
   - (*a*) C
   - (*b*) S
   - (*c*) B
   - (*d*) W
3. XSNICY
   - (*a*) Y
   - (*b*) C
   - (*c*) S
   - (*d*) I
4. ZAWBXC
   - (*a*) D
   - (*b*) C
   - (*c*) X
   - (*d*) W
5. MLONQPR
   - (*a*) R
   - (*b*) O
   - (*c*) Q
   - (*d*) L
6. DKRYFL
   - (*a*) L
   - (*b*) D
   - (*c*) R
   - (*d*) Y
7. LNQTWZCF
   - (*a*) C
   - (*b*) Q
   - (*c*) L
   - (*d*) F
8. XW, DC, CB, NM, PQ
   - (*a*) NM
   - (*b*) CB
   - (*c*) PQ
   - (*d*) XW
9. BEINSAI
   - (*a*) A
   - (*b*) E
   - (*c*) S
   - (*d*) I
10. ZTPKHF
    - (*a*) Z
    - (*b*) P
    - (*c*) T
    - (*d*) F

EXPLANATORY ANSWERS

1. (*c*) : The series is made with vowels only. AEIOU. I should be in place of H.

2. (*b*) : The letters in the series are moved five steps forward.

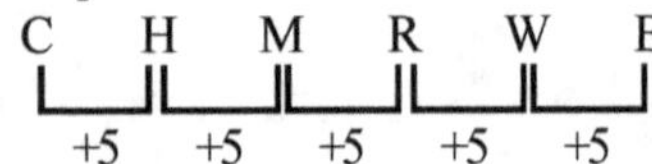

3. (*b*) : The pattern in the series is –5, *i.e.,*

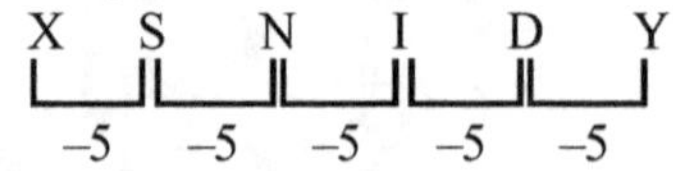

R should be in place of S
(The series restarts from A on reaching Z)

D should be in place of C.

4. (*d*) : There are two alternate series

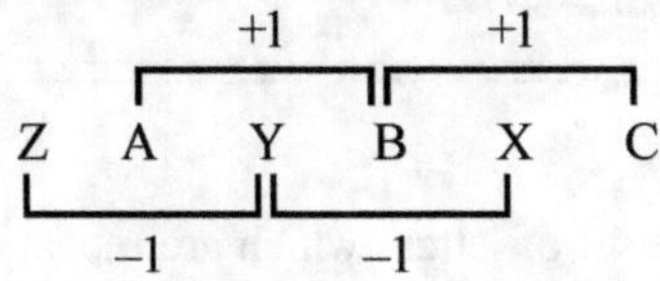

Series I : ZYX (reverse series)
Series II : ABC (natural series)
Y should be in place of W.

5. (*a*) : Two consecutive letters are written backwards.

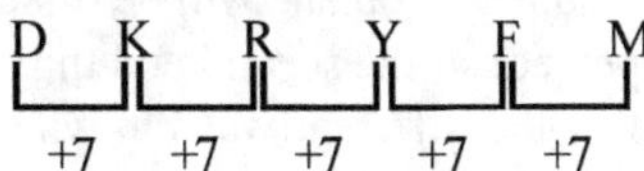

S should be in place of R.

6. (*a*) : The pattern in this series in moving the letters seven steps forward.

D K R Y F M
+7 +7 +7 +7 +7

M should be in place of L.

7. (*c*) : The pattern in the series is +3

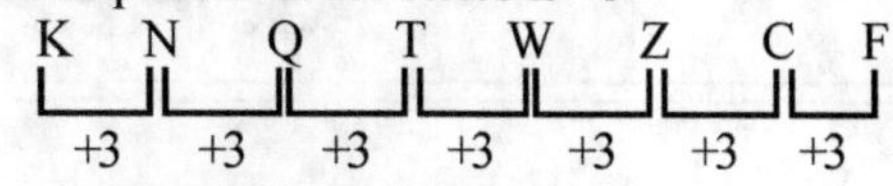

K should be in place of L.

8. (*c*) : The series is made with any two consecutive letters written backwards.

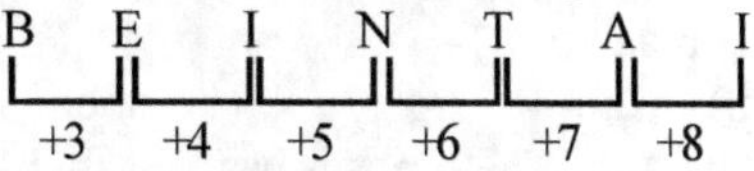

Q should come before P in the series.

9. (*c*) : The difference between the letters is increased by one at each step.

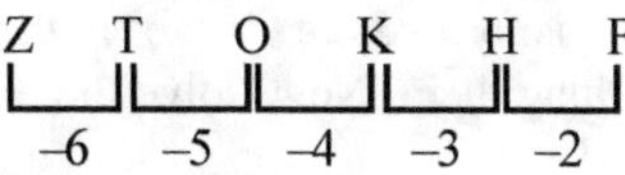

T should be in place of S.

10. (*b*) : The difference between the letters is decreased by one at each step.

Z T O K H F
–6 –5 –4 –3 –2

O should be in place of P.

3. REPEAT SERIES

In this type of series, small letters of the alphabet are used to make a set of letters which are repeated. The candidate has to find the set of letters which will fit the blanks left in the given series in such a manner that one section of the series is further repeated in the same manner.

SOLVED EXAMPLE

1. Which of the following groups of letters will complete the given series?
   ba-b-aab-a-b
   (*a*) baab   (*b*) abba   (*c*) abaa   (*d*) babb
   Ans. (*b*) : The series is baab, baab, baab. Here the section 'baab' is repeated in the series.

Solving steps **:** The candidate has to look for clues to solve such series pattern. 'aab' in the Series indicates that 'b' in this series is preceded by two 'a' so, the first blank and the last blank will be filled by 'a'. Now the first set is formed, *i.e.,* 'baab' in the beginning. This set is repeated, so the second and third blanks will have 'b' filling them. Now, solve the exercise given below to know the different ways in which these series are formed.

EXERCISE

Directions : *Which of the following groups of letters will complete the given series?*

1. ab---b-bbaa-
   (*a*) babba   (*b*) abaab
   (*c*) abbab   (*d*) baaab
2. aa-ab--aaa-a
   (*a*) baaa   (*b*) abab
   (*c*) aaab   (*d*) aabb
3. -baa-aab-a-a
   (*a*) baab   (*b*) abab
   (*c*) aaba   (*d*) aabb
4. -a cca-ccca-acccc-aaa
   (*a*) ccaa   (*b*) acca
   (*c*) caac   (*d*) caaa
5. c-bbb--abbbb-abbb-
   (*a*) abccb   (*b*) bacbb
   (*c*) aabcb   (*d*) abacb
6. ac-cab-baca-aba-acac
   (*a*) bcbb   (*b*) aacb
   (*c*) babb   (*d*) acbc
7. --aba--ba-ab
   (*a*) abbab   (*b*) bbaba
   (*c*) baabb   (*d*) abbba
8. --babbba-a--
   (*a*) bbaba   (*b*) babbb
   (*c*) baaab   (*d*) ababb
9. k-mk-lmkkl-kk-mk
   (*a*) lklm   (*b*) lkmk
   (*c*) lkmm   (*d*) lkml
10. abc-d-bc-d-b-dd
    (*a*) decdb   (*b*) dadac
    (*c*) cdabe   (*d*) bacde
11. b-abbc-bbca-bcabb-ab
    (*a*) acba   (*b*) acaa
    (*c*) cacc   (*d*) cabc
12. aca-ac--a-ac
    (*a*) babc   (*b*) aaac
    (*c*) cacc   (*d*) caca
13. ba-cb-b-bab-?
    (*a*) acbb   (*b*) bcaa
    (*c*) cabb   (*d*) bacc
14. ab-aa-caab-aab-a
    (*a*) bcbc   (*b*) bbca
    (*c*) cbcc   (*d*) caba

15. -bbcaa-bcaa-bc-a-bca
(a) bacab (b) abbab
(c) abcba (d) bcaab

16. a-bccb-ca-cca-baab-c
(a) accab (b) abcaa
(c) bacaa (d) ababc

17. b-dabbcd-b-c-ab
(a) cabd (b) bcad
(c) dcba (d) acbd

18. a-ba-caacb-bc-
(a) acbb (b) cbab
(c) cbaa (d) cbba

19. c-baa-aca-cacab-acac-bca
(a) acbaa (b) cbaac
(c) bccab (d) bbcaa

20. -bcc-ac-aabb-ab-cc
(a) bacab (b) abaca
(c) aabca (d) bcaca

21. ab-ccca-bccc-bbcc-
(a) abbc (b) bbac
(c) bbca (d) cabc

22. -cbc-a-bcaac-ca
(a) aaba (b) caab
(c) bcab (d) aacb

23. ab-ba--ba-
(a) abba (b) baab
(c) baba (d) abab

24. yx-yx-yxz-xzy-zyxz
(a) zzyx (b) xxzy
(c) yyzx (d) yzxz

25. xxxy-y-xxy-yxx-
(a) xyxy (b) yxyx
(c) yyxx (d) xxyy

EXPLANATORY ANSWERS

1. (d) : The series is abbaab, abbaab.
2. (c) : The series is aaaaba, aaaaba.
3. (b) : The series is aba, aba, aba, aba.
4. (d) : The series is c,a,cc,aa, ccc, aaa, cccc, aaaa.
5. (a) : The series is cabbbb, cabbbb, cabbbb.
6. (b) : The series is acac, abab, acac, abab, acac.
7. (a) : The series is ab, ab, ab, ab, ab, ab.
8. (b) : The series is bababb, bababb.
9. (d) : The series is klmk, klmk, klmk, klmk.
10. (b) : The series is abcdd, abcdd, abcdd.
11. (d) : The series is bcab, bcab, bcab, bcab, bcab.
12. (c) : The series is ac, ac, ac, ac, ac, ac.
13. (d) : The series is babc, babc, babc.
14. (c) : The series is abca, abca, abca, abca.
15. (b) : The series is abbca, abbca, abbca, abbca.
16. (d) : The series is aabcc, bbcaa, ccabb, aabcc.
17. (a) : The series is bcdab, bcdab, bcdab.
18. (c) : The series is acbabca, acbabca.
19. (a) : The series is cabaac, acabca, cabaac, acabca.
20. (a) : The series is bbccaa, ccaabb, aabbcc.
21. (b) : The series is abbccc abbccc.
22. (d) : The series is acbca acbca acbca.
23. (d) : The series is ab ab ab ab ab.
24. (a) : The series is yxz yxz yxz yxz yxz yxz.
25. (b) : The series is xxx yyy xxx yyy xxx.

4. NUMBER SERIES

In this type of series, the set of given numbers in a series are related to one another in a particular pattern or manner. The relationship between the numbers may be (i) consecutive odd/even numbers; (ii) consecutive prime numbers; (iii) squares/cubes of some numbers with/without variation of addition or subtraction of some number; (iv) sum/product/difference of preceding numbers; (v) addition/subtraction/multiplication/ division by some number; and (vi) many more combinations of the relationships given above.

EXERCISE

Directions : *In the following questions, select the number(s) from the given options for completing the given series.*

1. 7776, 1296, 216, 36, 6, ?
   - (a) 6
   - (b) 0
   - (c) 3
   - (d) 1
2. 29282, 2662, 242, 22, ?
   - (a) 1
   - (b) 2
   - (c) 0
   - (d) 11
3. 1, 2, 2, 4, 16, ?, 65536
   - (a) 276
   - (b) 64
   - (c) 256
   - (d) 198
4. 3, 5, 9, 15, 23, ?, 45
   - (a) 37
   - (b) 35
   - (c) 31
   - (d) 33
5. 7, 21, 35, 49, 63, ?
   - (a) 70
   - (b) 77
   - (c) 81
   - (d) 108
6. 10, 14, 23, 39, 64, ?, 149
   - (a) 78
   - (b) 128
   - (c) 103
   - (d) 100
7. 6, 24, 29, 116, 121, ?, 489
   - (a) 468
   - (b) 484
   - (c) 243
   - (d) 363

8. 5, 50, 45, 450, 445, ?, 4445
   - (a) 4450
   - (b) 4600
   - (c) 4550
   - (d) 4500
9. 6.25, 9, 12.25, 16, 20.25, 25, 30.25?
   - (a) 36
   - (b) 32
   - (c) 28.25
   - (d) 40.25
10. 243, 5, 81, 15, 27, 45, 9, ?
    - (a) 5
    - (b) 15
    - (c) 135
    - (d) 27
11. 2, 7, 14, 23, ?, 47
    - (a) 31
    - (b) 38
    - (c) 28
    - (d) 34
12. 0, 1, 8, 27, 64, ?
    - (a) 125
    - (b) 128
    - (c) 256
    - (d) 121
13. 37, 47, 58, ?, 79, 95
    - (a) 71
    - (b) 69
    - (c) 68
    - (d) 67
14. 4, –8, 14, –22, 32, ?
    - (a) –44
    - (b) 42
    - (c) –42
    - (d) 44
15. 6, 7, 9, 11, 15, 15, 24, 19, ?
    - (a) 32
    - (b) 34
    - (c) 36
    - (d) 37

EXPLANATORY ANSWERS

1. *(d)* : The numbers in this sequence are divided by 6 each time.
2. *(b)* : The numbers in the series are divided by 11 at each step.
3. *(c)* : The number in the series is product of all the numbers preceding it.

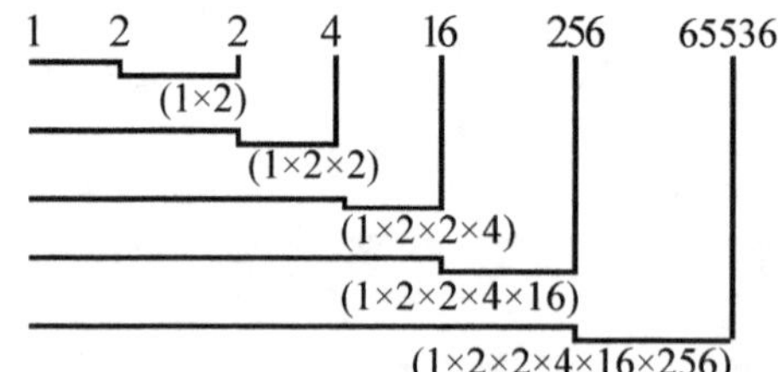

4. *(d)* : The difference between consecutive numbers increases by 2 at each step.

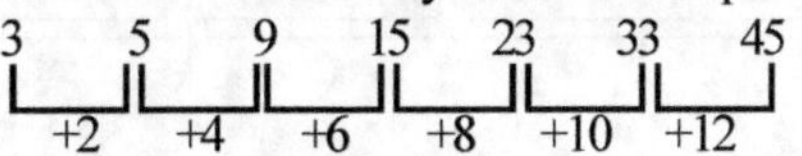

5. *(b)* : The series is multiplication of 7 by odd numbers starting from 3.

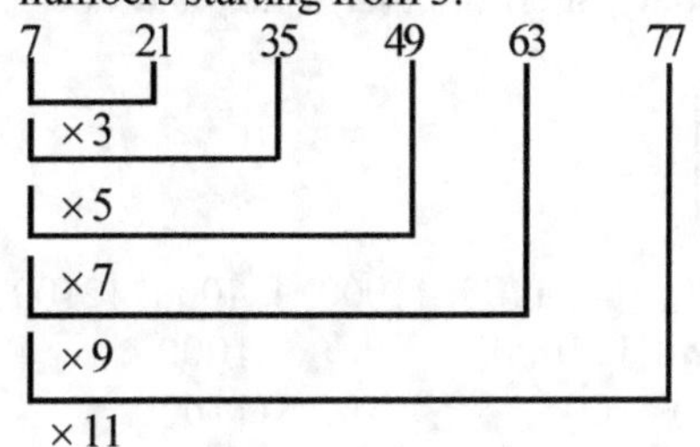

6. *(d)* : The number plus the square of numbers in natural order starting from 2 gives the next number in the series.

10   14   23   39   64   100   149

$+2^2$ $+3^2$ $+4^2$ $+5^2$ $+6^2$ $+7^2$

7. *(b)* : The sequence in the series is ×4, +5, which is repeated.

8. *(a)* : The sequence in the series is ×10, −5, which is repeated.

9. *(a)* : There are two alternate series :

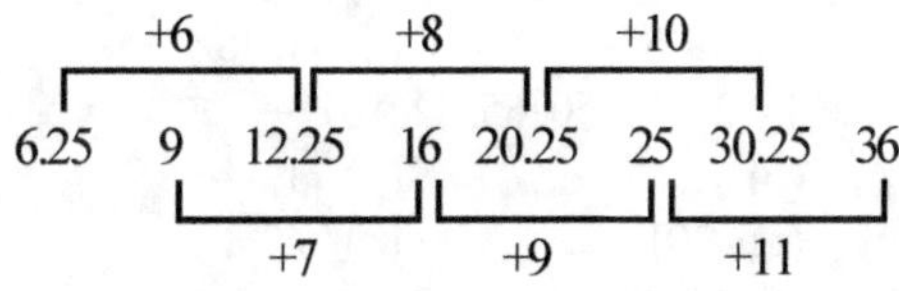

Series I : 6.25, 12.25, 20.25, 30.25 (sequence is +6, +8, +10)

Series II : 9, 16, 25, 36 (sequence is +7, +9, +11)

10. *(c)* : There are two alternate series :

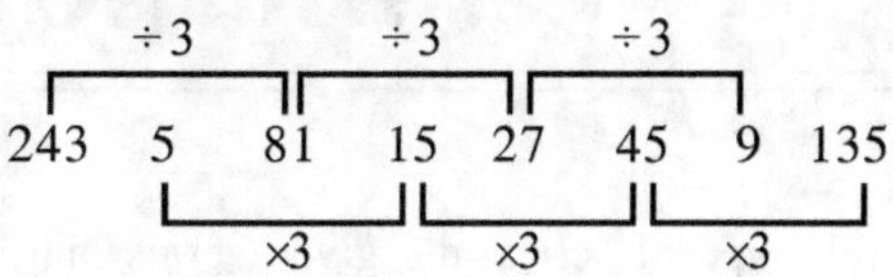

Series I : 243, 81, 27, 9 (division by 3)

Series II : 5, 15, 45, 135 (multiplication by 3)

11. *(d)* : The difference between two consecutive numbers is increasing by 2 starting from 5.

2   7   14   23   34   47

+5   +7   +9   +11   +13

12. *(a)* : The numbers are cubes of numbers in natural order.

13. *(a)* : The sum of the digits of the number is added to the number to obtain the next number in the series.

37   47   58   71   79   95

+(3+7) +(4+7) +(5+8) +(7+1) +(7+9)

14. *(a)* : Alternate numbers are marked positive and negative, but the difference between their magnitude increases by 2 at each step.

4   −8   14   −22   32   −44

4   6   8   10   12

15. *(c)* : There are two alternate series :

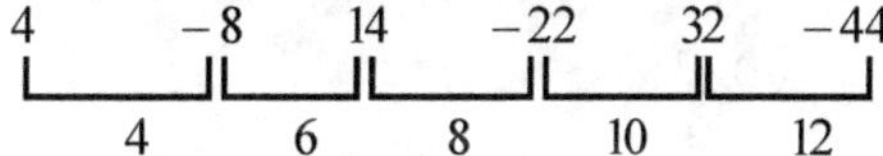
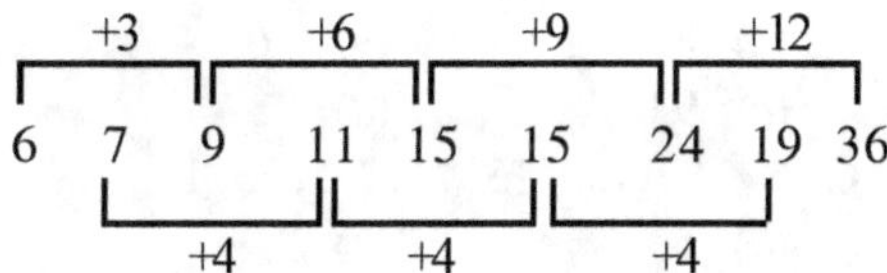

Series I : 6, 9, 15, 24, 36 (sequence is +3, +6, +9, +12)

Series II : 7, 11, 15, 19 (addition of 4 at each step)

5. WRONG NUMBER SERIES

In this type of series, the given series may be complete but what needs to be identified is the number in the given completed series which is disturbing the sequential pattern of that series and does not fit in with the relationship shared between the other numbers.

EXERCISE

Directions : *In the given series find the number which is wrong.*

1. 5, 25, 120, 625, 3125, 15625
   - (a) 15625
   - (b) 625
   - (c) 120
   - (d) 5

2. 4, 8, 11, 22, 18, 36, 24, 50
   - (a) 8
   - (b) 22
   - (c) 36
   - (d) 24

3. 2, 4, 12, 24, 72, 142, 432
   - (a) 432
   - (b) 12
   - (c) 142
   - (d) 72

4. 2, 3, 4, 4, 6, 8, 9, 12, 16
   - (a) 3
   - (b) 9
   - (c) 6
   - (d) 12

5. 97, 91, 86, 83, 79, 77, 76, 76
   - (a) 86
   - (b) 76
   - (c) 91
   - (d) 83

6. 7, 11, 11, 9, 15, 7, 19, 5, 23, 1
   - (a) 5
   - (b) 7
   - (c) 1
   - (d) 9

7. 3, 7, 12, 28, 48, 118, 192, 448
   - (a) 12
   - (b) 118
   - (c) 28
   - (d) 7

8. 10, 100, 1100, 11000, 111000, 1210000
   - (a) 1210000
   - (b) 11000
   - (c) 100
   - (d) 111000

9. 24576, 6144, 1536, 386, 96, 24
   - (a) 386
   - (b) 6144
   - (c) 96
   - (d) 1536

10. 11, 13, 15, 17, 19, 23, 29, 31, 37
    - (a) 13
    - (b) 23
    - (c) 15
    - (d) 31

11. 36, 43, 49, 54, 60, 61, 63, 64
    - (a) 60
    - (b) 63
    - (c) 54
    - (d) 43

12. 3, 10, 41, 206, 1236, 8660
    - (a) 10
    - (b) 41
    - (c) 206
    - (d) 1236

13. 17, 25, 37, 50, 65, 82, 101
    - (a) 25
    - (b) 17
    - (c) 101
    - (d) 65

14. 12, 20, 38, 42, 56, 72
    - (a) 20
    - (b) 38
    - (c) 56
    - (d) 72

15. 5, 6, 11, 22, 42, 88, 176
    - (a) 5
    - (b) 42
    - (c) 176
    - (d) 11

EXPLANATORY ANSWERS

1. (c) : The numbers in the series are multiplied by 5 to get the next number.

∴ 125 should be in place of 120.

2. (d) : Two numbers form a pair. The first number increases by 7 for the next pair and the second number is the double of first number.

$$\begin{array}{cccc} 4\ \ 8 & 11\ \ 22 & 18\ \ 36 & 25\ \ 50 \\ \times 2 & \times 2 & \times 2 & \times 2 \end{array}$$

$$+7 \qquad +7 \qquad +7$$

∴ 25 should be in place of 24.

3. (c) : There are two alternate series and in each series, the numbers are multiplied by 6 to get the next number.

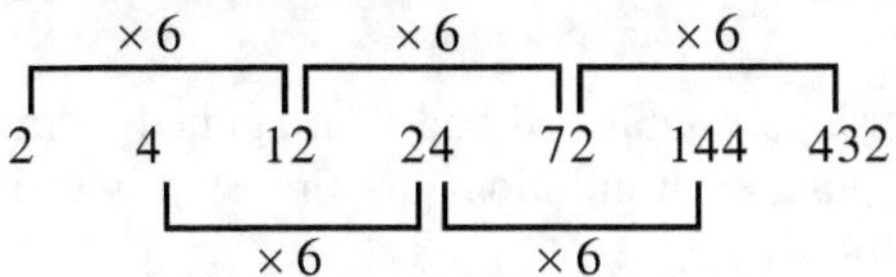

∴ 144 should be in place of 142.

4. (b) : There are three alternate series and in each series, the numbers are multiplied by 2 to get the next number.

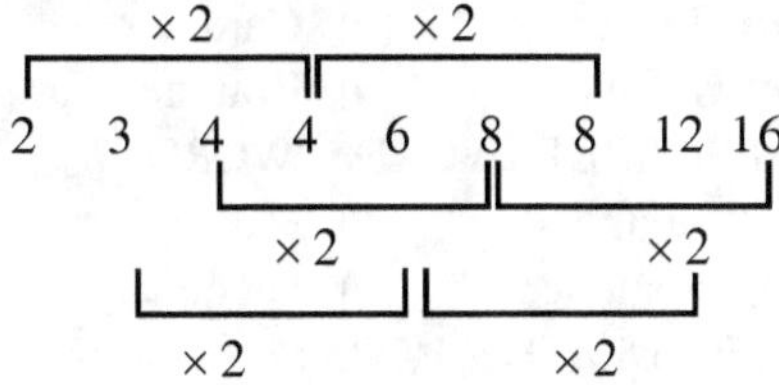

Series I : 2, 4, 8   *Series II* : 3, 6, 12
Series III : 4, 8, 16
∴ 8 should be in place of 9.

5. (d) : The difference between the consecutive numbers in the series decreases by 1 at each step.

97 91 86 82 79 77 76 76
  −6 −5 −4 −3 −2 −1 −0

∴ 82 should be in place of 83.

6. (c) : There are two alternate series :

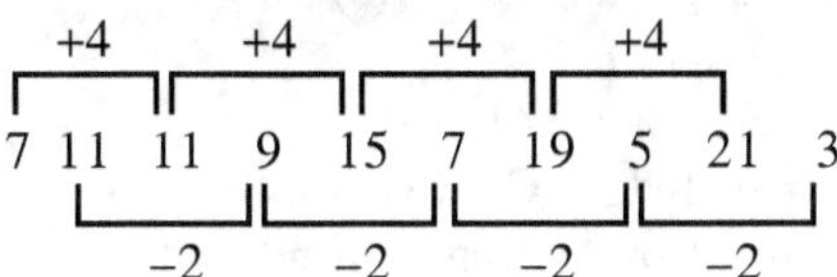

Series I : 7, 11, 15, 19, 23 (addition of 4)
Series II : 11, 9, 7, 5, 3 (subtraction of 2)
∴ 3 should be in place of 1.

7. (b) : There are two alternate series and in each series, the numbers are multiplied by 4 to get the next number.

3   7   12   28   48   112   192   448

∴ 112 should be in place of 118.

8. (d) : The numbers in this series are multiplied by 10 and 11 alternately is, *i.e.,* × 10, × 11.

10 100 1100 11000 121000 1210000
× 10 × 11 × 10 × 11 × 10
∴ 121000 should be in place of 111000.

9. (a) : The numbers in this series are divided by 4 to get the next number.

24576 6144 1536 384 96 24
÷ 4 ÷ 4 ÷ 4 ÷ 4 ÷ 4
∴ 384 should be in place of 386.

10. (c) : The series comprises of prime numbers in increasing order. Only 15 is an exception.

11. (a) : The difference between two consecutive numbers is decreasing by 1 at each step.

36 43 49 54 58 61 63 64
+7 +6 +5 +4 +3 +2 +1
∴ 58 should be in place of 60.

12. (d) : The sequence followed in this series is :
$3 \times 3 + 1 = 10$, $10 \times 4 + 1 = 41$
$41 \times 5 + 1 = 206$, $206 \times 6 + 1 = 1237$; and
$1237 \times 7 + 1 = 8660$
∴ 1237 should be in place of 1236.

13. (a) : The numbers in the series are 1 plus the squares of numbers in natural order starting from 4.

17 26 37 50 65 82 101
$4^2 + 1$ $5^2 + 1$ $6^2 + 1$ $7^2 + 1$ $8^2 + 1$ $9^2 + 1$ $10^2 + 1$
∴ 26 should be in place of 25.

14. (b) : The sequence followed in this series is :
$3 \times 4 = 12$, $4 \times 5 = 20$, $5 \times 6 = 30$,
$6 \times 7 = 42$, $7 \times 8 = 56$, $8 \times 9 = 72$
∴ 30 should be in place of 38.

15. (b) : The numbers in the series are the sum of all the numbers preceding them.

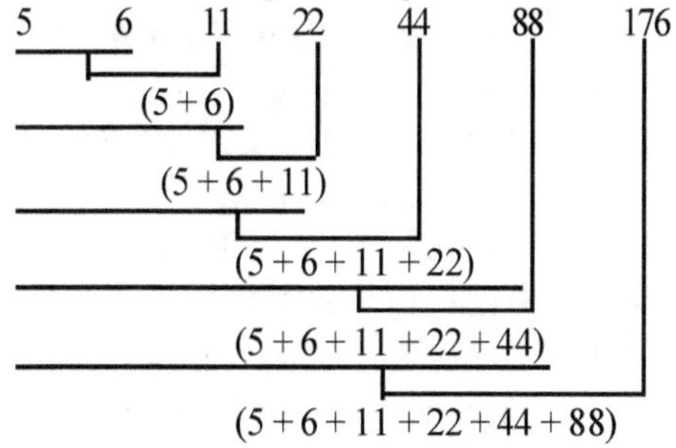

∴ 44 should be in place of 42.

6. WORD ANALOGY

In Analogy Tests, the relationship between two given words is established and then applied to the other words. The type of relationship may vary, so while attempting such questions the first step is to identify the type of relationship, which can be any one of the following.

EXERCISE

Directions : *In the questions given below one term is missing. Based on the relationship of the two given words find the missing term from the given options.*

1. HUNGER : FOOD : : THIRST : ?
   - (*a*) Water
   - (*b*) Drink
   - (*c*) Tea
   - (*d*) Coffee

2. HUNTER : GUN : : WRITER : ?
   - (*a*) Book
   - (*b*) Pen
   - (*c*) Poem
   - (*d*) Page

3. WOOL : SHEEP : : SILK : ?
   - (*a*) Saree
   - (*b*) String
   - (*c*) Silkworm
   - (*d*) Moth

4. FOOD : STOMACH : : FUEL : ?
   - (*a*) Engine
   - (*b*) Automobile
   - (*c*) Rail
   - (*d*) Aeroplane

5. WATER : SAND : : OCEAN : ?
   - (*a*) Island
   - (*b*) River
   - (*c*) Desert
   - (*d*) Waves

6. ADULT : BABY : : FLOWER : ?
   - (*a*) Seed
   - (*b*) Bud
   - (*c*) Fruit
   - (*d*) Butterfly

7. WRITER : READER : : PRODUCER : ?
   - (*a*) Creator
   - (*b*) Contractor
   - (*c*) Creature
   - (*d*) Consumer

8. ENTRANCE : EXIT : : LOYALTY : ?
   - (*a*) Treachery
   - (*b*) Patriotism
   - (*c*) Fidelity
   - (*d*) Reward

9. MOTHER : MATERNAL : : FATHER : ?
   - (*a*) Eternal
   - (*b*) Detrimental
   - (*c*) Paternal
   - (*d*) Formidable

10. PEARL : NECKLACE : : FLOWER : ?
    - (*a*) Plant
    - (*b*) Garden
    - (*c*) Petal
    - (*d*) Bouquet

11. ALPHABET : WORD : : WORD : ?
    - (*a*) Sound
    - (*b*) Music
    - (*c*) Sentence
    - (*d*) Dictionary

12. LIFE : DEATH : : HOPE : ?
    - (*a*) Cry
    - (*b*) Pain
    - (*c*) Despair
    - (*d*) Sad

13. GOOD : BAD : : VIRTUE : ?
    - (*a*) Blame
    - (*b*) Sin
    - (*c*) Despair
    - (*d*) Vice

14. BIRD : FLY : : SNAKE : ?
    - (*a*) Timid
    - (*b*) Clatter
    - (*c*) Crawl
    - (*d*) Hole

15. CAT : MOUSE : : BIRD : ?
    - (*a*) Cage
    - (*b*) Trap
    - (*c*) Eagle
    - (*d*) Worm

16. STATE : EXILE
    - (*a*) Police : Arrest
    - (*b*) Judge : Convict
    - (*c*) Constitution : Amendment
    - (*d*) Church : Excommunicate

17. CAPRICIOUSNESS : RELIABILITY
    - (*a*) Extemporaneous : Predictability
    - (*b*) Unreliable : Inhuman
    - (*c*) Tenacious : Practicality
    - (*d*) Arbitrary : Whimsical

18. LOATH : COERCION
    - (*a*) Detest : Caressing
    - (*b*) Irritate : Caressing
    - (*c*) Irate : Antagonism
    - (*d*) Reluctant : Persuasion

19. SCALES : FISH
   (*a*) Lady : Dress   (*b*) Tree : Leaves
   (*c*) Bird : Feather (*d*) Skin : Man
20. TREE : SAPLING
   (*a*) Hut : Mansion
   (*b*) Giant : Dwarf
   (*c*) Horse : Foal
   (*d*) Ant : Elephant
21. CHALK : BLACKBOARD
   (*a*) Door : Handle
   (*b*) Table : Chair
   (*c*) Ink : Paper
   (*d*) Type : Paint
22. PRIMEVAL : MEDIEVAL
   (*a*) Dinosaur : Dragon
   (*b*) Gorilla : Soldier
   (*c*) Evolution : Revelation
   (*d*) Thorn : Rose
23. TRILOGY : NOVEL
   (*a*) Rice : Husk
   (*b*) Milk : Cream
   (*c*) Fabric : Weaving
   (*d*) Serial : Episode
24. PEDANT : ERUDITION
   (*a*) Prude : Modesty
   (*b*) Blunt : Politician
   (*c*) Diplomats : Tactless
   (*d*) Enemy : Friendly
25. FURY : IRE
   (*a*) Convulsion : Spasm
   (*b*) Amusement : Happiness
   (*c*) Joke : Laugh
   (*d*) Dispassion : Emotion

EXPLANATORY ANSWERS

1. (*a*) : Hunger is satiated by food, thirst by water.

2. (*b*) : Weapon of a hunter is a gun, weapon of a writer is a pen.

3. (*c*) : Wool is obtained from sheep, silk is obtained from silkworm.

4. (*a*) : Food is consumed in stomach, fuel is consumed in engine.

5. (*c*) : The related words are near opposites.

6. (*b*) : The youngone of an adult is a baby and that of a flower is a bud.

7. (*d*) : A writer aims to please the readers by his writings, a producer aims to please the consumers by his products.

8. (*a*) : The related words are opposites.

9. (*c*) : Relations on the mother's side are maternal and on the father's side paternal.

10. (*d*) : Many pearls make a necklace, many flowers make a bouquet.

11. (*c*) : More than one alphabet make a word, more than one word make a sentence.

12. (*c*) : The related words are opposites.

13. (*d*) : The related words are opposites.

14. (*c*) : Birds fly, snakes crawl.

15. (*d*) : Cat chases the mouse, bird chases the worm.

16. (*d*) : Punishment of leaving the State is exile, punishment of leaving the Church is excommunication.

17. (*c*) : The related words are antonyms.

18. (*d*) : Loathing is the result of constant coersion, reluctance is the result of constant persuasion.

19. (*d*) : Covering of the fish is scales, covering of man is skin.

20. (*c*) : Young tree is a sapling, young horse is a foal.

21. (*c*) : Chalk is used to write on blackboard, ink is used to write on paper.

22. (*a*) : The related words represent almost the same time period and answer option represents almost the same sized creatures.

23. (*d*) : Trilogy is section of a novel, episode is a section of a serial.

24. (*a*) : The related words are synonyms.

25. (*b*) : Fury causes ire, amusement causes happiness.

7. NUMBER ANALOGY

In number analogy also, the relationship between the given numbers is detected and then applied to the second part to find the missing numbers. This relationship between the numbers can be based on any of the following patterns : *(i)* numbers can be odd/even/prime numbers; *(ii)* numbers can be multiples of one number; *(iii)* numbers can be squares/cubes of different numbers; *(iv)* some numbers can be added to/subtracted from/multiplied to/divided into the first number to get the second number; *(v)* the second number can be the sum/product/difference of the digits of first number; and *(vi)* combinations of any mathematical calculations given above can apply to the relationship between the two given numbers.

EXERCISE

Directions : *In the following questions, select the number from the given options which follows the same relationship as shared between the first two numbers.*

1. $1 : 11 :: 2 : ?$

    (a) 20   (b) 22

    (c) 24   (d) 44

2. $\dfrac{1}{7} : \dfrac{1}{14} :: \dfrac{1}{9} : ?$

    (a) $\dfrac{1}{88}$ (b) $\dfrac{1}{80}$

    (c) $\dfrac{1}{81}$ (d) $\dfrac{1}{18}$

3. $0.16 : 0.0016 :: 1.02 : ?$

    (a) 10.20   (b) 0.102

    (c) 0.0102   (d) 1.020

4. $663 : 884 :: 221 : ?$

    (a) 332   (b) 554

    (c) 773   (d) 442

5. $16 : 0.16 :: ?$

    (a) $2 : 0.02$ (b) $7 : 0.007$

    (c) $1.3 : 0.13$ (d) $0.01 : 0.001$

6. $3 : \dfrac{1}{3} :: ?$

    (a) $6 : 12$ (b) $5 : 2/15$

    (c) $8 : 1/8$ (d) $9 : 27$

7. $65 : 13 :: 180 : ?$

    (a) 93   (b) 36

    (c) 133   (d) 102

8. $125 : 27 :: 343 : ?$

    (a) 729   (b) 64

    (c) 216   (d) 512

9. $357 : 73 :: ?$

    (a) $429 : 94$

    (b) $201 : 21$

    (c) $138 : 38$

    (d) $93 : 39$

10. $731 : 902 :: 655 : ?$

    (a) 646   (b) 800

    (c) 793   (d) 556

11. $162 : 9 :: 310 : ?$

    (a) 33   (b) 27

    (c) 16   (d) 4

12. $13 : 17 :: 15 : ?$

    (a) 19   (b) 11

    (c) 21   (d) 16

13. $225 : 15 :: 256 : ?$

    (a) 26   (b) 16

    (c) 20   (d) 28

14. $46 : 48 :: 54 : ?$

    (a) 59   (b) 40

    (c) 67   (d) 62

15. $33 : 36 :: 21 : ?$

    (a) 9   (b) 18

    (c) 25   (d) 32

EXPLANATORY ANSWERS

1. (b) : The first number is repeated to obtain the second number.

2. (d) : The first fraction is multiplied by half to obtain the second fraction.

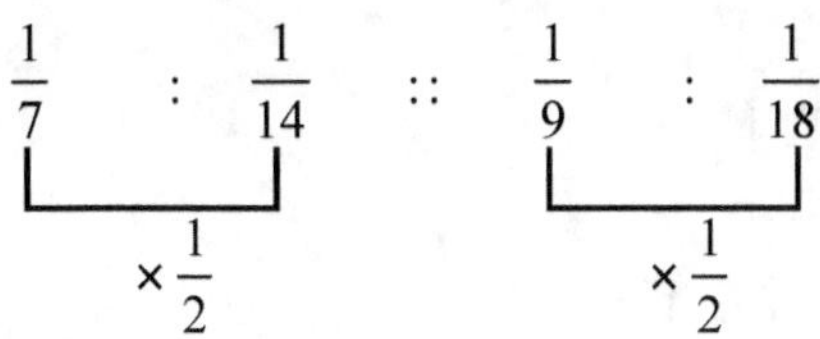

$$\frac{1}{7} \;:\; \frac{1}{14} \;::\; \frac{1}{9} \;:\; \frac{1}{18}$$

with each pair $\times \dfrac{1}{2}$

3. (c) : The decimals are divided by 100.

$$0.16 \;:\; 0.0016 \;::\; 1.02 \;:\; 0.0102$$

with each pair $\div 100$

4. (d) : The digits at tens and hundreds place is same but the digit at the units place is half the other identical digits.

$$\underline{66}\,\underline{3} \;:\; \underline{88}\,\underline{4} \;::\; \underline{22}\,\underline{1} \;:\; \underline{44}\,\underline{2}$$

5. (a) : Of the two related numbers, the second number is the result of first number divided by 100.

$$16 \;:\; 0.16 \;::\; 2 \;:\; 0.02$$

with each pair $\div 100$

6. (c) : Of the two related numbers, the second number is the part fraction of the first number, *i.e.* 3 is related to one-third $\left(\dfrac{1}{3}\right)$.

Similarly, 8 will be related to one-eighth $\left(\dfrac{1}{8}\right)$.

7. (b) : The first number is divided by 5 to get the second number.

$$65 \;:\; 13 \;::\; 180 \;:\; 36$$

with each pair $\div 5$

8. (a) : The numbers are cubes of different odd numbers.

$$125 \;:\; 27 \;::\; 343 \;:\; 729$$

$$5^3 \qquad 3^3 \qquad 7^3 \qquad 9^3$$

9. (a) : The central digit of the first number is left out and the corner digits written in reverse order to get the second number.

$$357 \;:\; 73 \;::\; 429 \;:\; 94$$

10. (a) : The sum of the digits of both the numbers is same.

$$731 : 902 \to 7 + 3 + 1$$
$$= 9 + 0 + 2 \; i.e. \; 11 = 11$$
$$655 : 646 \to 6 + 5 + 5$$
$$= 6 + 4 + 6 \; i.e. \; 16 = 16$$

11. (d) : The sum of the digits of the first number is the second number.

$$162 \;:\; 9 \;::\; 310 \;:\; 4$$
$$1 + 6 + 2 \qquad\qquad 3 + 1 + 0$$

12. (a) : First number plus 4 gives the second number.

$$13 \;:\; 17 \;::\; 15 \;:\; 19$$

with each pair $+4$

13. (b) : The root of first number is the second number.

$$225 \;:\; 15 \;::\; 256 \;:\; 16$$
$$\sqrt{225} \qquad\qquad \sqrt{256}$$

14. (b) : The product of the digits of first number is multiplied by 2 to get the second number.

$$46 \;:\; 48 \;::\; 54 \;:\; 40$$
$$(4 \times 6)\,2 \qquad\qquad (5 \times 4)\,2$$

15. (a) : The square of the sum of the digits of the first number is the second number.

$$33 \;:\; 36 \;::\; 21 \;:\; 9$$
$$(3 + 3)^2 \qquad\qquad (2 + 1)^2$$

8. ODD ONE OUT

In this type of classification, four words are given out of which three are almost same in matter or meaning and only one word is different from the common three. One has to find out the word which is different from the rest.

EXERCISE

Directions : *In each of the following questions, three words are alike in some manner. Spot the odd one out.*

1. (a) Green   (b) Red
   (c) Colour   (d) Orange
2. (a) Stable   (b) Hole
   (c) Canoe   (d) Sty
3. (a) Nose   (b) Eyes
   (c) Skin   (d) Teeth
4. (a) Venus   (b) Moon
   (c) Pluto   (d) Mars
5. (a) Happy   (b) Gloomy
   (c) Lively   (d) Cheerful

Directions : *Three of the following four in each question are alike in a certain way and so form a group. Select the group of letters that does not belong to that group.*

6. (a) ACE   (b) LOR
   (c) GIK   (d) VXZ
7. (a) TSR   (b) LKJ
   (c) PQO   (d) HGF
8. (a) EF LM   (b) KJ SR
   (c) XW HG   (d) ED YX
9. (a) JOPK   (b) BOPC
   (c) QOPR   (d) TOPS
10. (a) DfH   (b) MoQ
    (c) UwY   (d) lnO

Directions : *In each of the following questions, there are four options. Three numbers, in these options, are alike in certain manner. Only one number does not fit in. Choose the one which is different from the rest.*

11. (a) 1948   (b) 2401
    (c) 966   (d) 1449

12. (a) 182   (b) 169
    (c) 130   (d) 158
13. (a) 129   (b) 130
    (c) 131   (d) 132
14. (a) 3215   (b) 9309
    (c) 4721   (d) 2850
15. (a) 1776   (b) 2364
    (c) 1976   (d) 3776

Directions : *In the following questions select the pair which is different from the other three.*

16. (a) Chair - Furniture
    (b) Shirt - Garment
    (c) Necklace - Jewellery
    (d) Bogie - Engine
17. (a) Crayon - Paper
    (b) Pencil - Lead
    (c) Pen - Ink
    (d) Brush - Paint
18. (a) War - Peace
    (b) Real - Natural
    (c) Premiere - First
    (d) Wrath - Anger
19. (a) Finger - Thimble
    (b) Head - Cap
    (c) Waist - Tiara
    (d) Foot - Shoe
20. (a) Day - Night
    (b) Clever - Foolish
    (c) Clear - Blurred
    (d) Arrive - Come

(1673)-Reas.–3-II

Directions : *In the following questions, which of the following pair of letters is different from the other three?*

21. (a) FGH - HIJ (b) PQR - RST
 (c) MNO - OPQ (d) CDE - DEF
22. (a) JuM - jUm (b) iLo - Ilo
 (c) PSa - psA (d) ZeX - zEx

23. (a) NQT - JMP (b) CFI - RUX
 (c) ADG - FGH (d) SVY - ORU
24. (a) DXD - XDX (b) KUK - UKU
 (c) FHF - EHE (d) RSR - SRS
25. (a) AYT - BZU (b) FNG - EMF
 (c) RWO - QVN (d) HJD - GIC

EXPLANATORY ANSWERS

1. *(c)* : All others are types of colour.
2. *(c)* : Canoe is a boat. Others are resting places of birds/animals.
3. *(d)* : All others are sense organs.
4. *(b)* : All others are planets.
5. *(b)* : All others are expressions of joy.
6. *(b)* : The sequence in each group is +2. Only option (b) has sequence in +3, *i.e.,*

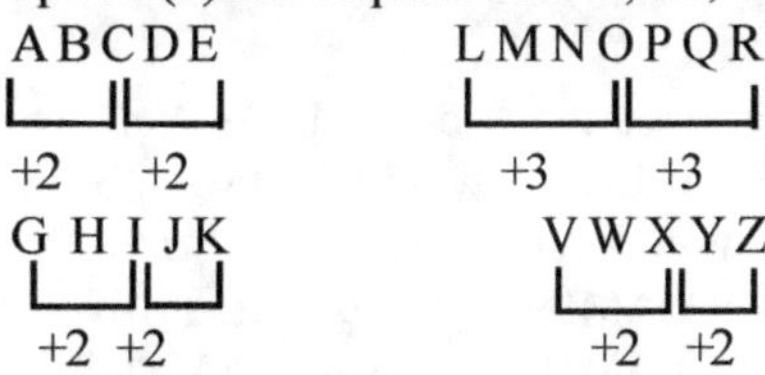

7. *(c)* : The sequence of alphabet in each group is in reverse order. Only option (c) has sequence in disturbed order.
8. *(a)* : Two consecutive alphabet in each group are in reverse sequence (–1), *i.e.,*

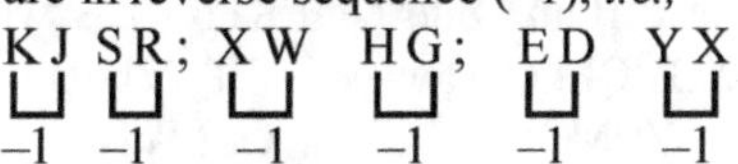

Only in option (a) the sequence is in natural order (+1), *i.e.,*

9. *(d)* : In each group, letters 'OP' are common. The two corner alphabet are in natural order (+1); *i.e.,*

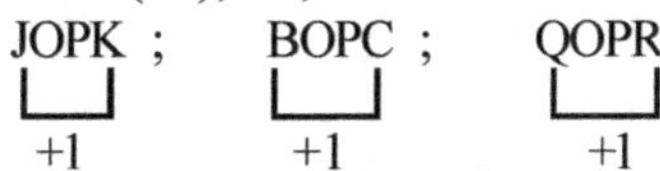

Only in option (d) they are in reverse order (–1); *i.e.,*

10. *(d)* : In other groups, only the alphabet in the centre is of lower case. In this option letter 'L' on the left is also in lower case.
11. *(a)* : Other numbers are divisible by 7.
12. *(d)* : Other numbers are multiples of 13.
13. *(c)* : 131 is a prime number.
14. *(b)* : In other numbers, no digit is repeated.
15. *(b)* : In other numbers, the last two digits are same.
16. *(d)* : Bogie is a part of train which is a type of conveyance. Chair, Shirt and Necklace are types of furniture, garment and jewellery respectively.
17. *(a)* : The medium used for writing with pencil is lead, with pen it is ink and with brush, it is paint. With crayon it should be wax.
18. *(a)* : The pair of words are opposite. Other pairs are synonyms.
19. *(c)* : Tiara is worn on the head.
20. *(d)* : Other words are opposite to each other.
21. *(d)* : In all other groups, the letters are in natural series and the last letter of first part is the first letter of the second part.
22. *(b)* : In all other groups, only the vowel is in lower case in the first part and in second part the case is reversed.
23. *(c)* : In all other groups, the letters jump two letters in between them.
24. *(c)* : In all other groups, the single letter in first part is repeated in the second and vice versa.
25. *(a)* : In all other groups, the letters in the first part are one step forward than the corresponding letters in the second part.

9. CODING AND DECODING

Coding is a secretive language which is used to change the representation of the actual term/word/value. This coded language can be framed by *(i)* moving the letters one or more steps forward or backward; *(ii)* substituting numbers for letters and vice–versa; *(iii)* writing the letters of the given word in reverse order in part or in whole; and *(iv)* replacing the letters in their natural series by the same positioned letters in their reverse series.

There is variety in ways of coding. Coding language is not only for words and numbers but also for hiding a group of words, statements or even sentences. This form of coding pattern may appear to be confusing but after solving only a few questions it is very easy to understand. Questions based on this coding pattern require no moving of steps or straining efforts of calculations, but only quick tallying or comparing ability. The codes can be letters or numbers.

EXERCISE

Directions : *In the following questions select the right option which indicates the correct code for the word or letter given in the question.*

1. If MUSK is coded as 146816, then ZERO will be coded as :
   - (a) 113811
   - (b) 122912
   - (c) 15915
   - (d) 2651815

2. If BAD is coded as 7, HIS as 9, LOW will be coded as :
   - (a) 50
   - (b) 8
   - (c) 23
   - (d) 5

3. In a certain code LIBERATE is written as 56403170, TRIBAL will be written in the same code as :
   - (a) 734615
   - (b) 736415
   - (c) 136475
   - (d) 034615

4. In certain military code, SYSTEM is written as SYSMET, and NEARER as AENRER, what will be the code for FRACTION?
   - (a) CRAFNOIT
   - (b) FRCAITNO
   - (c) CARFNOIT
   - (d) FRACNOIT

5. If CRUDE is written as BSTED, then MOIST will be coded as :
   - (a) NNJRU
   - (b) LNHRS
   - (c) NPJTU
   - (d) LPHTS

6. In a certain code ALPACA is written as ACAPLA. How will ANIMAL be written in that code?
   - (a) LAMINA
   - (b) ALAMIN
   - (c) LAMNIA
   - (d) AAMLIN

7. In a certain code FINGER is written as DGLECP. What will be the code for KIDNEY?
   - (a) IGBLCW
   - (b) IGCLBW
   - (c) IBCGLE
   - (d) IGBKCV

8. In a certain code QUESTION is written as NXBVQLLQ. How will REPLY be coded?
   - (a) YHMOV
   - (b) OBMVI
   - (c) VHSOB
   - (d) OHMOV

9. If in a certain code SKEW is coded as PNCY, then what will JXQV will stand for?
   - (a) MUTS
   - (b) MUST
   - (c) MTSU
   - (d) STUM

10. In a certain code LONDON is written as MPOEPO. What will IVOHSZ mean in the same code?
    - (a) HUNGRY
    - (b) HUNDRY
    - (c) GRUNHY
    - (d) HONDUS

11. In a certain code language 8514 is a code for HEAD, 3945 for RIDE and 057 for BEG. What will be the code for GRADE?
    - (a) 71345
    - (b) 73415
    - (c) 74135
    - (d) 73145

12. If MOTHERLAND is coded as 9501623748, how will DREAM be coded?
    (*a*) 82697   (*b*) 86297
    (*c*) 82769   (*d*) 82679
13. If OATH is coded in a certain language as TEYL, then how will WORD be coded?
    (*a*) BWRH   (*b*) HRWB
    (*c*) BSWH   (*d*) CSXI
14. If FINANCE is coded as GKQESIL, then how will BANK be coded in the same manner?

15. PLANNING is coded in a certain language as UFFHSCSA. How will AUTHORITY be coded in the same language?
    (*a*) FOYBTLNND
    (*b*) FYOTBNNLT
    (*c*) FBOYTLNTN
    (*d*) FBOYTNLTN

(*a*) CBOL   (*b*) CDRP
(*c*) CCQO   (*d*) CCPN

EXPLANATORY ANSWERS

1. *(b)* : The coded number signifies the position of the alphabet in its reverse order of the alphabetical series (ZYXW...)

    M U S K → MUSK
    ↓ ↓ ↓ ↓
    14th 6th 8th 16th → 146816

    Similarly,

    Z E R O → ZERO
    ↓ ↓ ↓ ↓
    1st 22nd 9th 12th → 122912

2. *(d)* : The coded number is the sum of number digits signifying the position of the alphabet in the natural order.

    B A D
    ↓ ↓ ↓
    2nd 1st 4th *i.e.,* $2 + 1 + 4$ = 7

    Similarly,

    H I S
    ↓ ↓ ↓
    8th 9th 19th *i.e.,* $8 + 9 + 19$ = 36
                         further, $3 + 6$ = 9

    Also,

    L O W
    ↓ ↓ ↓
    12th 15th 23rd *i.e.,* $12 + 15 + 23$ = 50
                         further, $5 + 0$ = 0

3. *(b)* : The letters of the word TRIBAL are picked from LIBERATE. So will be the coded numbers.

    L I B E R A T E → given word
    5 6 4 0 3 1 7 0 → codes

    Similarly,

    T R I B A L → word to be coded
    7 3 6 4 1 5 → answer codes

4. *(c)* : The word is divided into two equal parts and the letters of each part are written in reverse order.

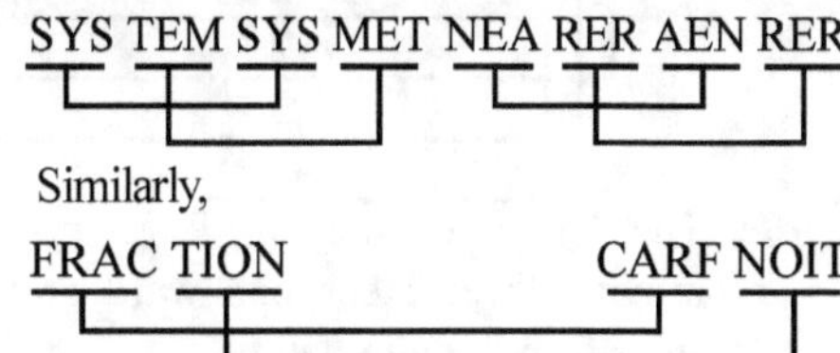

5. *(d)* : The code is formed by moving the letters one step backwards and one step forward alternately.

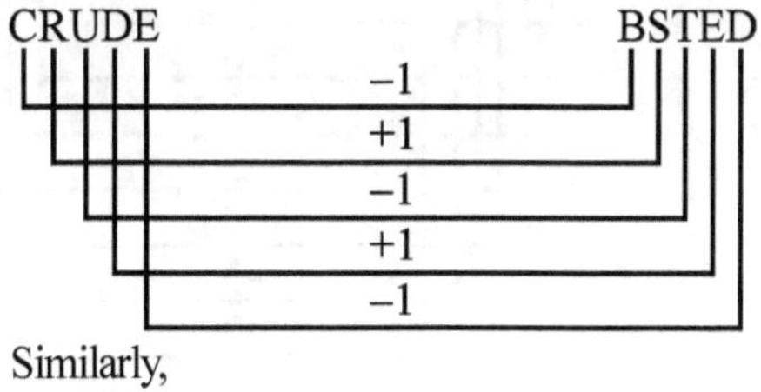

Similarly,

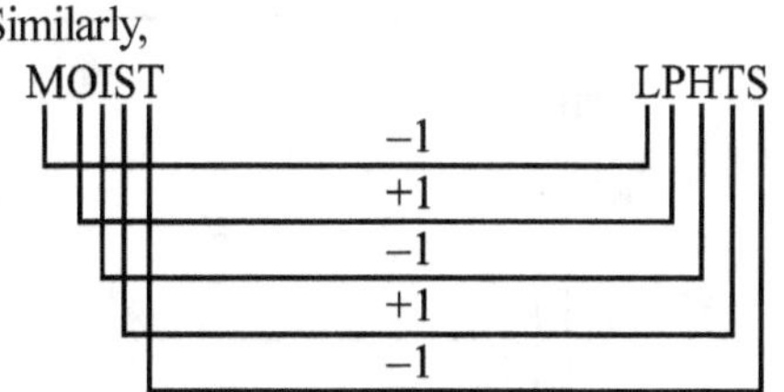

6. *(a)* : The letters of the word are written backwards.

Similarly,

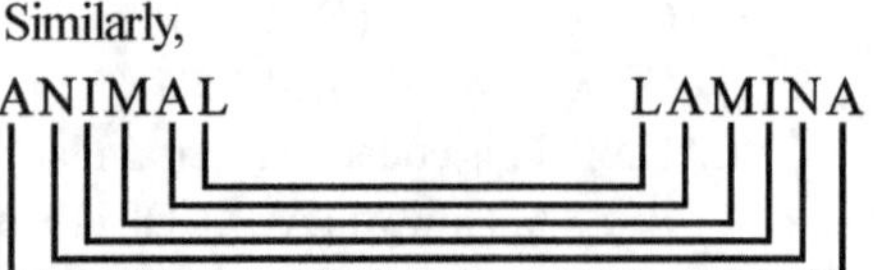

7. (a) : The word is coded by moving the letters two steps backwards.

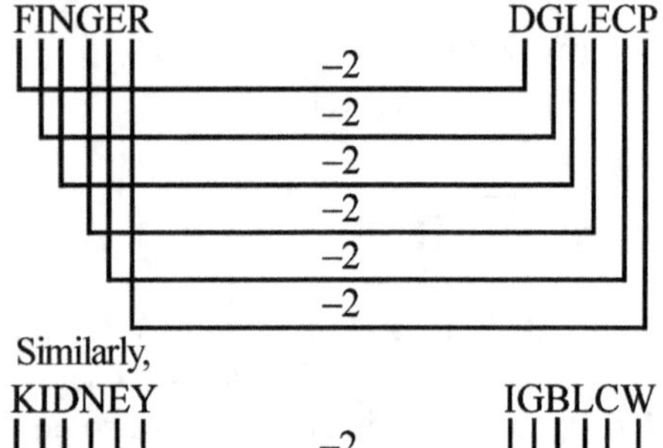

Similarly,

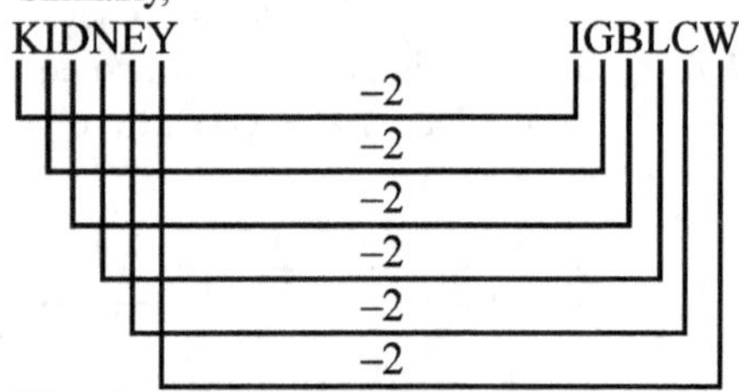

8. (d) : The letters of the word are coded by moving three steps backward and three steps forward alternately.

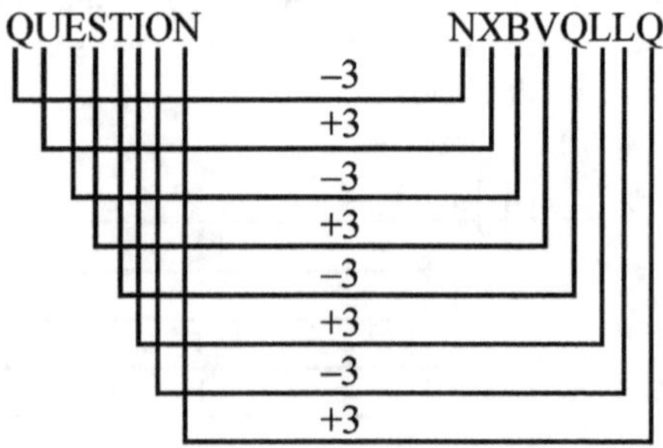

Similarly,

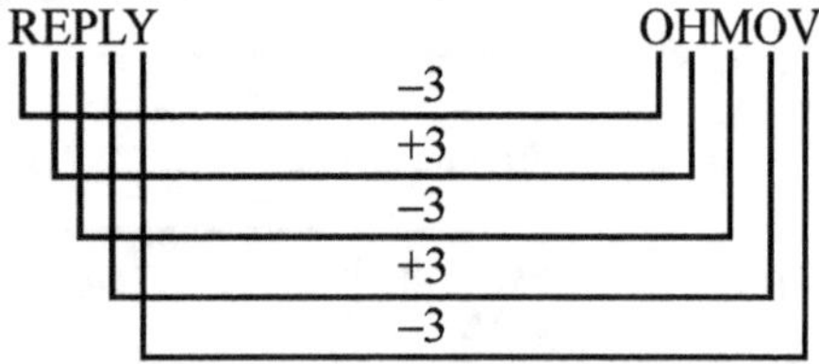

9. (b) : The letters are decoded by moving the letters +3, –3, +2 and –2 steps respectively.

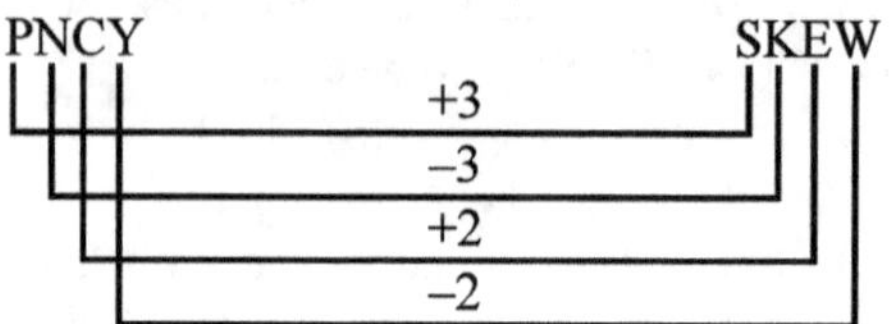

Similarly,

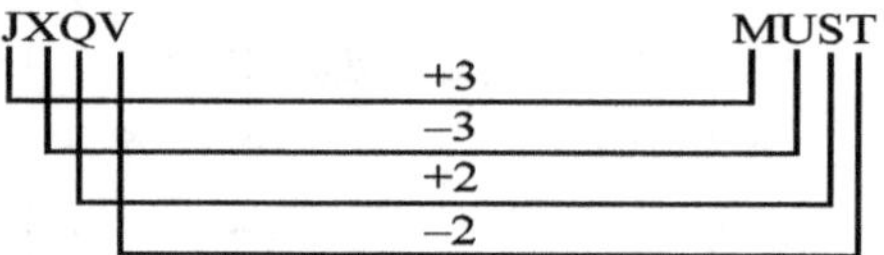

10. (a) : The letters of the coded word are moved one step backward.

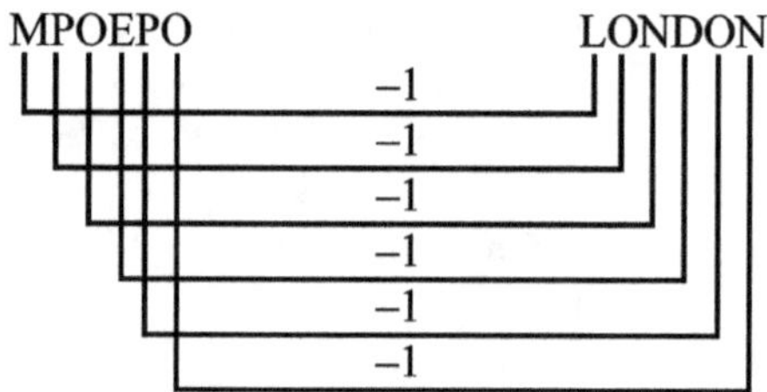

Similarly,

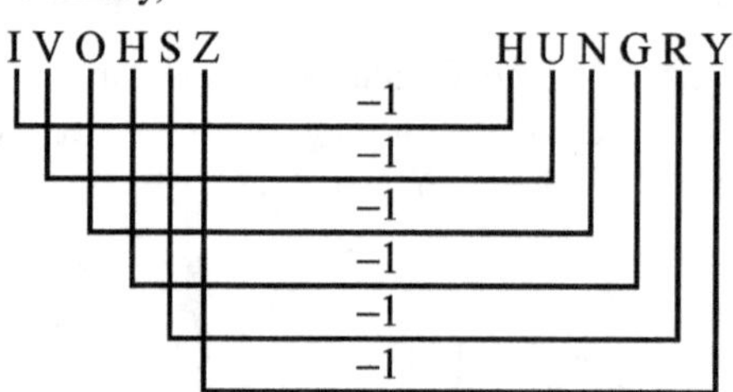

11. (d) : The word GRADE is framed by letters in the given words. So, in order to find the code for GRADE select the respective number codes.

H E A D   R I D E   B E G → letters
8 5 1 4   3 9 4 5   0 5 7 → codes

So,

G R A D E → letters
7 3 1 4 5   → answer codes

12. (d) : The letters of the word are coded by numbers. So to find the code for DREAM select the respective numbers.

M O T H E R L A N D → letters
9 5 0 1 6 2 3 7 4 8 → codes

So,   D R E A M → letters
      8 2 6 7 9 → answer codes

13. *(c)* : The letters are coded by moving five and four steps forward alternately.

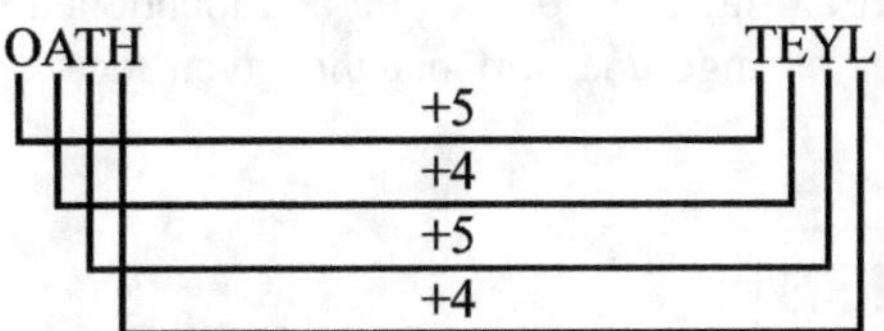

OATH ————— TEYL
+5
+4
+5
+4

Similarly,

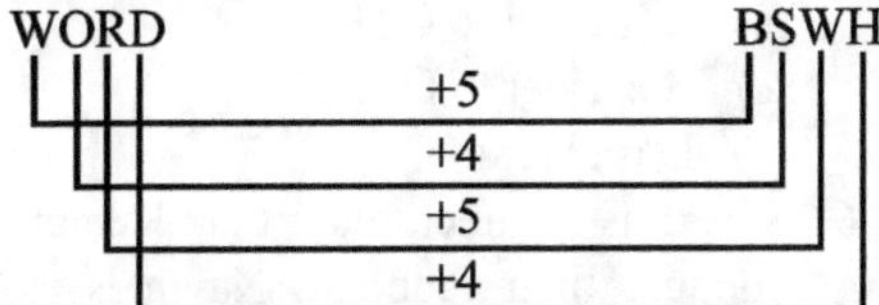

WORD ————— BSWH
+5
+4
+5
+4

14. *(c)* : The letters of the word are coded by moving one step ahead and increasing the difference by one.

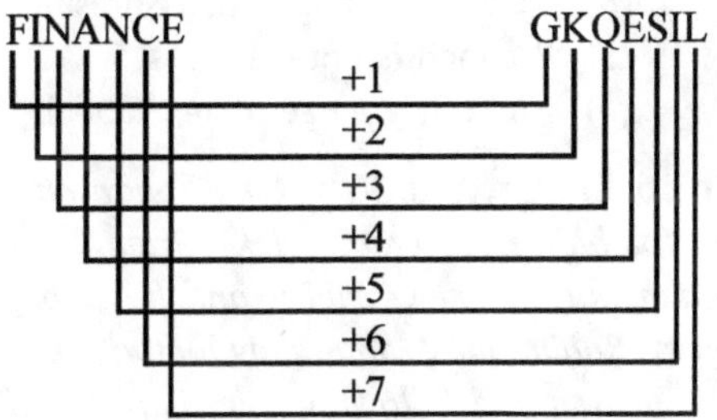

FINANCE ————— GKQESIL
+1
+2
+3
+4
+5
+6
+7

Similarly,

BANK ————— CCQO

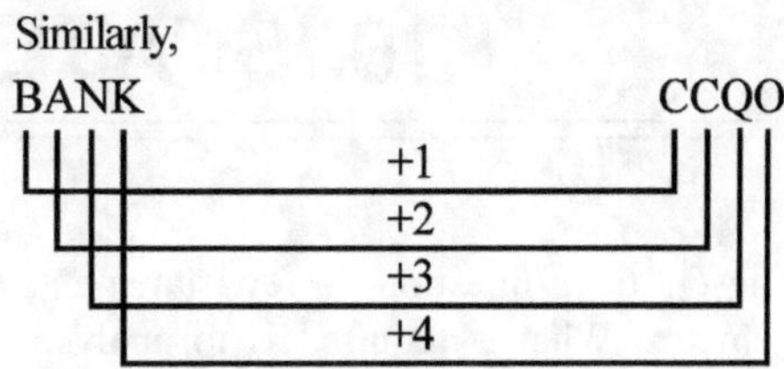

+1
+2
+3
+4

15. *(a)* : The letters of the word are coded by moving five steps forward and six steps backward alternately.

PLANNING ————— UFFHSCSA

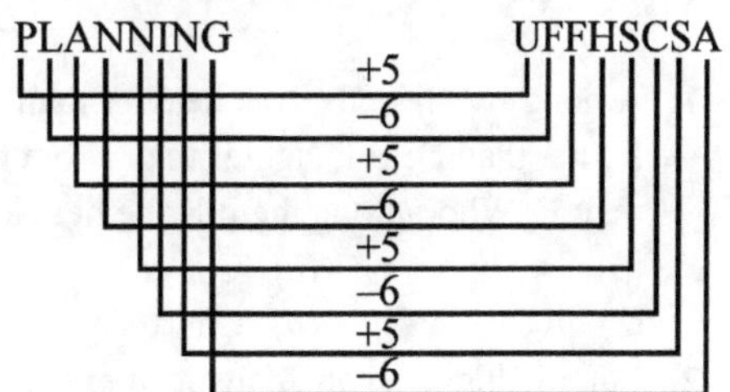

+5
−6
+5
−6
+5
−6
+5
−6

Similarly,

AUTHORITY ————— FOYBTLNND

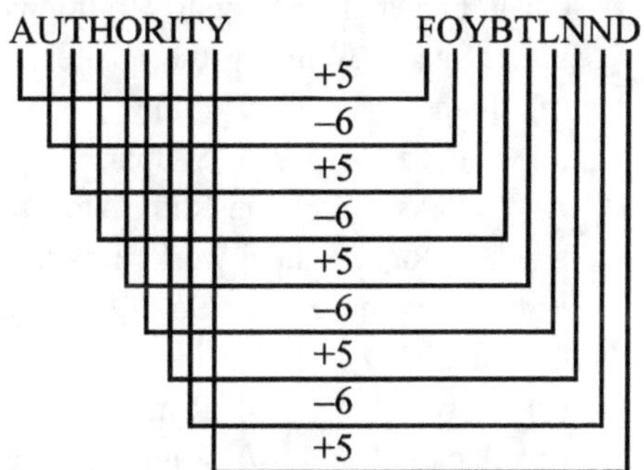

+5
−6
+5
−6
+5
−6
+5
−6
+5

10. STATEMENT ANALYSIS

In these type of questions, a few statements are given. Certain facts are broken up and mentioned in these statements. What is required is to analyse the statements, arrange and sort out the given facts and then answer the questions related to the given statements.

EXERCISE

1. Among five friends, A is heavier than B; C is lighter than D; B is lighter than D but heavier than E. Who among them is the heaviest?
   - (a) B
   - (b) C
   - (c) A
   - (d) Can't say

2. Pune is bigger than Jhansi, Sitapur is bigger than Chittor. Raigarh is not as big as Jhansi, but is bigger than Sitapur. Chittor is not as big as Sitapur. Which is the smallest?
   - (a) Jhansi
   - (b) Pune
   - (c) Chittor
   - (d) Sitapur

3. Ajay works more than Ram. Alok works as much as Raju. Pankaj works less than Alok. Ram works more than Alok. Who works the most of all?
   - (a) Ajay
   - (b) Ram
   - (c) Alok
   - (d) Raju

4. Among five friends P, Q, R, S and T, who is the youngest? To arrive at the answer which of the following information given in the statements (A) and (B) is sufficient?
   (A) R is younger than P and T.
   (B) S is younger than Q.
   - (a) Only A alone is sufficient
   - (b) Either A or B is sufficient
   - (c) Both A and B together are needed
   - (d) Both A and B together are not sufficient

5. A is elder to B while C and D are elder to E who lies between A and B. If C be elder to B, which one of the following statements is necessarily true?
   - (a) E is elder to B
   - (b) A is elder to C
   - (c) C is elder to D
   - (d) D is elder to C

6. Suresh is as much older than Kamal as he is younger than Prabodh. Navin is as old as Kamal. Which of the following statements is wrong?
   - (a) Suresh is older than Navin
   - (b) Kamal is younger than Suresh
   - (c) Prabodh is not the oldest
   - (d) Navin is younger than Prabodh

Directions (Qs. 7 to 9) : *Ram, Sohan and Mohan play football, hockey and cricket. Ram, Ramesh and Mohan play hockey, cricket and basketball. Ram, Sohan, Rahim and Mohan play football and cricket. Now answer the following questions based on the above statements :*

7. Which game is played by all the boys?
   - (a) Football
   - (b) Hockey
   - (c) Cricket
   - (d) Basketball

8. Which two boys play all the games?
   - (a) Ram, Sohan
   - (b) Ram, Ramesh
   - (c) Sohan, Mohan
   - (d) Ram, Mohan

9. Who does not play football?
   - (a) Ramesh
   - (b) Sohan
   - (c) Rahim
   - (d) Mohan

Directions (Qs. 10 to 12) : *Read the following directions and answer the questions given below :*
There are five persons in a group. Out of these two are men. Only three persons know swimming, of

which one is a man. There is a couple, of which the husband knows swimming. A is the younger sister of D and B is the husband of E. C is a swimming champion.

10. Who is the other man in the group?
  (*a*) C (*b*) B
  (*c*) A (*d*) D

11. The two women who know how to swim are:
  (*a*) A and C (*b*) C and D
  (*c*) D and E (*d*) A and E

12. The two persons who do not know how to swim are :
  (*a*) B and D (*b*) D and E
  (*c*) A and E (*d*) A and D

Directions (Qs. 13 to 15) : *Read the following statements and answer the questions given below :*
Rajat, Sushil and Nagesh play football, hockey and cricket. Rajat, Ramu and Nagesh play hockey, cricket and basketball. Rajat, Sushil, Mayank and Nagesh play football and cricket.

13. Which game is played by all the boys?
  (*a*) Hockey (*b*) Basketball
  (*c*) Football (*d*) Cricket

14. Who does not play football?
  (*a*) Rajat (*b*) Nagesh
  (*c*) Sushil (*d*) Ramu

15. Which of the following two boys play all the games?
  (*a*) Nagesh, Rajat (*b*) Mayank, Ramu
  (*c*) Ramu, Nagesh (*d*) Sushil, Mayank

EXPLANATORY ANSWERS

1. (*d*) : The five friends in descending order of weight are : A/D, B/C, E or A/D, B, C/E. Either A or D is the heaviest.

2. (*c*) : The order of cities in descending order of size is : Pune, Jhansi, Raigarh, Sitapur, Chittor.

3. (*a*) : On the basis of doing work, the descending order will be : Ajay, Ram, Alok/Raju, Pankaj.

4. (*d*) : Statements are not inter-related.

5. (*a*) : The order in descending seniority will be : A/C/D, E, B.

6. (*c*) : On the basis of age the descending order will be : Prabodh, Suresh, Kamal/Navin.

Chart for Answers 7 to 9

Boy	Games Played
Ram	Football, Hocky, Cricket, Basketball
Sohan	Football, Hockey, Cricket
Mohan	Football, Hockey, Cricket, Basketball
Ramesh	Hockey, Cricket, Basketball
Rahim	Football, Cricket.

7. (*c*) 8. (*d*)   9. (*a*)

For Answers 10 to 12 the information chart will be :

A. Woman ((younger sister of D); knows swimming.

B. Man (husband of E); knows swimming

C. Woman; Swimming champion

D. Man (brother of A)

E. Woman (wife of B)

From the couple B & E, B (husband) knows swimming. C is a swimming champion. Three persons know how to swim of which only B is a man. So, the two women who know how to swim are C and A (the younger sister of D). There are two men in the group of five. One is B and the other will be D.

10. (*d*)   11. (*a*)   12. (*b*)

Chart for Answers 13 to 15

Boy	Games Played
Rajat	— Football, Hockey, Cricket, Basketball
Sushil	— Football, Hockey, Cricket, Basketball
Nagesh	— Football, Hockey, Cricket, Basketball
Ramu	— Hockey, Cricket, Basketball
Mayank	— Football, Cricket

13. (*d*)   14. (*d*) 15. (*a*)

11. PLACE ARRANGEMENT

Place arrangement generally refers to the positioning of persons or objects in a manner indicated by set of information given. One has to understand the order of placement and then attempt questions following the given information.

EXERCISE

Directions : *In the following questions, understand the arrangement pattern and then select the right answer from the given options :*

1. Five boys are sitting in a row. Raghu is not adjacent to Shyam or Amit. Ajay is not adjacent to Shyam. Raghu is adjacent to Mayank. If Mayank is at the middle in the row, then Ajay is adjacent to whom out of the following?
   (*a*) Amit   (*b*) Raghu
   (*c*) Mayank   (*d*) Shyam

2. Mini is to the right of Rajni but to the left of Ananta. Saya is to the right of Mini but to the left of Jaya. Who is on the extreme left if all the girls are facing North?
   (*a*) Jaya   (*b*) Mini
   (*c*) Rajni   (*d*) Saya

3. O, P, Q, R, S and T are standing on a bench according to their height. P is taller than O but shorter than S. Only S is taller than T. R is shorter than P but taller than Q. Who is the shortest?
   (*a*) O   (*b*) Q
   (*c*) P   (*d*) Cannot be said

4. Five personalities are living in a multistoried building. Mr. Effortless lives in a flat above Mr. Active, Mr. Charge lives in a flat below Mr. Diligent, Mr. Active lives in a flat above Mr. Diligent and Mr. Behaved lives in a flat below Mr. Charge. Who lives in the topmost flat?
   (*a*) Mr. Charge   (*b*) Mr. Diligent
   (*c*) Mr. Effortless (*d*) Mr. Behaved

5. Six friends are sitting in a circle and playing cards. Kenny is to the left of Danny. Michael is in-between Bob and John. Roger is in between Kenny and Bob. Who is sitting to the right of Michael?
   (*a*) Danny   (*b*) John
   (*c*) Kenny   (*d*) Bob

6. Four girls A, B, C and D are sitting in a circle. B and C are facing each other. Which of the following is definitely true?
   (*a*) A is to the left of C
   (*b*) D is to the left of C
   (*c*) A and D are facing each other
   (*d*) A is not between B and C

7. Brijesh, Jayesh, Amar and Praveer are playing a game of cards. Amar is to the right of Jayesh who is to the right of Brijesh. Who is to the right of Amar?
   (*a*) Brijesh
   (*b*) Praveer
   (*c*) Brijesh or Praveer
   (*d*) Jayesh

8. In a pile of 10 books there are 3 of History, 3 of Hindi, 2 of Maths, and 2 of English. Taking from above there is an English book between a History and Maths book, a History book between a Maths and an English book, a Hindi book between an English and a Maths book, a Maths book between two Hindi books, and two Hindi books between a Maths and a History book. Book of which subject is at the sixth position from the top?
   (*a*) English   (*b*) Hindi
   (*c*) History   (*d*) Maths

9. Five persons A, B, C, D and E are sitting in a row facing you such that D is on the left of C and B is on the right of E. A is on the right of C and B is on the left of D. If E occupies a corner position, then who is sitting in the centre?

(*a*) A   (*b*) B

(*c*) C   (*d*) D

10. Six friends A, B, C, D, E and F are standing in a circle. B is between F and C; A is between E and D; F is to the left of D. Who is between A and F?

(*a*) C   (*b*) B

(*c*) D   (*d*) E

EXPLANATORY ANSWERS

1. *(b)* : The order of sitting is :

Amit, Shyam, Mayank, Ajay, Raghu

or

Ajay, Raghu, Mayank, Amit, Shyam

2. *(c)* : The order in which the girls are positioned is :

Rajni, Mini, Ananta, Saya, Jaya

or

Saya, Jaya, Ananta

or

Saya, Ananta, Jaya

3. *(d)* : In descending order of height, the standing positions are :

S		S
T		T
P	*or*	P
R		R
O		Q
Q		O

Either O or Q is the shortest. The informa-tion given is not enough to clarify the answer.

4. *(c)* : The personalities living in flats in multi-storied building are in order given below :

Mr. Effortless

Mr. Active

Mr. Diligent

Mr. Charge

Mr. Behaved

5. *(d)* : The order in which the friends are sitting is :

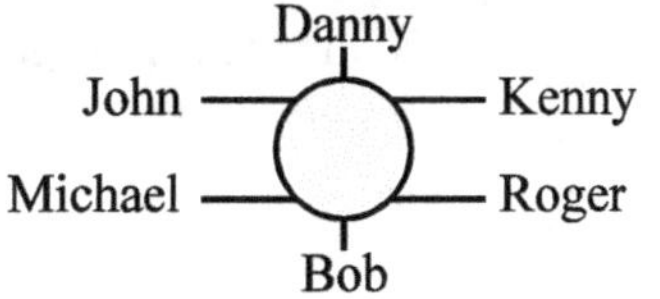

6. *(c)* : The sitting positions are :

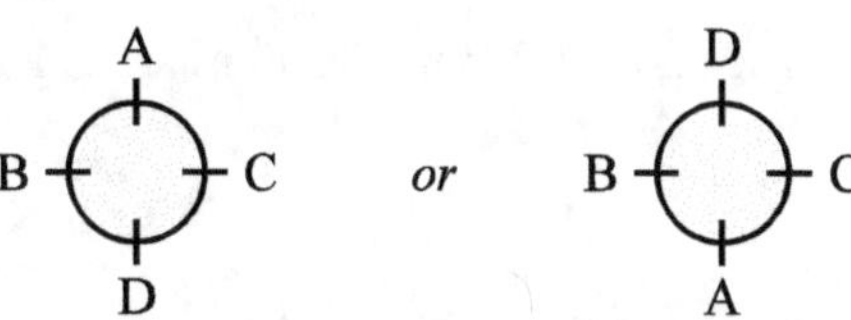

7. *(b)* : The order from left to right is :

Brijesh, Jayesh, Amar, Praveer

8. *(b)* : The pile of books is in the order :

1st — History

English

Maths

History

English

6th — Hindi

Maths

Hindi

Hindi

10th — History

9. *(d)* : Sitting order while facing us is :

A, C, D, B, E

10. *(c)* : The pattern of standing is :

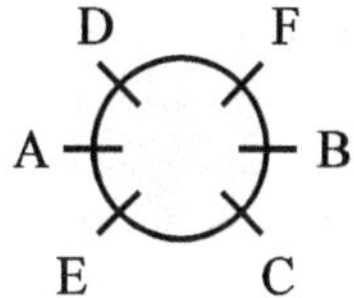

12. DIRECTION SENSE

In these type of tests, the directions in questions needs to be perceived. Such questions are based on the direction chart.

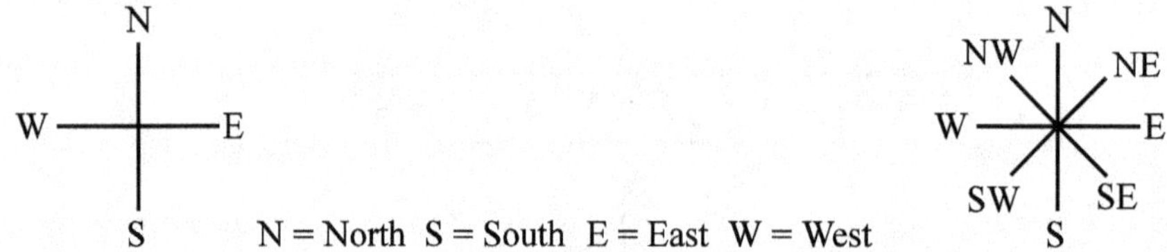

The sense of the different directions are guided by the left and right turns or angular turns.

EXERCISE

Directions : *In the following questions, select the right answer from the given options to depict the correct direction/distance.*

1. Kittu walks towards East and then towards South. After walking some distance he turns towards West and then turns to his left. In which direction is he walking now?
   (*a*) North   (*b*) South
   (*c*) East   (*d*) West

2. A person is driving towards West. What sequence of directions should he follow so that he is driving towards South?
   (*a*) left, right, right
   (*b*) right, right, left
   (*c*) left, left, left
   (*d*) right, right, right

3. Richa drives 8 km to the South, turns left and drives 5 km. Again, she turns left and drives 8 km. How far is she from her starting point?
   (*a*) 3 km   (*b*) 5 km
   (*c*) 8 km   (*d*) 13 km

4. Dingi runs 40 km towards North then turns right and runs 50 km. He turns right and runs 30 km, and once again turns right and runs 50 km. How far is he from his starting point?
   (*a*) 90 km   (*b*) 50 km
   (*c*) 10 km   (*d*) 5 km

5. If North is called North-West, North-West is called West, West is called South-West and so on. What will South-East be called?
   (*a*) East   (*b*) West
   (*c*) North-East   (*d*) South-East

6. A man travels 100 km towards South. From there he turns right and travels 100 km and again turns right to travel 50 km. Which direction is he in from his starting point?
   (*a*) North   (*b*) North-East
   (*c*) East   (*d*) South-West

7. A train runs 120 km in West direction, 30 km in South direction and then 80 km in east direction before reaching the station. In which direction is the station from the train's starting point?
   (*a*) South-West   (*b*) North-West
   (*c*) South-East   (*d*) South

8. Facing the West direction, Priya jogs for 20 m, turns left and goes further 40 m. She turns left again and jogs for 20 m. Then she turns right to go 20 m to reach the park. How far is the park from her starting point and in which direction?
   (*a*) 20 m South   (*b*) 40 m West
   (*c*) 60 m South   (*d*) 100 m East

9. If all the directions are rotated, *i.e.,* if North is changed to West and East to North and so on, then what will come in place of North-West?
  (*a*) South-West   (*b*) North-East
  (*c*) East-North   (*d*) East-West
10. A and B start together from one point. They walk 10 km towards North. A turns left and covers 5 km whereas B turns right and covers 3 km. A turns left again and covers 15 km whereas B turns right and covers his 15 km. How far is A from B?
  (*a*) 18 km   (*b*) 10 km
  (*c*) 5 km   (*d*) 8 km

EXPLANATORY ANSWERS

1. (*b*) :

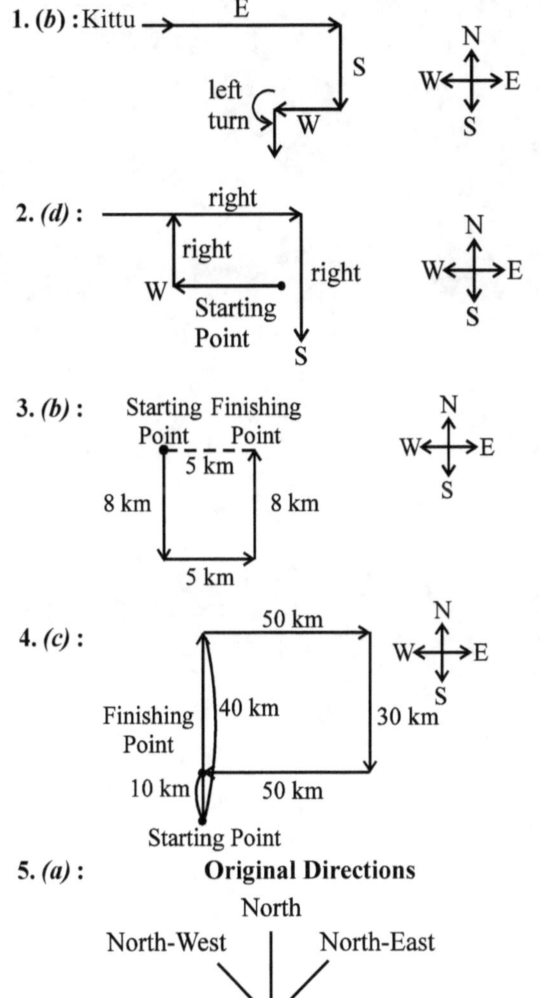

2. (*d*) :

3. (*b*) :

4. (*c*) :

5. (*a*) : **Original Directions**

Changed Directions

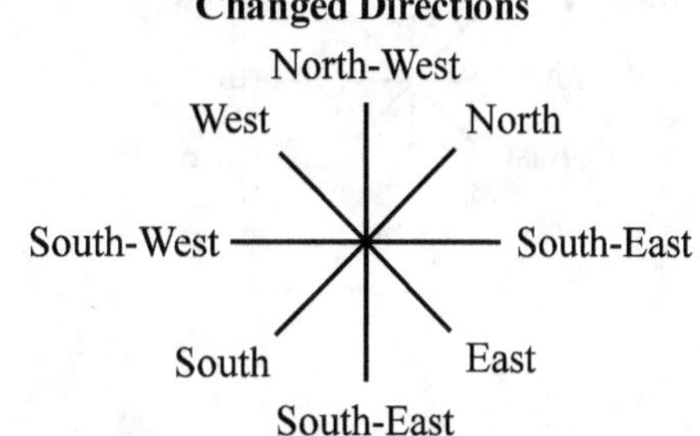

6. (*d*) :

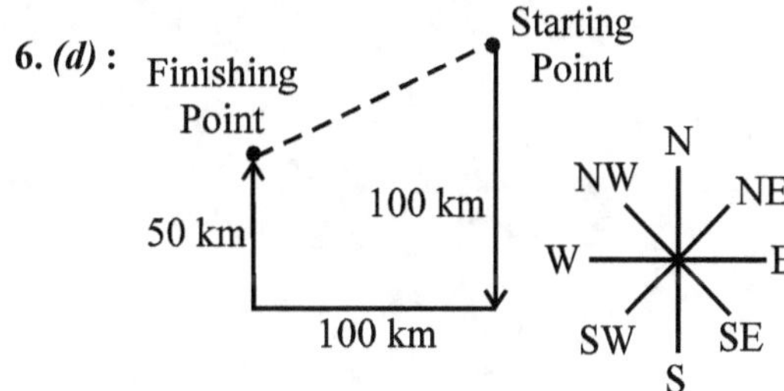

7. (*a*) :

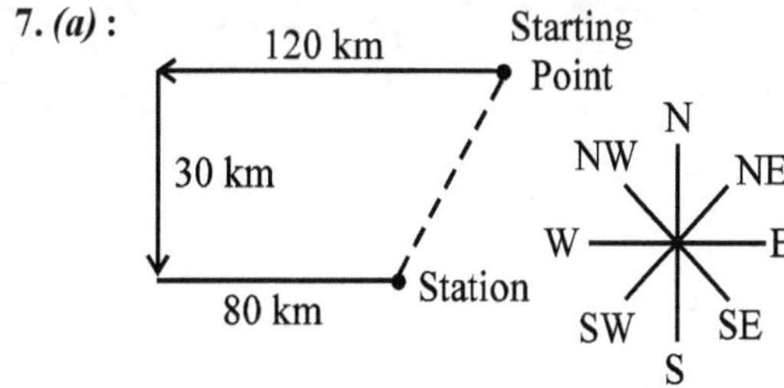

8. (*c*) : $(40 + 20) = 60$ metres South

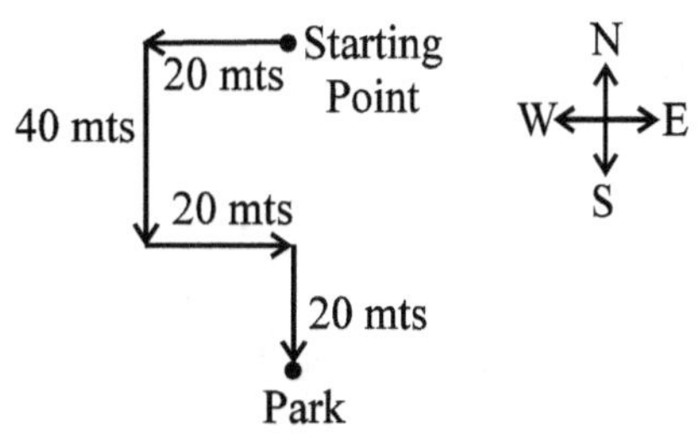

9. *(a)* : Original Directions

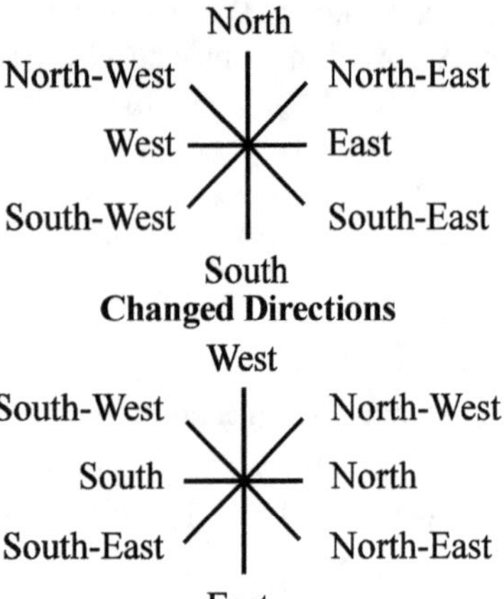

10. *(d)* :

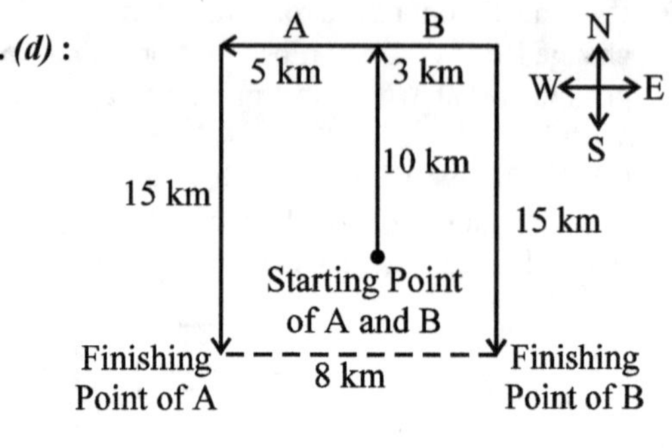

13. BLOOD RELATIONSHIPS

While attempting questions on blood relations, one should be clear of all the relation patterns that can exist between any two individuals. These type of questions are given mainly to test one's relationship ability.

Very well-known relations are :

Mother	Grandmother	Father	Grandfather	Son	Grandson
Daughter	Granddaughter	Brother	Brother-in-law	Sister	Sister-in-law
Niece	Father-in-law	Nephew	Mother-in-law	Uncle	Son-in-law
Aunt	Daughter-in-law	Husband	Cousin	Wife	

The patterns of some relationships which help in solving questions in these tests are :

Father's *or* Mother's Father	—	Grandfather (Paternal *or* Maternal)
Father's *or* Mother's Mother	—	Grandmother (Paternal *or* Maternal)
Father's *or* Mother's Son	—	Brother
Father's *or* Mother's Daughter	—	Sister
Father's Brother	—	Paternal Uncle
Father's Sister	—	Paternal Aunt
Mother's Brother	—	Maternal Uncle
Mother's Sister	—	Maternal Aunt
Uncle *or* Aunt's Son *or* Daughter	—	Cousin
Son's Wife	—	Daughter-in-law
Daughter's Husband	—	Son-in-law
Husband's *or* Wife's Brother	—	Brother-in-law
Husband's *or* Wife's Sister	—	Sister-in-law
Brother's Wife	—	Sister-in-law
Sister's Husband	—	Brother-in-law
Brother's Son	—	Nephew
Brother's Daughter	—	Niece

EXERCISE

Directions : *In each of the following questions keenly study the relationship mentioned between the persons, and then from the given options select the right relationship as the answer.*

1. A lady said, "The person standing there is my grandfather's only son's daughter". How is the lady related to the standing person?
   (*a*) Sister   (*b*) Mother
   (*c*) Aunt   (*d*) Cousin

2. Ajay is the brother of Vijay. Mili is the sister of Ajay. Sanjay is the brother of Rahul and Mehul is the daughter of Vijay. Who is Sanjay's Uncle?
   (*a*) Rahul   (*b*) Ajay
   (*c*) Mehul   (*d*) Data inadequate

3. A man introduced the boy coming with him as "He is son of the father of my wife's daughter". What relation did the boy bear to the man?
   (*a*) Son-in-law   (*b*) Son
   (*c*) Brother   (*d*) Father

4. If Amit's father is Billoo's father's only son and Billoo has neither a brother nor a

daughter, what is the relationship between Amit and Billoo?
(a) Uncle — Nephew
(b) Father — Daughter
(c) Father — Son
(d) Cousins

5. Pointing to a woman in the photograph a man said, "She is the daughter of my grandmother's only son." How is the woman related to the man?
(a) Mother   (b) Daughter
(c) Sister-in-law   (d) Sister

6. Pointing to a photograph, a woman said, "She is the only daughter of my mother's father." How is the woman related to the person in the photograph?
(a) Mother
(b) Grandmother
(c) Daughter
(d) Cannot be determined

7. Ram is the brother of Shyam and Mahesh is the father of Ram. Jagat is the brother of Priya and Priya is daughter of Shyam. Who is the uncle of Jagat ?
(a) Shyam   (b) Mahesh
(c) Ram   (d) Data insufficient

8. Introducing a man, a woman said, "His wife is the only daughter of my father". How is the man related to the woman?
(a) Husband   (b) Father
(c) Father-in-law   (d) Brother

9. If Maya is the only daughter of Richa's grandmother's brother, how is Maya's daughter related to Richa?
(a) Niece   (b) Cousin
(c) Aunt   (d) Mother

10. Pointing to a woman, a man said, "Her husband's mother is the wife of my father's only son". How is the man related to the woman?
(a) Son   (b) Brother-in-law
(c) Uncle   (d) Father-in-law

EXPLANATORY ANSWERS

1. (a) : Grandfather

Father (only son)

Daughter (standing person) ⟶ Lady (sister)

Lady's grandfather's son is lady's father and father's daughter will only be lady's sister.

2. (d) : 1. Mili ⟶ Ajay ⟶ Vijay
(sister)   (brother) ↓
           Mehul

2. Sanjay ⟶ Rahul (daughter)
(brother)

There are two sets of relationship. Information given is incomplete and no relation can be established between the two sets.

3. (b) : The relationship chart based on problem is :

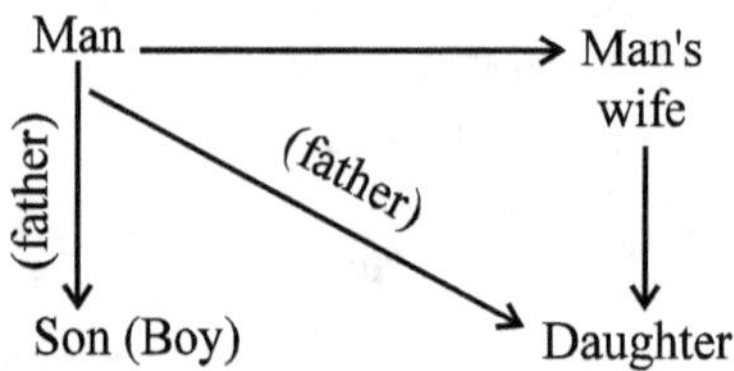

'Father of the man's wife's daughter' is the man himself and the boy in question is the man's son.

4. (c) : The relationship chart based on problem is :

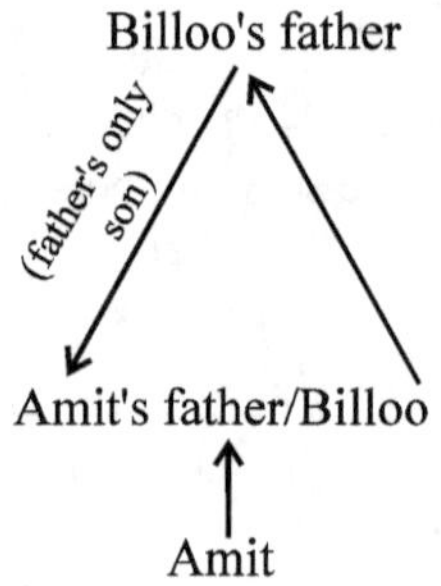

Amit's father is Billoo's father's only son means Billoo is the only son in question also, he is the father of Amit. It must be noted that Billoo has no brother which means he is single and also, when he has no daughter, Amit is his only son.

5. (d) :

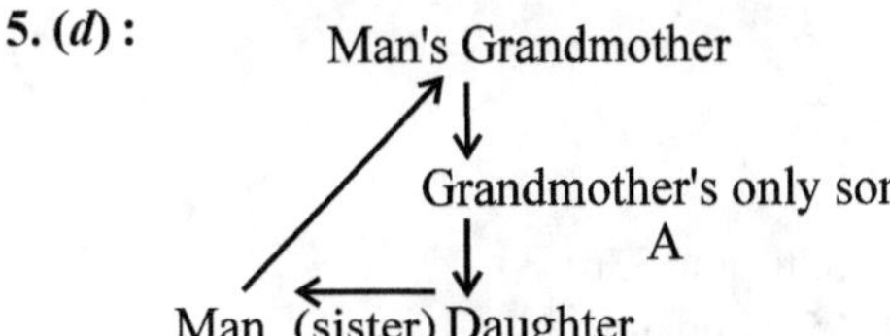

'My grandmother's only son' is the father of the man, and 'daughter of my grandmother's only son' is the sister of the man.

6. (c) :

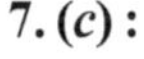

'Only daughter of my mother's father' is the person in the photograph and she is also the mother of the woman. So, the woman is the daughter of the person in the photograph.

7. (c) :

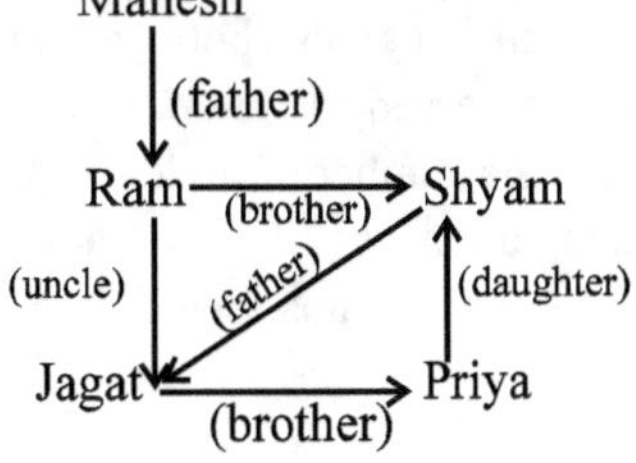

Jagat is brother of Priya and Priya is daughter of Shyam. So Shyam is also the father of Jagat. Ram is the brother of Shyam. So, Jagat's father's brother Ram is the uncle of Jagat.

8. (a) :

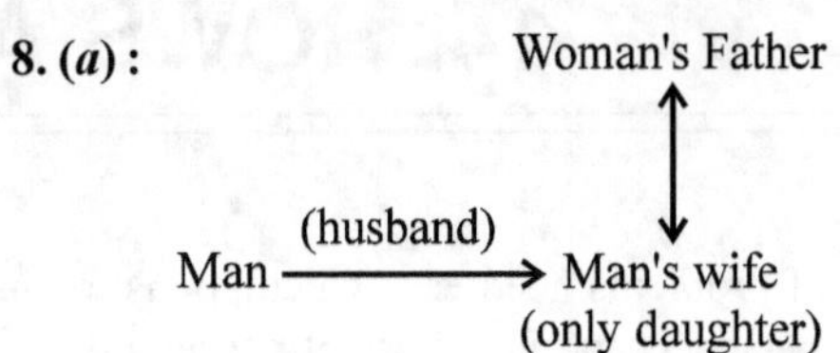

'Only daughter of my father' is the woman herself and the man is her husband.

9. (b) :

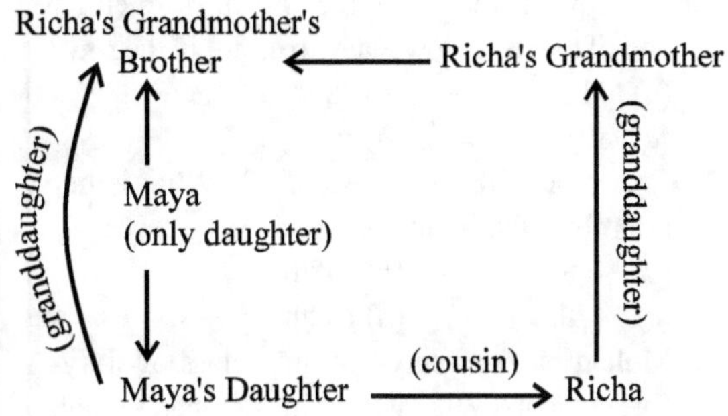

Both Maya's Daughter and Richa are granddaughters of a brother and a sister respectively. So Maya's daughter is the cousin of Richa.

10. (d) :

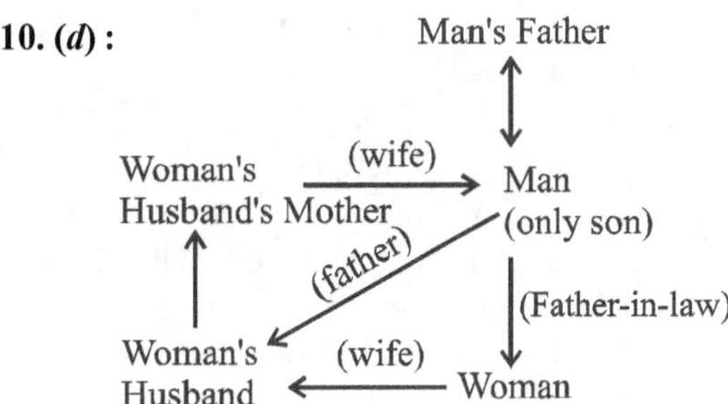

'My father's only son' is the man himself. 'Her husband's mother' is the wife of the man and so the man is the father of the woman's husband. As the woman is the wife of man's son, the man is the father-in-law of the woman.

14. ROWS AND RANKS

These type of problems need easy calculations to find out the number of objects in a row, lane or queue or to find a person's rank in a class of certain number of students; or to find the total number of students.

EXERCISE

1. In a row of trees, one tree is fifth from either end of the row. How many trees are in the row?
   (a) 11   (b) 8
   (c) 10   (d) 9

2. Jaya ranks 5th in a class of 53. What is her rank from the bottom in the class?
   (a) 49th   (b) 48th
   (c) 47th   (d) 50th

3. Mohan ranks twenty-first in a class of sixty-five students. What will be his (Mohan's) rank if the lowest candidate is assigned rank 1?
   (a) 44th   (b) 45th
   (c) 46th   (d) Data inadequate

4. If Rahul finds that he is 12th from the right in a line of boys and 4th from the left, how many boys should be added to the line such that there are 28 boys in the line?
   (a) 12   (b) 14
   (c) 20   (d) 13

5. In a row of boys, Rajan is tenth from the right and Suraj is tenth from the left. When Rajan and Suraj interchange their positions, Suraj will be twenty-seventh from the left. Which of the following will be Rajan's position from the right?
   (a) Tenth
   (b) Twenty-sixth
   (c) Twenty-ninth
   (d) None of these

6. Mahesh and Suresh are ranked 11th and 12th respectively from the top in a class of 41 students. What will be their respective ranks from the bottom?
   (a) 32nd and 33rd
   (b) 29th and 30th
   (c) 30th and 31st
   (d) 31st and 30th

7. Uma ranked 8th from the top and 37th from bottom in a class. How many students are there in the class?
   (a) 47   (b) 46
   (c) 45   (d) None of these

8. In a queue, Sadiq is 14th from the front and Joseph is 17th from the end, while Jane is in between Sadiq and Joseph. If Sadiq be ahead of Joseph and there be 48 persons in the queue, how many persons are there between Sadiq and Jane?
   (a) 5   (b) 6
   (c) 7   (d) 8

9. Rohan ranked eleventh from the top and twenty-seventh from the bottom among the students who passed the annual examination in a class. If the number of students who failed in the examination was 12, how many students appeared for the examination?
   (a) 48
   (b) 49
   (c) 50
   (d) Cannot be determined

10. Some boys are sitting in a row. P is sitting fourteenth from the left and Q is seventh from the right. If there are four boys between P and Q, how many boys are there in the row?
   (a) 19   (b) 21
   (c) 25   (d) 23

EXPLANATORY ANSWERS

1. (*d*):

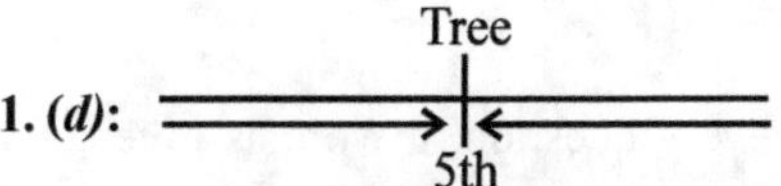

Total number of trees in the row are :
$(5 + 5) - 1 = 9$.

2. (*a*) :

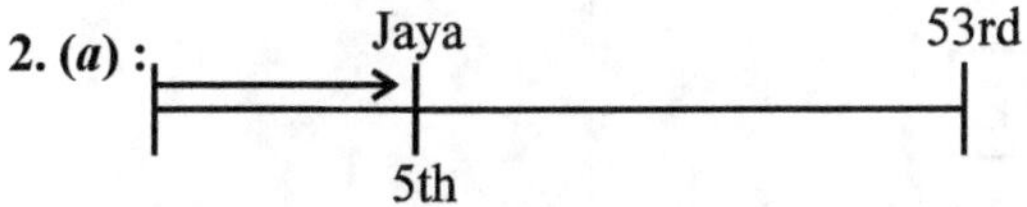

Jaya's rank from the bottom is :
$(53 - 5) + 1 = 49$th.

3. (*b*) :

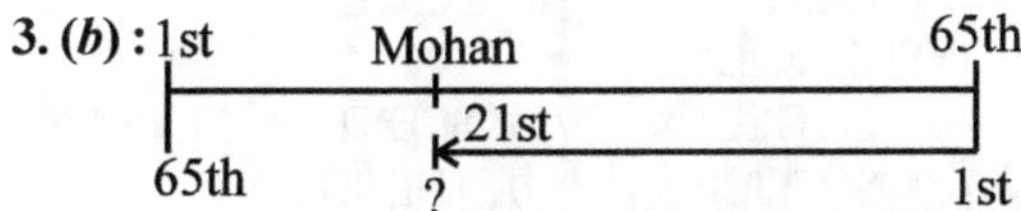

Note : Mohan's rank from the last or the question asked means the same.

Mohan's rank is $(65 - 21) + 1 = 45$th.

4. (*d*) :

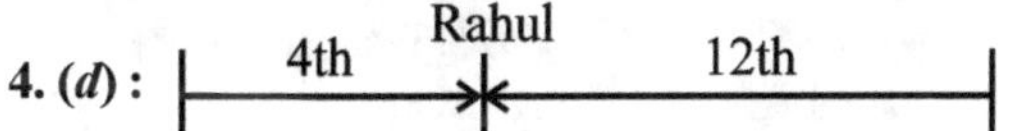

The number of boys in the line are :
$(4 + 12) - 1 = 15$

To make a line of 28 boys, $(28 - 15)$ *i.e.* 13 more boys are needed.

5. (*d*) :

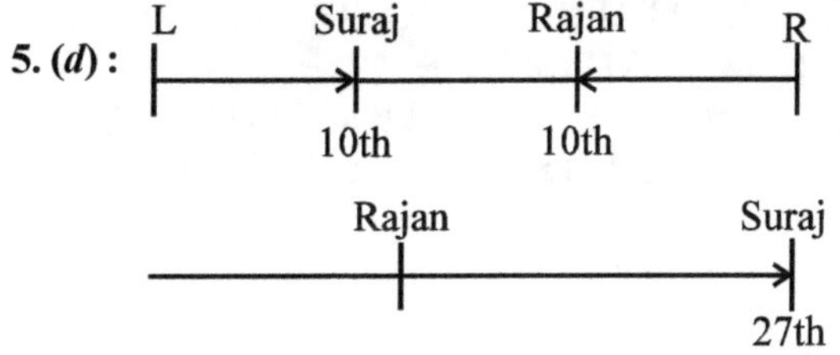

As the position of boys is equal from both ends, Rajan will also be 27th from the right after changing positions.

6. (*d*) :

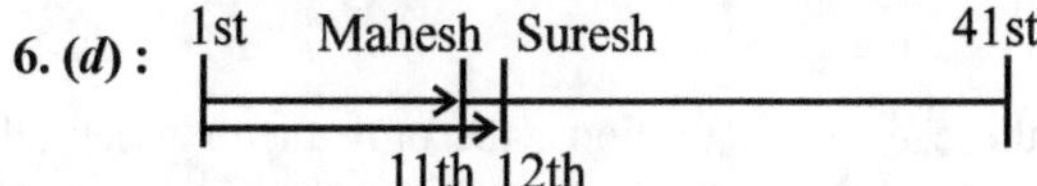

Mahesh's position from bottom is :
$(41 - 11) + 1 = 31$st

Suresh's position from bottom is :
$(41 - 12) + 1 = 30$th.

7. (*d*) :

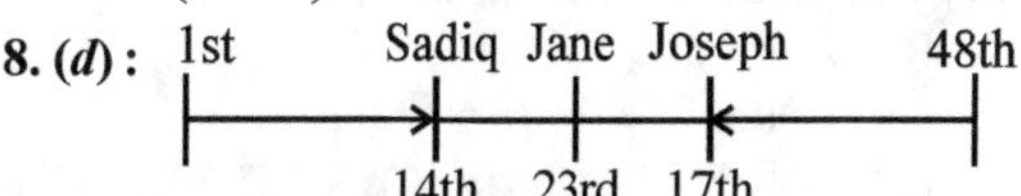

Total number of students in the class are :
$(8 + 37) - 1 = 44$.

8. (*d*) :

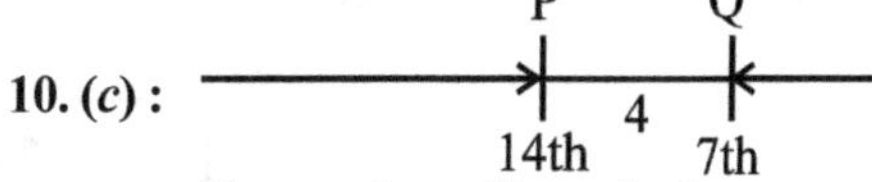

Sadiq's position from front : 14th

Joseph's position from last :
17th or $48 - 17 + 1 = 32$nd from front.

Middle postion between Sadiq & Joseph
$$= \frac{(32 - 14)}{2} + 14 = 23 \text{ rd.}$$

Hence, Jane position is 23rd from front

Person between Sadiq & Jane
$$= 23 - 14 - 1 = 8.$$

9. (*b*) :

Number of students who passed the examination $(11 + 27) - 1 = 37$

Those who failed $= 12$

Total number of students who appeared in the examination $= 37 + 12 = 49$.

10. (*c*) :

The number of boys in the row are :
$(14 + 4 + 7) = 25$.

15. PERMUTATIONS AND COMBINATIONS

In these type of questions, the only factor essential is alertness. In every question, a word is given. By using the letters of this given word the options are formed. The candidates are required to find from the given options the word *(i)* which cannot be formed by using the letters of the given word or *(ii)* which can be formed by using the letters of the given word.

EXERCISE

Directions : *Find out the one word among the options which cannot be formed by using the letters of the word as given in each question.*

1. ROTATION
   - *(a)* TORN
   - *(b)* NOTE
   - *(c)* TART
   - *(d)* RAIN
2. PHILOSOPHY
   - *(a)* SOIL
   - *(b)* SHIP
   - *(c)* SOLO
   - *(d)* SPIN
3. SLAVATION
   - *(a)* SNORT
   - *(b)* LATVIA
   - *(c)* SALIVA
   - *(d)* AVAIL
4. ACADEMY
   - *(a)* DEMY
   - *(b)* MACE
   - *(c)* DIRE
   - *(d)* MADE
5. INCOGNITO
   - *(a)* GOING
   - *(b)* INACTION
   - *(c)* IGNITION
   - *(d)* TONGO
6. JUDICIARY
   - *(a)* INJURY
   - *(b)* CADDY
   - *(c)* DICY
   - *(d)* ACRID
7. DOCTRINE
   - *(a)* CRUST
   - *(b)* DOCTOR
   - *(c)* TIRED
   - *(d)* CREED
8. EDUCATED
   - *(a)* DATE
   - *(b)* CUTE
   - *(c)* EAST
   - *(d)* DUCT
9. INSUFFICIENT
   - *(a)* ENTICE
   - *(b)* SCENT
   - *(c)* SUFFICE
   - *(d)* THENCE
10. DECEMBER
    - *(a)* REDEEM
    - *(b)* DECREE
    - *(c)* BRACED
    - *(d)* MEMBER
11. FUGITIVE
    - *(a)* EXIT
    - *(b)* FIVE
    - *(c)* GIVE
    - *(d)* GIFT
12. CATASTROPHE
    - *(a)* TASTE
    - *(b)* CHEAP
    - *(c)* POUCH
    - *(d)* STARE
13. TORRENTIAL
    - *(a)* TRAIL
    - *(b)* MENTAL
    - *(c)* LEARN
    - *(d)* RETAIL
14. INFRASTRUCTURE
    - *(a)* RAPTURE
    - *(b)* INSECURE
    - *(c)* CRAFTS
    - *(d)* STRUCTURE
15. RECOMMEND
    - *(a)* MEND
    - *(b)* ROME
    - *(c)* CANE
    - *(d)* OMEN

ANSWERS

1	2	3	4	5	6	7	8	9	10
(b)	*(d)*	*(a)*	*(c)*	*(b)*	*(a)*	*(a)*	*(c)*	*(d)*	*(c)*

11	12	13	14	15
(a)	*(c)*	*(b)*	*(a)*	*(c)*

16. SYMBOL SUBSTITUTION

Questions in these category are easy to attempt. Candidates must be quick in substituting symbols and calculations. The common pattern of questions asked are given below.

EXERCISE

1. If "+" means "–"; "–" means "×"; "×"means "÷" and "÷" means "+", then
   $15 \times 5 \div 10 + 5 - 3 = ?$
   (a) 9.5   (b) 0
   (c) –2   (d) 24

2. If "+" means "×"; "–" means "÷"; "÷"means "+" and "×" means "–", then what will be the value of $20 \div 40 - 4 \times 5 + 6 = ?$
   (a) 60   (b) 1.67
   (c) 150   (d) 0

3. If × stands for addition, < for subtraction, + stands for division, > for multiplication, – stands for equal to, ÷ for greater than, and = stands for less than, state which of the following is true?
   (a) $5 \times 3 < 7 \div 8 + 4 \times 1$
   (b) $3 \times 4 > 2 - 9 + 3 < 3$
   (c) $5 > 2 + 2 = 10 < 4 \times 8$
   (d) $3 \times 2 < 4 \div 16 > 2 + 4$

4. If → stands for subract, ← stands for add, •↑↑ stands for multiply, ↓↓ stands for divide, ↔ for greater than, ⟷ stands for equal to, then which of the following alternatives is true?
   (a) $4 \leftarrow 6 \uparrow\uparrow 2 \longleftrightarrow 3 \rightarrow 12 \leftarrow 12$
   (b) $10 \downarrow\downarrow 5 \uparrow\uparrow 5 \longleftrightarrow 9 \rightarrow 3 \leftarrow 4$
   (c) $15 \uparrow\uparrow 2 \rightarrow 5 \longleftrightarrow 12 \downarrow\downarrow 4 \leftarrow 3$
   (d) $13 \downarrow\downarrow 13 \leftarrow 1 \leftrightarrow 20 \rightarrow 5 \uparrow\uparrow 2$

5. If Δ denotes =; + denotes >, – denotes <, □ denotes ≠, × denotes > and ÷ denotes < then
   a + b – c denotes
   (a) b Δ c □ a
   (b) b □ a ÷ c
   (c) a ÷ b × c
   (d) b – a + c

6. If '✳' denotes '×', 'Δ' denotes '÷', '□' denotes '–', '●' denotes '+', 'α' denotes '=' and 'β' denotes ≠, then which of the following euations is correct?
   (a) $2 \square 10 ✳ 4 \triangle 5 \alpha 5 ● 12 \triangle 6$
   (b) $27 \triangle 9 ● 6 \beta 3 ✳ 6 \square 9$
   (c) $4 \triangle 2 ✳ 0 \alpha 7 \triangle 1 ✳ 0$
   (d) $5 ● 6 \triangle 3 \square 2 \alpha 8 \triangle 4 ✳ 3$

7. If ↓ stands for '÷', ↑ stands for '×', → stands for '+' and ← stands for '–', then
   $25 \downarrow 5 \rightarrow 3 \uparrow 6 \leftarrow 8 = ?$
   (a) 9   (b) 12
   (c) 16   (d) 15

8. If the + and × signs of the following equations are interchanged, which will be the correct equation?
   (a) $7 \times 5 + 3 = 20$
   (b) $4 + 9 \times 1 = 42$
   (c) $6 \times 5 + 8 = 46$
   (d) $2 + 11 \times 4 = 28$

9. If '+' stands for multiplication, '×' stands for addition, '÷' stands for subtraction and '–' stands for division, then what will be the result of the following equation?
   $7 \times 4 \div 10 \times 2 + 5 = ?$
   (a) 7   (b) 0
   (c) 11   (d) 15

10. If 'A' means '÷', 'B' means '+', 'C' means '×' and 'D' means '–', then
    $12\,C\,4\,A\,24\,D\,10\,B\,1 = ?$
    (a) $11\frac{1}{3}$ (b) 23
    (c) –7   (d) $16\frac{4}{5}$

EXPLANATORY ANSWERS

1. (c) : $15 \div 5 + 10 - 5 \times 3$
$3 + 10 - 15 = -2$

2. (d) : $20 + 40 \div 4 - 5 \times 6$
$20 + 10 - 30 = 0$

3. (c) :
(a) $\quad 5 + 3 - 7 > 8 \div 4 + 1$
$\quad\quad 1 > 3$
(b) $\quad 3 + 4 \times 2 = 9 \div 3 - 3$
$\quad\quad 11 = 0$
(c) $\quad 5 \times 2 \div 2 < 10 - 4 + 8$
$\quad\quad 5 < 14$
(d) $\quad 3 + 2 - 4 > 16 \times 2 \div 4$
$\quad\quad 1 > 8$

4. (b) :
(a) $\quad 4 + 6 \times 2 = 3 - 12 + 12$
$\quad\quad 16 = 3$
(b) $\quad 10 \div 5 \times 5 = 9 - 3 + 4$
$\quad\quad 10 = 10$
(c) $\quad 15 \times 2 - 5 = 12 \div 4 + 3$
$\quad\quad 25 = 6$
(d) $\quad 13 \div 13 + 1 > 20 - 5 \times 2$
$\quad\quad 2 > 10$

5. (d) : What is given is $a > b < c$
The equations are :
(a) $\quad b = c \neq a$ which is wrong
(b) $\quad b \neq a < c$ which is wrong
(c) $\quad a < b > c$ which is wrong
(d) $\quad b < a > c$ which is correct
Therefore, (d) is the answer.

6. (c) : The solved equations will be :
(a) $\quad 2 - 10 \times 4 \div 5 = 5 + 12 \div 6$
$\quad\quad 2 - 8 = 5 + 2$
$\quad\quad -6 = 7$ which is wrong
(b) $\quad 27 \div 9 + 6 \neq 3 \times 6 - 9$
$\quad\quad 3 + 6 \neq 18 - 9$
$\quad\quad 9 \neq 9$ which is wrong
(c) $\quad 4 \div 2 \times 0 = 7 \div 1 \times 0$
$\quad\quad 2 \times 0 = 7 \times 0$
$\quad\quad 0 = 0 \quad$ which is correct
(d) $\quad 5 + 6 \div 3 - 2 = 8 \div 4 \times 3$
$\quad\quad 5 = 6 \quad$ which is wrong

7. (d) : $25 \div 5 + 3 \times 6 - 8$
$5 + 18 - 8 = 15$

8. (c) : After interchanging the signs the equations are :
(a) $\quad 7 + 5 \times 3 = 22 \quad$ which is wrong
(b) $\quad 4 \times 9 + 1 = 37 \quad$ which is wrong
(c) $\quad 6 + 5 \times 8 = 46 \quad$ which is correct
(d) $\quad 2 \times 11 + 4 = 26 \quad$ which is wrong

9. (c) : $7 + 4 - 10 + 2 \times 5$
$7 + 4 - 10 + 10 = 11$

10. (c) : $12 \times 4 \div 24 - 10 + 1$
$2 - 10 + 1 = -7$

17. MISSING NUMBERS

Playing with numbers and mathematical skills are needed to attempt these type of tests. The candidates have to work out the right combination of arithmetical symbols to arrive at the answer options which will take the place of the interrogation sign in the given questions.

EXERCISE

Directions: *In each question given below which one number can be placed at the sign of interrogation?*

1. 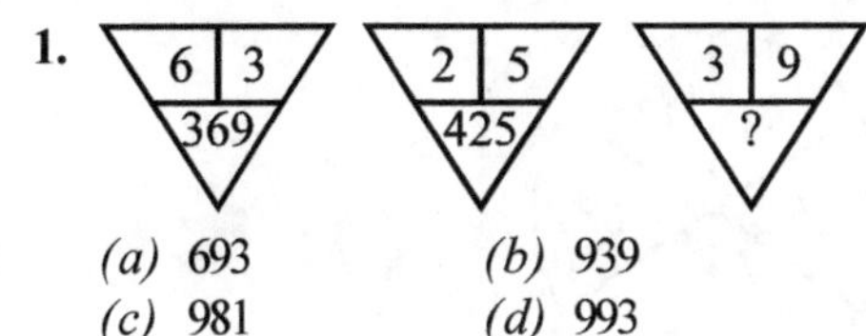

   (a) 693   (b) 939
   (c) 981   (d) 993

2. 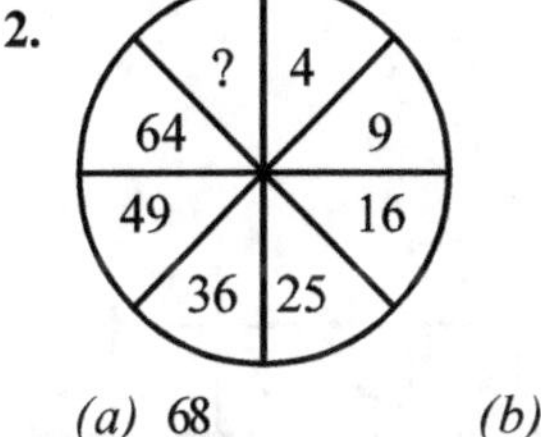

   (a) 68   (b) 100
   (c) 72   (d) 81

3. 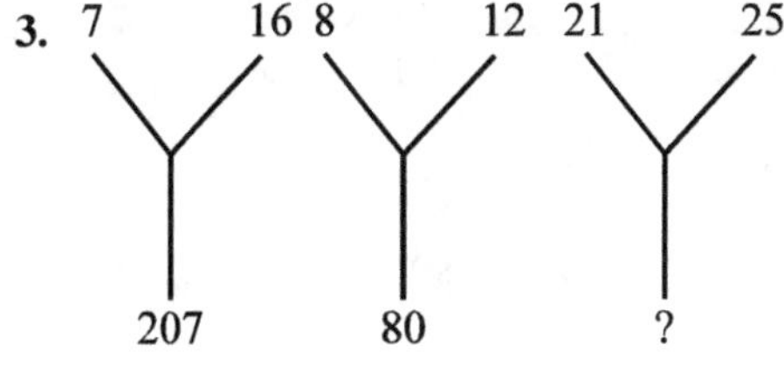

   (a) 425   (b) 184
   (c) 241   (d) 210

4. 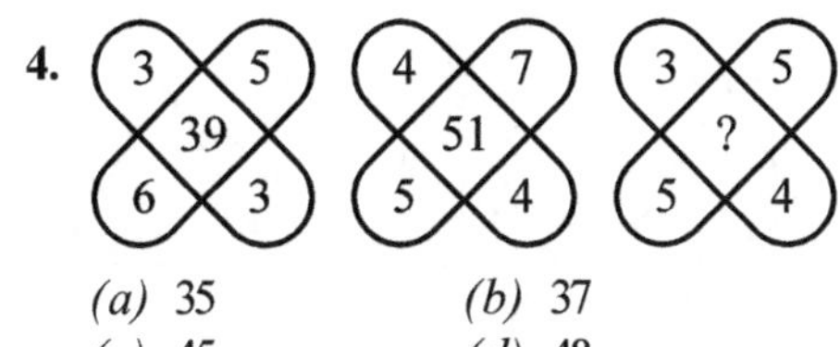

   (a) 35   (b) 37
   (c) 45   (d) 48

5. 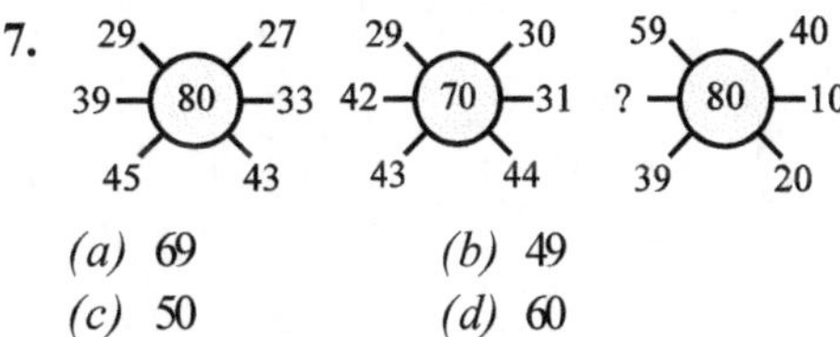

   (a) 4   (b) 8
   (c) 20   (d) 14

6.
14	9	4
12	7	2
10	5	0
16	11	?

   (a) 9   (b) 6
   (c) 3   (d) 7

7. 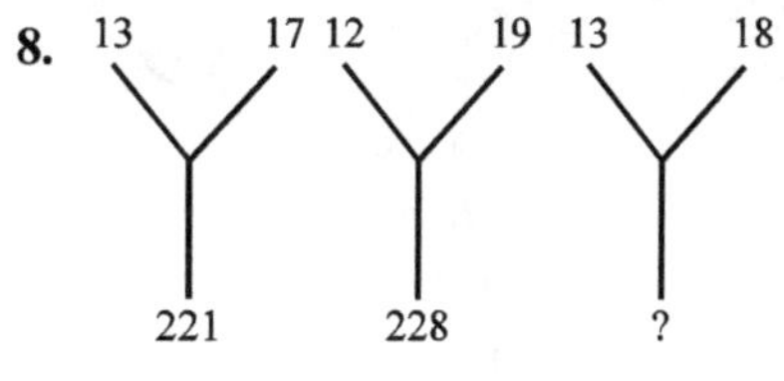

   (a) 69   (b) 49
   (c) 50   (d) 60

8. 

   (a) 31   (b) 229
   (c) 234   (d) 312

9. 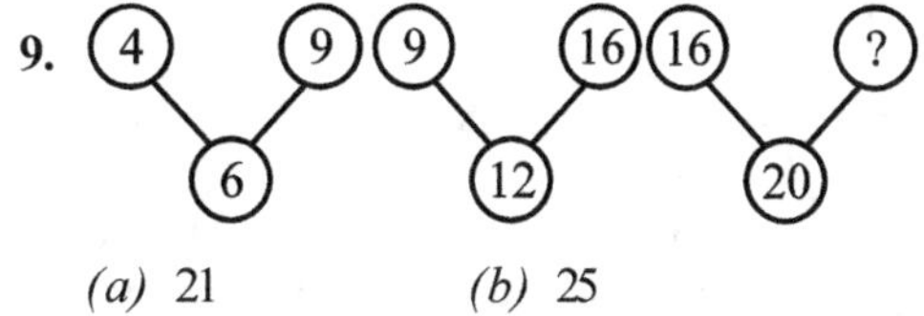

   (a) 21   (b) 25
   (c) 50   (d) 60

10.

51	(11)	61
64	(30)	32
35	(?)	43

(a) 25   *(b)* 27
(c) 32   *(d)* 37

11. 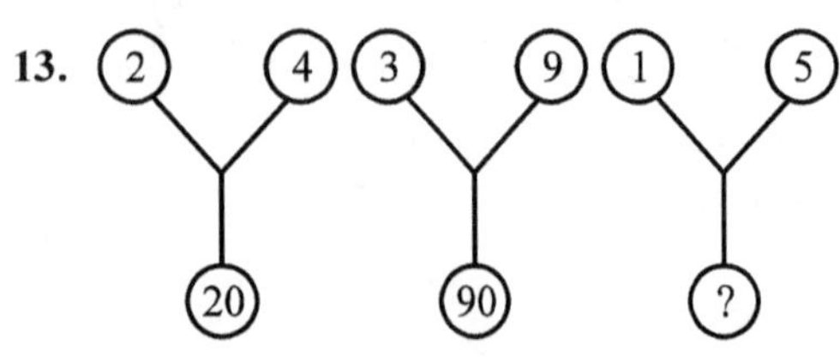

(a) 5   *(b)* 6
(c) 8   *(d)* 9

12.

(a) 8   *(b)* 14
(c) 10   *(d)* 6

13.

(a) 20   *(b)* 25
(c) 26   *(d)* 75

14.

27	22	50
13	12	26
9	2	?

(a) 12   *(b)* 39
(c) 18   *(d)* 24

15.

(a) 25   *(b)* 47
(c) 37   *(d)* 41

16. 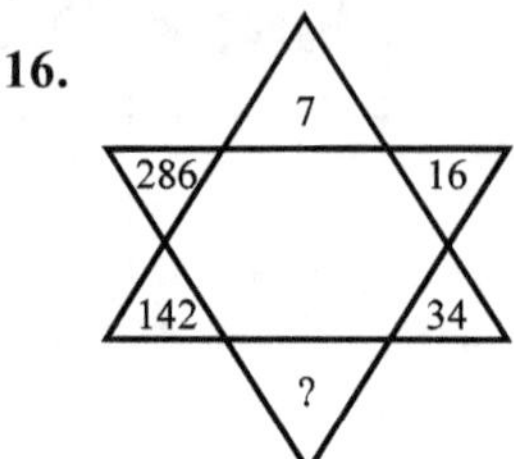

(a) 70
(b) 68
(c) 56
(d) 92

17.

(a) 41   *(b)* 37
(c) 29   *(d)* 25

18.

(a) 72   *(b)* 68
(c) 82   *(d)* 96

19.

42	(21)	22
78	(?)	84
162	(18)	99

(a) 12
(b) 13
(c) 60
(d) 72

20. 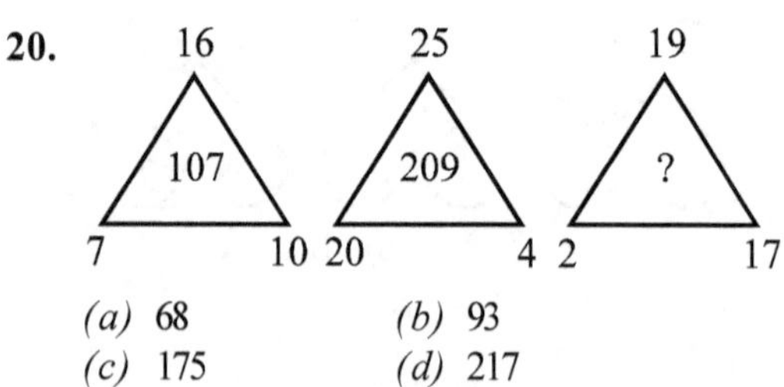

(a) 68   *(b)* 93
(c) 175   *(d)* 217

EXPLANATORY ANSWERS

1. (c) : The squares of two numbers on the top placed side by side gives the number inside the bottom triangle, *i.e.*,
6^2 and $3^2 = 369$
2^2 and $5^2 = 425$, similarly
3^2 and $9^2 = 981$.

2. (d) : Starting from number 4 the numbers are the squares of numbers in natural order *i.e.*, $2^2 = 4, 3^2 = 9, 4^2 = 16 \ldots \ldots 9^2 = 81$.

3. (b) : The number at the bottom is the difference of the squares of two numbers at the top, *i.e.*,
$16^2 - 7^2 = 256 - 49 = 207$
$12^2 - 8^2 = 144 - 64 = 80$, similarly
$25^2 - 21^2 = 625 - 441 = 184$.

4. (b) : The number in the centre is the sum of the products of diagonal numbers, *i.e.*,
$(3 \times 3) + (5 \times 6) = 39$
$(4 \times 4) + (7 \times 5) = 51$, similarly
$(3 \times 4) + (5 \times 5) = 37$.

5. (d) : Sum of two numbers on the top divided by 2 gives the third number, *i.e.*,
$(7 + 5) \div 2 = 6$
$(5 + 21) \div 2 = 13$, similarly
$(24 + 4) \div 2 = 14$.

6. (b) : The numbers in 2nd and 3rd columns are 5 less than the nunbers in 1st and 2nd columns respectively, *i.e.*,
$14 - 5 = 9$ and $9 - 5 = 4$
$12 - 5 = 7$ and $7 - 5 = 2, \ldots$ similarly
$16 - 5 = 11$ and $11 - 5 = 6$.

7. (a) : The sum of 3 numbers in each line in one figure is same, *i.e.*,
$29 + 80 + 43$ or $39 + 80 + 33$
     or $45 + 80 + 27 = 152$
$29 + 70 + 44$ or $42 + 70 + 31$
     or $43 + 70 + 30 = 143$,
similarly $59 + 80 + 20$ or $39 + 80 + 40 = 159$.
The missing number is :
     $159 - (80 + 10) = 69$.

8. (c) : The number at the bottom is the product of two numbers at the top, *i.e.*,
$13 \times 17 = 221$
$12 \times 19 = 228$, similarly

$13 \times 18 = 234$.

9. (b) : Square of number at the bottom is equal to the product of two numbers at the top, *i.e.*,
$6^2 = 4 \times 9, i.e., 36$
$12^2 = 9 \times 16, i.e., 144$, similarly
$20^2 = 16 \times ?, i.e., 400$. The missing number is $400 \div 16 = 25$.

10. (b) : The sum of the products of the digits of numbers in 1st and 3rd columns is the number in the 2nd column, *i.e.*,
$(5 \times 1) + (6 \times 1) = 11$
$(6 \times 4) + (3 \times 2) = 30$, similarly
$(3 \times 5) + (4 \times 3) = 27$.

11. (d) : The sum of numbers on right and centre subtracted from the number on the left gives the number at the bottom, *i.e.*,
$93 - (27 + 63) = 3$
$79 - (38 + 37) = 4$, similarly
$67 - (16 + 42) = 9$.

12. (c) : The number inside each triangle is the difference of the numbers at its base *i.e.*
$10 - 4 = 6, 18 - 4 = 14$ and $18 - 10 = 8$
$14 - 8 = 6, 22 - 8 = 14$ and $22 - 14 = 8$, similarly
$11 - 5 = 6, 15 - 5 = 10$ and $15 - 11 = 4$.

13. (c) : The sum of squares of two numbers at the top gives the third number below, *i.e.*,
$2^2 + 4^2 = 20$
$3^2 + 9^2 = 90$, similarly
$1^2 + 5^2 = 26$.

14. (a) : The sum of numbers in 1st and 2nd column plus 1 is the number in the 3rd column, *i.e.*,
$27 + 22 + 1 = 50$
$13 + 12 + 1 = 26$, similarly
$9 + 2 + 1 = 12$.

15. (d) : The product of numbers on either side of the triangle plus the number at the base is the number inside the triangle, *i.e.*,
$(5 \times 3) + 4 = 19$
$(6 \times 4) + 5 = 29$, similarly
$(7 \times 5) + 6 = 41$.

16. *(a)* : Clockwise starting from number 7, the next number is obtained by doubling the number and adding 2, *i.e.,*
$(7 \times 2) + 2 = 16$
$(16 \times 2) + 2 = 34 \ldots$, similarly
$(34 \times 2) + 2 = 70$
$(70 \times 2) + 2 = 142$
$(142 \times 2) + 2 = 286.$

17. *(c)* : The difference between the numbers in opposite sectors is 13, *i.e.,*
$26 - 13 = 13$
$68 - 55 = 13$, similarly
The missing number is $42 - 13 = 29$
$(42 + 13 = 55$ is not given as option$)$.

18. *(b)* : The number at the bottom is obtained by subtracting the sum of two numbers in the centre grid line from the square of the number at the top, *i.e.,*
$7^2 - (2 + 7) = 40$
$5^2 - (8 + 3) = 14$, similarly
$9^2 - (7 + 6) = 68.$

19. *(b)* : The number inside the brackets is obtained by multiplying the number on the left by 2 and then dividing the product by the sum of digits of number on the right, *i.e.,*
$(42 \times 2) \div (2 + 2) = 21$
$(162 \times 2) \div (9 + 9) = 18$, similarly
$(78 \times 2) \div (8 + 4) = 13.$

20. *(a)* : Subtracting the sum of squares of two numbers at the base from the square of number at the apex gives the number inside the triangle, *i.e.,*
$16^2 - (7^2 + 10^2) = 107$
$25^2 - (20^2 + 4^2) = 209$, similarly
$19^2 - (2^2 + 17^2) = 68.$

18. ALPHABET PROBLEMS

Alphabet problems are fun to attempt. They are based on alphabetical series in natural as well as reverse order.

Natural Order

A B C D E F G H I J K L M N O P Q R S T U V W X Y Z

Reverse Order

Z Y X W V U T S R Q P O N M L K J I H G F E D C B A

> **Note :** The series starts from A on reaching Z and from Z on reaching A. Of these A E I O U are vowels and the rest are consonants.

EXERCISE

1. Which letter should be ninth letter to the left of ninth letter from the right if the first half of the alphabet is reversed?
   - (a) I
   - (b) D
   - (c) F
   - (d) E

2. Starting from the fifth letter from the left, if twelve letters are written in reverse order, then which letter will be the seventh to the left of the fourteenth letter from the right?
   - (a) N
   - (b) H
   - (c) L
   - (d) O

3. What letter will come in the centre of sixth letter from the right and thirteenth letter from the left?
   - (a) Q
   - (b) R
   - (c) P
   - (d) S

4. If in the word "DISTURBANCE", the first letter is interchanged with the last letter, the second letter is interchanged with the tenth letter and so on, which letter would come after the letter "T" in the newly formed word?
   - (a) I
   - (b) U
   - (c) N
   - (d) S

5. If it is possible to make a meaningful word with the third, the fifth, the seventh and the tenth letters of the word PROJECTION. If no such word can be made, give 'O' as the answer. If more than one such word can be made, give 'M' as the answer.
   - (a) T
   - (b) N
   - (c) O
   - (d) M

6. A meaningful word is made if we take the first, fourth, fifth, seventh, tenth, eleventh and the twelfth letters of the word "FELICITATIONS". Which of the following will be the fifth letter of that word from the right end of that word?
   - (a) T
   - (b) C
   - (c) N
   - (d) I

7. On rearranging the jumbled spelling of the word SKARTINS, a language is obtained. What is the fifth letter from the right of the rearranged word?
   - (a) N
   - (b) K
   - (c) R
   - (d) S

8. If the 1st, 3rd, 5th, 7th, 10th and 13th letters of the word "ENTERTAINMENT" are used to make a meaningful word, then what two letters will come in the centre?
   - (a) A M
   - (b) T T
   - (c) RE
   - (d) N A

9. On rearranging the jumbled spelling of the word GRUBY a sport is obtained. What is the letter in the centre?
   - (a) R
   - (b) B
   - (c) G
   - (d) U

10. If the letters 'ERVSECI' can be rearranged to form a meaningful word what will be the fifth letter from the right?

   (a) R   *(b)* V

   (c) E   *(d)* None of these

11. From the word HASTEN how many independent meaningful English words can be made without changing the order of the letters and using each letter only once?

   (a) 1   *(b)* 2

   (c) 3   *(d)* 4

EXPLANATORY ANSWERS

1. *(d)* : MLKJIGHFEDCBANOPQRSTUVWXYZ

    9th   9th

2. *(d)* : ABCDPONMLKJIHGFEQRSTUVWXYZ

    7th   14th

3. *(a)* :

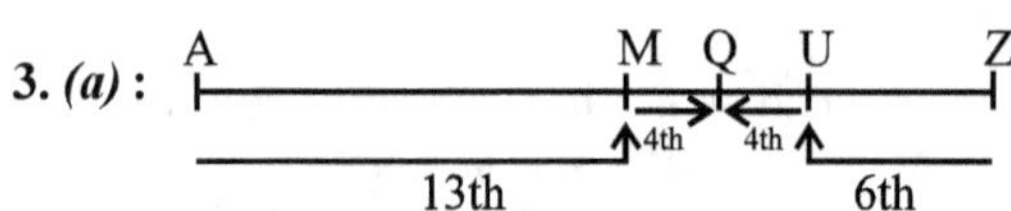

13th letter from left is 'M' and 6th letter from right is 'U'. The letter in the centre of 'M' and 'U' is 'Q'.

4. *(d)* : ECNABRUTSID

5. *(d)* : PROJECTION

The 3rd, 5th, 7th and 10th letters are OETN.

The words formed are TONE and NOTE.

6. *(b)* : FELICITATIONS

The 1st, 4th, 5th, 7th, 10th, 11th and 12th lettes are FICTION.

The word is FICTION and 5th letter from right is 'C'.

7. *(d)* : The word is SANSKRIT and 5th letter from right is 'S'.

8. *(b)* : ENTERTAINMENT

The 1st, 3rd, 5th 7th, 10th and 13th letters are ETRAMT.

The word formed is MATTER.

9. *(c)* : The sport is RUGBY. The letter in the centre is 'G'.

10. *(a)* : The word is SERVICE and fifth letter from right is 'R'.

11. *(b)* : The words formed are : HAS, TEN.

19. LOGICAL DIAGRAM

In these type of questions, a set of five different figures is given as options. Each figure represents a logical pattern of certain groups of related words wherein each word represents a class. One has to identify the most appropriate logical figure for the set of words given. Some of the relationships represented by these diagrams are given below. Understand the relationship patterns and then attempt the exercise following the explanation.

EXERCISE

Directions : *From the five logical Diagrams, select one which best illustrates the relationship among three given classes in the questions 1 to 10.*

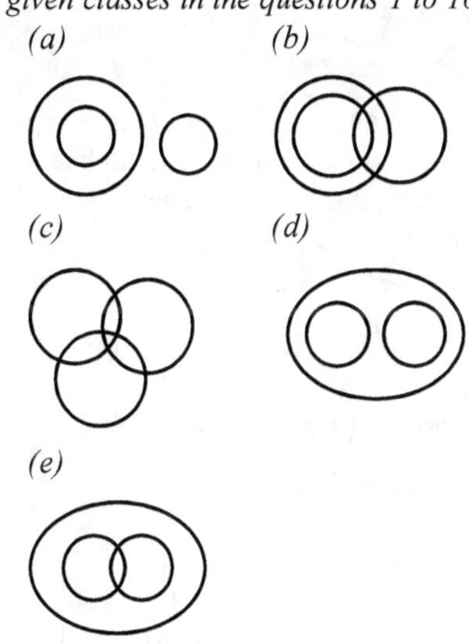

1. Birds, fruits, mangoes
2. Criminals, lawyers, bandits
3. Swimmers, bachelors, men
4. Smart, engineers, women
5. Vegetables, potatoes, brinjals
6. Grapes, sweet, fruit
7. Doctors, architects, humans
8. Scholars, people, Indians
9. Children, naughty, studious
10. Pens, pencils, stationery

Directions : *From the five logical diagrams select*

Directions : *one which best illustrates the relationship among three given classes in questions 11 to 20.*

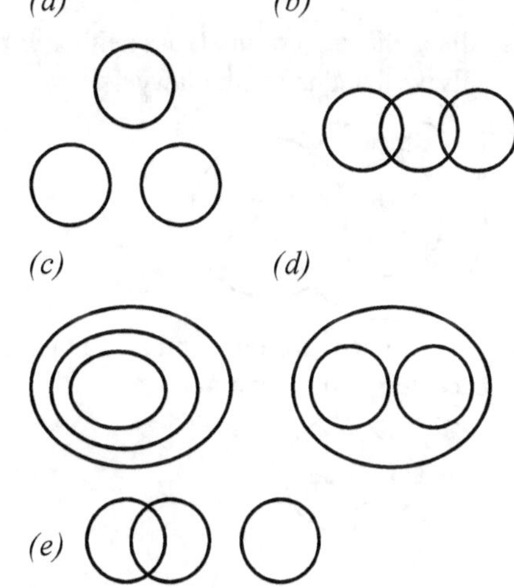

11. Ink, crayons, red
12. Canines, dogs, pups
13. Table, chair, stool
14. Ripe, mangoes, basket
15. Scholars, studious, illiterates
16. Cars, ships, means of conveyance
17. Age, number, thirteen
18. Country, state, continent
19. Father, parent, mother
20. Iron, metal, mercury

EXPLANATORY ANSWERS

1. (a) :

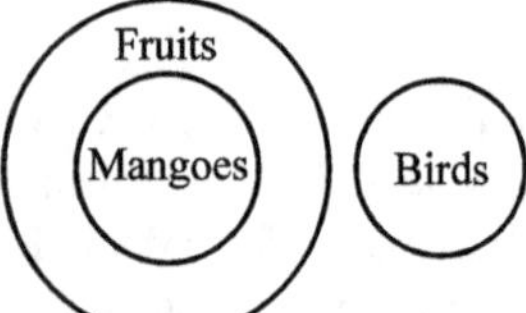

All mangoes are fruits, but neither fruits, nor mangoes can be birds.

2. (a) :

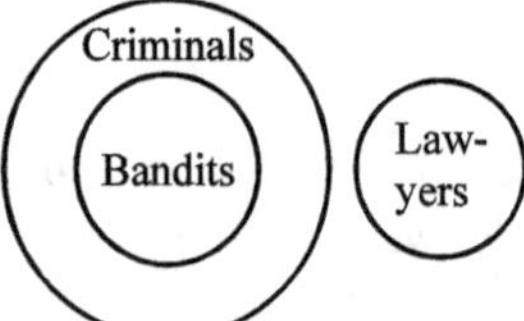

All bandits are criminal, but neither criminals nor bandits can be lawyers.

3. (b) :

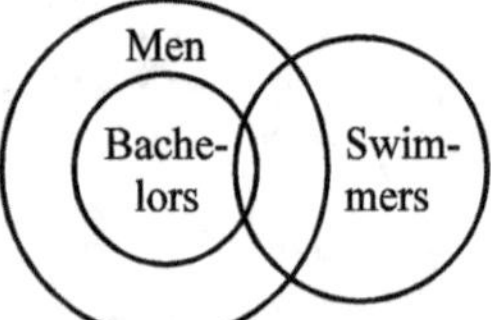

All bachelors are men and some men and bachelors can be swimmers.

4. (c) :

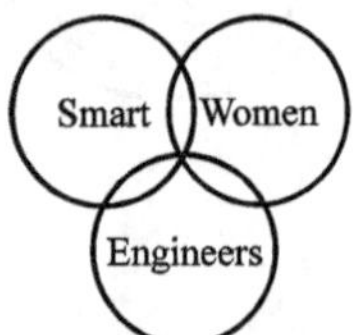

Some women can be smart and some women can be engineers and vice–versa. Some engineers can be women and some engineers can be smart and vice–versa.

5. (d) :

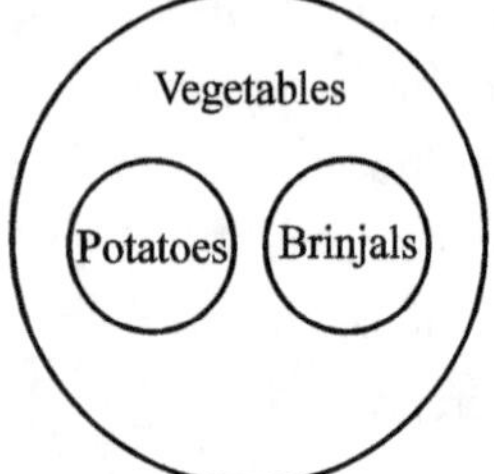

Potatoes and brinjals are vegetables but they have nothing in common. Some vegetables are potatoes and some are brinjals.

6. (b) :

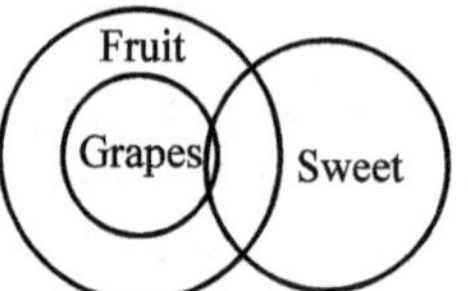

Some grapes are sweet and all grapes are fruit. But not all that is sweet is fruit.

7. (d) :

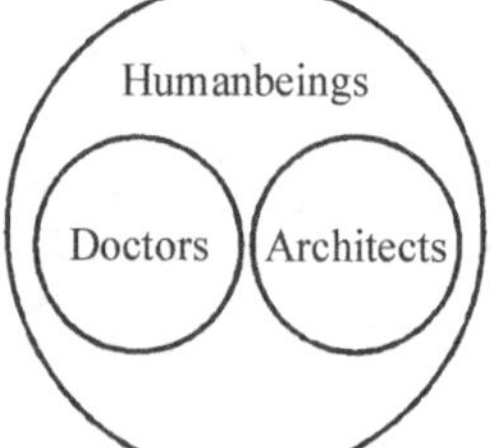

Doctors and architects are two separate classes, but all doctors and architects are humans and some humans are either doctors or architects.

8. (e) :

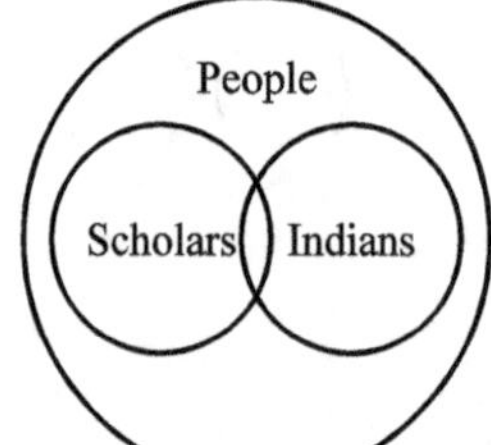

Some Indians can be scholars and some scholars can be Indians. All scholars and Indians are people.

9. (c) :

Some children can be naughty and some can be studious, some studious can be children and some naughty. Some naughty can be studious and some children.

10. *(d)* :

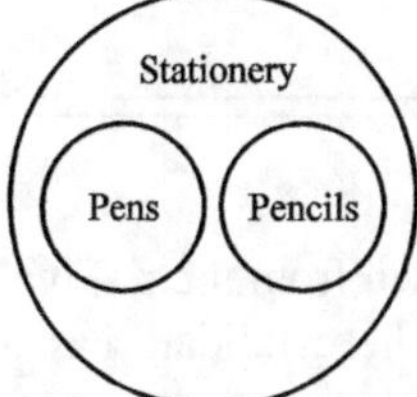

Pens and pencils both are items of stationery and some stationery is pens and pencils, but pens and pencils are two separate classes.

11. *(b)* :

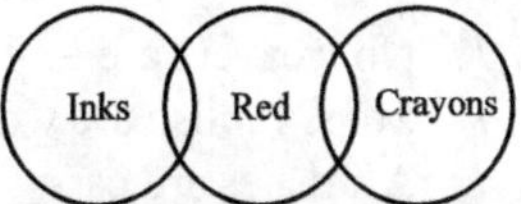

Some ink and some crayons can be red and some red units can be inks and crayons, but ink and crayon have nothing in common.

12. *(c)* :

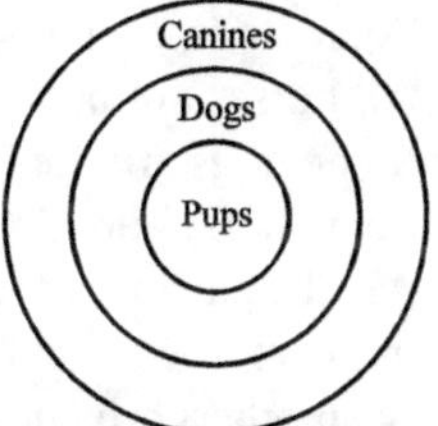

All pups are dogs and all dogs are canines. Some canines are dogs, of which some are pups.

13. *(a)* :

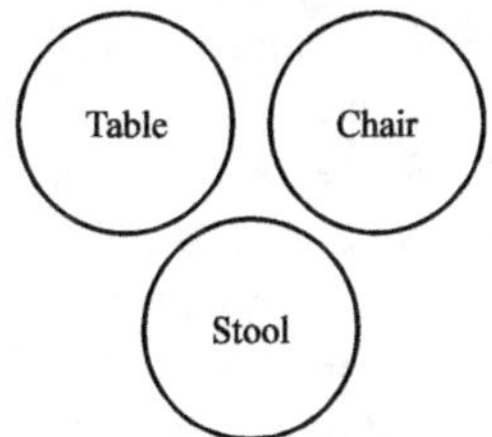

All three are different classes.

14. *(e)* :

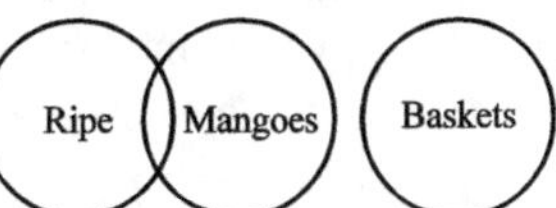

Some mangoes are ripe and some ripe units are mangoes, but neither ripe units nor mangoes can be baskets.

15. *(e)* :

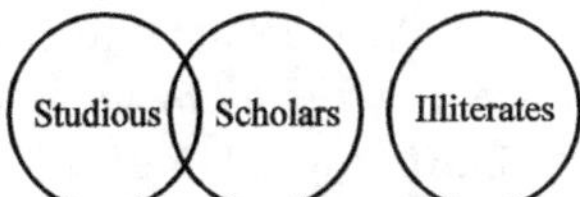

Some studious can be scholars and some scholars can be studious, but neither studious nor scholars can be illiterates.

16. *(d)* :

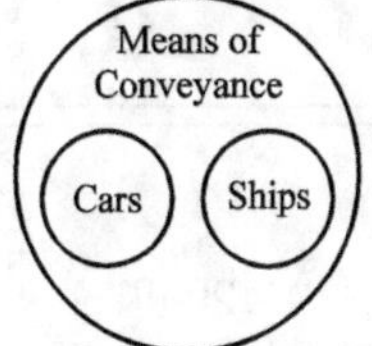

All cars and all ships are means of conveyance, but neither is contained in the other. Some means of conveyance are cars and some ships.

17. *(b)* :

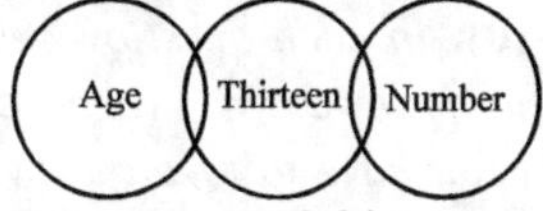

Some are aged thirteen and some numbers are thirteen. Some thirteen units are numbers and some ages. Age and number have nothing in common.

18. *(c)* :

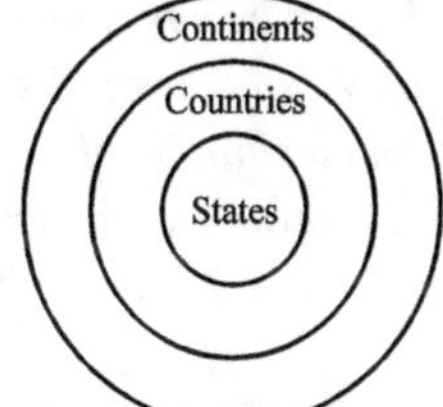

All continents contain countries within it and each country contains states within it.

19. *(d)* :

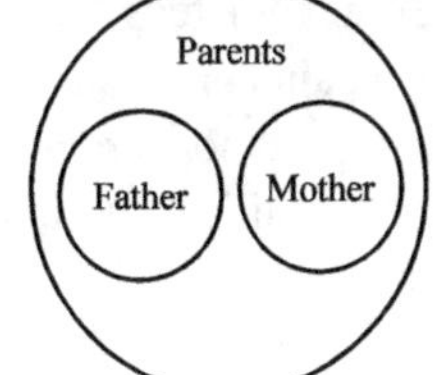

All fathers and mothers are parents, but they are two separate classes. Some of the parents are fathers and some are mothers.

20. *(d)* :

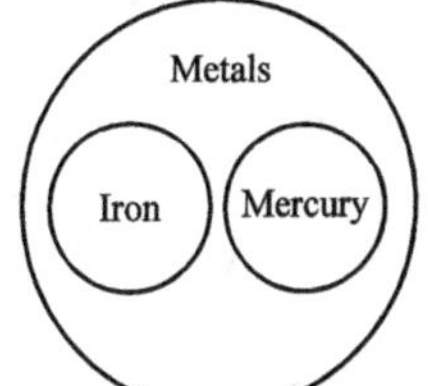

Iron and mercury are metals, but they have nothing in common. Some metals are iron and some mercury.

20. SYLLOGISM

In this reasoning pattern, the two premises are followed by two conclusions drawn from them. Five options *(a)*, *(b)*, *(c)*, *(d)* and *(e)* are given as answers. Based on the two statements the candidate has to select the right option as answer.

EXERCISE

Directions (Qs. 1-10): *In each question below are given two statements followed by two conclusions numbered I and II. You have to take the two given statements to be true even if they seem to be at variance from commonly known facts and then decide which of the given conclusions logically follows from the two given statements, disregarding commonly known facts. Read both the statements and—*

Give answer (a) if only conclusion I follows; give answer (b) if only conclusion II follows; give answer (c) if either I or II follows; give answer (d) if neither I nor II follows and give answer (e) if both I and II follows.

1. Statements   I: All tomatoes are red.
             II: All grapes are tomatoes.
  Conclusions I: All grapes are red.
             II: Some tomatoes are grapes.

2. Statements   I: All painters are smilling.
             II: Some authors are painters.
  Conclusions I: All smiling authors are painters.
             II: Some authors are smiling.

3. Statements   I: All peons in this office are efficient.
             II: Ramu is not efficient.
  Conclusions I: Ramu is not peon in this office.
             II: Ramu should be more efficient.

4. Statements   I: All weavers are hard working.
             II: No hard working men are foolish.
  Conclusions I: No weavers are foolish.
             II: Some foolish are weavers.

5. Statements   I: All fishes are cars.
             II: All cars are vegetables.
  Conclusions I: Some vegetables are cars.
             II: Some vegetables are fishes.

6. Statements   I: Some dogs are pups.
             II: All horses are pups.
  Conclusions I: Some dogs are horses.
             II: Some horses are dogs.

7. Statements   I: All beautiful women are mothers.
             II: All mothers are understanding.
  Conclusions I: All beautiful women are understanding.
             II: All mothers are beautiful women.

8. Statements   I: Some toys are tables.
             II: No table is black.
  Conclusions I: Some toys are black.
             II: Some toys are not black.

9. Statements   I: All rivers are mountains.
             II: Some rivers are deserts.
  Conclusions I: Some mountains are deserts.
             II: Some deserts are not mountains.

10. Statements   I: All men are horses.
             II: All horses are elephants.
  Conclusions I: All men are elephants.
             II: All elephants are men.

Directions (Qs. 11-15): *In the following questions, select the set of conclusion which logically follows from the given statements.*

11. *Statements* *I:* All foxes are plates.
    II: All plates are trees.
    Conclusions I: All foxes are trees.
    II: All trees are foxes.
    III: Some trees are foxes.
    IV: Some trees are plates.
    (a) All conclusions are correct.
    (b) Only conclusions I, III, and IV follow.
    (c) Only conclusions II, III, and IV follow.
    (d) Only conclusions I and IV follow.
    (e) None of the above.
12. *Statements* *I:* Some cubes are squares.
    II: All squares are circles.
    Conclusions I: All cubes are circles.
    II: Some circles are cubes.
    III: Some circles are squares.
    IV: All squares are cubes.
    (a) Only conclusion I follows.
    (b) Only conclusion I, II and III follow.
    (c) All conclusions are correct.
    (d) Only conclusions II and III follow.
    (e) None of the above.
13. *Statements* *I:* All cups are goats.
    II: All goats are tins.
    Conclusions I: All goats are cups.
    II: All tins are goats.
    III: No cups are tins.
    IV: No tins are cups.

(a) Only conclusions III and IV follow.
(b) Only conclusios I and II follow.
(c) Only conclusions I, II and III follow.
(d) All conclusions are correct.
(e) None of the above.
14. *Statements* *I:* All bombs are bags.
    II: Some bags are jets.
    Conclusions I: All bombs are jets.
    II: All jets are bombs.
    III: Some jets are bombs.
    IV: Some bombs are jets.
    (a) Only conclusion III follows.
    (b) Only conclusions I and II follow.
    (c) All conclusions are correct.
    (d) Only conclusions III and IV follow.
    (e) None of these.
15. *Statements* *I:* Some thorns are jackets.
    II: Some jackets are boats.
    Conclusions I: No thorns are boats.
    II: All jackets are boats.
    III: Some boats are thorns.
    IV: No jackets are thorns.
    (a) Either conclusion I or IV follows.
    (b) Either conclusion I or II follows.
    (c) Either conclusion I or III follows.
    (d) No conclusion is correct.
    (e) All conclusions are correct.

EXPLANATORY ANSWERS

1. *(e)* : When all tomatoes are red and all grapes are tomatoes, then all grapes are also red. When all grapes are tomatoes, then some tomatoes must be grapes. Therefore, both conclusions I and II are correct.

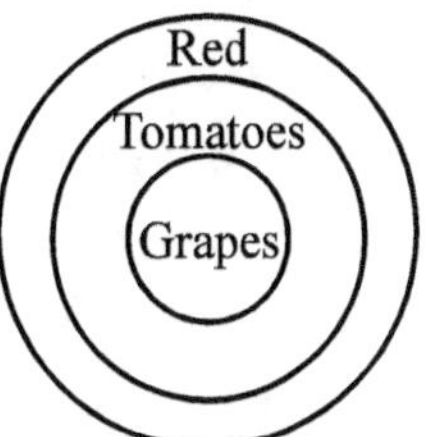

2. *(b)* : When all painters are smiling and some authors are painters, then some authors are smiling. Therefore, only conclusion II is correct.

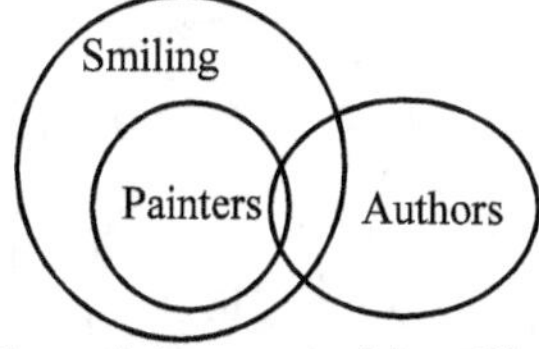

3. *(a)* : When all the peons of the office are efficient, then Ramu cannot be a peon in this office. Therefore, only conclusion I is correct.

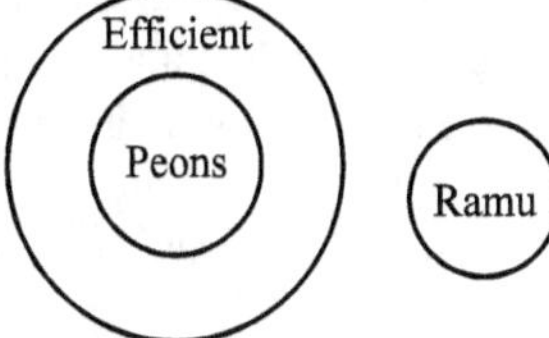

4. (a) : When all weavers are hardworking and no hardworking men are foolish, then no weavers are foolish. Therefore, only conclusion I is correct.

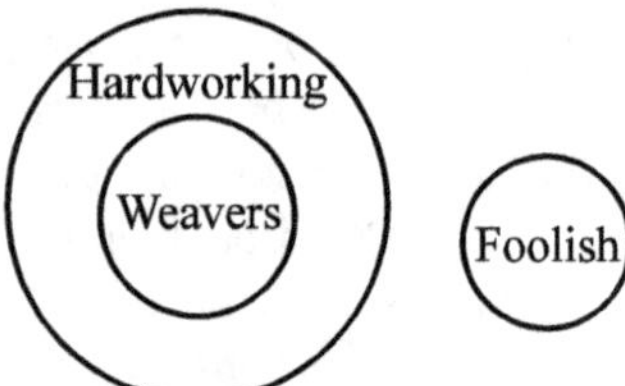

5. (e) : When all fishes are cars and all cars are vegetables, then all fishes will naturally be vegetables. This means that some vegetables are fishes. And when all cars are vegetables, then some vegetables will be cars naturally. Therefore, both the conclusions I and II are correct.

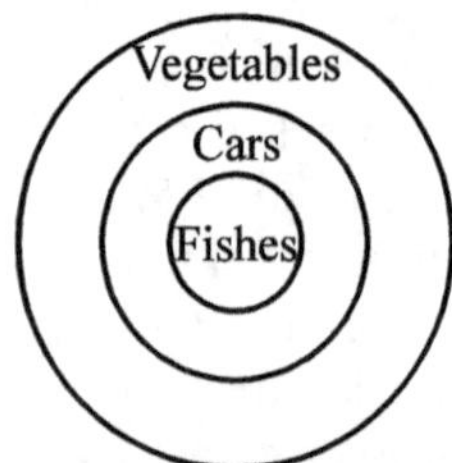

6. (d) : No relationship can be established between the two statements. Therefore, neither conclusion I nor conclusion II is correct.

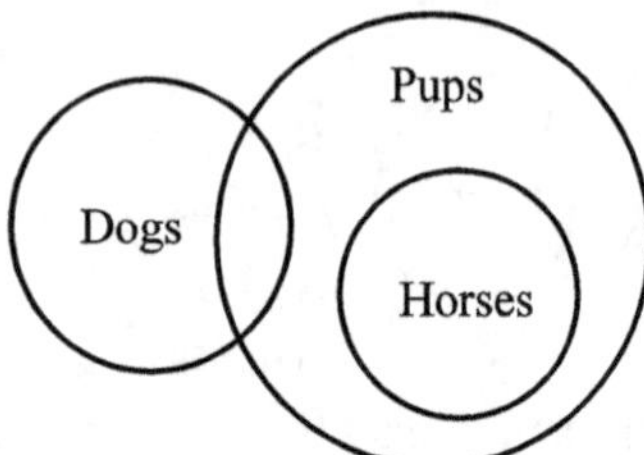

7. (a) : When all beautiful women are mothers and all mothers are understanding, then naturally all beautiful women are understanding. All mothers need not be beautiful women. Therefore, only conclusion I is correct.

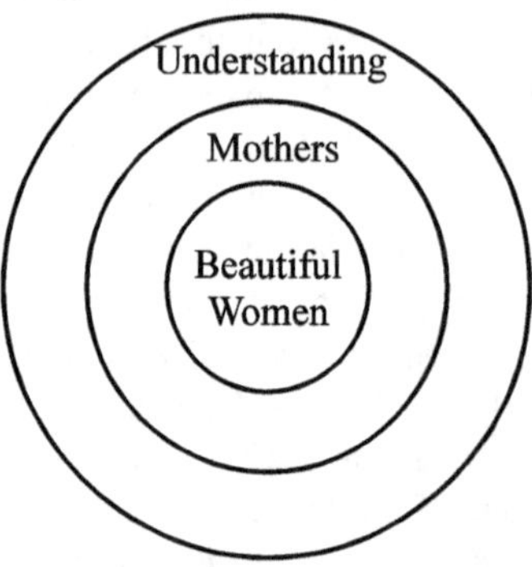

8. (c) : When some toys are tables and no table is black, then it is indicated that some toys can be black, as all toys are not tables. On the other hand, some toys may not be black. Therefore, there is a possibility that some toys may or may not be black. As such, either conclusion I or conclusion II can be correct.

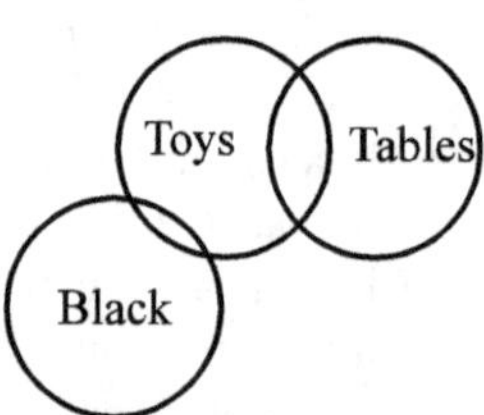

9. (e) : When all rivers are mountains and some rivers are deserts, then some deserts cannot be mountains and also, some mountains need not be deserts. Therefore, both conclusion I and conclusion II are correct.

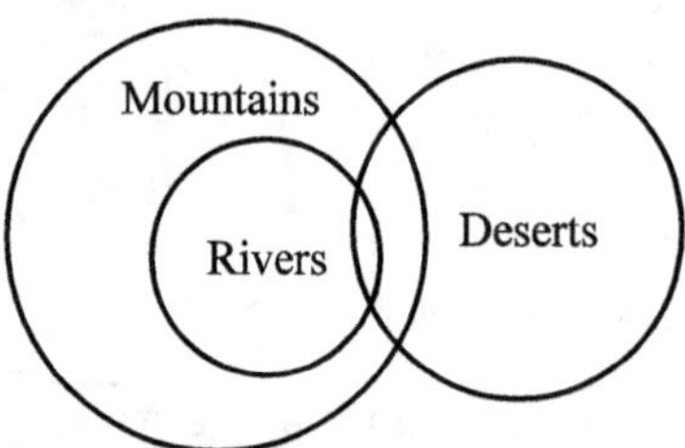

10. (a) : When all men are horses and all horses are elephants then, naturally all men are elephants, but all elephants need not be men. Therefore, only conclusion I is correct.

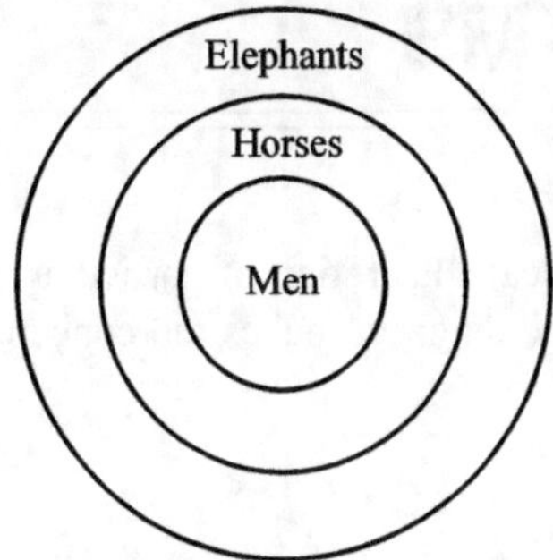

11. *(b)* :

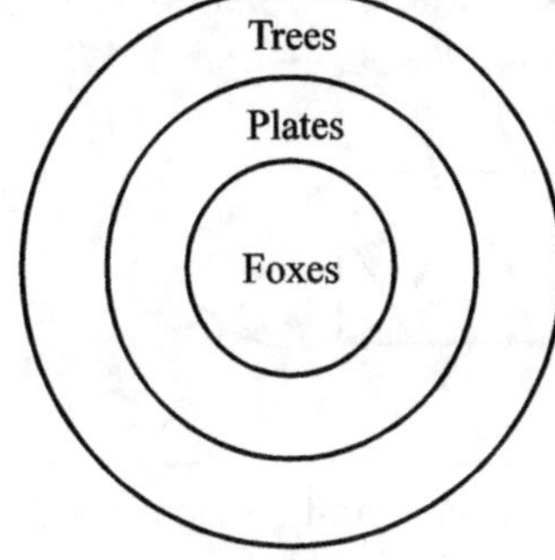

When all foxes are plates and all plates are trees, then naturally all foxes will be trees and some trees will then have to be foxes. And when all plates are trees then some trees will have to be plates. Therefore, only conclusions I, III and IV are correct.

12. *(d)* : When it is given that some cubes are squares and all squares are circles, then some cubes will naturally be circles, though all cubes cannot be circles. When some cubes are circles, then some circles will have to be cubes. And when all squares are circles, then some circles will have to be squares. As per given statement II, all squares are circles. Therefore all squares cannot be cubes. As such only conclusions II and III are correct.

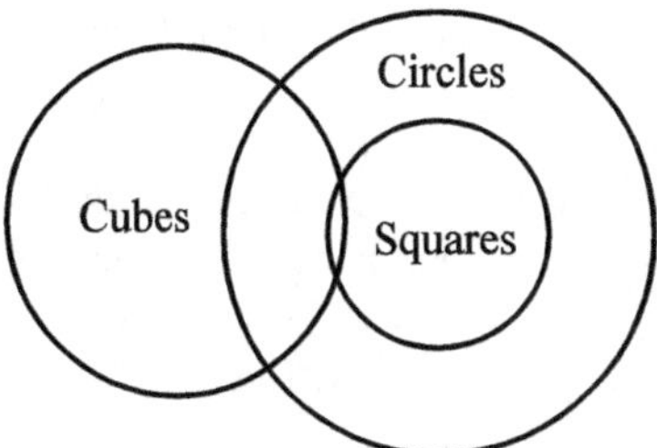

13. *(e)* : When all cups are goats, then only some goats can be cups. When all goats are tins, then only some tins can be goats. When all cups are goats and all goats are tins, then naturally all cups are tins and some tins must be cups. Therefore, all the conclusions are incorrect.

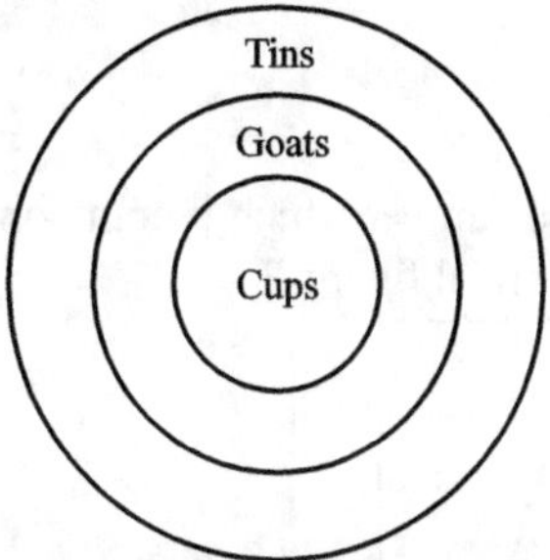

14. *(e)* : When all bombs are bags and some bags are jets then all bombs cannot be jets. 'Some bags' indicate that there is no chance of some bombs being jets, or some jets being bombs. Further all jets cannot be bombs. Therefore, all conclusions are incorrect.

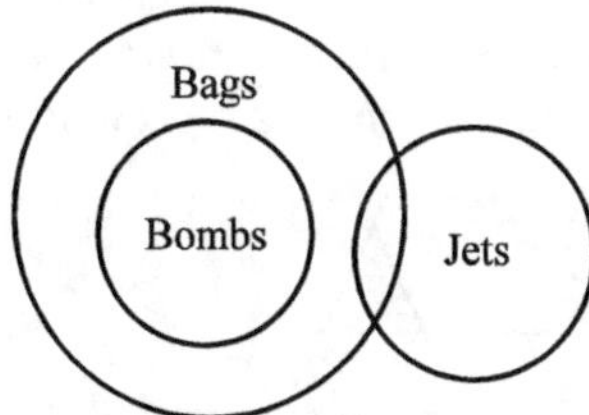

15. *(d)* : When some thorns are jackets and some jackets are boats, then some thorns may be boats but some boats cannot be thorns. As per Statement I, some thorns are jackets, some jackets need to be thorns. When Statement II conveys that some jackets are boats, then it is clear that all jackets cannot be boats. Therefore, no particular given conclusion can be drawn from the given statements.

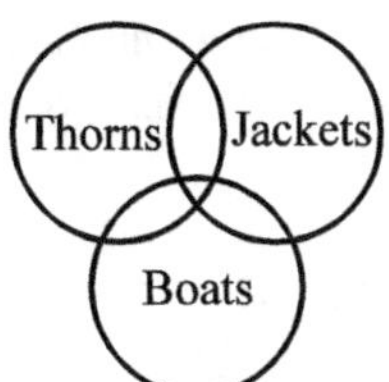

21. VENN DIAGRAMS

In these type of questions, diagrammatic representation presents a logical illustration of particular class or statements based on which the questions are asked. A clear view of the diagram makes the concepts clear for attempting such questions.

EXERCISE

1. What is the number which is common to only two geometrical figures?

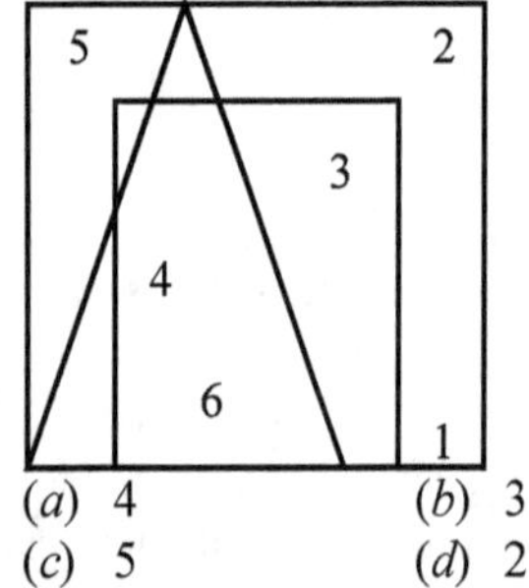

(a) 4 (b) 3
(c) 5 (d) 2

Directions (Qs. 2 and 3) : *In the following diagram, rectangle represents Hindi Announcers, circle represents English Announcers, square represents French Announcers, and triangle represents German Announcers.*

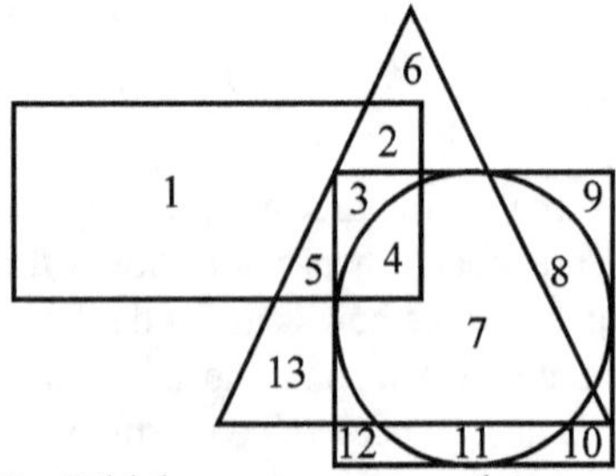

2. Which area represents those announcers who can present programmes in Hindi, French and German only?

(a) 1 (b) 2
(c) 3 (d) 4

3 Which area represents those announcers who can present programmes in French and English only?

(a) 7 (b) 9
(c) 11 (d) 13

Directions (Qs. 4 and 5) : *Study the diagram to answer these questions.*

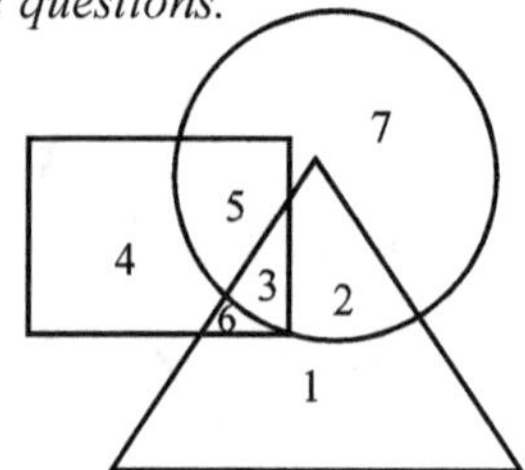

4. Which number is in all the geometrical figures?

(a) 5 (b) 6
(c) 2 (d) 3

5. Number 6 is in :

(a) Rectangle and triangle
(b) Circle and traingle
(c) Rectangle and circle
(d) Rectangle only

Directions (Qs. 6 to 9) : *In the following diagram*

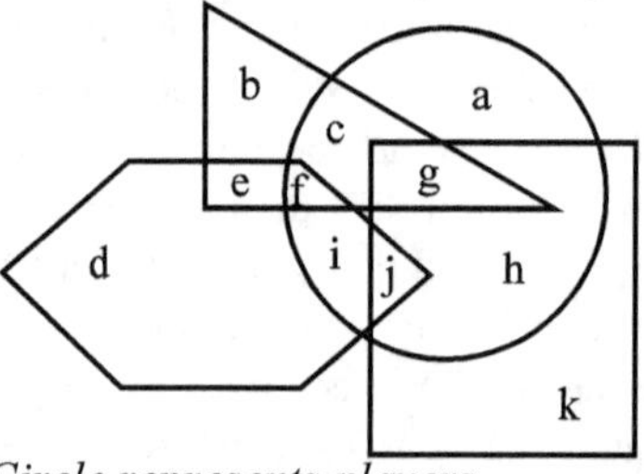

The Circle represents players
The Triangle represents outdoor games
The Hexagon represents indoor games and
The Square represents national level players
Study the diagram and answer the questions given below :

6. The letter in the section representing the players who play indoor games at national level is :

(a) f (b) i
(c) j (d) g

7. The letter representing the section of outdoor as well as indoor game players who do not play at the national level is :

(*a*) c   (*b*) f

(*c*) e   (*d*) i

8. The section representing national level players who do not play either outdoor or indoor games but still come under the category of players is :

(*a*) k   (*b*) g

(*c*) c   (*d*) h

9. Persons who play outdoor games but do not come under the category of players are represented in the section marked :

(*a*) b   (*b*) c

(*c*) a   (*d*) d

Direction (Qs. 10) : *Study the diagram given below.*

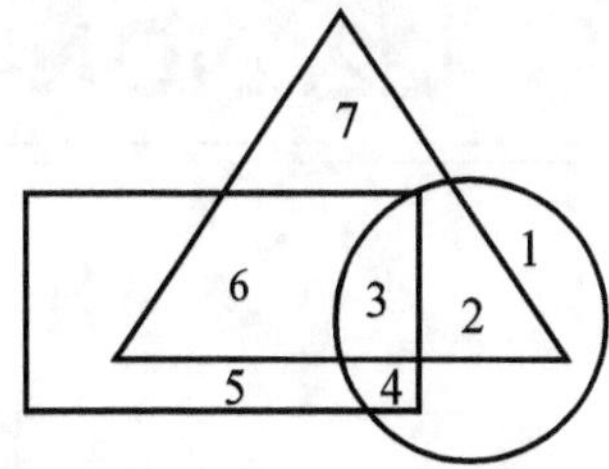

A college provides three different activities, students union represented by triangle, literary society represented by rectangle and social service league represented by circle.

10. Those who take part in both literary society and social service league but not in students union are represented by :

(*a*) 3 & 4   (*b*) 5 & 6

(*c*) 5 & 1   (*d*) 4

EXPLANATORY ANSWERS

1. *(b)* :

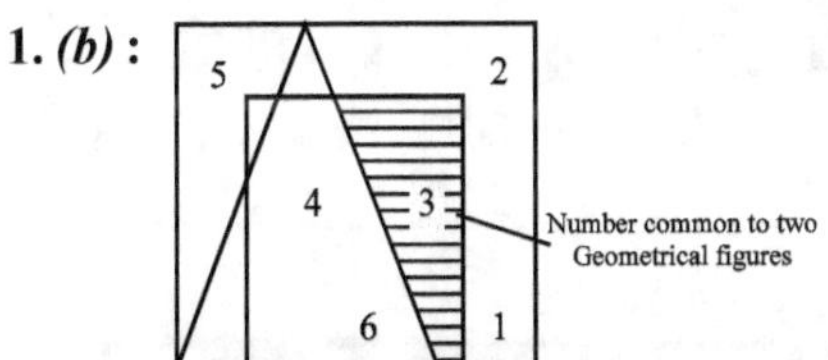

Note : Numbers 4 and 6 are common to all three geometrical figures.

2. *(c)*,   3. *(c)* :

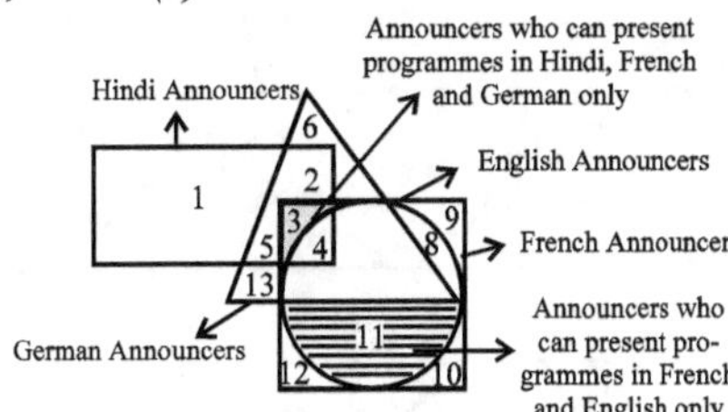

4. *(d)*,   5. *(a)* :

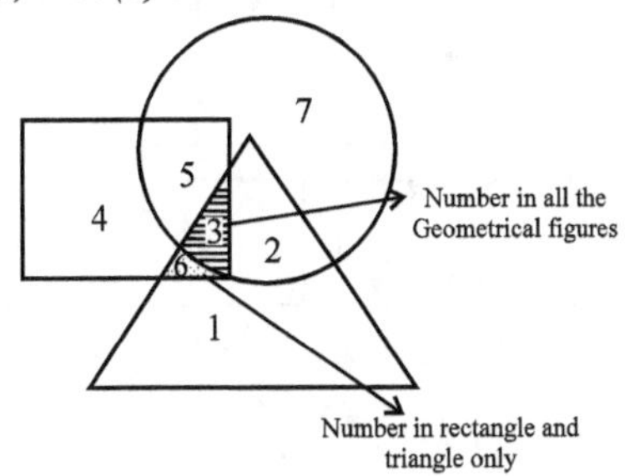

6. *(c)*,   7. *(b)*,   8. *(d)*,   9. *(a)* :

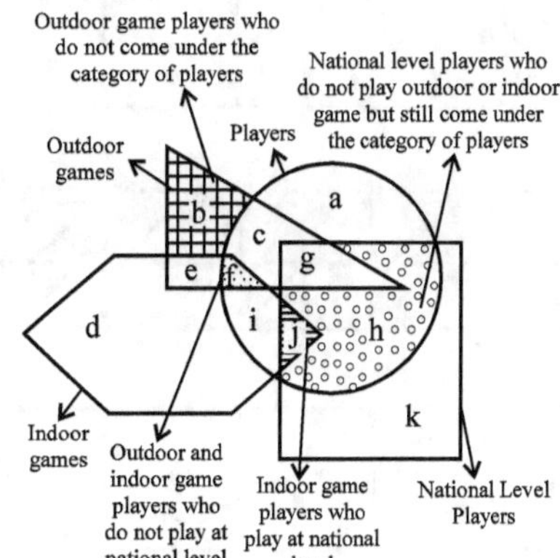

10. *(d)*

22. NON-VERBAL SERIES

Directions (Q. 1–10) : *In each of the following questions which one of the five answer figures given below should come after the problem figures if the sequence are continued?*

Problem Figures   Answer Figures

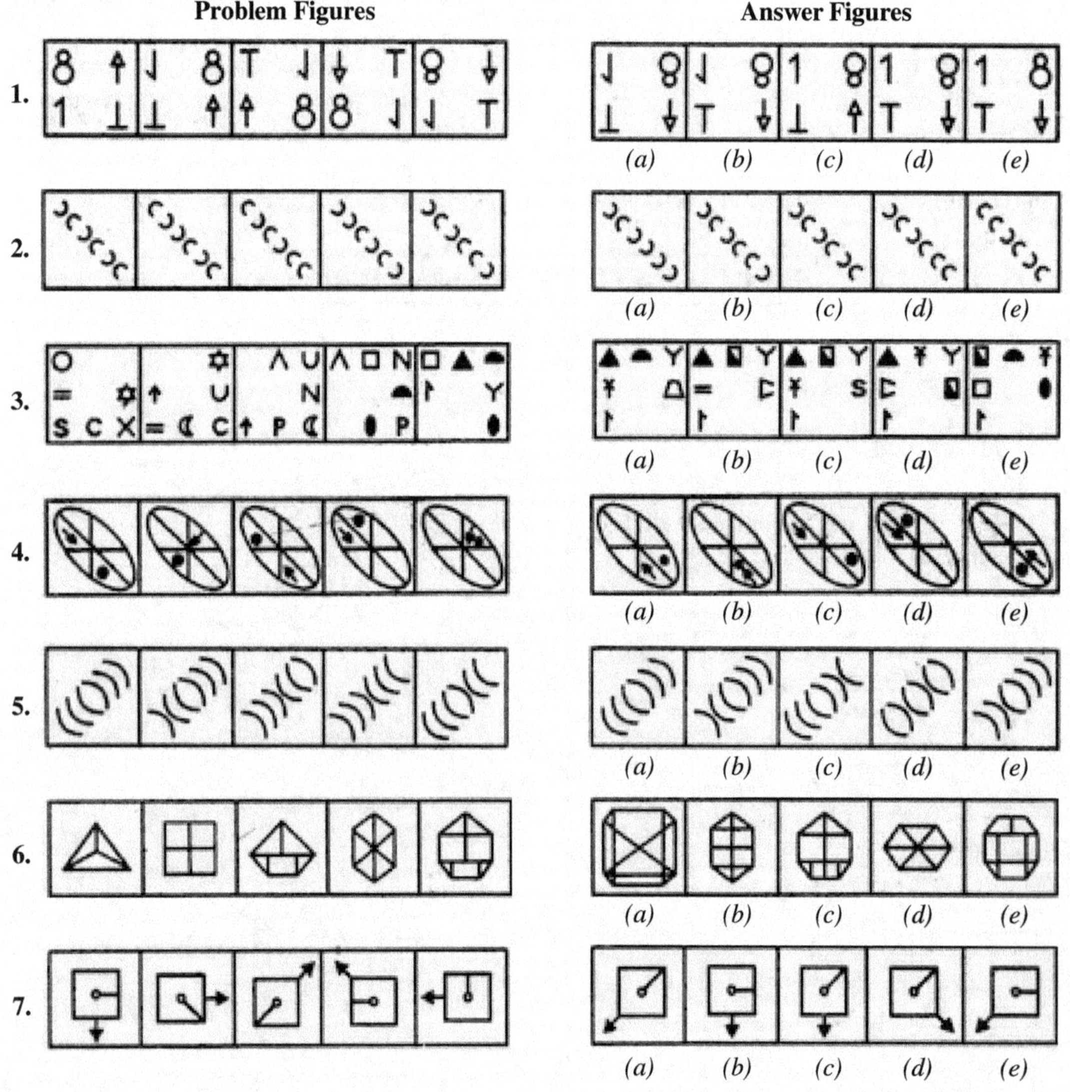

Problem Figures **Answer Figures**

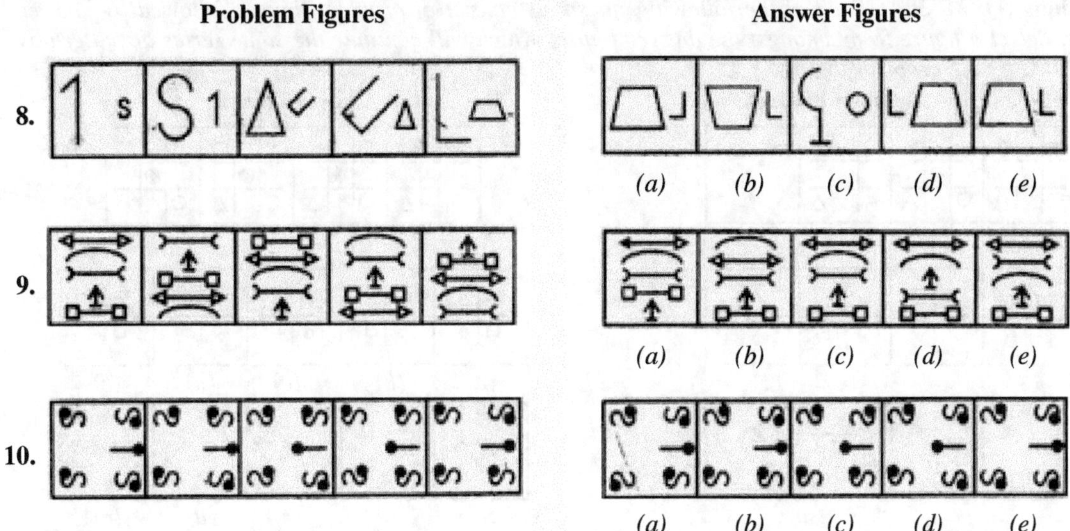

Directions (Q. 11-20) : *In each of these questions, a series begins with an unmarked figure on the extreme left in the row of figures. One and only one of the five lettered figures in the series does not fit into the series. The two unmarked figures, one on the extreme left and the other on the extreme right fit into the series. Take as many aspects into account as possible of the figures in the series and find out the one and only of the five marked figures which does not fit into the series. The letter of that figure is the answer.*

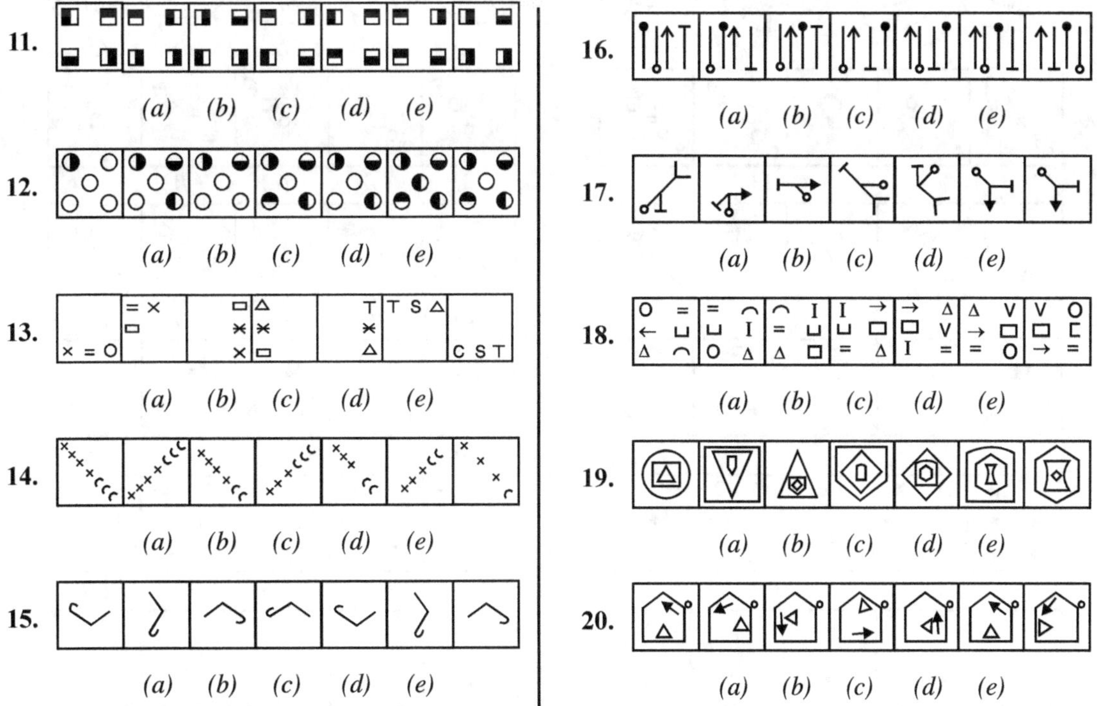

Directions (Q. 21–30) : *Each of the following questions consist of problem figures followed by answer figures. Select a figure from amongst the answer figures which will continue the same series or pattern as established by the problem figures.*

Problem Figures   **Answer Figures**

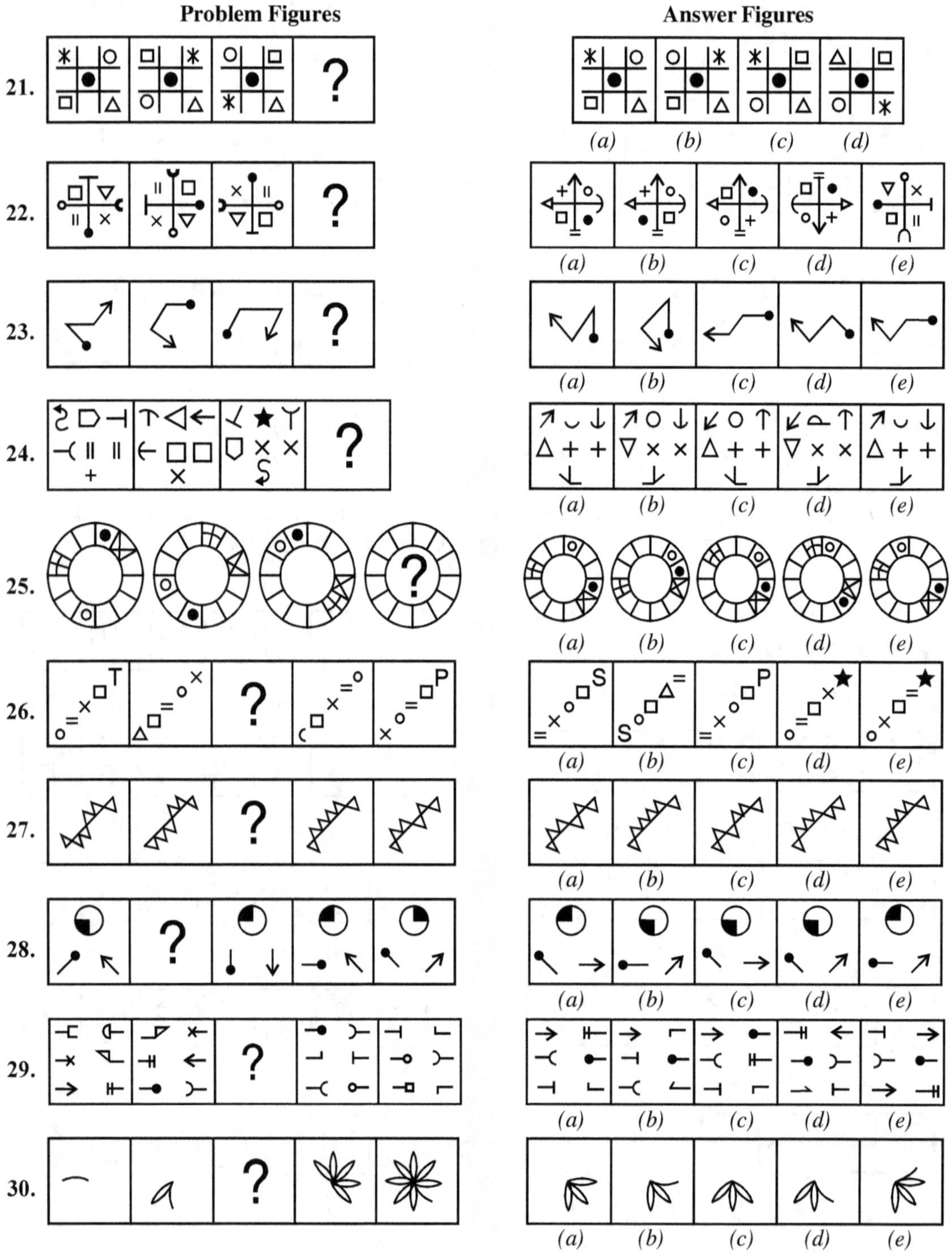

EXPLANATORY ANSWERS

1. (d) : In each step, all the elements move to the adjacent corner (of the square boundary) in a CW direction and the element that reaches the upper-left corner gets vertically inverted.

2. (c) : We can label the arcs as shown  . The arcs get inverted in the sequence (1 & 2), (3, 4 & 5), (6 & 1), (2, 3 & 4), (5 & 6), ...

3. (d) : All the elements move half-a-side of the square boundary in ACW direction in each step. Also, first, third and fifth elements are replaced by new elements in one step and second, fourth and sixth elements are replaced by new elements in the next step. The two steps are repeated alternately.

4. (a) : In each step, the dot moves one space CW and the arrow moves two spaces CW.

5. (c) : One arc and four arcs get inverted alternately.

6. (e) : The number of parts increases by one along with the number of sides in the figure.

7. (c) : The pin rotates 45°CW and 90°CW alternately and moves one space (each space is equal to half-a-side of the square) and two spaces CW alternately. The arrow rotates 90°ACW and 45°ACW alternately and moves two spaces and one space.

8. (e) : In one step, the two elements interchange positions and the smaller element gets enlarged while the larger element gets reduced in size. In the next step, the smaller element is replaced by a new small element and the larger element is replaced by a new large element.

9. (c) : In each step, the elements move in the order

10. (b) : The upper-left element gets laterally inverted in first, third, fifth. .... steps; the upper-right element gets rotated through 180° is first, fourth, seventh,.... steps; the lower-left element gets laterally inverted in second, fourth, sixth, ... steps; the lower-right element gets rotated through 180° in third, sixth,... steps and the pin at the middle-right position gets laterally inverted in every second step.

11. (a) : The shade in the top left square is moved one step clockwise till figure B and then reversed, the process is repeated. The shade in the top right square is moved one step anticlockwise till figure D and then reversed. The shade in the bottom left square is moved one step clockwise in alternate figures and the shade in bottom right square is moved one step clockwise after two figures. In figure 'A' the rule is isolated by the shade in the bottom left square.

12. (e) : In alternate figures a new circle is shaded clockwise. The pattern of the shade is also moved clockwise. In figure 'E' right half of the circle in the centre should have been shaded.

13. (a) : The three elements are placed either horizontally or vertically. In option 'A' neither of the placements can be applied.

14. (c) : The placement of elements is same in alternate figures. The number and type of elements is same in two subsequent figures. In this manner, figure 'C' should have four crosses and two C shapes.

15. (c) : The element is moved one step anticlockwise and the arc at one end is turned outside and inside alternately. In figure 'C' the element should be on the right side with the arc turned outside on the top side.

16. (e) : The left most element, line segment with the dot is moved one step towards right till figure C where it reaches the extreme right position. This process is repeated from figure D where the element on the extreme left, line segment with a circle, is moved. In figure 'E' the placement of the elements does not follow the rule of the series.

17. *(e)* : The 'T' line is rotated 45° clockwise and the line with the circle 45° anticlockwise. The 'Y' shape and the arrow are repeated twice after two figures. In option E, the 'T' shape and the line with the circle are rotated by 90°.

18. *(e)* : First the elements in the four corners are moved one step anticlockwise, next the four elements from the top are moved one step anticlockwise and then the four elements from the bottom are moved one step anticlockwise. Of the remaining two elements, the one on the left is made new each time and then their places are interchanged. This process is repeated from figure D. In option 'E' open square should have been in place of circle to continue the series.

19. *(a)* : At each step the outermost figure is removed and a new figure is placed right in the centre of other two figures. In option 'A' the triangle is turned upside down, which violates the rule of the series.

20. *(a)* : The arrow is moved one step anticlockwise and the triangle one step clockwise. In figure 'A' the triangle should have been on the left side of the figure.

21. *(a)* : The places of star, circle and square are moved one step clockwise at each step.

22. *(e)* : The elements in the four quadrants are moved one step clockwise and the elements at the ends of the cross are moved one step anticlockwise in this series.

23. *(a)* : In alternate figures, the line with the dot is turned 90° clockwise and the arrow 180° clockwise.

24. *(e)* : In alternate figures, the element in the top left position is horizontally inverted and moved one and half steps anticlockwise, the top middle element is turned 90° clockwise and moved one step anticlockwise, the top right element is turned 135° clockwise and moved one step anticlockwise, the element at the bottom is replaced by a new element and moved to the top middle position, and the two identical elements are replaced by two new identical elements.

25. *(a)* : The cross and the circle move one and two steps clockwise respectively (at each step), the plus moves 3, 4 and 5 steps clockwise, and the dot 6, 5 and 4 steps clockwise.

26. *(a)* : At first step, the fifth or the bottom most element is moved to the second place from top, the second element moved to the fourth place, the fourth element is moved to the third place, the third element is moved to the first or the topmost place and the element on the top, which is made new, is moved to the last or the fifth place. At second step i.e., from second problem figure to third problem figure the above process is reversed. The bottom most element is the first and the top most element is the last or fifth. Hereafter, the process is repeated from the beginning. Option 'A' is the right answer.

27. *(c)* : Starting from the bottom, one triangle is moved to the opposite side at each step in upward order. Option 'C' fits into the question marked space.

28. *(c)* : The shade inside the circle is rotated clockwise in alternate figures; the line segment with a dot is rotated 135° clockwise in alternate figures and the arrow is rotated 135° anticlockwise in alternate figures. By this process answer figure 'C' completes the series.

29. *(a)* : At each step the elements are moved diagonally upward and then laterally inverted, and the top two elements are made new and placed at the bottom line. By this process, option figure 'A' completes the series.

30. *(a)* : The number of arcs making the petals of the flower are increased by one, one and half, two, two and half respectively at each step. Also, the flower is turned 45° anticlockwise. By this process, option 'A' is the right answer.

23. NON-VERBAL ANALOGY

EXERCISE

TYPE-I

Directions (Q. 1-15): *The second figure in the first unit of the Problem Figures bears a certain relationship to the first figure. Similarly, one of the figures in the Answer Figures bears the same relationship to the first figures in the second unit of the Problem Figures. Locate the figure which would fit the questions marks.*

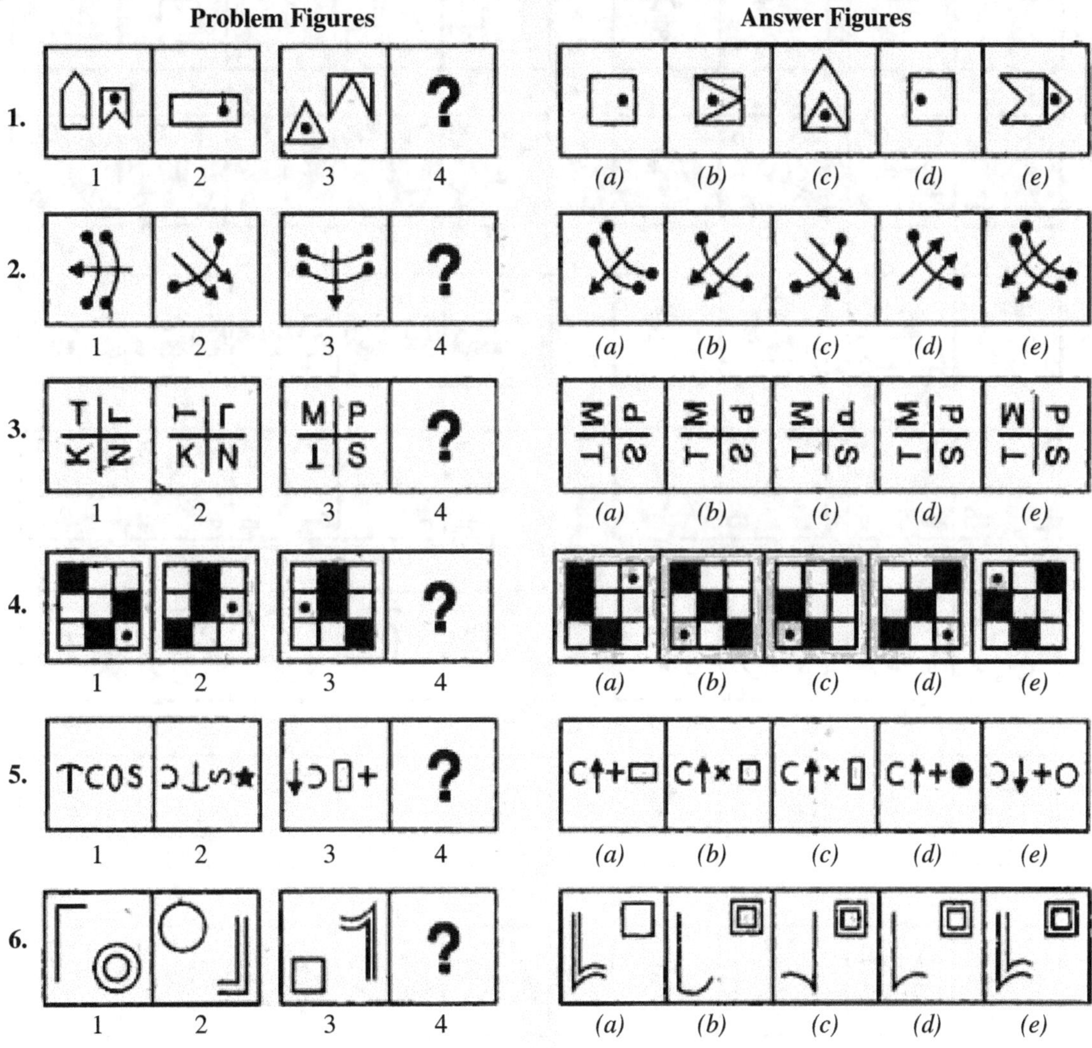

Problem Figures　　　　　　　**Answer Figures**

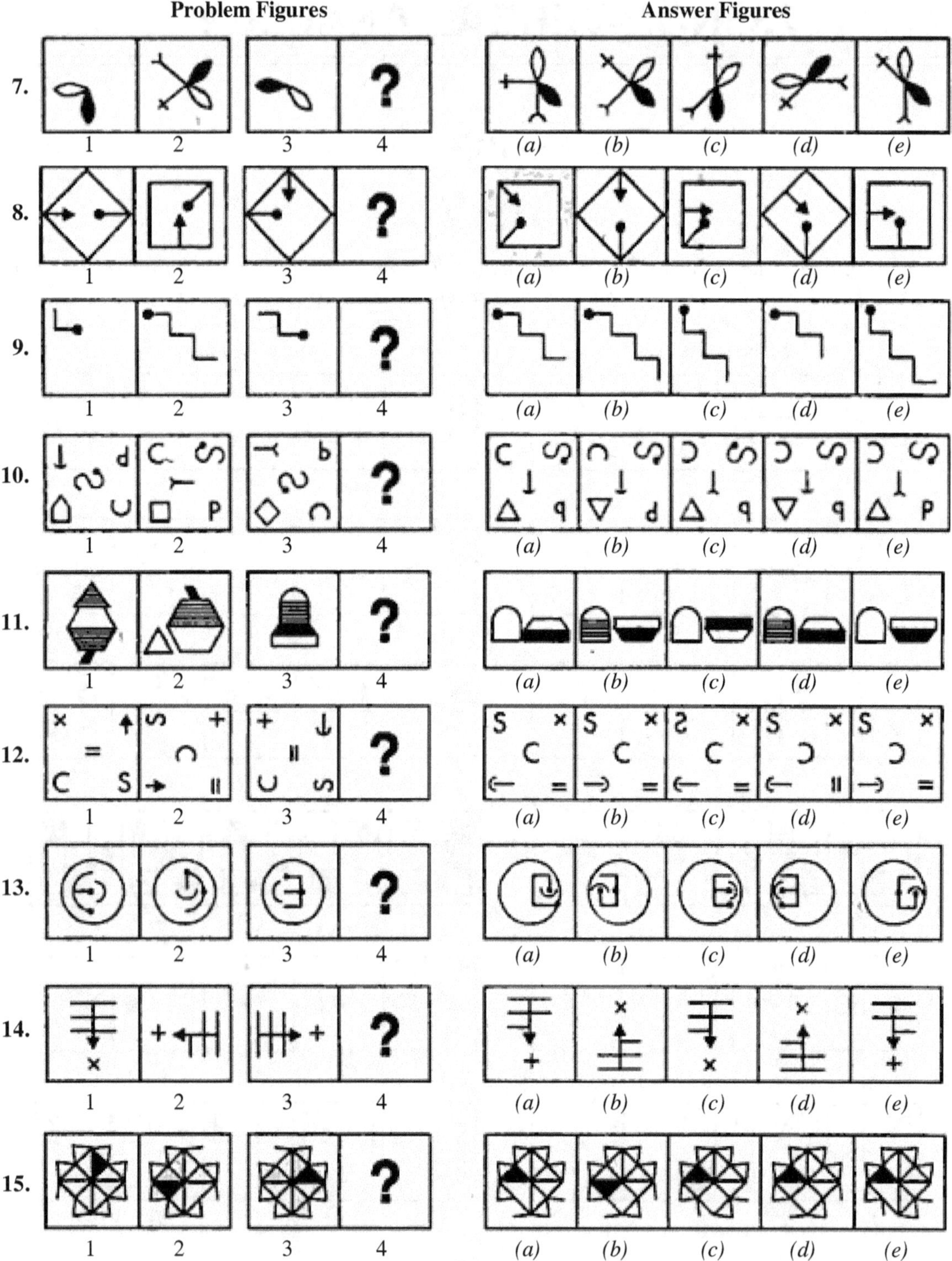

TYPE-II

Directions (Q. 16–30): *In each of the following questions, a related pair of figures is followed by five numbered pairs of figures. Select the pair that has a relationship **similar** to that in the unnumbered pair.*

Problem Figure **Answer Figures**

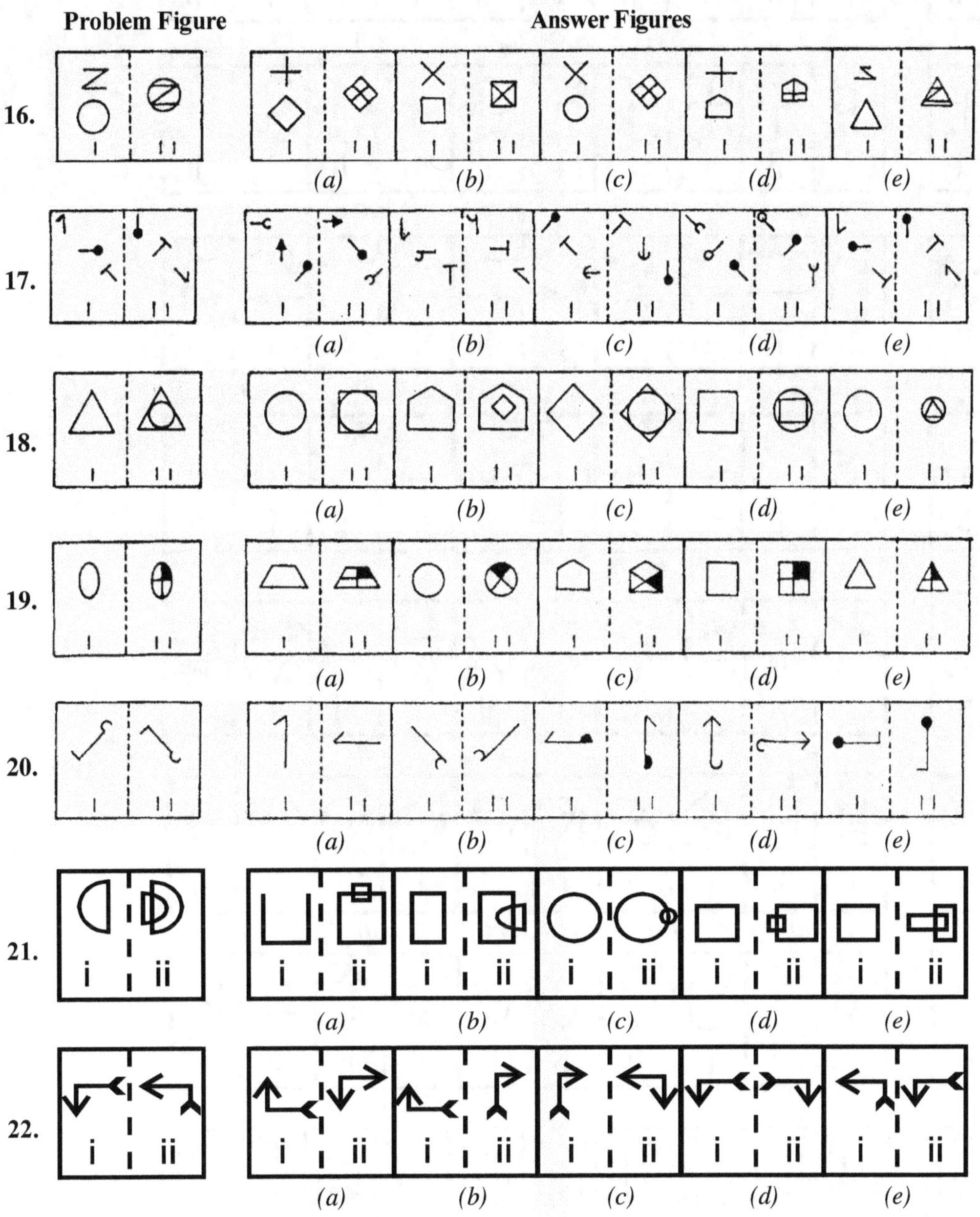

Problem Figure **Answer Figures**

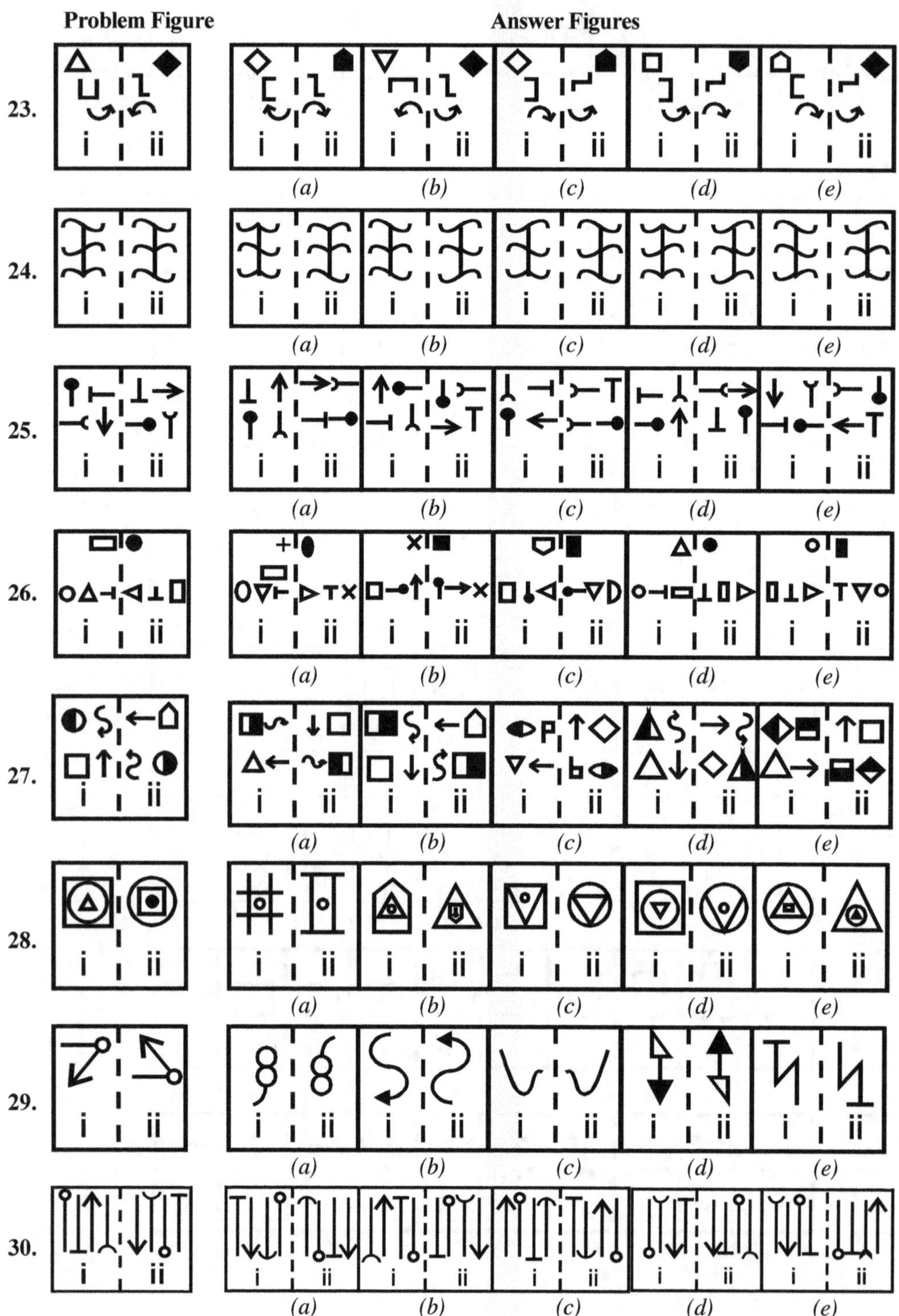

EXPLANATORY ANSWERS

1. *(b)* **:** The R.H.S. figure is fitted into the L.H.S. figure and the resulting figure is rotated 90° CW.

2. *(b)* **:** The figure rotates 45° ACW, the arrow changes to a curved line with dotted ends and the curved lines with dotted ends get converted to arrows.

3. *(d)* **:** The top left symbol rotates 90° ACW while all other symbols rotate 90° CW.

4. *(e)* **:** The black portion in top layer moves one step to the right; the black portions in the middle and the lower layers move one step to the left and the dot moves one step upwards.

5. *(d)* **:** The first and second symbols from the left interchange positions and the other two symbols also interchange positions. The symbol that reaches the first position from the left gets laterally inverted; the symbol that reaches the second position gets inverted, the third symbol rotates 90° CW and the fourth symbol gets replaced by a new one.

6. *(d)* **:** The single figure is replaced by a figure similar to the double figures and the double figures are replaced by figures similar to the single figure.

7. *(e)* **:** The figure rotates 135° ACW; a 'T' appears diagonally opposite to the black leaf and a 'Y' appears diagonally opposite to the white leaf.

8. *(c)* **:** The square rotates through 45°. The arrow moves 90° ACW and the pin moves 45° ACW.

9. *(b)* **:** The figure rotates through 180° and three lines forming a zig-zag, get attached to its lower end.

10. *(d)* **:** The symbols move in the order

The symbol that reaches the central position rotates 90° CW and its arc gets inverted; the 'P' shaped symbol rotates through 180°; the 'C' shaped symbol rotates 90° CW; the 'S' Shaped symbol gets laterally inverted and the fifth symbol gets replaced by a new one.

45°, the symbol that reaches the lower right corner rotates 90° ACW and a new symbol appears in middle-left position.

11. *(e)* **:** The upper and the lower parts of the figure get separated. Shading is removed from the upper part and the lower part is inverted. The two parts are then placed side by side.

12. *(a)* **:** The symbols move in the order

The symbol that reaches the top-left corner rotates 90° ACW; the symbol in the top-right corner rotates through 45°; the symbols in the lower-left corner and in the central positions rotates 90° CW and the symbol that reaches the lower-right corner rotates through 90°.

13. *(e)* **:** The figure gets laterally inverted. The dot on the larger arc, the pin and the small arc rotate 90° ACW. Also, the pin gets inverted.

14. *(c)* **:** The figure rotates 90° CW. One half of one of the lines on the arrow is lost. The figure in front of the arrowhead rotates through 45°.

15. *(d)* **:** The missing line segment in the first figure is replaced in second. Then moving ACW, the third line segment is removed along the two next consecutive sides of the square. Shaded portion in the first figure moves three steps ACW. Similarly, the third figure gives figure (D).

16. *(b)* **:** The uppermost design enters into innerside side of the lower design from Ist figure to the IInd figure.

17. *(a)* **:** In element I to II upper left design comes at lower right rotating 135° C.W. Middle design goes to upper left and rotates 90° CW. While lower right design goes to middle and it also rotates 90° C.W. The same changes occur in option A.

18. *(e)* **:** In element I to II and ellipse is put in the triangle. Similarly in option E a triangle is put in the ellipse.

19. *(d)* **:** From first figure to IInd figure, design is divided into four equal parts and right side of the upper portion becomes shaded.

20. *(e)* **:** From Ist figure to IInd figure, design is reversed after moving 90° anticlockwise direction.

21. *(d)* **:** The figure in the first part is laterally inverted and a similar but smaller design is placed on its left side in the second part.

22. *(e)* **:** The element in first part is moved by 90° and the places of short and long line segments are interchanged.

23. *(c)* **:** The number of sides making the top left figure is increased by one and a new figure is made, shaded and moved to the top right position. The element in the centre is turned 90° anticlockwise and the small line on the other side is turned by 180°. The element in the bottom right is turned upside down and moved to the bottom left position.

24. *(a)* **:** The direction of both arcs on the top, are on the middle right and arc on the bottom left in first part are turned to the other side in the second part.

25. *(b)* **:** From part one to part two, the element in the top left is turned 90° clockwise and the other three 90° anticlockwise, also the elements are moved one step anticlockwise.

26. *(b)* **:** From part one to part two, the top right element is turned by 90° and moved down, the lower right and middle elements are turned 90° clockwise and 90° anticlockwise respectively and moved to the left and the lower left element is shaded and moved up.

27. *(a)* **:** All the four elements exchange place diagonally and in doing so the top left element is laterally inverted, the top right element is horizontally inverted, the bottom right element is turned 90° anticlockwise and the number of lines making the element in bottom left is increased by one.

28. *(e)* **:** The innermost figure is removed and the new innermost figure also encloses the other two figures. The innermost and smallest figure is then shaded.

29. *(b)* **:** The design in the first part is horizontally inverted in the second.

30. *(b)* **:** All the elements in the first part are turned upside down and then 1st, 2nd, 3rd and 4th positioned elements become 3rd, 4th, 1st and 2nd elements in the second part.

24. ODD MAN OUT

In this type of reasoning a statement is followed by inferences drawn from it. From these inferences only one definitely follows which is the hidden proposition of the sentence and it is the right answer to the question.

EXERCISE

Directions (Q. 1–10) : *In each question below five figures are given. Four are similar in a certain way and so form a group. The question is— which one of the figures **does not** belong to that group?*

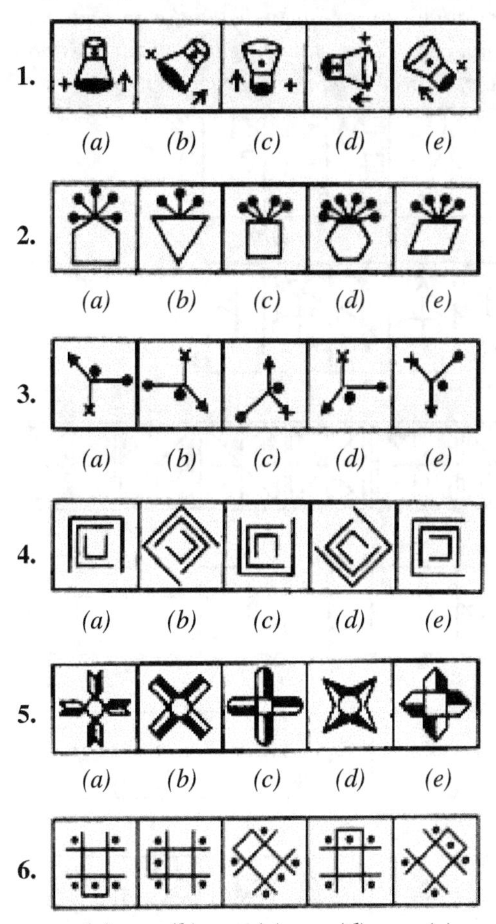

Directions (Q. 11–20) : *In each of the following questions, in four out of the five figures, element I is related to element II in the same particular way. Find out the figure in which the element I is **not** so related to element II.*

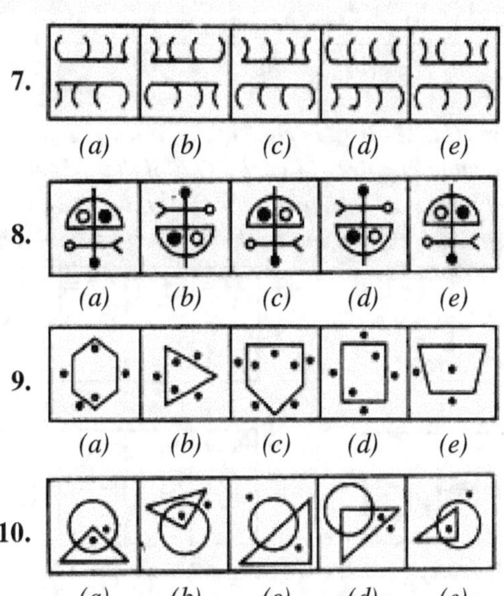

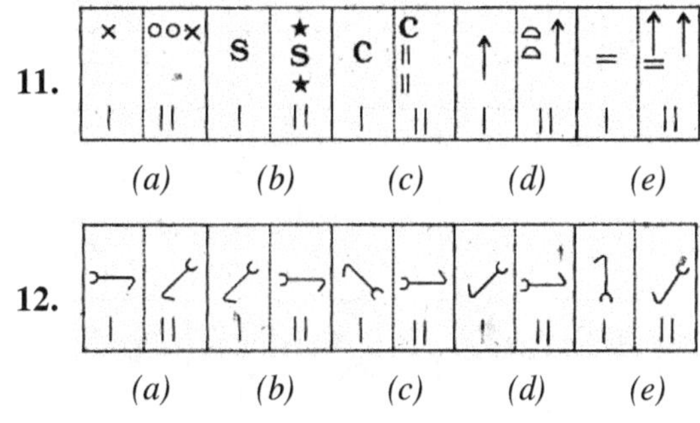

(1673)-Reas.–9

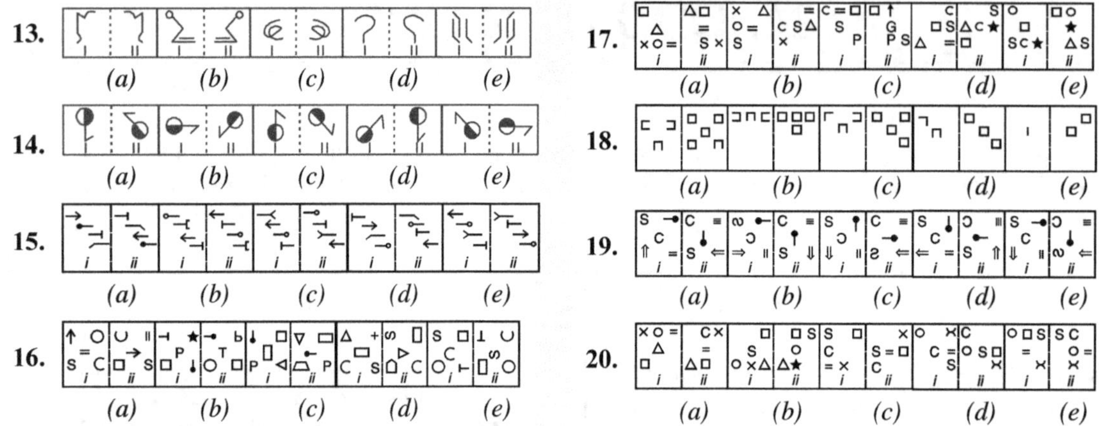

13.   (a)   (b)   (c)   (d)   (e)

14.   (a)   (b)   (c)   (d)   (e)

15.   (a)   (b)   (c)   (d)   (e)

16.   (a)   (b)   (c)   (d)   (e)

17.   (a)   (b)   (c)   (d)   (e)

18.   (a)   (b)   (c)   (d)   (e)

19.   (a)   (b)   (c)   (d)   (e)

20.   (a)   (b)   (c)   (d)   (e)

Directions (Q. 21–30) : *In each of the following questions, a related pair of figures (unnumbered) is followed by five numbered pairs of figures. Out of these five, four have relationship similar to that in the unnumbered pair. Only one pair of figures does not have similar relationship. Select that pair of figures which does not have a similar relationship to that in the unnumbered pair. Number of that pair is your answer.*

21. 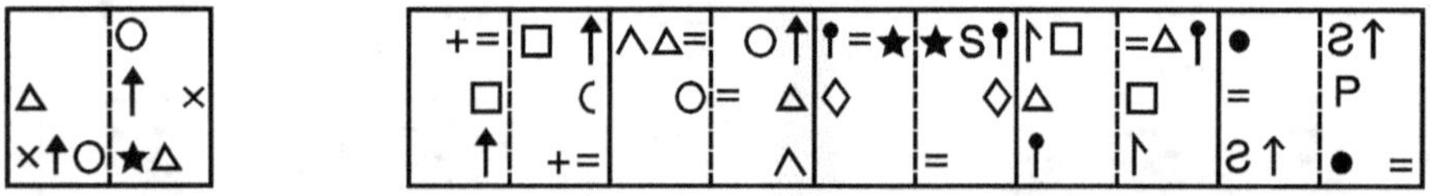   (a)   (b)   (c)   (d)   (e)

22. 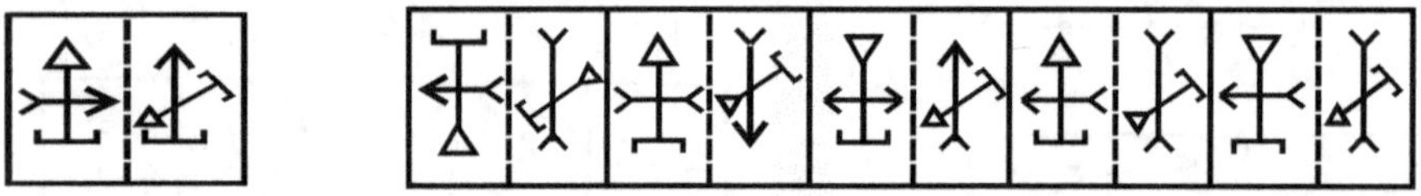   (a)   (b)   (c)   (d)   (e)

23. 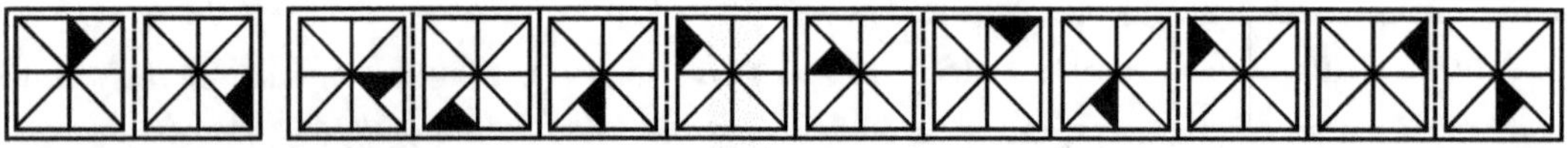   (a)   (b)   (c)   (d)   (e)

24. 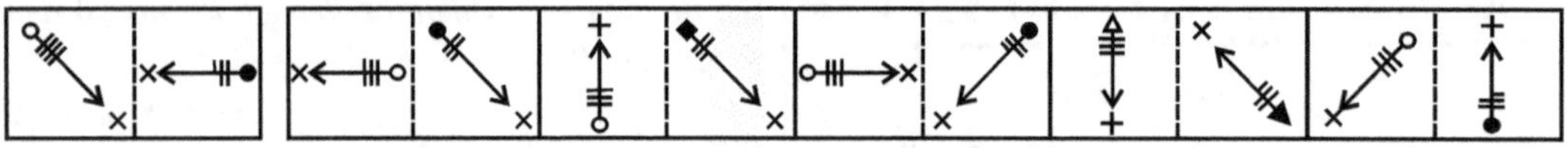   (a)   (b)   (c)   (d)   (e)

25. 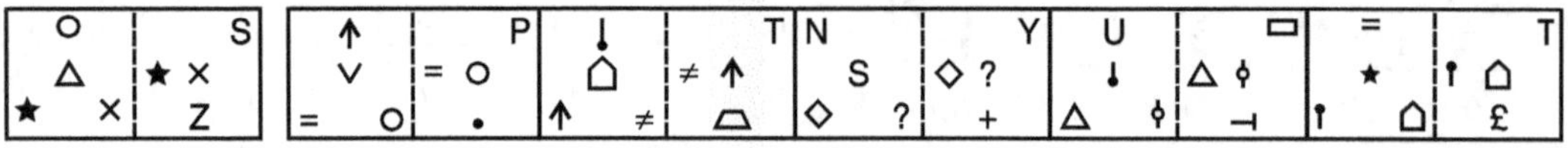   (a)   (b)   (c)   (d)   (e)

26.    (a)   (b)   (c)   (d)   (e)

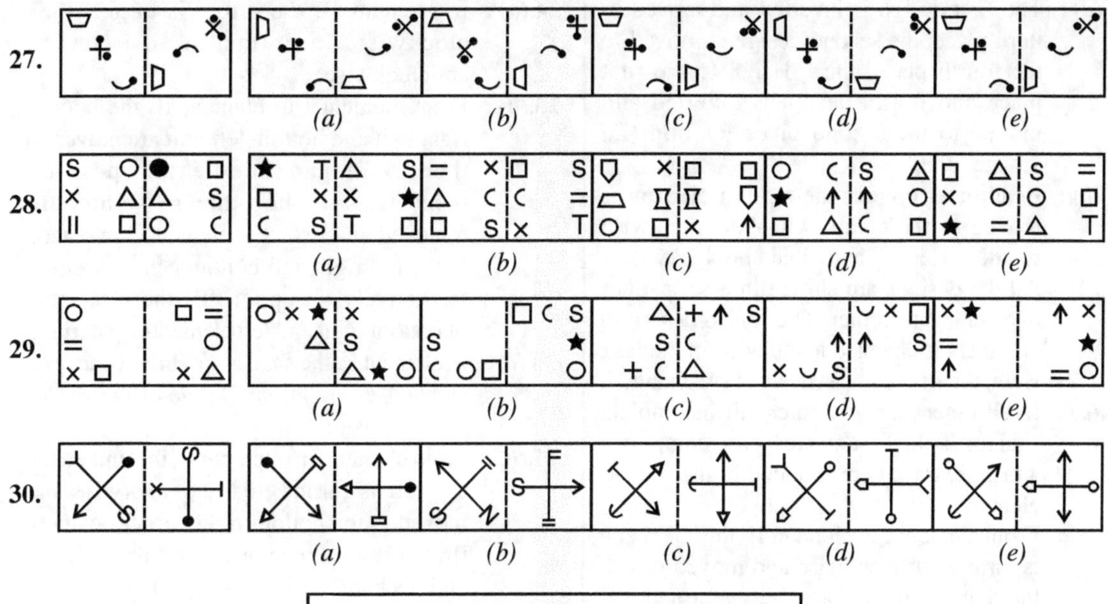

27. (a)　(b)　(c)　(d)　(e)

28. (a)　(b)　(c)　(d)　(e)

29. (a)　(b)　(c)　(d)　(e)

30. (a)　(b)　(c)　(d)　(e)

EXPLANATORY ANSWERS

1. (d) : In all other figures, the arrow and the + sign lie towards the black end of the main figure.

2.(a) : The pins, equal in number of sides in the main figure are attached to the midpoint of a side of the main figure in case of figures (B), (C), (D) and (E). In figure (A), these pins are attached to a vertex of the main figure.

3.(c) : In all other figures, the dot appears in the angle formed between the arrow and the pin.

4.(a) : All other figures can be rotated into each other. (In each figure except figure (A), the middle element is obtained by rotating the outer element through 90° CW and the inner element is obtained by rotating the middle element through 90° CW).

5.(c) : All other figures have at least one line of symmetry.

6.(c) : All other figures can be rotated into each other.

7.(e) : In each one of the other four figures, four arcs are curved towards the left and four other arcs are curved towards the right.

8.(c) : All other figures can be rotated into each other.

9.(d) : In all other figures, the number of dots outside the main figure is one more than the number of dots inside the main figure.

10.(a) : In all other figures, one of the dots lies outside the triangle as well as the circle.

11.(e) : Except in figure (B), in all other figures, from element I to II two new designs are added in one side of the main design.

12.(c) : In each figure from element I to II the main design rotates through 135° clockwise or anticlockwise. Except in figure (C), in all other figures, the smaller line segment moves to other side from element I to II.

13.(a) : In all other figures the element II can be obtained by the lateral inversion of the element I. In figure (A), the lower design has not been inverted.

14.(b) : In figure (B), the small segment is on the same side as that of the half shaded circle in both the elements.

15.(d) : The first design is inverted and moved to third place, the second design is moved to the fourth place, third design to the first place and fourth design is inverted and moved to the second place. Option (D) violates this.

16.(b) : In all other options the top-left element is moved to the centre with 90° clockwise rotation. Here, it is rotated anticlockwise.

17.(d) : All the designs are shifted in a set pattern one behind the other. The fourth design in all others is changed and placed in the last. Here, the fifth and last designs are changed.

18.(a) : In all other pair of figures, all incomplete squares in the first elements are completed and an extra square is added in the second element.

19.(a) : From element I to element II, the 'S' shape is turned 90° clockwise and moved down, the double arrow shape '⇒' is turned 90° clockwise and moved to the right, the two parallel lines one turned by 90°; one parallel line is added and all three lines are moved up, the line with a dot is turned 90° clockwise and moved to the centre and the 'C' shape in the centre is turned by 180° and moved to top left position. Here, the double arrow is turned anticlockwise.

20.(c) : Starting from one unit, all units are moved in a set pattern, the places of last two units moved are interchanged and the last unit is then made new. Here, no changes are made in the last two units.

21.(d) : From element I to element II clockwise the first unit is moved 2 steps forward, the second unit 1 step forward, the third unit 2½ steps forward and the fourth unit 3 steps forward. In option 'D' the third unit violates the rule.

22.(e) : From element I to element II, the horizontal bar is turned 135° anticlockwise and the unit at the lower end is turned by 180°. The vertical bar is turned 90° anticlockwise and the unit at the lower end is turned by 180°. In option 'E' one more unit at the top is turned by 180°.

23.(e) : In element II, the shade is moved two sections clockwise and shifted from the centre to the base. In option 'E' it is not so.

24.(a) : In element II, the arrow is turned 135° clockwise. In option 'A' it is turned anticlockwise.

25.(b) : From element I to element II, the bottom right unit and bottom left unit are moved to the centre and middle left position respectively. The other two units are removed and two new elements are placed in the top right and bottom centre position respectively. In option 'B' the placement of bottom right and left elements is not right.

26.(c) : In element II, the shades are shifted one petal clockwise. In option 'C' one of the shades is not moved.

27.(b) : From element I to element II, the unit on the top left is turned 90° anticlockwise and moved to the bottom right corner position, the unit in the centre is turned 135° anticlockwise and moved to the top right position, and the unit in the bottom right is turned by 180° and moved to the centre. In option 'B', the middle unit is turned 135° clockwise.

28.(a) : From element I to element II, a new unit is placed in the top left position, the top left unit is moved to the middle right position, the middle right unit is moved to the left position, the middle left unit is replaced by a new unit and placed in bottom right position, the bottom right unit is moved to the top right position, and the top right unit is moved diagonally to replace the bottom left unit. In option 'A', the middle left unit is not changed when moved to the bottom right position.

29.(e) : From element I to element II starting anticlockwise, the first and second units are moved 1½ steps clockwise respectively, the third unit ½ step anticlockwise, the fourth unit 2 steps clockwise, and a new unit is placed ahead of the first unit. Option 'E' violates the rules.

30.(e) : In element II, the cross is turned 135° clockwise and then the positions of left and top units on the cross are interchanged. In option 'E' it is not so.

ARITHMETICAL AND NUMERICAL ABILITY

NUMBER SYSTEM

1. There are four numbers A, B, C and D. Average of the first three i.e., A, B and C is 15 and that of B, C and D is 16. If the last number, i.e., D is 19, then the first number is—
   A. 15   B. 16
   C. 17   D. 18

2. Of the three numbers, the first is twice the second and thrice the third. If the average of three is 22, the three numbers are—
   A. 12, 18, 36   B. 18, 12, 36
   C. 36, 12, 18   D. 36, 18, 12

3. If a person is standing on the sixth number in the queue from both the ends, the total persons in the queue are—
   A. 9   B. 11
   C. 12   D. 13

4. A number 'x' when multiplied by 5 and added to three times its own gives 64, the number is—
   A. 8   B. 12
   C. 14   D. 18

5. A number which when multiplied by 11 is as much above 180 as it was originally below it. The number is—
   A. 25   B. 30
   C. 40   D. 45

6. The sum of a number and its reciprocal is thrice the difference of the number and its reciprocal. Find the number.
   A. $\sqrt{2}$ B. $\sqrt{3}$
   C. $\sqrt{5}$ D. $\sqrt{7}$

7. A boy was asked to find $\dfrac{7}{9}$ of a fraction. He made a mistake of dividing the fraction by $\dfrac{7}{9}$ and so got an answer which exceeded the correct answer by $\dfrac{8}{21}$. Find the correct answer.
   A. $\dfrac{2}{3}$ B. $\dfrac{5}{7}$
   C. $\dfrac{7}{12}$ D. $\dfrac{7}{15}$

8. There are 408 boys and 312 girls in a school, which are to be divided into equal sections of either boys or girls alone. Find the maximum number of boys or girls that can be placed in a section. Also find the total number of sections thus formed.
   A. 10, 20   B. 24, 30
   C. 24, 40   D. 30, 30

9. The sum of all possible two-digit number formed from three different one-digit natural numbers, when divided by the sum of the original three numbers is equal to—
   A. 11   B. 18
   C. 22   D. 36

10. There are four prime numbers written in ascending order. The product of the first three is 385 and that of the last three is 1001. The last number is—
    A. 19   B. 17
    C. 13   D. 11

11. If the number 357 ★ 25 ★ is divisible by both 3 and 5, then the missing digits in the unit's place and thousandth place respectively are—
    A. 0, 4   B. 5, 4
    C. 5, 6   D. 0, 6

12. The difference between two numbers is 1365. When the larger number is divided by the smaller one, the quotient is 6 and the remainder is 15. The smaller number is:

A. 360   B. 295
C. 270   D. 240

13. When a number is divided by 31, the remainder is 29. When the same number is divided by 16, what will be the remainder?
A. 15   B. 13
C. 11   D. Data inadequate

14. In dividing a number by 585, a student applied the method of short division. He divided the number successively by 5, 9 and 13 (factor of 585) and got the remainders 4, 8 and 12. If he had divided the number by 585, the remainder would have been:
A. 584   B. 292
C. 144   D. 24

15. When a number divided by 6 leaves a remainder 3. When the square of the same number is divided by 6, the remainder is:
A. 3   B. 2
C. 1   D. zero

ANSWERS

1	2	3	4	5	6	7	8	9	10
B	D	B	A	B	A	C	B	C	C

11	12	13	14	15
C	C	D	A	A

SOME SELECTED EXPLANATORY ANSWERS

1. $\dfrac{A+B+C}{3} = 15,$

or, $A + B + C = 15 \times 3 = 45$ ... (i)

$\dfrac{B+C+D}{3} = 16,$

or $B + C + D = 48$ ... (ii)

$D = 19$

$\therefore \ B + C + 19 = 48$

or, $B + C = 48 - 19 = 29$

But, $A + B + C = 45$

Putting the value of $B + C = 29$ in the above equation (i), we get $A + 29 = 45$

$\therefore \ A = 45 - 29 = 16.$

2. Let the third number $= x$

$\therefore$ First number $= 3x$

Second number $= \dfrac{3x}{2}$

$\therefore \dfrac{1}{3}\left[x + 3x + \dfrac{3x}{2}\right] = 22 \ \Rightarrow \ \dfrac{11}{2}x = 66$

$\Rightarrow x = \dfrac{66 \times 2}{11} = 12 = $ Third number,

$12 \times 3 = 36 = $ First number,

$\dfrac{12 \times 3}{2} = 18 = $ Second number.

3. If the person is standing at sixth number in the queue from both sides, that means there are five persons ahead and five persons behind him. Hence, total number of persons in the queue is $5 + 1 + 5 = 11.$

4. $5 \times x + 3x = 64 \quad \Rightarrow 8x = 64$

$\therefore \qquad x = \dfrac{64}{8} = 8.$

5. Let the number is x

$\therefore \qquad 180 - x = 11x - 180$

$\Rightarrow \qquad 180 + 180 = 11x + x$

$\Rightarrow \qquad 360 = 12x,$

$\Rightarrow \qquad x = \dfrac{360}{12} = 30.$

6. Let the no. $= x$ then its reciprocal $= \dfrac{1}{x}$

By the question, $\left(x + \dfrac{1}{x}\right) = 3\left(x - \dfrac{1}{x}\right)$

$\Rightarrow \qquad \dfrac{x^2+1}{x} = \dfrac{3(x^2-1)}{x}$

$\Rightarrow \qquad x^2 + 1 = 3x^2 - 3$

$\Rightarrow \qquad 3x^2 - x^2 = 3 + 1$

$\therefore \qquad x = \sqrt{2}.$

7. Let the required fraction $= x$

then, by the question $\quad x \div \dfrac{7}{9} - x \times \dfrac{7}{9} = \dfrac{8}{21}$

$\Rightarrow \qquad x \times \dfrac{9}{7} - \dfrac{7x}{9} = \dfrac{8}{21}$

$\Rightarrow \qquad \dfrac{32x}{63} = \dfrac{8}{21}$

$\Rightarrow \qquad x = \dfrac{8}{21} \times \dfrac{63}{32} = \dfrac{3}{4}$

Hence, the correct answer $= \dfrac{3}{4} \times \dfrac{7}{9} = \dfrac{7}{12}.$

8.

```
      312) 408(1
           312
           ___
       96) 312 (3
           288
           ___
       24) 96 (4
           96
           __
           ×
```

$\therefore$ Maximum number of girls or boys that can be placed in a section $= 24$ and total

number of such section $= \dfrac{408}{24} + \dfrac{312}{24}$

$= 17 + 13 = 30$

9. Let three different one digit natural numbers be x, y and z.

Then, sum of all possible two digits numbers

$= (10x + y) + (10y + x) + (10x + z)$

$\qquad + (10z + x) + (10y + z) + (10z + y)$

$= 22x + 22y + 22z = 22\,(x + y + z)$

Hence, required number $= 22$.

10. Let four prime numbers be a, b, c and d respectively.

Now, $\dfrac{abc}{bcd} = \dfrac{385}{1001} \qquad \Rightarrow \dfrac{c}{d} = \dfrac{5}{13}$

Hence, $a = 5$ and $d = 13$

11. $357 \star 25 \star$

For divisible by 5, the last digit must be either 0 or 5.

If last digit is 0, then other required digit will be 2 or 5 or 8

Hence, the numbers are $(0, 2)$ or $(0, 5)$ or $(0, 8)$

If last digit is 5, then other required digit will be 0 or 3 or 6 or 9

Hence, the numbers are $(5, 0)$ or $(5, 3)$ or $(5, 6)$ or $(5, 9)$

So, correct option is (c).

12. Here, $(x + 1365) = 6x + 15$

$\Rightarrow 5x = 1350$

$\therefore \quad x = \dfrac{1350}{5} = 270$

Hence, the smaller number $= 270$.

13. The number $= 31x + 29$.

Here, given data is inadequate.

14.

```
   5 | a
   9 | b − 4
  13 | c − 8
     | 1 − 12
```

Now, $\quad c = 13 \times 1 + 12 = 25$

$b = 9c + 8 = 9 \times 25 + 8 = 233$

$a = 5b + 4 = 5 \times 233 + 4$

$\qquad\qquad\qquad = 1165 + 4 = 1169$

$1169 = 585 \times 1 + 584$

Hence, required remainder $= 584$.

15. The number $= 6x + 3$

Now, $(6x + 3)^2 = 36x^2 + 36x + 9$

$= (36x^2 + 36x + 6) + 3$

$= 6(6x^2 + 6x + 1) + 3$

Hence, required remainder $= 3$.

LCM AND HCF

1. The L.C.M. and H.C.F. of two numbers are 4284 and 32 respectively. If one of the numbers is 204, the other is
   A. 672   B. 576
   C. 676   D. 572

2. Two numbers are in the ratio of 8 : 15. If their H.C.F. is 4, the numbers are
   A. 32 and 60   B. 16 and 30
   C. 80 and 150   D. 64 and 120

3. The greatest number that will divide 366, 513 and 324 leaving the same remainder in each case is
   A. 21   B. 18
   C. 27   D. 42

4. The L.C.M. of two numbers is 45 times their H.C.F. If the sum of the L.C.M. and the H.C.F. of these two numbers is 1150 and one of the numbers is 125, then the other number is
   A. 256   B. 225
   C. 250   D. 255

5. The H.C.F. and the L.C.M. of two numbers are 50 and 250 respectively. On dividing one of these numbers by 2, 50 is obtained as quotient. The numbrs are
   A. 100, 125   B. 80, 100
   C. 125, 100   D. 200, 250

6. Three bells ring respectively at an interval of 15 seconds, 20 seconds and 24 seconds. If they ring continuously for 12 minutes then how many times, during this period, will they ring together?
   A. 2 times   B. 6 times
   C. 5 times   D. 3 times

7. If the sum of two numbers is 55 and the H.C.F. and L.C.M. of these numbers are 5 and 120 respectively. Find the sum of their reciprocals.
   A. $\dfrac{120}{11}$ B. $\dfrac{11}{120}$
   C. $\dfrac{601}{55}$ D. $\dfrac{55}{601}$

8. The LCM of two numbers is 48. The numbers are in the ratio of 2 : 3. The sum of the numbers is
   A. 64   B. 40
   C. 32   D. 28

9. Find the greatest number that will divide 43, 91 and 183 so as to leave the same remainder in each case.
   A. 13   B. 9
   C. 7   D. 4

10. The greatest possible length which can be used to measure exactly the length 7m, 3m 85cm, 12m 95 cm is
    A. 42 cm   B. 35 cm
    C. 25 cm   D. 15 cm

11. A, B and C start at the same time in the same direction to run around a circular park. A completes a round in 252 seconds, B in 308 seconds and C in 198 seconds, all starting at the same point. After what time will they meet again at the starting point?
    A. 46 minutes 12 seconds
    B. 45 minutes
    C. 42 minutes 36 seconds
    D. 26 minutes 18 seconds

12. Which of the following has most numbers of divisors?
A. 182   B. 176
C. 101   D. 99

13. Which is of the following is a co-primes?
A. $(23, 92)$ B. $(21, 35)$
C. $(18, 25)$ D. $(16, 62)$

14. Let N be the greatest number that will divide 1305, 4665 and 6905, leaving the same remainder in each case. Then find the sum of the digits in N.
A. 8   B. 6
C. 5   D. 4

15. The greatest number which one dividing 1657 and 2037 leaves remainder 6 and 5 respectively, is:
A. 305   B. 235
C. 127   D. 123

ANSWERS

1	2	3	4	5	6	7	8	9	10
A	A	A	B	A	B	B	B	D	B

11	12	13	14	15
A	B	C	D	C

SOME SELECTED EXPLANATORY ANSWERS

1. 1st number × 2nd number = LCM × HCF
∴   204 × 2nd number = 4284 × 32
∴   2nd number = $\dfrac{4284 \times 32}{204}$ = 672
∴   2nd number = 672

2. Let the numbers be $8x$ and $15x$
$8x = 2 \times 2 \times 2 \times x$
$15x = 3 \times 5 \times x$
∴ LCM of $8x$ and $15x = 2 \times 2 \times 2 \times x \times 3 \times 5$
$= 120x$
Now, 1st number × 2nd number = HCF × LCM
$\Rightarrow$ $8x \times 15x = 4 \times 120x$
$\Rightarrow$ $120x^2 = 4 \times 120x$
$\Rightarrow$ $x = 4$
∴   Numbers are $8 \times 4 = 32$ and $15 \times 4 = 60$

3. Difference between 366 and 513 = 513 − 366
$= 147$
and difference between 513 and 324
$= 513 - 324 = 189$
∴ HCF of 147 and 189

```
147) 189 (1
     147
   × 42) 147 (3
       126
     × 21) 42 (2
         42
         ×
```
∴ The required largest number is 21.

4. LCM of the two numbers = 45 × HCF
and   LCM + HCF = 1150
$\Rightarrow$ 45 × HCF + HCF = 1150
$\Rightarrow$ HCF(45 + 1) = 1150
$\Rightarrow$ HCF = $\dfrac{1150}{46}$ = 25
∴   LCM = 45 × 25 = 1125
∵ 1st number × 2nd number = LCM × HCF
∴ 125 × 2nd number = 1125 × 25
∴   2nd number = $\dfrac{1125 \times 25}{125}$ = 225.

5. According to the condition of the problem, 50 is obtained on dividing one of the numbers by 2
∴ One of the numbers = 50 × 2 = 100
Now, 1st number × 2nd number = LCM × HCF
∴   100 × 2nd number = 250 × 50
∴   2nd number = $\dfrac{250 \times 50}{100}$ = 125

Hence, numbers are 100 and 125.

6. LCM of 15, 20 and 24

```
5 | 15, 20, 24
4 |  3,  4, 24
3 |  3,  1,  6
  |  1,  1,  2
```
LCM = 5 × 4 × 3 × 2 = 120

$\because$ 12 minutes = 12×60 = 720 seconds

$\therefore$ Number of times the bells will ring together during 12 minutes

$$= \frac{720}{120} = 6 \text{ times.}$$

7. Let the number be x and y.

Then, $x + y = 55$;

xy = HCF $\times$ LCM = 5×120

$\therefore$ Sum of their reciprocals

$$= \frac{1}{x} + \frac{1}{y} = \frac{x+y}{xy} = \frac{55}{5 \times 120} = \frac{11}{120}.$$

8. Let the two numbers be $2x$ and $3x$;

their LCM = $6x$

Now, $\quad 6x = 48 \qquad \therefore \quad x = 8$

Hence, the numbers are 2×8, $3 \times 8 = 16, 24$

Their sum = $16 + 24 = 40$.

9.

```
2240) 3360 (1        1120) 5600 (5
      2240                 5600
1120 ) 2240 (2              ×
       2240
        ×
```

Hence, N = HCF of 3360,

2240 and 5600 = 1120

Sum of digits in N = $1 + 1 + 2 + 0 = 4$.

10. 7m = 700 cm;

3m 85 = 385 cm;

12m 95cm = 1295 cm

```
385) 700 (1
     385
     315) 385 (1
          315
          70) 315 (4
              280
              35 ) 70 (2
                   70
                    ×
35) 1295 (37
    105
    245
    245
     ×
```

Hence, required length = HCF of 700 cm, 385 cm, 1295 cm = 35 cm.

11.

```
 2 | 252,  308,  198
 2 | 126,  154,   99
 3 |  63,   77,   99
 3 |  21,   77,   33
 7 |   7,   77,   11
11 |   1,   11,   11
   |   1,    1,    1
```

Hence, LCM = $2 \times 2 \times 3 \times 3 \times 7 \times 11 = 2772$

Hence, A, B, C will meet again at the starting point after 2772 sec. = 46 min 12 sec.

12.

Numbers	Their divisors
182	$\rightarrow$ 1, 2, 7, 13, 14, 26, 91 and 182
176	$\rightarrow$ 1, 2, 4, 8, 16, 22, 44, 88 and 176
101	$\rightarrow$ 1 and 101
99	$\rightarrow$ 1, 3, 9, 11, 33 and 99

Therefore, 176 has the most number of divisors.

13. HCF of 23 and 92 = 23

HCF of 21 and 35 = 7

HCF of 18 and 25 = 1

HCF of 16 and 62 = 2

Hence, 18 and 25 are co-prime numbers.

14. N = HCF of $(4665 - 1305)$,

$(6905 - 4665)$ and $(6905 - 1305)$

= HCF of 3360, 2240 and 5600 = 112

Sum of digit of $1 + 1 + 2 = 4$.

15. Required number = HCF of $(1657 - 6)$ and

$(2037 - 5)$ = HCF of 1651 and 2032 = 127.

```
1651) 2032 (1
      1651
      381) 1651 (4
           1524
           127) 381 (3
                381
                 ×
```

AVERAGE

1. One-third of a certain journey was covered at the rate of 25 km per hour, one-fourth at the rate of 30 km per hour and the rest at the 50 km per hour. What is the average speed per hour for whole journey?

   A. $33\dfrac{1}{3}$ kmph

   B. $44\dfrac{1}{4}$ kmph

   C. $22\dfrac{1}{2}$ kmph

   D. 33 kmph

2. A batsman has a certain average of runs for 16 innings. In the 17th innings, he makes a score of 85 runs thereby increasing his average by 3. What is the average after the 17th inning?
   A. 33 runs
   B. 34 runs
   C. 37 runs
   D. 36 runs

3. The average of 6 observations is 12. A new seventh observation is included and the new average is decreased by 1. The seventh observation is
   A. 1
   B. 3
   C. 5
   D. 6

4. The average age of 30 students in a class is 12 years. The average age of a group of 5 of the students is 10 years and that of another group of 5 of them is 14 years. The average age of the remaining students is
   A. 8 years
   B. 10 years
   C. 12 years
   D. 14 years

5. Out of the three given numbers, the first number is twice the second and thrice the third. If the average of three numbers is 121, what is the difference between the first and third number?
   A. 144
   B. 77
   C. 99
   D. 132

6. If the average marks of three batches of 55, 60 and 45 students is 50, 55 and 60, then average marks of all the students is:
   A. 55
   B. 54
   C. 54.68
   D. 55.68

7. The average of 8 numbers is 20. The average of first two numbers is $15\dfrac{1}{2}$ and that of the next three is $21\dfrac{1}{3}$. If the sixth number is less than the seventh and eighth numbers by 4 and 7 respectively, then the eighth number is:
   A. 27
   B. 25
   C. 22
   D. 18

8. A pupil's marks were wrongly entered as 83 instead of 63. Due to that the average marks for the class got increased by half. What is the number of pupils in the class?
   A. 73
   B. 40
   C. 40
   D. 10

9. A cricketer whose bowling average is 12.4 runs per wicket takes 5 wickets for 26 runs and thereby decreases his average by 0.4. The number of wickets taken by him till the last match was:
   A. 85
   B. 80
   C. 72
   D. 64

10. The average weight of a class of 24 students is 35 kg. If the weight of the teacher is included, the average rises by 400 g. What is the weight of the teacher?
    A. 55 kg
    B. 53 kg
    C. 50 kg
    D. 45 kg

11. Nine men went to a hotel. Eight of them spent Rs. 3 for each over their meals and the ninth spent Rs. 2 more than the average expenditure of all the nine. What is the total money spent by them?
A. Rs. 29.25   B. Rs. 29.50
C. Rs. 29   D. Rs. 30

12. The average age of 24 students in a class is 10. If the teacher's age is included, the average increases by one. The age of the teacher is
A. 25   B. 30
C. 35   D. 40

13. The average of 5 consecutive even numbers A, B, C, D and E is 34. What is the product of B and D?

A. 1152   B. 1368
C. 1224   D. 1088

14. The average of 50 numbers is 30. If two numbers, 35 and 40 are discarded, then the average of the remaining numbers is nearly:
A. 29.68   B. 29.27
C. 28.78   D. 28.32

15. The average monthly salary of 20 employees of an organisation is Rs. 1500. If the manager's salary is added, then the average salary increases by Rs. 100. Find the manager's monthly salary?
A. Rs. 4800   B. Rs. 3600
C. Rs. 2400   D. Rs. 2000

ANSWERS

1	2	3	4	5	6	7	8	9	10
A	C	C	C	D	C	B	B	A	D

11	12	13	14	15
A	C	A	A	B

SOME SELECTED EXPLANATORY ANSWERS

1. Let the total distance covered during journey
= 60 km

$\frac{1}{3}$ of the distance covered during journey

$$= 60 \times \frac{1}{3} = 20 \text{ km}$$

$\frac{1}{4}$ of the distance covered during journey

$$= \frac{1}{4} \times 60 = 15 \text{ km}$$

∴ The distance covered during the rest of journey = 60 − (20 + 15) = 25 km
Time taken to cover 20 km at 25 km/h

$$= \frac{20}{25} \text{ hours} = \frac{4}{5} \text{ hour}$$

Time taken to cover 15 km at 30 km/h

$$= \frac{15}{30} \text{ hours} = \frac{1}{2} \text{ hour}$$

Time taken to cover 25 km at 50 km/h

$$= \frac{25}{50} \text{ hours} = \frac{1}{2} \text{ hour}$$

Total time taken $= \dfrac{4}{5} + \dfrac{1}{2} + \dfrac{1}{2}$

$$= \frac{9}{5} \text{ hours}$$

Hence average speed per hour $= 60 \div \dfrac{9}{5}$

$$= \frac{60 \times 5}{9} = \frac{100}{3} \text{ km/h}$$

$$= 33\frac{1}{3} \text{ km/h}$$

2. Average increase in the score of 17 innings
= 3 runs
Total increase in the score of 17 innings
= 3 × 17 = 51 runs
∴ His average of 16 innings = 85 − 51
= 34 runs

Hence, average after the 17th innings
$$= 34 + 3 = 37 \text{ runs}$$

3. Seventh observation $= (7 \times 11 - 6 \times 12) = 5$

4. Let, the required average age be x
Then, $5 \times 10 + 5 \times 14 + 20 \times x = 30 \times 12$
$$\Rightarrow \quad 20x = 360 - 120$$
$$\Rightarrow \quad 20x = 240$$
$$\Rightarrow \quad x = 12$$

5. Let the three numbers be x, $\dfrac{x}{2}$ and $\dfrac{x}{3}$ respectively,

Now, $\dfrac{1}{3}\left(x + \dfrac{x}{2} + \dfrac{x}{3}\right) = 121$

$$\Rightarrow \dfrac{11x}{6} = 121 \times 3$$

$$\therefore \quad x = \dfrac{121 \times 3 \times 6}{11} = 198$$

Hence, required difference $= x - \dfrac{x}{3} = \dfrac{2x}{3}$

$$= \dfrac{2}{3} \times 198 = 132$$

6. Required average Marks

$$= \dfrac{55 \times 50 + 60 \times 55 + 45 \times 60}{55 + 60 + 45} = \dfrac{8750}{160} = 54.68$$

7. Let the sixth, seventh and eighth numbers are x, $x + 4$ and $x + 7$.
Sum of last three numbers

$$= 8 \times 20 - \left(2 \times \dfrac{31}{2} + 3 \times \dfrac{64}{3}\right)$$

$$\Rightarrow x + x + 4 + x + 7 = 160 - 95$$
$$\Rightarrow 3x + 11 = 65$$
$$\Rightarrow 3x = 54 \qquad \therefore x = 18$$
New eighth number $= x + 7 = 18 + 7 = 25$

8. Let the total number of pupils in the class be x; then,

$$\dfrac{83 - 63}{x} = \dfrac{1}{2} \qquad \Rightarrow \dfrac{20}{x} = \dfrac{1}{2} \qquad \therefore x = 40$$

9. Let the number of wickets taken by him be x till the last match.

Then, $\dfrac{x \times 12.4 + 26}{x + 5} = 12$

$$\Rightarrow 12.4x + 26 = 12x + 60$$

$$\Rightarrow 0.4x = 34 \quad \therefore \quad x = \dfrac{340}{4} = 85$$

10. Let the weight of the teacher be x kgs, then

$$\dfrac{24 \times 35 + x}{25} = 35.4$$

$$\Rightarrow 840 + x = 885 \qquad \therefore \quad x = 45 \text{ kgs}$$

12. Age of the teacher $= (25 \times 11 - 24 \times 10)$ years
$$= 35 \text{ years}$$

13. Let 5 consecutive even numbers A, B, C, D and E be x, $x + 2$, $x + 4$, $x + 6$ and $x + 8$ respectively.

Now, $\dfrac{x + x + 2 + x + 4 + x + 6 + x + 8}{5} = 34$

$$\Rightarrow 5x + 20 = 170$$
$$\Rightarrow 5x = 150 \qquad \therefore x = 30$$
Then, $B = x + 2 = 30 + 2 = 32$;
$D = x + 6 = 30 + 6 = 36$
Hence, their product $= 32 \times 36 = 1152$

14. The average of remaining 48 numbers

$$= \dfrac{50 \times 30 - (35 + 40)}{48} = \dfrac{1500 - 75}{48}$$

$$= \dfrac{1425}{48} = 29.68$$

15. Let manager's salary be Rs. x, then

$$\dfrac{20 \times 1500 + x}{21} = 1600$$

$$\Rightarrow 30{,}000 + x = 33600$$
$$\therefore \quad x = \text{Rs. } 3600$$

PROBLEMS BASED ON AGES

1. The ratio of ages of A and B is 3 : 11. After 3 years the ratio becomes 1 : 3. What are the ages of A and B?
   A. 9 years, 33 years   B. 10 years, 40 years
   C. 9 years, 27 years   D. None of these

2. Two years ago, the ratio of Ram's and Mohan's age was 3 : 2 and at present 7 : 5. What are their present ages?
   A. 14 years, 10 years   B. 15 years, 10 years
   C. 13 years, 9 years   D. None of these

3. The ages of Samir and Saurabh are in the ratio of 8 : 15 respectively. After 9 years the ratio of their ages will be 11 : 18. What is the difference between their ages in years?
   A. 20 years   B. 21 years
   C. 22 years   D. 24 years

4. The present age of father is 34 years more than that of his son. 12 years ago, father's age was 18 times the age of his son. The present age of son in years is:
   A. 12   B. 14
   C. 16   D. 18

5. A mother is 25 years older than her daughter. Five years ago, the age of the mother was 6 times the age of the daughter. What is the present age of mother?
   A. 25 years   B. 29 years
   C. 32 years   D. 35 years

6. The difference between the present ages of P and Q is 4 years. The ratio of their ages after 5 years will be 9 : 8. The present age of P is:
   A. 24 years   B. 30 years
   C. 32 years   D. None of these

7. Ten years ago, the age of Divya was half of the age of Namrata. If the ratio of present ages of both is 3 : 4, the sum of their present ages is:
   A. 35 years   B. 30 years
   C. 25 years   D. 18 years

8. The ratio between the present ages of A and B is 5 : 3 respectively. The ratio between A's age 4 years ago and B's age 4 years hence is 1 : 1. The ratio between A's age 4 years hence and B's age 4 years ago is:
   A. 4 : 1   B. 3 : 1
   C. 2 : 1   D. 1 : 3

9. Ram got married 8 years ago. His present age is $\frac{6}{5}$ times his age at the time of marriage.

   Ram's sister was 10 years younger to him at the time of his marriage. What is the present age of Ram's sister?
   A. 40 years   B. 38 years
   C. 36 years   D. 32 years

10. A father said to his son, "I was as old as you are at present at the time of your birth." If the father's age is 38 years now. Five years ago the age of son was:
    A. 38 years   B. 33 years
    C. 19 years   D. 14 years

$$\boxed{\textbf{ANSWERS}}$$

1	2	3	4	5	6	7	8	9	10
A	A	B	B	D	D	A	B	B	D

SOME SELECTED EXPLANATORY ANSWERS

1. Let the ages of A and B be $3x$ and $11x$ years; then

$$\frac{3x+3}{11x+3} = \frac{1}{3} \quad \Rightarrow \quad 9x + 9 = 11x + 3$$

$$\Rightarrow 2x = 6 \qquad \therefore \quad x = 3$$

Hence, their present age, $3x = 3 \times 3 = 9$ years;
$11x = 11 \times 3 = 33$ years

2. Let the present ages of Ram and Mohan are $7x$ and $5x$ years; then

$$\frac{7x-2}{5x-2} = \frac{3}{2} \quad \Rightarrow \quad 14x - 4 = 15x - 6$$

$$\therefore \ x = 2$$

Hence, their present ages : $7 \times 2 = 14$ years
and $5 \times 2 = 10$ years

3. Let the present ages of Samir and Saurabh are $8x$ and $15x$ years respectively; then

$$\frac{8x+9}{15x+9} = \frac{11}{18} \quad \Rightarrow \quad 144x + 162 = 165x + 99$$

$$\Rightarrow 21x = 63 \quad \therefore \quad x = 3$$

Hence, difference of their ages $= 15x - 8x = 7x$
$= 7 \times 3 = 21$ years

4. Let the present ages of father and his son be $x + 34$ and x years respectively; then
$18(x - 12) = x + 34 - 12$
$\Rightarrow \ 18x - 216 = x + 22$
$\Rightarrow 17x = 238 \qquad \therefore \ x = 14$
Hence, present age of his son $= 14$ years

5. Let the present ages of mother and her daughter are $(x + 25)$ and x years respectively; then
$6(x - 5) = x + 25 - 5$
$\Rightarrow \qquad 6x - 30 = x + 20$
$\Rightarrow \qquad \qquad 5x = 50 \qquad \therefore x = 10$
Hence, the age of the mother $= 10 + 25$
$= 35$ years

6. Let the present ages of P and Q be $(x + 4)$ and x years;

then, $\dfrac{x+4+5}{x+5} = \dfrac{9}{8} \quad \Rightarrow \quad 8x + 72$
$= 9x + 45 \qquad \therefore \ x = 27$
Hence, present age of P $= 27 + 4 = 31$ years

7. Let the present ages of Divya and Namrata are $3x$ and $4x$ years respectively; then

$$\frac{3x-10}{4x-10} = \frac{1}{2}$$

$\Rightarrow \ 6x - 20 = 4x - 10$
$\Rightarrow \qquad 2x = 10 \quad \therefore \ x = 5$
Hence, sum of their ages $= 3x + 4x = 7x$
$= 7 \times 5 = 35$ years

8. Let the present ages of A and B are $5x$ and $3x$ years respectively; then,

$$\frac{5x-4}{3x+4} = 1 \qquad \Rightarrow \ 5x - 4 = 3x + 4$$

$\Rightarrow 2x = 8 \qquad \therefore \ x = 4$
Hence, their present ages are 20 years and 12 years.
So, required ratio $= (20 + 4) : (12 - 4)$
$= 24 : 8 = 3 : 1$

9. Let the present age of Ram be x years; then

$$\frac{x}{x-8} = \frac{6}{5} \qquad \Rightarrow \qquad 5x = 6x - 48$$

$\therefore \quad x = 48$
Hence, present age of Ram's sister
$= 48 - 10 = 38$ years.

10. Let the age of father was x years at the time of his son's birth, then present age of father and his son will be $2x$ and x years,
Now, $\qquad 2x = 38 \qquad \therefore \ x = 19$ years
Hence, 5 years ago the age of son was $19 - 5$
$= 14$ years

CHAIN RULE

1. A fort has provision for 50 days. After 15 days a reinforcement of 150 men arrives and the provision now lasts 25 days. How many men were there in the fort?
   A. 300   B. 225
   C. 275   D. 200

2. In a fort there is provisions for 40 days for 275 persons. If after 16 days 125 persons leave the fort for how many more days the provisions will last?
   A. 35 days   B. 44 days
   C. 45 days   D. 53 days

3. 60 men could complete a work in 250 days. They worked together for 200 days. After that the work had to be stopped for 10 days due to bad weather. How many more men should be engaged to complete the work in time?
   A. 20   B. 18
   C. 15   D. 10

4. A contractor undertook to complete a project in 90 days and employed 60 men on it. After 60 days, he found that $\frac{3}{4}$ of the work has already been completed. How many men can he discharge so that the project may completed exactly on time?
   A. 15   B. 20
   C. 30   D. 40

5. A flagstaff 17.5 m high casts a shadow of length 40.25 m. The height of the building, which casts a shadow of length 28.75m under similar condition will be:
   A. 21.25 m   B. 17.5 m
   C. 12.5 m   D. 10 m

6. If 5 men or 9 women can do a piece of work in 19 days, then 3 men and 6 women will do the same work in how many days?
   A. 21   B. 18
   C. 15   D. 12

7. A certain number of men can finish a piece of work in 100 days. If there were 10 men less, it will take 10 days more for the work to be finished. How many men were there originally?
   A. 110   B. 100
   C. 82   D. 75

8. Some persons can do a piece of work in 12 days. Two times the number of such persons will do half of that work in:
   A. 12 days   B. 3 days
   C. 6 days   D. 4 days

9. 2 men and 7 boys can do a piece of work in 14 days; 3 men and 8 boys can do the same in 11 days. Then 8 men and 6 boys can do three times of this work in
   A. 30 days   B. 4 days
   C. 21 days   D. 18 days

10. If 3 men or 6 boys, working 7 hours a day can do a piece of work in 10 days; how many days will it take to complete a piece of work twice as large with 6 men and 2 boys working together for 8 hours a day?
    A. 9   B. $8\frac{1}{2}$
    C. $7\frac{1}{2}$ D. $6\frac{1}{2}$

11. If 15 men can do a certain amount of work in 20 days working 8 hours a day, in how many days will 10 men do three times the work working 6 hours a day?
A. 120 days
B. 70 days
C. 100 days
D. None of these

12. 40 men consume 60 kgs of rice in 15 days, then in how many days will 30 men consume 12 kgs of rice?

A. 9 days
B. $6\dfrac{1}{4}$ days

C. 4 days
D. $3\dfrac{1}{4}$ days

13. 56 men can complete a piece of work in 24 days. In how many days can 42 men complete the same piece of work?

A. 48
B. 32
C. 20
D. 16

14. Running at the same constant rate, 6 identical machines can produce a total of 270 bottles per minute. At this rate, how many bottles could 10 such machines produce in 4 minutes?
A. 1400
B. 1600
C. 1800
D. 2000

15. 400 persons, working 9 hours a day complete $\dfrac{1}{4}th$ of the work in 10 days. The number of additional persons, working 8 hours a day, required to complete the remaining work in 20 days, is:
A. 275
B. 250
C. 675
D. 200

ANSWERS

1	2	3	4	5	6	7	8	9	10
B	B	C	B	C	C	A	B	C	C

11	12	13	14	15
A	C	B	C	C

SOME SELECTED EXPLANATORY ANSWERS

1.

Days	Men
35↑	x ↓
25	$x + 150$

$$\Rightarrow \frac{x+150}{x} = \frac{35}{25} \qquad \Rightarrow 1 + \frac{150}{x} = \frac{35}{25}$$

$$\Rightarrow \frac{150}{x} = \frac{10}{25}$$

$$\therefore x = \frac{25}{10} \times 150 = 375$$

Required number of men = 375 – 150 = 225

2.

Persons	Days
275↑	24 ↓
150	x

$$\Rightarrow \frac{x}{24} = \frac{275}{150} \qquad \therefore x = \frac{275}{150} \times 24 = 44 \text{ days}$$

3.

Days	Men
50↑	60 ↓
40	x

$$\Rightarrow \frac{x}{60} = \frac{50}{40} \qquad \therefore x = \frac{50}{40} \times 60 = 75 \text{ men}$$

Hence, number of additional men = 75 – 60
= 15

4.

Work	Days	Men
$\dfrac{3}{4}$ ↓	60 ↑	60 ↓
$\dfrac{1}{4}$	30	x

$$\Rightarrow \frac{x}{60} = \frac{60}{30} \times \frac{1/4}{3/4}$$

$$\therefore x = \frac{60}{30} \times \frac{1}{3} \times 60 = 40 \text{ days}$$

Hence, number of men to be discharged
= 60 – 40 = 20

5.

Shadow (m)	Object (m)
40.25 ↓	17.5 ↓
28.75 ↓	x ↓

$$\Rightarrow \quad \frac{x}{17.5} = \frac{28.75}{40.25}$$

$$\therefore \quad x = \frac{28.75 \times 17.5}{40.25} = 12.5 \text{ m}$$

6. 5 men $\equiv$ 9 women

$$\therefore \quad 3 \text{ men} = \frac{9}{5} \times 3 = \frac{27}{5} \text{ women}$$

Hence, 3 men and 6 women $= \dfrac{27}{5} + 6$

$$= \frac{57}{5} \text{ women}$$

Women	Days
9 ↑	19 ↓
$\dfrac{57}{5}$ ↑	x ↓

$$\Rightarrow \quad \frac{x}{19} = \frac{9 \times 5}{57}$$

$$\therefore \quad x = \frac{9 \times 5}{57} \times 19 = 15 \text{ days}$$

7.

Days	Men
100 ↑	x ↓
110 ↑	$x - 10$ ↓

$$\Rightarrow \quad \frac{x-10}{x} = \frac{100}{110} \qquad \Rightarrow \quad 110x - 1100 = 100x$$

$$\Rightarrow \quad 10x = 1100 \qquad \therefore \quad x = 110$$

Hence, initially the number of men = 110

8.

Work	Persons	Days
1 ↓	x ↑	12 ↓
$\dfrac{1}{2}$ ↓	$2x$ ↑	a ↓

$$\Rightarrow \quad \frac{a}{12} = \frac{x}{2x} \times \frac{1}{2} \qquad \therefore \quad a = \frac{1}{4} \times 12 = 3 \text{ days}$$

9. Here, 14×2 men $+ 14 \times 7$ boys $\equiv 11 \times 3$ men
$$+ 11 \times 8 \text{ boys}$$

$$\Rightarrow 28 \text{ men} + 98 \text{ boys} \equiv 33 \text{ men} + 88 \text{ boys}$$

$\Rightarrow$ 5 men = 10 boys $\therefore$ 1 man = 2 boys

Then, 2 men and 7 boys $\equiv$ 4 boys + 7 boys
$$= 11 \text{ boys}$$

& also, 8 men and 6 boys $\equiv$ 16 boys + 6 boys
$$= 22 \text{ boys}$$

Work	Boys	Days
1 ↓	11 ↑	14 ↓
3 ↓	22 ↑	x ↓

$$\Rightarrow \quad \frac{x}{14} = \frac{11}{22} \times \frac{3}{1}$$

$$\therefore \quad x = \frac{1}{2} \times 3 \times 14 = 21 \text{ days}$$

12.

Men	Rice (kgs)	Days
40 ↑	60 ↓	15 ↓
30 ↑	12 ↓	x ↓

$$\Rightarrow \quad \frac{x}{15} = \frac{12}{60} \times \frac{40}{30}$$

$$\therefore \quad x = \frac{12}{60} \times \frac{40}{30} \times 15 = 4 \text{ days}$$

14.

Machines	Time (minutes)	Bottles
6 ↓	1 ↓	270 ↓
10 ↓	4 ↓	x ↓

$$\Rightarrow \quad \frac{x}{270} = \frac{4}{1} \times \frac{10}{6}$$

$$\therefore \quad x = \frac{4 \times 10}{6} \times 270 = 1800 \text{ bottles}$$

15.

Work	Hours	Days	Persons
$\dfrac{1}{4}$ ↓	9 ↑	10 ↑	400 ↓
$\dfrac{3}{4}$ ↓	8 ↑	20 ↑	x ↓

$$\Rightarrow \quad \frac{x}{400} = \frac{10}{20} \times \frac{9}{8} \times \frac{3/4}{1/4}$$

$$\therefore \quad x = \frac{1}{2} \times \frac{9}{8} \times 3 \times 400 = 675$$

Hence, number of additional persons
$$= 675 - 400 = 275$$

TIME AND DISTANCE

1. Starting from a point at a speed of 4 km/hr a man reaches at a cerain place and returns back to the point from where he had started journey on bicycle at the speed of 16 km/hr. His average speed during the entire journey will be :
   A. 6.4 km/h
   B. 8.4 km/h
   C. 5.4 km/h
   D. 10 km/h

2. A motorist covers a certain distance at a average speed of 48 km/h in 45 minutes. What speed in km/h he must maintain to cover the same distance in 30 minutes?
   A. 66 km/h
   B. 79 km/h
   C. 80 km/h
   D. 72 km/h

3. A policeman saw a thief at a distance of 200 m. The policeman and the thief started running at the same time. If the policeman runs at a speed of $4\frac{1}{6}$ m per second and the thief at a speed of $3\frac{1}{3}$ m per second, after what time the policeman will catch the thief?
   A. 12 min
   B. 10 min
   C. 9 min
   D. 4 min

4. A monkey wants to climb up a glazed pole. He climbs 12 metres in 1 minute and then he slips back 3 metres in the next minute. If the pole is 63 metre high, how long does he take to climb at the top of the pole?
   A. $11\frac{1}{4}$ min
   B. $12\frac{1}{2}$ min
   C. $12\frac{3}{4}$ min
   D. $14\frac{3}{4}$ min

5. The distance between two stations A and B is 300 km. A train leaves the station A with a speed of 40 km/hr. At the same time another train departs from the station B with a speed of 50 km/hr. How much time will these two trains take to cross each other?
   A. 3 hrs 40 min
   B. 3 hrs 20 min
   C. 2 hrs 20 min
   D. 3 hrs 45 min

6. Nilesh goes to school from his village at the speed of 4 km/hr and returns from school to village at the speed of 2 km/hr. If he takes 6 hours in all, then what is the distance between the village and the school?
   A. 8 km
   B. 6 km
   C. 5 km
   D. 4 km

7. By increasing the speed of the bus by 10 km/hr the time of journey for 72 km is reduced by 36 minutes. What was the original speed of the bus?
   A. 30 km/hr
   B. 35 km/hr
   C. 40 km/hr
   D. 45 km/hr

8. A train covers a distance in 50 minutes, if it runs at a speed of 48 km/hr on an average. The speed at which the train must run to reduce the time of journey to 40 minutes will be:
   A. 70 km/hr
   B. 60 km/hr
   C. 55 km/hr
   D. 50 km/hr

9. A certain distance is covered by a vehicle at a certain speed. If half of this distance is covered by another vehicle in double the time, the ratio of the speeds of the two vehicles is:
   A. 4 : 1
   B. 1 : 4
   C. 2 : 1
   D. 1 : 2

10. A is faster than B. A and B each walk 24 km. The sum of their speeds is 7 km/hr and sum of times taken by them is 14 hours. What is the speed of A?
    A. 7 km/hr
    B. 5 km/hr
    C. 4 km/hr
    D. 3 km/hr

ANSWERS

1	2	3	4	5	6	7	8	9	10
A	D	D	C	B	A	A	B	A	C

SOME SELECTED EXPLANATORY ANSWERS

1. Average speed during the entire journey

$$= \frac{2xy}{x+y} = \frac{2 \times 4 \times 16}{4+16} = \frac{8 \times 16}{20} = 6.4 \text{ km/hr.}$$

2. Let required speed be x km/hr; then

$$x \times \frac{1}{2} = 48 \times \frac{3}{4} \quad \therefore \quad x = 48 \times \frac{3}{4} \times 2$$

$$= 72 \text{ km/hr}$$

3. Suppose the policeman will catch the thief after t seconds

then, $\left(\dfrac{25}{6} - \dfrac{10}{3}\right) t = 200 \Rightarrow \dfrac{5}{6} t = 200$

$$\therefore t = \frac{200 \times 6}{5} = 240 \text{ sec} = 4 \text{ min.}$$

4. The monkey climbs 12 metres in 1 minute and then he slips back 3 metres in the next minute
∴ The monkey climbs in the first 2 minutes
= 12 – 3 = 9 metres
∴ In the first 12 minutes the monkey climbs
= 9 × 6 = 54 metres
Remaining height of the pole to be covered by the monkey = 63 – 54 = 9 metre
∴ The monkey will climb the height of 9 metres in the 13th minute
∵ The monkey climbs 12 metres in 1 minute

∴ The monkey will climb 9 metres in $\dfrac{1}{12} \times 9$

$$= \frac{3}{4} \text{ minute}$$

∴ Time spent in climbing at the top of the

pole $= \left(12 + \dfrac{3}{4}\right)$ minutes $= 12\dfrac{3}{4}$ minutes

5. The two trains are moving in the opposite directions

∴ Relative speed = 40 + 50 = 90 km/hr.

∴ Time taken to cross each other $= \dfrac{300}{90} = 3\dfrac{1}{3}$

hours or, 3 hours 20 minutes.

6. Let x km be the distance between village and the school; then

$$\frac{x}{4} + \frac{x}{2} = 6 \qquad \Rightarrow \frac{3x}{4} = 6$$

$$\therefore \quad x = \frac{6 \times 4}{3} = 8 \text{ km}$$

8. Let x km/hr be the required speed of the train; then

$$x \times \frac{40}{60} = 48 \times \frac{50}{60}$$

$$\therefore \quad x = \frac{48 \times 50}{40} = 60 \text{ km/hr}$$

9. Let x km/hr and t hr be the certain speed and certain time.

Then, ratio of their speeds $= \dfrac{x}{t} : \dfrac{x}{2 \times 2t} = 1 : \dfrac{1}{4}$

$= 4 : 1$

10. Let speeds of A and B are x_1 and x_2 km/hr and times taken by them are t_1 and t_2 hrs, then
$$x_1 + x_2 = 7 \text{ km/hr} \qquad \qquad \text{...(i)}$$
$$t_1 + t_2 = 14 \text{ hrs} \qquad \qquad \text{...(ii)}$$

Now, $\dfrac{24}{x_1} + \dfrac{24}{x_2} = 14 \quad \Rightarrow \quad \dfrac{24\left(x_1 + x_2\right)}{x_1 x_2} = 14$

$$\therefore \quad x_1 x_2 = \frac{24 \times 7}{14} = 12$$

Then, $x_1 - x_2 = \sqrt{\left(x_1 + x_2\right)^2 - 4 x_1 x_2}$

$$= \sqrt{(7)^2 - 4 \times 12} = 1 \qquad \text{...(iii)}$$

Solving *(i)* and *(iii)* we get $x_1 = 4$ km/hr

TIME AND WORK

1. A and B working together complete a work in 35 days. If A takes 60 days to complete it, how long would B alone take to complete it?
   A. 64 days
   B. 72 days
   C. 81 days
   D. 84 days

2. A few children working together can do a piece of work in 18 days. If the number of children employed on the work is made double, how long would they take to complete half of the work?

   A. $4\frac{1}{2}$ days
   B. $2\frac{1}{3}$ days

   C. $8\frac{3}{4}$ days
   D. $6\frac{1}{2}$ days

3. 10 men or 18 boys can do a piece of work in 15 days. In how many days would 25 men and 15 boys complete the same work working together?

   A. $5\frac{1}{2}$ days
   B. $4\frac{1}{2}$ days

   C. $6\frac{2}{3}$ days
   D. $2\frac{1}{3}$ days

4. A cistern is filled by a tap in $3\frac{1}{2}$ hours. Due to a leak in the bottom of the cistern, it takes half an hour longer to fill the cistern. If the cistern is full, how long will it take the leak to empty it?
   A. 28 hours
   B. 29 hours

   C. $31\frac{1}{3}$ hours
   D. 38 hours

5. A is twice as good a workman as B and thrice as good a workman as C. If C alone can do a piece of work in 24 days, how long would the three persons take to finish the work working together?

   A. $3\frac{3}{11}$ days
   B. $4\frac{4}{7}$ days

   C. $4\frac{4}{11}$ days
   D. $3\frac{4}{11}$ days

6. If 3 men and 5 women can do a piece of work in 8 days and 2 men and 7 boys can do the same work in 12 days. Find the number of boys, the work done by whom can equate the work done by 10 women.
   A. 19 boys
   B. 21 boys
   C. 23 boys
   D. 15 boys

7. 8 men alone can complete a piece of work in 12 days. 4 women alone can complete the same piece of work in 48 days and 10 children alone can complete the piece of work in 24 days. In how many days can 10 men, 4 women and 10 children together complete the piece of work?
   A. 6
   B. 8
   C. 10
   D. 15

8. A works twice as fast as B. If B can complete a piece of work independently in 12 days. Find in how many days A and B together can complete the work?
   A. 8 days
   B. 6 days
   C. 4 days
   D. 18 days

9. A contractor undertook to complete a project in 90 days and employed 60 men on it. After 60 days, he found that $\frac{3}{4}$ of the work has already been completed. How many men can he discharge so that the project may be completed exactly on time?

A. 15   B. 20
C. 30   D. 40

10. A can do a piece of work in 25 days and B can do it in 20 days. They work together for 5 days and then A goes away. In how many days will B finish the remaining work?
A. 33 days   B. 20 days
C. 11 days   D. 10 days

ANSWERS

1	2	3	4	5	6	7	8	9	10
D	A	B	A	C	B	A	C	B	C

SOME SELECTED EXPLANATORY ANSWERS

1. (A + B)'s 1 day's work = $\dfrac{1}{35}$

and also, A's 1 day's work = $\dfrac{1}{60}$

Hence, B's 1 day's work = $\dfrac{1}{35} - \dfrac{1}{60} = \dfrac{5}{420} = \dfrac{1}{84}$

So, B will do the whole work in 84 days.

3. 10 men $\equiv$ 18 boys

25 men $\equiv \dfrac{18}{10} \times 25 = 45$ boys

Hence, 25 men + 15 boys = 45 + 15 = 60 boys
Now, 18 boys can do a piece of work in 15 days.
Hence, 60 boys will do a piece of work in

$\dfrac{15 \times 18}{60} = \dfrac{9}{2}$ days = $4\dfrac{1}{2}$ days.

4. In 1 hour $\dfrac{2}{7}$ cistern is filled by the tap.

Hence, in $\dfrac{1}{2}$ hour $\dfrac{2}{14} = \dfrac{1}{7}$ cistern is filled by the tap.

So, $\dfrac{1}{7}$ cistern is emptied by the leakage in 4 hours.
So, 1 cistern will be emptied by the leakage in 28 hours.

6. Here, (3 men + 5 women) × 8
$\equiv$ (2 men + 7 boys) × 12

$\Rightarrow$ 40 women $\equiv$ 84 boys

$\therefore$ 10 women $\equiv \dfrac{84}{40} \times 10 = 21$ boys

Hence, work done by 10 women
= work done of 21 boys.

7. B's 1 day's work = $\dfrac{1}{4} - \dfrac{1}{12} = \dfrac{2}{12} = \dfrac{1}{6}$

Hence, B alone will complete the work in 6 days.

8. Ratio of efficiency of A and B = 2 : 1
Then, ratio of their time taking = 1 : 2
Hence, if B can complete the work in 12 days, then A in 6 days.

Now, (A + B)'s 1 day's work = $\dfrac{1}{6} + \dfrac{1}{12} = \dfrac{3}{12} = \dfrac{1}{4}$

So, A and B together can complete the work in 4 days.

9. After 60 days remaining work = $1 - \dfrac{3}{4} = \dfrac{1}{4}$

In 60 days $\dfrac{3}{4}$ work has been done by 60 men

In 30 days $\dfrac{1}{4}$ work will be done by

$60 \times \dfrac{4}{3} \times \dfrac{1}{4} \times \dfrac{60}{30} = 40$ men.

Hence, required number of men = 60 – 40 = 20 (which are to be discharged).

BOATS AND STREAMS

1. A boat goes 6 km upstream and back to the starting point in 2 hours. If the current of the stream runs at the rate of 4 km/hr, find the speed of the boat in still water.
   A. 6 km/hr
   B. 8 km/hr
   C. 10 km/hr
   D. 12 km/hr

2. A boat covers 24 km upstream and 36 km downstream in 6 hours, while it covers 36 km upstream and 24 km downstream in 6½ horus. Find the speed of the current.
   A. 2 km/hr
   B. 4 km/hr
   C. 6 km/hr
   D. 8 km/hr

3. A man can row 5 km/hr in still water and the speed of the stream is 1.5 km/hr. He takes an hour when he travels upstream to a place and back again to the starting point. How far is the place from the starting point?
   A. 2.275 km
   B. 3.5 km
   C. 1.5 km
   D. None of these

4. The speed of a boat in still water is 6 km/hr and the speed of the stream is 1.5 km/hr. A man rows to a place at a distance of 22.5 km and comes back to the starting point. Find the total time taken by him.
   A. 8 hours
   B. 10 hours
   C. 12 hours
   D. 4 hours

5. A boat covers 20 km downstream and 6 km upstream in 3 hours, while it covers 30 km downstream and 12 km upstream in 5 hours. What is the speed of boat in still water?
   A. 6 km/hr
   B. 8 km/hr
   C. 10 km/hr
   D. 12 km/hr.

6. Samir can travel 12 miles downstream in a certain river in 6 hours less than it takes him to travel the same distance upstream. But when he could double his rowing rate for his 24-mile round trip, the downstream 12 miles would then take only one hour less than the upstream 12 miles. Find the speed of the current in miles/hour.
   A. $2\dfrac{2}{3}$
   B. $2\dfrac{1}{3}$
   C. $1\dfrac{2}{3}$
   D. $1\dfrac{1}{3}$

7. A boat takes 6 hours to travel from place M to N downstream and back from N to M upstream. If the speed of the boat in still water is 4 km/hr; what is the distance between two places?
   A. 6 kms
   B. 8 kms
   C. 12 kms
   D. Data inadequate

8. A man can row upstream at 8 km/hr and downstream at 13 km/hr. The speed of the stream is:
   A. 2.5 km/hr
   B. 4.2 km/hr
   C. 5 km/hr
   D. 10.5 km/hr

9. A man's speed with the current is 15 km/hr and the speed of the current is 2.5 km/hr. The man's speed against the current is:
   A. 12.5 km/hr
   B. 10 km/hr
   C. 9 km/hr
   D. 8.5 km/hr

10. A motorboat, whose speed is 15 km/hr in still water goes 30 km downstream and comes back in a total of 4 hours 30 minutes. What is the speed of the stream (in km/hr)?
    A. 10
    B. 6
    C. 5
    D. 4

ANSWERS

1	2	3	4	5	6	7	8	9	10
B	A	A	A	B	B	D	A	B	C

SOME SELECTED EXPLANATORY ANSWERS

1. Let the speed of a boat in still water = x km/hr; then

$$\frac{6}{x-4}+\frac{6}{x+4}=2 \quad \Rightarrow \quad \frac{2x}{x^2-16}=\frac{1}{3}$$

$\Rightarrow x^2 - 6x - 16 = 0$

$\Rightarrow (x-8)(x+2) = 0$

Hence, the speed of the boat = 8 km/hr.

2. Let x km/hr and y km/hr be the speeds of the boat in still water and the speed of the current respectively, then

$$\frac{24}{x-y}+\frac{36}{x+y}=6 \Rightarrow \frac{4}{x-y}+\frac{6}{x+y}=1 \quad ...(i)$$

And, $\quad \dfrac{36}{x-y}+\dfrac{24}{x+y}=\dfrac{13}{2} \qquad ...(ii)$

Solving these two equations, we get

$\quad x + y = 12;\ x - y = 8$

Hence, $y = \dfrac{1}{2}(12-8)=2$ km/hr.

3. Let required distance be x km, then

$$\frac{x}{5-1.5}+\frac{x}{5+1.5}=1 \Rightarrow \frac{x\times2}{7}+\frac{x\times2}{13}=1$$

$\Rightarrow\ 40x = 91 \qquad \therefore\ x = 91/40 = 2.275$ km

4. Required time period $= \dfrac{22.5}{6+1.5}+\dfrac{22.5}{6-1.5}$

$$=\frac{45}{15}+\frac{45}{9}\ = 8 \text{ hours.}$$

5. Let x km/hr and y km/hr be the speed of boat in still water and speed of current respectively; then

$$\frac{20}{x+y}+\frac{6}{x-y}=3 \qquad\qquad ...(i)$$

and also, $\quad \dfrac{30}{x+y}+\dfrac{12}{x-y}=5$

$$\Rightarrow \frac{15}{x+y}+\frac{6}{x-y}=\frac{5}{2} \qquad\qquad ...(ii)$$

Solving equations *(i)* & *(ii)*, we get $x + y = 10$ and $x - y = 6$

Since, $x = \dfrac{1}{2}$ (10 + 6) = 8 km/hr.

6. Let x km/hr and y km/hr be the speed of rowing in still water and speed of the current respectively; then

$$\frac{12}{x-y}-\frac{12}{x+y}=6 \quad \Rightarrow \quad \frac{24y}{x^2-y^2}=6$$

$$\Rightarrow\ x^2 = y^2 + 4y \qquad\qquad ...(i)$$

Again, $\quad \dfrac{12}{2x-y}-\dfrac{12}{2x+y}=1$

$$\Rightarrow \frac{24y}{4x^2-y^2}=1 \quad \Rightarrow x^2=\frac{y^2+24y}{4} \quad ...(ii)$$

From equations (i) and (ii), we get

$$y^2 + 4y = \frac{y^2+24y}{4} \ \Rightarrow 3y^2 = 8y$$

$$\therefore\ \ y=\frac{8}{3}=2\frac{1}{3}\ \text{ miles/hr.}$$

8. The speed of the stream $= \dfrac{1}{2}(13-8)=\dfrac{5}{2}$

$$= 2.5 \text{ km/hr.}$$

9. The man's speed in still water

$\quad = 15 - 2.5 = 12.5$ km/hr

Hence, the men's speed against the current

$\quad = 12.5 - 2.5 = 10$ km/hr

10. Let speed of the stream be x km/hr, then

$$\frac{30}{15+x}+\frac{30}{15-x}=4\frac{1}{2} \Rightarrow \frac{30\times30}{225-x^2}=\frac{9}{2}$$

$$\Rightarrow \frac{200}{225-x^2}=1 \qquad \Rightarrow\ x^2 = 225-200$$

$\Rightarrow x^2 = 25 \qquad\qquad \therefore\ \ x = 5$ km/hr.

ALLIGATION OR MIXTURE

1. A shopkeeper buys 26 kgs of milk @ Rs. 16 per kg. He also buys from another source an inferior quality of milk @ Rs. 10 per kg. How much quantity of the latter should he buy to mix it with the former so that he can sell the mixture @ Rs. 14 per kg without making any loss?
   A. 13 kgs
   B. 12 kgs
   C. 14 kgs
   D. 16 kgs

2. Two vessels A and B contain mixture of milk and water in the ratio 4 : 1 and 9 : 11 respectively. They are mixed in the ratio of 3 : 2. Find the ratio of milk : water in the resulting mixture.
   A. 34 : 16
   B. 33 : 17
   C. 16 : 34
   D. 17 : 33

3. A shopkeeper has 50 kgs of rice. He sells a part of it at 20% profit and the rest at 40% profit. If he gains 25% on the whole, find the quantity of each part.
   A. 12.5 kgs and 37.5 kgs
   B. 37.5 kgs and 12.5 kgs
   C. 23.5 kgs and 21.5 kgs
   D. 21.5 kgs and 23.5 kgs

4. A man bought a certain quantity of sugar for Rs. 8000. He sells one-fourth of it at 20% loss. At what per cent profit should he sell the remainder stock so as to make an overall profit of 20%?
   A. 20%
   B. 30%
   C. 35%
   D. 40%

5. Rs. 675 was divided among 75 boys and girls. Each boy gets Rs. 20 whereas a girl gets Rs. 5. Find the number of boys and girls.
   A. 20, 55
   B. 15, 60
   C. 25, 50
   D. 30, 45

6. A vessel contains mixture of liquids A and B in the ratio 3 : 2. When 20 litres of the mixture is taken out and replaced by 20 litres of liquid B, the ratio changes to 1 : 4. How many litres of liquid A was there initially present in the vessel?
   A. 12 litres
   B. 18 litres
   C. 24 litres
   D. 22 litres

7. A container is full of milk. One-third of milk is taken out of it and replaced by same quantity of water. Then again one-third of the mixture is taken out of it and replaced by the same quantity of water. The process is repeated 4 times. If 16 litres of milk is left in the container at the end of 4th operation, find the capacity of the container.
   A. 76 litres
   B. 81 litres
   C. 82 litres
   D. 85 litres

8. The cost of type-I rice is Rs. 15 per kg and type-II is Rs. 20 per kg. If both type I and type II are mixed in the ratio of 2 : 3, then find the price per kg of the mixed variety.
   A. Rs. 19.50
   B. Rs. 19
   C. Rs. 18.50
   D. Rs. 18

9. In what ratio must a grocer mix two varieties of tea worth Rs. 60 a kg and Rs. 65 a kg so that by selling the mixture at Rs. 68.20 a kg he may gain 10%?
   A. 4 : 5
   B. 3 : 5
   C. 3 : 4
   D. 3 : 2

10. A vessel contains 80 litres of milk. 16 litres of milk was taken out of the vessel and replaced by water. Then 16 litres of mixture was withdrawn and again replaced by water. The operation was repeated for third time. How much milk is now left in the vessel?

A. 96.40 litres   B. 50.36 litres
C. 40.96 litres   D. 32.76 litres

ANSWERS

1	2	3	4	5	6	7	8	9	10
A	B	B	B	A	B	B	D	D	C

SOME SELECTED EXPLANATORY ANSWERS

1.

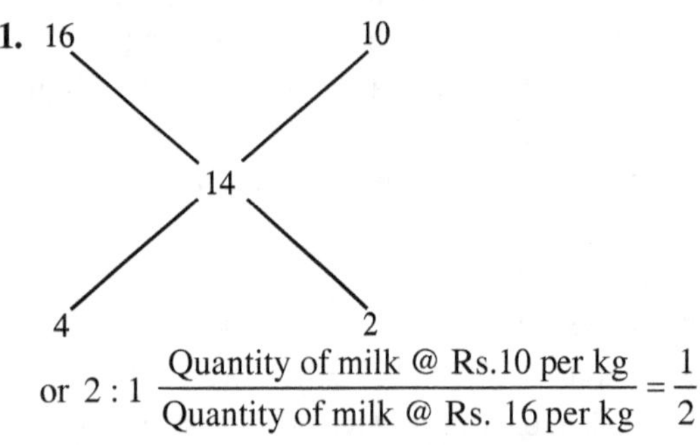

or 2 : 1 $\dfrac{\text{Quantity of milk @ Rs.10 per kg}}{\text{Quantity of milk @ Rs. 16 per kg}} = \dfrac{1}{2}$

So, quantity of milk @ Rs. 10 per kg. $= \dfrac{26}{2}$
$= 13$ kgs.

2. Fraction is

	Milk	Water
A :	$\dfrac{4}{5}$	$\dfrac{1}{5}$
B :	$\dfrac{9}{20}$	$\dfrac{11}{20}$

$(3A + 2B) = $ A and B : $\left(\dfrac{12}{5}+\dfrac{9}{10}\right)\left(\dfrac{3}{5}+\dfrac{11}{10}\right)$

$$\dfrac{33}{10} \qquad \dfrac{17}{10}$$

So, Ratio of milk : water in the resulting mixture $= 33 : 17$.

3.

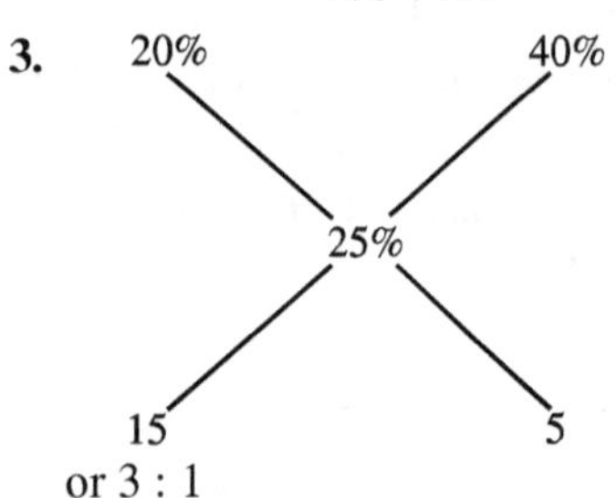

or 3 : 1

Quantity sold at 20% profit $= \dfrac{3}{3+1} \times 50$
$= 37.5$ kgs.
Quantity sold at 40% profit $= (50 - 37.5)$
$= 12.5$ kgs.

4. Let the remainder stock be sold at $x\%$ profit.

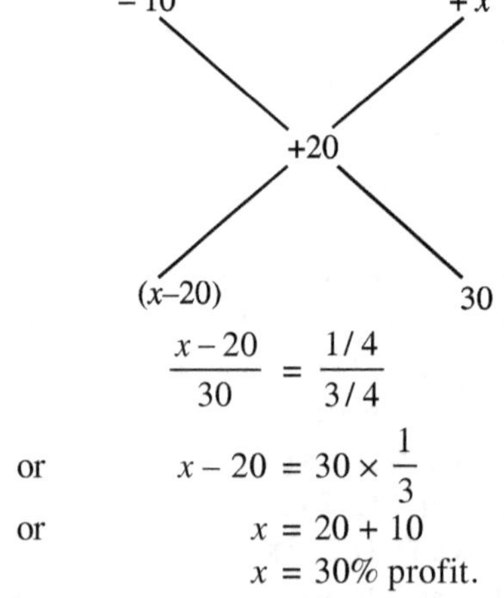

$\dfrac{x-20}{30} = \dfrac{1/4}{3/4}$

or $\qquad x - 20 = 30 \times \dfrac{1}{3}$

or $\qquad x = 20 + 10$
$x = 30\%$ profit.

5. Average money per head (boy or girl)
$= $ Rs. $\dfrac{675}{75} = $ Rs. 9

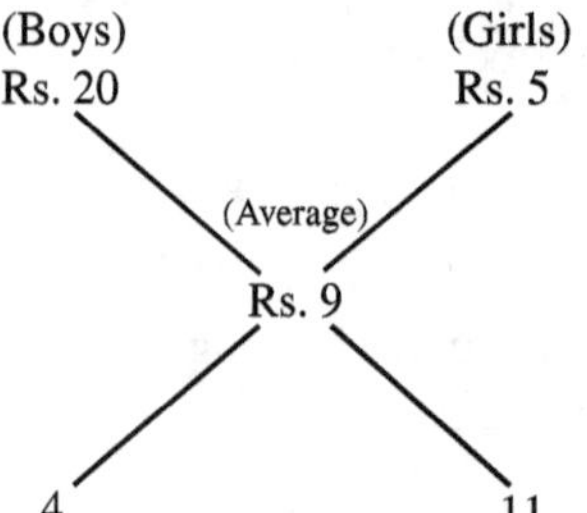

$$\text{Number of boys} = \frac{4}{4+11} \times 75 = 20$$

$$\text{Number of girls} = \frac{11}{4+11} \times 75 = 55.$$

6. % of liquid B initially present in the vessel

$$= \frac{2}{3+2} \times 100 = 40\%$$

% of liquid B finally present in the vessel

$$= \frac{4}{1+4} \times 100 = 80\%$$

The second solution is liquid B which is being mixed and it has 100% liquid B.

80% of liquid B present in the resultant mixture may be taken as average percentage. So, using rule of alligation on liquid B per cent, we can write,

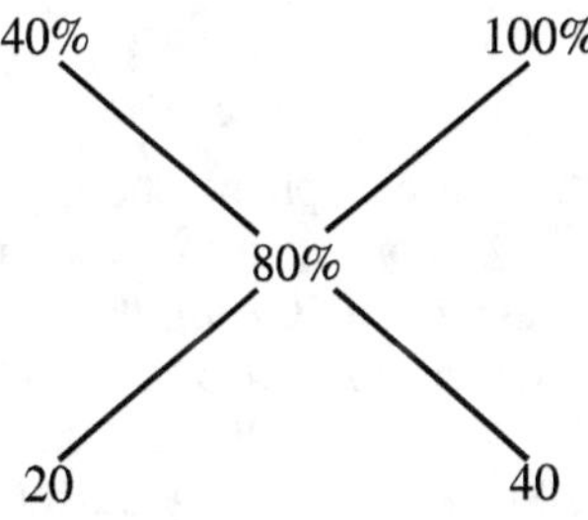

or   1 : 2

The ratio of liquid left in the vessel to liquid B being mixed = 1 : 2

Since the quantity of liquid B being mixed is 20 litres, the quantity of liquid left in the vessel is 10 litres.

Therefore, the total quantity of liquid initially present in the vessel

$$= 10 + 20 = 30 \text{ litres}$$

$$\text{Quantity of liquid A} = \frac{3}{2+3} \times 30$$

$$= 18 \text{ litres.}$$

7. Let capacity of the container be x litre; then

$$x(1 - 1/3)^4 = 16 \quad \Rightarrow \quad x\left(\frac{2}{3}\right)^4 = 16$$

$$\Rightarrow x \times \frac{16}{81} = 16 \qquad \therefore \quad x = 81 \text{ litres}$$

8. Let the price per kg of mixed variety be Rs. x; then

By the rule of alligation,

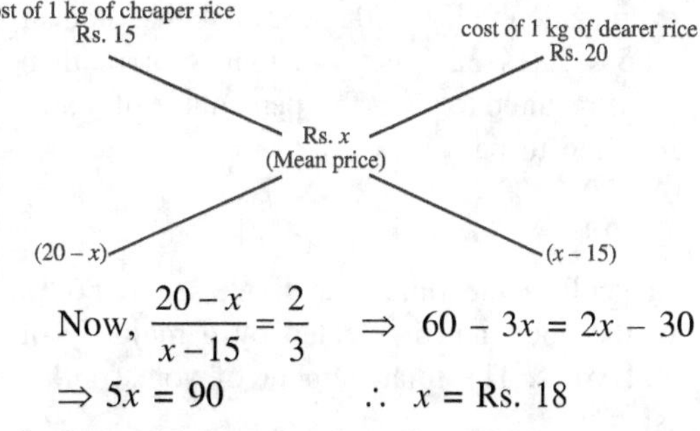

$$\text{Now, } \frac{20-x}{x-15} = \frac{2}{3} \quad \Rightarrow \quad 60 - 3x = 2x - 30$$

$$\Rightarrow 5x = 90 \qquad \therefore \quad x = \text{Rs. } 18$$

9. S.P. of 1 kg mixture = Rs. 68.20, Gain % = 10%

$$\text{Hence, C.P. of 1 kg mixture} = \frac{100}{110} \times \text{Rs. } 68.20$$

$$= \text{Rs. } 62$$

By the rule of alligation

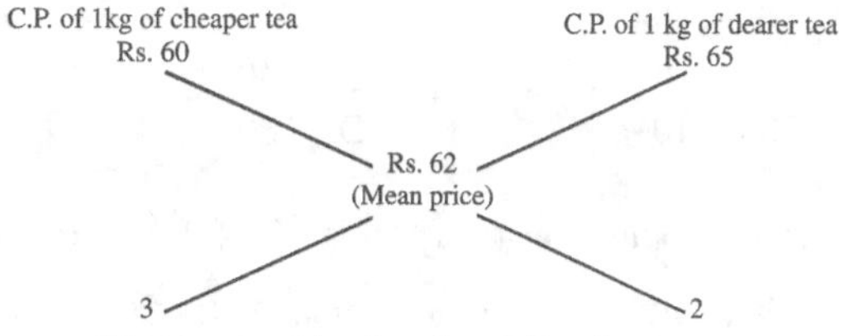

Hence, required ratio = 3 : 2

10. Amount of milk left $= 80\left(1 - \frac{16}{80}\right)^3$

$$= 80\left(\frac{4}{5}\right)^3$$

$$80 \times \frac{64}{125} = 40.96 \text{ litres.}$$

PERCENTAGE

1. A student who secures 20% marks in an examination fails by 30 marks. Another student who secures 32% gets 42 marks more than those required to pass. The percentage of marks required to pass is:
   A. 20   B. 25
   C. 28   D. 30

2. In a college election, a candidate secured 62% of the votes and is elected by a majority of 144 votes. The total number of votes polled is:
   A. 600   B. 800
   C. 925   D. 1200

3. In an organisation, 40% of the employees are matriculates, 50% of the remaining are graduates and the remaining 180 are postgraduates. How many employees are graduates?
   A. 360   B. 240
   C. 300   D. 180

4. The population of a village is 4500. $\frac{5}{9}$th of them are males and rest females. If 40% of the males are married, then the percentage of married female is :
   A. 35   B. 40
   C. 50   D. 60

5. A's income is 10% more than B's. How much per cent is B's income is less than A's?
   A. 10%   B. 7%
   C. $9\frac{1}{11}\%$ D. $6\frac{1}{2}\%$

6. If the price of a television set is increased by 25%, then by what percentage should the new price be reduced to bring the price back to original level?
   A. 15%   B. 20%
   C. 25%   D. 30%

7. In an election one of the two candidates gets 40% votes and loses by 100 votes. Total number of votes is :
   A. 500   B. 400
   C. 600   D. 1000

8. The gross income of a person is Rs. 20000. 10% of his income is exempted from income tax and his net income is Rs. 19100. The rate of income tax is :
   A. 3%   B. 2%
   C. 4%   D. 5%

9. The owner of a cell phone shop charges his customer 32% more than the cost price. If a customer paid Rs. 6600 for the cell phone, then what was the cost price of the cell phone?
   A. Rs. 5000   B. Rs. 5500
   C. Rs. 5800   D. Rs. 6100

10. If the cost of pins reduced by Rs. 4 per dozen, 12 more pins can be purchased for Rs. 48. The cost of pins per dozen after reduction is:
    A. Rs. 8   B. Rs. 12
    C. Rs. 16   D. Rs. 20

11. In an examination 80% of the students passed in Mathematics and 70% passed in English, while 10% students failed in both the subjects. If 360 students passed in both the subjects, find the total number of students who appeared in the examination.
    A. 400   B. 600
    C. 630   D. 640

12. Electric tax is increased by 20% and its consumption is decreased by 20%. The change in the expenditure is:
    A. 4% decrease   B. 4% increase
    C. 5% decrease   D. 5% increase

13. The selling price of certain commodity was reduced by 25%. As a result of it, the sales increased by 30%. What was the effect of it on cash collected by daily sales?
A. 2.5% decrease   B. 2.5% increase
C. 5% decrease   D. 5% increase

14. The wheat sold by a grocer contained 10% low quality wheat. What quantity of good quality wheat should be added to 150 kgs of wheat so that the percentage of low quality wheat becomes 5%?

A. 50 kgs   B. 85 kgs
C. 135 kgs   D. 150 kgs

15. Nilam spends 15% of her monthly income on household expenses. She spends 17% of the monthly income in travelling and 6% on medical expenses and saves the rest Rs. 15,500. What is her monthly income?
A. Rs. 20,000
B. Rs. 25,000
C. Rs. 30,000
D. Rs. 35,000

ANSWERS

1	2	3	4	5	6	7	8	9	10
B	A	D	C	C	B	A	D	A	B

11	12	13	14	15
B	A	A	D	B

SOME SELECTED EXPLANATORY ANSWERS

1.   20% of $x + 30 = 32\%$ of $x - 42$

$\Rightarrow \quad 12\%$ of $x = 72$

$\Rightarrow \quad x = \dfrac{72 \times 100}{12} = 600$

Pass Mark $= 20\%$ of $600 + 30 = 150$

Pass percentage $= \left(\dfrac{150}{600} \times 100\right)\% = 25\%$

2. $(62\%$ of $x - 38\%$ of $x) = 144$

$\Rightarrow 24\%$ of $x = 144 \quad \Rightarrow \quad x = \dfrac{144 \times 100}{24} = 600$

3.   Matriculates $= \dfrac{40}{100} x = \dfrac{2x}{5}$

Remaining $= \left(x - \dfrac{2x}{5}\right) = \dfrac{3x}{5}$

Graduates $= \dfrac{50}{100} \times \dfrac{3x}{5} = \dfrac{3x}{10}$

Remaining $= \dfrac{3x}{5} - \dfrac{3x}{10} = \dfrac{3x}{10}$

Now, $\dfrac{3x}{10} = 180$

$\therefore \ x = \dfrac{10 \times 180}{3} = 600$

$\therefore$ Graduates $= \dfrac{3 \times 600}{10} = 180$.

4. Males $= \left(\dfrac{5}{9} \times 4500\right) = 2500$

Females $= 2000$

$\therefore \quad$ Married males $= \dfrac{40}{100} \times 2500 = 1000$

and married females $= 1000$

$\therefore$ Percentage of married females

$= \left(\dfrac{1000}{2000} \times 100\right)\% = 50\%$.

5. Required percentage $= \left[\dfrac{10}{(100 + 10)} \times 100\right]\%$

$= 9\dfrac{1}{11}\%$.

6. Required reduction $= \dfrac{25}{100 + 25} \times 100 = 20\%$.

7. Out of 100, difference in votes = (60 – 40) = 20

20% of x = 100

$$\therefore x = \frac{100 \times 100}{20} = 500 .$$

8. Gross income = Rs. 20000

Income exempted from income tax = 10% of gross income

$\therefore$ Income on which income tax is chargeable

= (100 – 10%) = 90% of gross income

$$= 20000 \times \frac{90}{100} = Rs. 18000$$

$\therefore$ Total income tax paid on

$$= Rs. 20000 – Rs. 19100$$
$$= Rs. 900$$

$$\therefore \text{Rate per cent of income tax} = \frac{900}{18000} \times 100$$

$$= 5\%$$

9. Let cost price of the cell phone be Rs. x; then

$$x + \frac{32}{100} \times x = 6600 \quad \Rightarrow \quad \frac{132x}{100} = 6600$$

$$\therefore \quad x = \frac{100 \times 6600}{132} = Rs. 5000.$$

10. Let reduced price by Rs. x per dozen, then

$$\frac{48}{x} - \frac{48}{x+4} = 1 \quad \Rightarrow \quad \frac{48 \times 4}{x^2 + 4x} = 1$$

$$\Rightarrow \quad x^2 + 4x - 192 = 0$$
$$\Rightarrow \quad (x + 16)(x - 12) = 0$$
$$\therefore \qquad\qquad x = Rs. 12.$$

11. Here, percentage of students failed in Mathematics and English be 30% and 20% respectively.

Percentage of students failed either one or both subjects = 30 + 20 – 10 = 40%

Hence, percentage of pass students = 100 – 40

$$= 60\%$$

Now, 60% = 360

$$\therefore 100\% = \frac{360}{60} \times 100 = 600.$$

12. Let initially electric tax is Rs. 100 and consumption = 100 units

Decrease in consumption

$$= 100 \times 100 – 120 \times 80 = Rs. 400$$

Hence, decrease percentage = $\dfrac{400 \times 100}{100 \times 100} = 4\%$.

13. Let the selling price of a commodity be Rs. 100 and number of sales = 100 units

Decrease in daily cash = $100 \times 100 – 75 \times 130$

$$= Rs. 250$$

Hence, decrease percentage

$$= \frac{250 \times 100}{100 \times 100} = 2.5\,\%.$$

14. Let x kg of good wheat be added; then

$$\frac{10}{100} \times 150 = \frac{5}{100}(150 + x)$$

$$\Rightarrow 150 + x = 300 \quad \therefore \quad x = 150\,kg.$$

15. Let her monthly income be Rs. x; then

$$x - \left(\frac{15}{100} \times x + \frac{17}{100} \times x + \frac{6}{100} \times x\right) = 15,500$$

$$\Rightarrow x - \frac{38x}{100} = 15500 \quad \Rightarrow \quad \frac{62x}{100} = 15500$$

$$\therefore \quad x = \frac{15500 \times 100}{62} = Rs. 25000.$$

PROFIT AND LOSS

1. Ashok bought 25 kg of rice at the rate of Rs. 6 per kg and 35 kg of rice at the rate of Rs. 7 per kg. He mixed the two and sold the mixture at the rate of Rs. 6.75 per kg. What was his gain or loss in the transaction?
   A. Rs. 16 gain
   B. Rs. 16 loss
   C. Rs. 10 gain
   D. None of these

2. Profit after selling a commodity for Rs. 425 is same as loss after selling it for Rs. 355. The cost of the commodity is :
   A. Rs. 285
   B. Rs. 390
   C. Rs. 295
   D. Rs. 400

3. Ram bought 4 dozen apples at Rs. 12 per dozen and 2 dozen at Rs. 16 per dozen. He sold all of them to earn 20%. At what price per dozen did he sell the apples?
   A. Rs. 14.40
   B. Rs. 16.00
   C. Rs. 16.80
   D. Rs. 16.20

4. At what price must Kantilal sell a mixture of 80 kg sugar at Rs. 6.75 per kg with 120 kg at Rs. 8 per kg to gain 20%?
   A. Rs. 7.50 per kg
   B. Rs. 8.20 per kg
   C. Rs. 8.35 per kg
   D. Rs. 9 per kg

5. A person bought an article and sold it at a loss of 10%. If he had bought it for 20% less and sold it for Rs. 55 more, he would have had a profit of 40%. The C.P. of the article is :
   A. Rs. 200
   B. Rs. 225
   C. Rs. 250
   D. None of these

6. A dealer sold a machine to a shopkeeper at 20% profit. The shopkeeper sold the machine to a customer so as to get 25% profit for himself. The difference between the selling price of the dealer and that of the shopkeeper was found to be Rs. 129. What is the initial price of the machine?
   A. Rs. 410
   B. Rs. 420
   C. Rs. 430
   D. Rs. 440

7. A man bought a horse and cart. If he sold the horse at 10% loss and the cart at 20% gain he would not loss anything. If he sold the horse at 5% loss and the cart at 5% gain he would lose Rs. 10 in the bargain. What did he pay for each?
   A. Rs. 400, Rs. 200
   B. Rs. 300, Rs. 300
   C. Rs. 250, Rs. 350
   D. Rs. 350, Rs. 250

8. The marked price of a radio is 20% more than its cost price. If a discount of 10% is given on the marked price, the gain percentage is:
   A. 8
   B. 10
   C. 12
   D. 15

9. A dishonest dealer sells his goods at the cost price and still earns a profit of 60% by underweight. What weight does he use for a kg?
   A. 625 gms
   B. 750 gms
   C. 800 gms
   D. 850 gms

10. A man sells two horses for Rs. 990 each. On one he gains 10% and the other he loses 10%. What is his total percentage of gain or loss in the transaction?
    A. 1% gain
    B. 1% loss
    C. 2% gain
    D. 2% loss

ANSWERS

1	2	3	4	5	6	7	8	9	10
C	B	B	D	C	C	A	A	A	B

SOME SELECTED EXPLANATORY ANSWERS

1. C.P. of 60 kg mixture = Rs. $(25 \times 6 + 35 \times 7)$
$$= \text{Rs. } 395$$
   S.P. of 60 kg mixtire = Rs. (60×6.75)
$$= \text{Rs. } 405$$
$\therefore$ Gain = Rs. $(405 - 395)$
$$= \text{Rs. } 10$$

2. Let C.P. = Rs. x
   Then, $425 - x = x - 355 \Rightarrow 2x = 780$
   $\therefore$ $x = $ Rs. 390

3. C.P. of 6 dozen apples = Rs. $(12 \times 4 + 16 \times 2)$
$$= \text{Rs. } 80$$
$\therefore$ S.P. = Rs. $\left(\dfrac{120}{100} \times 80\right)$
$$= \text{Rs. } 96$$
$\therefore$ S.P. per dozen = Rs. $\left(\dfrac{96}{6}\right) = $ Rs. 16

4. C.P. of 1 kg sugar = $\dfrac{80 \times 6.75 + 120 \times 8}{200}$
$$= \text{Rs. } 7.50$$
$\therefore$ S.P. of 1 kg = Rs. $\left(\dfrac{120}{100} \times 7.50\right)$
$$= \text{Rs. } 9 \text{ per kg}$$

5. Let C.P. = Rs. x,
   then S.P. = $\dfrac{90}{100} \times x = $ Rs. $\dfrac{9x}{10}$
   Now, when C.P. = Rs. $\dfrac{80x}{100} = $ Rs. $\dfrac{4x}{5}$;
   then S.P. = $\dfrac{140}{100} \times \dfrac{4x}{5} = $ Rs. $\dfrac{28x}{25}$
   But, $\dfrac{28x}{25} - \dfrac{9x}{10} = 55 \Rightarrow \dfrac{11x}{50} = 55$
   $\therefore$ $x = $ Rs. 250

6. Let the initial price = Rs. x; then C.P. for dealer
$$= \dfrac{120}{100} \times x = \text{Rs. } \dfrac{6x}{5}$$
   Again, C.P. for shopkeeper = $\dfrac{125}{100} \times \dfrac{6x}{5}$
$$= \text{Rs. } \dfrac{3x}{2}$$
   Now, $\dfrac{3x}{2} - \dfrac{6x}{5} = 129 \Rightarrow \dfrac{3x}{10} = 129$
   $\therefore$ $x = \dfrac{10 \times 129}{3} = $ Rs. 430

7. Here, 10% C.P. of horse = 20% C.P. of cart;
   Hence, C.P. of horse = $2 \times$ C.P. of cart;
   Let C.P. of cart and horse be Rs. x and Rs. $2x$ respectively; then,
$$\dfrac{5}{100} \times 2x - \dfrac{5}{100} \times x = 10 \Rightarrow \dfrac{1}{20}x = 10$$
   $\therefore x = 200$
   Hence, C.P. of a cart = Rs. 200 and C.P. of a horse = $2 \times 200 = $ Rs. 400

8. Let C.P. be Rs. 100; then marked price
$$= \text{Rs. } 120$$
   Since, S.P. = $\dfrac{90}{100} \times 120 = $ Rs. 108
   $\therefore$ Profit = $108 - 100 = $ Rs. 8, Hence, gain = 8%.

9. Required weight = $\dfrac{100}{160} \times 1000 = 625$ gms.

10. Here, loss % = $\left(\dfrac{10}{10}\right)^2 = 1\%$.

SIMPLE INTEREST

1. A lent a sum of Rs. 1250 to B at a certain rate of interest for 3 years and a sum of Rs. 1500 to C at the same rate of interest for 2 years. If he was paid total Rs. 258.75 as interest in both cases, find the rate of interest at which money was lent by him.

   A. $4\dfrac{1}{6}\%$
   B. $6\dfrac{1}{4}\%$
   C. $2\dfrac{1}{7}\%$
   D. $3\dfrac{5}{6}\%$

2. A invested Rs. 5000 at a certain rate of simple interest and Rs. 4000 for the same period at 1% higher rate of interest. If the interest in both cases is same, the former rate of interest is :

   A. 3%
   B. 4%
   C. 6%
   D. 5%

3. If a certain sum of money at simple interest amounts to Rs. 1900 in 3 years and to Rs. 2050 in 5 years, the rate per cent per annum is :

   A. 4½%
   B. 3½%
   C. 2½%
   D. 5¼%

4. A certain sum of money lent out on simple interest amounts to Rs. 1760 in 2 years and to Rs. 2000 in 5 years. Find the sum.

   A. Rs. 1650
   B. Rs. 1500
   C. Rs. 1580
   D. Rs. 1600

5. Out of the sum of Rs. 1550, a part was lent out at 5% p.a. simple interest and the remaining at 8% p.a. simple interest. If the total interest in both cases after 3 years is Rs. 300, the sum of money lent out at 8% p.a. simple interest was:

   A. Rs. 760
   B. Rs. 775
   C. Rs. 750
   D. Rs. 780

6. If simple interest on a certain sum of money for 4 years at 5% p.a. is same as the simple interest on Rs. 840 for 10 years at the rate of 4% p.a., the sum of money is:

   A. Rs. 1780
   B. Rs. 1660
   C. Rs. 1680
   D. Rs. 1620

7. What equal instalment of annual payment will discharge a debt which is due as Rs. 848 at the end of 4 years at 4% per annum simple interest?

   A. Rs. 200
   B. Rs. 212
   C. Rs. 225
   D. Rs. 250

8. Madhavi lent Rs. 5000 to Kamla for 5 years and Rs. 3000 to Vimla for 4 years. Find the rate of interest, if Madhavi gets an interest of Rs. 600 in the end.

   A. 1.62%
   B. 2.5%
   C. 3%
   D. 4%

9. A sum of money doubles itself in 7 years at simple interest. In how many years it will become four fold?

   A. 10 years
   B. 14 years
   C. 21 years
   D. 35 years

10. An amount doubles itself at the end of 8 years with a certain rate of simple interest. What will be the total simple interest on Rs. 8000 at that rate at the end of 4 years?

    A. Rs. 2000
    B. Rs. 4000
    C. Rs. 6000
    D. None of these

ANSWERS

1	2	3	4	5	6	7	8	9	10
D	B	A	D	C	C	A	A	C	B

SOME SELECTED EXPLANATORY ANSWERS

1. $\dfrac{1250 \times R \times 3}{100} + \dfrac{1500 \times R \times 2}{100} = 258.75$

$\Rightarrow 6750\ R = 25875$

$\therefore \quad R = \dfrac{25875}{6750} = \dfrac{23}{6} = 3\dfrac{5}{6}\%$

2. Here, $\dfrac{5000 \times R \times T}{100} = \dfrac{4000 \times (R+1) \times T}{100}$

$\Rightarrow 5R = 4R + 4 \quad \therefore \ R = 4\%$

3. Simple interest for 2 years
$\quad = $ Rs. 2050 – Rs. 1900 = Rs. 150

$\therefore$ Simple interest for 1 year = Rs. $\dfrac{150}{2}$

$\qquad\qquad\qquad\qquad = $ Rs. 75

Since simple interest for 3 years = Rs. 75 × 3

$\qquad\qquad\qquad\qquad\qquad = $ Rs. 225

$\therefore \quad$ Principal = Rs. 1900 – Rs. 225

$\qquad\qquad\qquad = $ Rs. 1675

Hence, $\quad$ Rate $= \dfrac{75 \times 100}{1675 \times 1} = 4\frac{1}{2}\%$

4. Interest for 3 years = Rs. 2000 – Rs. 1760

$\qquad\qquad\qquad = $ Rs. 240

$\therefore$ Interest for 1 year = Rs. $\dfrac{240}{3}$ = Rs. 80

And interest for 2 years = Rs. 80 × 2 = Rs. 160

$\therefore$ Principal = Rs. 1760 – Rs. 160 = Rs. 1600

5. Let Rs. x and Rs $(1550 - x)$ were lent out at 8% and 5% respectively; then

$\dfrac{x \times 8 \times 3}{100} + \dfrac{(1550 - x) \times 5 \times 3}{100} = 300$

$\Rightarrow 24x + 23250 - 15x = 30000$

$\Rightarrow 9x = 6750 \quad \therefore \ x = \dfrac{6750}{9} = $ Rs. 750

6. Here, $\dfrac{P \times 5 \times 4}{100} = \dfrac{840 \times 4 \times 10}{100} \Rightarrow 5P = 8400$

$\therefore P = \dfrac{8400}{5} = $ Rs. 1680

7. Let equal instalment be Rs. x; then

$x + \dfrac{x \times 4 \times 3}{100} + x + \dfrac{x \times 4 \times 2}{100} + x$

$\qquad\qquad\qquad + \dfrac{x \times 4 \times 1}{100} + x = 848$

$\Rightarrow 4x + \dfrac{24x}{100} = 848 \quad \Rightarrow \dfrac{106x}{25} = 848$

$\therefore \ x = \dfrac{848 \times 25}{106} = $ Rs. 200

8. $\dfrac{5000 \times R \times 5}{100} + \dfrac{3000 \times R \times 4}{100} = 600$

$\Rightarrow \quad 250\ R + 120\ R = 600$

$\Rightarrow \qquad\qquad 370R = 600$

$\therefore \qquad\qquad R = \dfrac{600}{370} = 1.62\%$

9. Let principal be Rs. x; then amount = Rs. $2x$,
Hence, I = $2x - x$ = Rs. x.

$R = \dfrac{x \times 100}{x \times 7} = \dfrac{100}{7}\%$ p.a.

Now, amount = Rs. $4x$; then I = $4x - x$

$\qquad\qquad\qquad\qquad = $ Rs. $3x$

Hence, T $= \dfrac{3x \times 100}{x \times \dfrac{100}{7}} = \dfrac{3 \times 100 \times 7}{100} = 21$ years

10. Let principal = Rs. x; then amount = Rs. $2x$;
I = $2x - x$ = Rs. x

$R = \dfrac{x \times 100}{x \times 8} = \dfrac{25}{2}\%$

Again, $\quad$ I $= \dfrac{8000 \times 25 \times 4}{100 \times 2} = $ Rs. 4000

COMPOUND INTEREST

1. The compound interest on a certain sum of money invested for 3 years at 5% per annum is Rs. 1891.50. What will be the simple interest on the same sum at the same rate for 2 years?
   A. Rs. 1700
   B. Rs. 1200
   C. Rs. 1500
   D. Rs. 2100

2. A sum of money lent out at a certain rate of simple interest amounts to Rs. 6600 in 2 years and to Rs. 6900 in 3 years. What will be the compound interest on the same sum of money if lent out at the same rate for 2 years?
   A. Rs. 605
   B. Rs. 715
   C. Rs. 615
   D. Rs. 595

3. A man deposits Rs. 1200 in a bank on the 1st day of each year. If the bank pays 5% per annum compound interest on deposited sum of money, what will be the amount to his credit on the 10th day of the second year?
   A. Rs. 2560
   B. Rs. 2460
   C. Rs. 2370
   D. Rs. 2860

4. If the difference between compound and simple interest on a certain sum of money for 3 years at 5% per annum is Rs. 244, the sum is :
   A. Rs. 40000
   B. Rs. 25000
   C. Rs. 30000
   D. Rs. 32000

5. A man purchased a sewing machine for Rs. 5000. If due to sustained use value of this sewing machine depreciates by 6% annually, find its value after 3 years.
   A. Rs. 3775.67
   B. Rs. 4152.92
   C. Rs. 4250.25
   D. Rs. 4356.25

6. Find the sum on which the difference between compound and simple interest for 3 years at 10% per annum will be Rs. 868.
   A. Rs. 29500
   B. Rs. 27625
   C. Rs. 28500
   D. Rs. 28000

7. Samir invested Rs. 15000 at the rate of interest 10% p.a. for 1 year. If the interest compound six months. What amount will Samir get at the end of the year?
   A. Rs. 16,500
   B. Rs. 16525.50
   C. Rs. 16537.50
   D. Rs. 18,150

8. The compound interest on a certain sum for 2 years at 10% per annum is Rs. 525. The simple interest on the same sum for double the time at half the rate per cent per annum is:
   A. Rs. 800
   B. Rs. 600
   C. Rs. 500
   D. Rs. 400

9. The least number of complete years in which a sum of money put at 20% compound interest will be more than doubled is:
   A. 6
   B. 5
   C. 4
   D. 3

10. On a sum of money, the simple interest for 2 years is Rs. 660, while the compound interest is Rs. 696.30, the rate of interest being the same in both cases. Find the rate of interest.
    A. Rs. 12%
    B. 11%
    C. 10%
    D. 9%

ANSWERS

1	2	3	4	5	6	7	8	9	10
B	C	B	D	B	D	C	C	C	B

SOME SELECTED EXPLANATORY ANSWERS

1. Here,

$$1891.50 = P\left[\left(1+\frac{5}{100}\right)^3 - 1\right]$$

$$\Rightarrow \quad 1891.50 = P\left[\left(\frac{21}{20}\right)^3 - 1\right]$$

$$\Rightarrow \quad 1891.50 = P\left(\frac{1261}{8000}\right)$$

$$\therefore P = \frac{1891.50 \times 8000}{1261} = \text{Rs. } 12000$$

Now, S.I. $= \dfrac{12000 \times 5 \times 2}{100} = \text{Rs. } 1200$

2. Here, 1 year's S.I. = Rs. 6900 – Rs. 6600
$$= \text{Rs. } 300$$
$\therefore$ 2 year's S.I. = 300 × 2 = Rs. 600
$\therefore$ Principal = Rs. 6600 – Rs. 600
$$= \text{Rs. } 6000$$

Hence, Rate $= \dfrac{600 \times 100}{6000 \times 2} = 5\%$

$$\therefore \quad \text{C.I.} = 6000\left[\left(1+\frac{5}{100}\right)^2 - 1\right]$$

$$= 6000\left[\left(\frac{21}{20}\right)^2 - 1\right] = \frac{6000 \times 41}{400} = \text{Rs. } 615$$

3. Required amount $= 1200\left(1+\dfrac{5}{100}\right) + 1200$

$$= 1200 \times \frac{21}{20} + 1200 = 1260 + 1200 = \text{Rs. } 2460$$

4. Here, $P\left[\left(1+\dfrac{5}{100}\right)^3 - 1\right] - \dfrac{P \times 5 \times 3}{100} = 244$

$$\Rightarrow P \times \frac{1261}{8000} - \frac{3P}{20} = 244 \Rightarrow P \times \frac{61}{8000} = 244$$

$$\therefore \quad P = \frac{244 \times 8000}{61} = \text{Rs. } 32000$$

5. Here, value of the machine after 3 years

$$= 5000\left(1-\frac{6}{100}\right)^3 = 5000 \times \frac{47}{50} \times \frac{47}{50} \times \frac{47}{50}$$

$$= \text{Rs. } 4152.92.$$

6. Here, $P\left[\left(1+\dfrac{10}{100}\right)^3 - 1\right] - \dfrac{P \times 10 \times 3}{100} = 868$

$$\Rightarrow P \times \frac{331}{1000} - \frac{3P}{10} = 868$$

$$\Rightarrow P \times \frac{31}{1000} = 868 \quad \therefore \quad P = \frac{868 \times 1000}{31}$$

$$= \text{Rs. } 28000$$

7. $A = 15000\left(1+\dfrac{5}{100}\right)^2 = 15000 \times \dfrac{441}{400}$

$$= \text{Rs. } 16537.50$$

8. Here, $P\left[\left(1+\dfrac{10}{100}\right)^2 - 1\right] = 525$

$$\Rightarrow P\left[\frac{121}{100} - 1\right] = 525 \Rightarrow P \times \frac{21}{100} = 525$$

$$\therefore \quad P = \frac{525 \times 100}{21} = \text{Rs. } 2500$$

Hence, required S.I. $= \dfrac{2500 \times 5 \times 4}{100} = \text{Rs. } 500$

9. Here, $P\left(1+\dfrac{20}{100}\right)^n > 2P \Rightarrow \left(\dfrac{6}{5}\right)^n > 2$

Hence, if $n = 4$ then, $\left(\dfrac{6}{5}\right)^4 = \dfrac{1296}{625} > 2$

So, $n = 4$ years

10. Here, S.I. for 1 year = Rs. 330
Since, simple interest of Rs. 330 for 1 year
= 696.30 – 660 = Rs. 36.30

Hence, required rate $= \dfrac{36.30 \times 100}{330 \times 1} = \dfrac{3630}{330}$

$$= 11\%$$

AREA AND PERIMETER

1. If side of a square is reduced by 50%, its area will be reduced by
   A. 50%
   B. 75%
   C. 80%
   D. 60%

2. If each side of a square is doubled, its area will become
   A. double
   B. four times
   C. three times
   D. eight times

3. Three sides of a triangle are in the ratio of 17 : 15 : 8. If the perimeter of this triangle is 40 m, find its area
   A. 50 sq. m.
   B. 49 sq. m.
   C. 60 sq. m.
   D. 69 sq. m.

4. If the length of a rectangle is increased by 20% and width is decreased by 15%, then its area
   A. decreases by 4%
   B. increases by 2%
   C. decreases by 2%
   D. increases by 3%

5. If the length of a rectangle is increased by 20%, then by how much per cent its breadth must be decreased so as to keep its area unaltered?
   A. 25%
   B. $8\frac{1}{3}\%$
   C. $16\frac{2}{3}\%$
   D. 20%

6. The ratio of length and breadth of a rectangular plot is 71 : 61 respectively. The area of the plot is 17324 m². What is perimeter of the plot?
   A. 264 m
   B. 284 m
   C. 528 m
   D. 614 m

7. If the length and breadth of a rectangular field are increased, the area increases by 50%. If the increase in length was 20%, by what percentage was the breadth increased?
   A. 20%
   B. 25%
   C. 30%
   D. 40%

8. The length and breadth of a varandah is 40 m and 15 m respectively. How many stone slabs of size 6 decimetre × 5 decimetre each are needed in flooring it:
   A. 1000
   B. 2000
   C. 3000
   D. 4000

9. The circumference of a circular plot is 396 m. What is the area of the circular plot?
   A. 9,446 m²
   B. 9,856 m²
   C. 12,474 m²
   D. 18,634 m²

10. If the sides of an equilateral triangle are increased by 20%, 30% and 50% respectively to form a new triangle, the increase in the perimeter of the equilateral triangle is:
    A. 25%
    B. $33\frac{1}{3}\%$
    C. 50%
    D. 100%

ANSWERS

1	2	3	4	5	6	7	8	9	10
B	B	C	B	C	C	B	B	C	B

SOME SELECTED EXPLANATORY ANSWERS

1. Area of the square $= x^2$ sq. m.

   Side of the new square $= x - 50\%$ of $x = \dfrac{x}{2}$ m

   $\therefore$ Area of the new square $= \left(\dfrac{x}{2}\right)^2 = \dfrac{x^2}{4}$ sq. m.

   $\therefore$ Reduction in area of the square $= x^2 - \dfrac{x^2}{4}$

   $\qquad\qquad = \dfrac{3x^2}{4}$ sq. m.

   $\therefore$ Percentage reduction $= \dfrac{3x^2/4}{x^2} \times 100 = 75\%$

2. Area of the square $= x^2$ sq. m

   Now, area of the new square $= (2x)^2 = 4x^2$ sq. m
   Hence, it is clear that if side of a square is doubled, its area becomes four times.

3. Suppose sides of the triangle are $17x$ m, $15x$ m and $8x$ metres

   $\therefore$ Perimeter $= 17x + 15x + 8x = 40x$
   Now, $\qquad 40x = 40$
   $\Rightarrow \qquad\qquad x = 1$ m
   Therefore, the sides are $17 \times 1 = 17$ m, 15×1
   $\qquad\qquad = 15$ m and $8 \times 1 = 8$ m
   $\because \qquad (17)^2 = (15)^2 + (8)^2,$
   i.e., it is a right angled triangle
   $\therefore$ Area of the right angled triangle

   $\qquad\qquad = \dfrac{1}{2} \times 8 \times 15 = 60$ sq.m.

4. Area of the rectangle $= xy$ sq. metre

   Area of the new rectangle $= \dfrac{120}{100} x \times \dfrac{85}{100} y$

   $\qquad\qquad = 1.020\ xy$ sq. metre
   $\therefore$ Increase in the area $= 1.02\ xy - xy$
   $\qquad\qquad = .02\ xy$ sq. m.

   $\therefore$ Percentage increase $= \dfrac{.02xy}{xy} \times 100 = 2\%$

5. Area of the rectangle $= xy$
   On reducing the breadth by $A\%$ and increasing the length by 20%

   Length of the new rectangle $= \dfrac{120x}{100} x = 1.2x$

   Breadth of the new rectangle $= y - A\%$ of y

   $\qquad\qquad = y\left(1 - \dfrac{A}{100}\right)$

   $\therefore$ Area of the new rectangle $= 1.2x \times y\left(1 - \dfrac{A}{100}\right)$

   Now, $xy = 1.2\ xy\left(1 - \dfrac{A}{100}\right) \Rightarrow 1 = 1.2\dfrac{(100-A)}{100}$

   $\Rightarrow \qquad\qquad 1.2\ A = 120 - 100$

   $\therefore \qquad\qquad A = \dfrac{20}{1.2} = 16\dfrac{2}{3}\%$

6. Let length and breadth of a rectangle be $71x$ and $61x$ m; then

   $71x \times 61x = 17324 \Rightarrow x^2 = \dfrac{17324}{71 \times 61} = 4$

   $\therefore \qquad x = 2$
   Hence, length $= 71 \times 2 = 142$ m; breadth
   $\qquad\qquad = 61 \times 2 = 122$ m
   Since, perimeter $= 2(142 + 122) = 2 \times 264$
   $\qquad\qquad = 528$ m

7. Here, $20 + x + \dfrac{20 \times x}{100} = 50 \quad \Rightarrow x + \dfrac{x}{5} = 30$

   $\Rightarrow \dfrac{6x}{5} = 30 \qquad\qquad \therefore\ x = \dfrac{5 \times 30}{6} = 25$

   Hence, breadth was increased by 25%

8. Required number of stone slabs $= \dfrac{40 \times 15}{\dfrac{6}{10} \times \dfrac{5}{10}}$

   $= \dfrac{40 \times 15 \times 100}{6 \times 5} = 2000$

9. Radius of circular plot $= \dfrac{396 \times 7}{2 \times 22} = 63$ m

   Area of the circular plot $= \dfrac{22}{7} \times 63 \times 63$

   $\qquad\qquad = 12{,}474$ m^2

VOLUME AND SURFACE AREA

1. If a solid sphere of 3 cm radius is melted and recast into a right circular cone whose base radius is same as that of the sphere, the height of the cone will be
   A. 8 cm
   B. 12 cm
   C. 6 cm
   D. 5 cm

2. Diameter of a roller is 2.4 m and it is 1.68 m long. If it takes 1000 complete revolutions once over to level a field, the area of the field is
   A. 12672 sq. m
   B. 12671 sq. m
   C. 12762 sq. m
   D. 11768 sq. m

3. If each edge of a cube is increased by 10%, then by how much per cent will the surface area of this cube be increased?
   A. 21%
   B. 18%
   C. 15%
   D. 20%

4. Height and base radius of a solid cylinder are 14 m and 4 m respectively. It is melted and recast into a solid cone of the same base radius as that of the cylinder, what will be the height of the cone?
   A. 21 m
   B. 42 m
   C. 48 m
   D. 54 m

5. A room is in the form of a cube of side 10 m. How many bales of cotton can be kept in it if each bale covers 5 cu m space?
   A. 100
   B. 175
   C. 200
   D. 225

6. Three cubes having side 2 cm, 3 cm and 4 cm respectively are melted together to form a new cube. The side of the new cube will be
   A. 3.526 cm
   B. 4.628 cm
   C. 4.626 cm
   D. 4.528 cm

7. If base diameter of a cylinder is increased by 50%, then by how much per cent its height must be decreased so as to keep its volume unaltered?
   A. 45.56%
   B. 55.56%
   C. 50.16%
   D. 62.33%

8. The surface area of a cube is 600 sq. m. Its diagonal is
   A. $10\sqrt{3}$ cm
   B. $5\sqrt{3}$ cm
   C. $4\sqrt{2}$ cm
   D. $10\sqrt{2}$ cm

9. The base diameter of a conical tomb is 28 m and its slant height is 50 m. Find the cost of white washing its curved surface at the rate of 80 paise per sq. m?
   A. Rs. 1860
   B. Rs. 1760
   C. Rs. 1950
   D. Rs. 1875

10. The volume of a cuboid is 1120 cu cm and its height is 5 cm while the length and the breadth of the cuboid are in the ratio 8 : 7. The length of this cylinder exceeds the breadth by
    A. 4 cm
    B. 2 cm
    C. 7 cm
    D. 5 cm

ANSWERS

1	2	3	4	5	6	7	8	9	10
B	A	A	B	C	C	B	A	B	B

SOME SELECTED EXPLANATORY ANSWERS

1. Volume of the cone = Volume of the sphere

$$\therefore \ \frac{1}{3}\pi(3)^2 \times h = \frac{4}{3}\pi \times 3^3 \Rightarrow h = 12 \text{ cm}$$

Hence, height of the cone = 12 cm.

2. Surface area of the roller = $2\pi rh$

$$= 2 \times \frac{22}{7} \times 1.2 \times 1.68 = 12.672 \text{ sq. m}$$

In one complete revolution, the roller covers 12.672 sq. m.

$\therefore$ It will cover in 1000 revolutions
$= 12.672 \times 1000 = 12672$ sq. m

Hence, area of the field = 12672 sq. m.

3. Percentage increase in the surface area of the

$$\text{cube} = \left(x + y + \frac{xy}{100}\right)\%$$

$$= \left(10 + 10 + \frac{10 \times 10}{100}\right)\% = 21\%.$$

4. Here,
volume of the cone = Volume of the cylinder

$$\Rightarrow \quad \frac{1}{3}\pi r^2 \times \text{height} = \pi r^2 \times 14$$

$$\therefore \qquad \text{Height} = 14 \times 3 = 42 \text{ m}$$

Thus, height of the cone = 42 m.

5. Volume of the cubical room $= (10)^3$
$$= 1000 \text{ cu m}$$

Number of cotton bales which can be placed in the room

$$= \frac{\text{Volume of the room}}{\text{Volume of each cotton bale}} = \frac{1000}{5} = 200.$$

6. Volume of the new cube $= 2^3 + 3^3 + 4^3$
$$= 8 + 27 + 64 = 99 \text{cu cm}$$

$\therefore$ Side of the new cube $= \sqrt[3]{99} = 4.626$ cm.

7. Change in the volume of the cylinder

$$= \left(x + y + (-z) + \frac{xy + y(-z) + (-zx)}{100} + \frac{xy(-z)}{100^2}\right)\%$$

Since volume of the cylinder remains unchanged.

$$\therefore \qquad \text{Change} = 0\%$$

Now, $\left(50 + 50 + (-z) + \frac{50 \times 50 - 50z - 50z}{100} + \frac{50 \times 50 \times (-z)}{100^2}\right) = 0$

$$\therefore \quad 100 - z + 25 - z - .25z = 0$$

$$\Rightarrow 2.25z = 125 \Rightarrow z = \frac{125}{2.25} = 55.56$$

$\therefore$ Height of the cylinder should be decreased by 55.56%.

8. Here, $\qquad 6 \times (\text{side})^2 = 600$
$$\Rightarrow \qquad \text{side}^2 = 100$$
$$\Rightarrow \qquad \text{side} = \sqrt{100} = 10 \text{ cm}$$

$\therefore$ Diagonal of the cube $= \sqrt{3} \times \text{side}$

$$= \sqrt{3} \times 10$$

$$= 10\sqrt{3} \text{ cm.}$$

9. Area of the curved surface of the cone

$$= \frac{22}{7} \times \frac{28}{2} \times 50 = 2200 \text{ sq. m.}$$

$\therefore$ Cost of white washing at 80 paise per sq. m

$$= 2200 \times \frac{80}{100} = \text{Rs. } 1760.$$

10. Suppose the length and the breadth of the cuboid are $8x$ cm and $7x$ cm

$\therefore$ Here, $\quad 8x \times 7x \times 5 = 1120$

$$\Rightarrow x^2 = \frac{1120}{280} = 4 = (2)^2 \quad \Rightarrow \quad x = 2$$

$\therefore$ Length of the cuboid $= 8 \times 2 = 16$ cm
Breadth of the cuboid $= 7 \times 2 = 14$ cm

Hence, it is clear that length of the cuboid exceeds the breadth by 2 cm.

AREA AND PERIMETER

1. The length of a plot is four times its breadth. A playground measuring 1200 square metres occupies a third of the total area of the plot. What is the length of the plot, in metres?
   A. 20
   B. 30
   C. 60
   D. None of these

2. The width of a rectangular hall is $\frac{3}{4}$ of its length. If the area of the hall is 300 m^2, then the difference between its length and width is:
   A. 3 m
   B. 4 m
   C. 5 m
   D. 15 m

3. The length and breadth of a rectangular piece of land are in ratio of 5 : 3. The owner spent ₹ 3000 for surrounding it from all the sides at ₹ 7.50 per metre. The difference between its length and breadth is:
   A. 50 m
   B. 100 m
   C. 150 m
   D. 200 m

4. A room 8 m × 6 m is to be carpeted by a carpet 2 m wide. The length of carpet required is:
   A. 12 m
   B. 36 m
   C. 24 m
   D. 48 m

5. The length of a rectangle is increased by 60%. By what per cent would the width have to be decreased to maintain the same area?
   A. $37\frac{1}{2}\%$
   B. 60%
   C. 75%
   D. 120%

6. A man walked 20 m to cross a rectangular field diagonally. If the length of the field is 16 m, the breadth of the rectangle is:
   A. 4 m
   B. 16 m
   C. 12 m
   D. Cannot be determined

7. If the ratio of the areas of two squares is 9 : 1, the ratio of their perimeters is:
   A. 9 : 1
   B. 3 : 1
   C. 3 : 4
   D. 1 : 3

8. The perimeter of both, a square and a rectangle are each equal to 48 m and the difference between their areas is 4 m^2. The breadth of the rectangle is:
   A. 10 m
   B. 12 m
   C. 14 m
   D. None of these

9. Area of a square with side x is equal to the area of a triangle with base x. The altitude of the triangle is:
   A. $\dfrac{x}{2}$
   B. x
   C. $2x$
   D. $4x$

10. If only the length of the rectangular plot is reduced to $\frac{2}{3}$rd of its original length, the ratio of original area to reduced area is:
    A. 2 : 3
    B. 3 : 2
    C. 1 : 2
    D. None of these

11. If the radius of a circle be reduced by 50%, its area is reduced by:
    A. 25%
    B. 50%
    C. 75%
    D. 100%

12. The perimeter of a rhombus is 52 m while its longer diagonal is 24 m. Its other diagonal is:
    A. 5 m
    B. 10 m
    C. 20 m
    D. 28 m

13. The circumference of a circle is 352 m, then its area in m^2 is:
    A. 9856
    B. 8956
    C. 6589
    D. 5986

ANSWERS

1	2	3	4	5	6	7	8	9	10
D	C	A	C	A	C	B	A	C	B

11	12	13
C	B	A

SOME SELECTED EXPLANATORY ANSWERS

1. Area of the plot $= 3 \times 1200 = 3600 \text{ m}^2$
   Let breadth be x m. Then length $= 4x$ m
   According to the question,
   $4x \times x = 3600 \Rightarrow x^2 = 900 \Rightarrow x = 30$
   Hence, length of the plot $= 4 \times 30 = 120$ m.

2. Let length be x m, then breadth $= \dfrac{3x}{4}$ m

   Area of the hall $= x \times \dfrac{3x}{4} = \dfrac{3x^2}{4}$

   According to the question,

   $\dfrac{3x^2}{4} = 300 \Rightarrow x^2 = 400 \Rightarrow x = 20$

   Length $= 20$ m and breadth $= \dfrac{3}{4} \times 20 = 15$ m

   Difference $= 20 - 15 = 5$ m

3. Let length $= 5x$ m and breadth $= 3x$ m
   Perimeter of rectangle $= 2(5x + 3x) = 16x$ m

   But perimeter $= \dfrac{\text{Total cost}}{\text{Rate}} = \dfrac{3000}{7.50} = 400$ m

   Now, $\quad 16x = 400 \Rightarrow x = 25$
   $\qquad$ length $= 5x = 5 \times 25 = 125$ m
   $\qquad$ breadth $= 3x = 25 \times 3 = 75$ m
   $\qquad$ Difference $= 125 - 75 = 50$ m

4. Length of the carpet $= \dfrac{8 \times 6}{2} = 24$ m.

7. Let the areas of the squares be $(9x^2) \text{ m}^2$ and $(x^2) \text{ m}^2$
   Then, their sides are $3x$ m and x m respectively

   Ratio of their perimeters $= \dfrac{12x}{4x} = 3 : 1$

9. According to the question,

   $$x^2 = \frac{1}{2} \times x \times h$$

   $\Rightarrow \qquad h = \dfrac{2x^2}{x} = 2x$

10. Let length $= x$ and breadth $= y$

    New length $= \dfrac{2}{3}x$

    $\therefore \dfrac{\text{Original area}}{\text{Reduced area}} = \dfrac{xy}{\dfrac{2}{3}xy} = \dfrac{3}{2} = 3 : 2$

11. Original area $= \pi r^2$, New area $= \pi\left(\dfrac{r}{2}\right)^2 = \dfrac{\pi r^2}{4}$

    Reduction in area $= \pi r^2 - \dfrac{\pi r^2}{4} = \dfrac{3\pi r^2}{4}$

    Reduction per cent $= \dfrac{3\pi r^2}{4} \times \dfrac{1}{\pi r^2} \times 100 = 75\%$

12. Side of rhombus $= \dfrac{52}{4} = 13$ m

    In $\triangle ABM$,
    $\qquad x^2 = (13)^2 - (12)^2$
    $\qquad x^2 = 169 - 144$
    $\qquad x^2 = 25$
    $\Rightarrow \quad x = 5$ m
    $\therefore$ Another diagonal
    $\qquad = 2 \times 5 = 10$ m

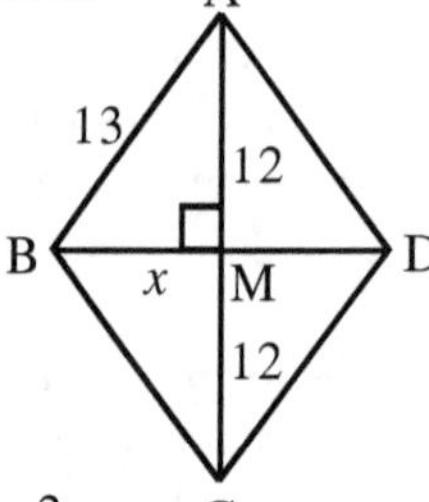

13. Circumference of a circle $= 2\pi r$

    $\Rightarrow \qquad 352 = 2 \times \dfrac{22}{7} \times r$

    $\Rightarrow \qquad r = \dfrac{352 \times 7}{44} = 56$ m

    Area of circle $= \pi r^2 = \dfrac{22}{7} \times 56 \times 56$

    $\qquad\qquad = 9856 \text{ m}^2$

ENGLISH LANGUAGE

1. <u>Comprehension Passages</u>

ENGLISH LANGUAGE COMPREHENSION

The objective of language comprehension test is to ascertain the ability of the candidates to understand the passage properly. Therefore candidates are required to take notice of the following points:

1. Read the full passage very attentively and intelligently.
2. Try to comprehend the gist of it.
3. Make a mental note of all the important details and points given in the passage.
4. Read the passage for the second time in case you have not been able to understand it satisfactorily.
5. Divide the time proportionately for all the passages.
6. Answer the questions on the basis of facts, as given in the paragraph.
7. Don't waste much time in answering the questions of any one passage.
8. Check all the answers once again, very carefully, to see whether any question is left unanswered by mistake.

MODEL QUESTIONS (FOR PRACTICE)

Directions: *Each of the following passages is followed by five questions. Read the passage carefully and then answer the questions that follow each. For each question, four probable answers A, B, C and D are given. Only one out of these is correct. Choose the correct answer.*

PASSAGE-1

The use of words like 'welcome', 'thank you', 'please', etc., at the right moment reflects a polite nature. The civic sense also lies within the scope of good manners. We should not shout or talk loudly in public places like hospitals and libraries and create disturbance. We should not cheat people or make fun of them. Cleanliness is also necessary. We must not throw the waste on roads and make use of dustbins. We should not harm the public property as it belongs to all of us. While in a queue, discipline should be maintained. We must give fair chance to others.

1. Expressions like 'welcome' 'thank you' and 'please' reflect
   - A. happiness
   - B. discipline
   - C. civic sense
   - D. polite nature

2. While in a library, we should
   - A. respect others
   - B. avoid arguments
   - C. talk in low tone
   - D. be courteous

3. A public property belongs to
   - A. nobody
   - B. all of us
   - C. government
   - D. one who maintains it

3

4. Discipline is
  A. the rule of proper conduct or action
  B. the rule of road sense
  C. making use of dustbins
  D. forming a queue

5. The most appropriate title for this passage would be
  A. Polite Nature
  B. Courtesy
  C. Good Manners
  D. Civic Sense

PASSAGE-2

There is an old proverb 'Early to bed and early to rise makes a man healthy and wise.' I am in the habit of getting up early in the morning and have formed the habit of taking long morning walks in the past two years. It is a light exercise and best for physical fitness. The morning air which is fresh and pure is beneficial for the lungs. The early rays of the rising sun are good for healthy skin. 'Health is wealth' and doctors also recommend morning walk to their patients for gaining sound health and freshness of energy.

1. What is good for lungs?
  A. Sunrays   B. Fresh air
  C. Sound sleep   D. Light exercise

2. What is a light exercise?
  A. Early to bed
  B. Early to rise
  C. Morning walk
  D. Gaining sound health

3. What is good for skin?
  A. Fresh air
  B. Morning air
  C. Morning walk
  D. Rising sun's rays

4. What is best for physical fitness?
  A. Light exercise
  B. Long morning walk
  C. Early to rise
  D. Fresh and pure air

5. Long morning walk
  A. bring sound sleep
  B. ensures physical fitness
  C. ensures healthy skin
  D. keeps healthy, wealthy and wise

PASSAGE-3

Mahatma Gandhi lived a splendid long life and has set great moral standards before us. He showed to the world the true way to peace. He wished to see India prosper but he became a martyr for the noble cause of Hindu-Muslim unity at the time of partition when a religious fanatic, Nathuram Godse, shot him dead on January 30, 1948. His last words were 'Hey Ram'. He lived and died for his country and countryman.

1. Mahatma Gandhi showed the world the true way to
  A. prosperity   B. love
  C. truth   D. peace

2. Mahatma Gandhi became a martyr for the noble cause of
  A. truth
  B. non-violence
  C. freedom of India
  D. Hindu-Muslim unity

3. Mahatma Gandhi was shot dead
  A. before India achieved independence
  B. by a mad man
  C. by an intolerant religious person
  D. by a non-religious person

4. Mahatma Gandhi set great moral standards. It means
  A. he was a great religious teacher
  B. he was a great moralist
  C. he made India morally stronger
  D. moral was everything to him

5. Gandhiji lived and died for his country and countryman. It means
  A. he was born in India and died in India
  B. he was a patriot
  C. he was a great moralist
  D. he sacrified his life for India and her people

PASSAGE-4

On one hot day a crow felt very thirsty. He flew from one place to another in search of water. After long hours of labour he found a pitcher. Eagerly, he perched on the mouth of the pitcher. He found that the water was at the bottom of the vessel. He tried his best to dip his beak but did not succeed. He did not know what to do. Suddenly some pebbles lying nearby gave him an idea. One by one he dropped the pebbles with his beak into the pitcher. The level of water slowly came up to the mouth of the pitcher. The crow then drank the water and quenched his thirst.

1. The crow found a pitcher
   A. as it flew
   B. after many hours of labour
   C. full of water
   D. which was empty

2. What is the moral of the passage?
   A. No pains, no gains
   B. God helps those who help themselves
   C. Necessity is the mother of invention
   D. Try and try again, you will succeed at last

3. The crow flew from place to place
   A. in search of pitcher
   B. in search of pebbles
   C. in search of water
   D. in search of a vessel

4. The pitcher, the crow found
   A. was full of water
   B. was dry
   C. had little water in the bottom
   D. had water up to its mouth

5. As the crow dropped pebbles into the pitcher, what happend?
   A. The pitcher broke down
   B. The water leaked one of the pitcher
   C. The level of water into the pitcher rose up slowly
   D. Water level immediately rose to the mouth of the pitcher

PASSAGE-5

Once upon a time a crane and a fox lived in a forest. They were good friend. One day the fox invited the crane to a feast. He made a tasty food and served it before the crane on a plate. The crane could not eat anything because of the long beak. But the fox licked all his food. The crane felt insulted. He decided to teach the fox a lesson.

Next day he invited the fox. He prepared the same tasty food and placed it in front of the fox inside a narrow glass. The crane ate easily while the fox looked on. Now, it was the fox's turn to remain hungry.

1. What is the moral of the passage?
   A. Beware of the wicked
   B. One good turn deserves another
   C. Be contented with what you have
   D. Tit for tat

2. The crane could not eat tasty food because the
   A. food was served in a shallow plate
   B. food was very hot
   C. food was served in a long jar
   D. crane was not hungry

3. The fox had to remain hungry because
   A. the food served was not enough in quantity
   B. the food was served inside a narrow glass
   C. the food served was not tasty
   D. the food was all liquid

4. Why did the crane feel insulted?
   A. Because he was invited to feast but he could not eat anything
   B. Because the food was served in a shallow plate and he could not eat
   C. Because the food was too hot
   D. Because the fox gulped all the food quickly

5. The crane successfully taught a lesson to the fox when he invited the fox to a feast and served the food
   A. in a narrow glass
   B. in a large plate
   C. in a broken plate
   D. in a long jar

PASSAGE-6

The family set down at the table and began to talk about the summer holidays. They had to decide a place to visit during the vacation. Should they go to their village or to a hill station? The parents preferred the village while the children wished to go the hill station. After few moments of discussion the elders decided to visit both the places. First they shall go to the village for a week and then stay at the hill station for the remaining days. For the first time the family shall be together during the holidays. The children were happy with the holiday plan.

1. The purpose for which the family set down at the table was
   A. to decide a place to visit during the vacation
   B. to educate the children how to carry articles during a visit to a hill station
   C. to decide the date when they should start their journey
   D. to tell the children that they will visit a hill station during this vacation

2. The final plan was to visit
   A. their village
   B. a hill station
   C. their village as well as a hill station
   D. their home town

3. The final decision was made by
   A. the boys   B. the girls
   C. the women   D. the elders

4. They decided first to go to their village and stay there for
   A. a day   B. a week
   C. ten days   D. a fortnight

5. Why were children happy?
   A. Because a hill station was included in their holiday plan
   B. Because a visit to their village was excluded from their holiday plan
   C. Because their choice prevailed
   D. Because they were going all alone to the hill station

1. Govind intended to go
   A. for a business trip
   B. to a hill station
   C. on a long journey to a sacred place
   D. to his home town for a long period

2. Why did Govind leave his box of jewellery with Mirind?
   A. Because it was not safe to take the box with him on a long journey
   B. Because Mirind was his fast friend
   C. Because the box was very heavy
   D. Because his house was unsafe

3. Why did Govind take Mirind to a lonely place?
   A. To tell him that the box contained valuable jewellery
   B. So that no third person could see box
   C. To show him what was within the box
   D. To tell him that the box will remain with him

4. Where did Govind hand over the box of jewellery to Mirind?
   A. At Mirind's house
   B. At his own house
   C. In a lonely place
   D. In a lonely place under a tree

5. It was not safe to leave the box in a lone house. Here the word 'lone house' means
   A. a house in a deserted place
   B. a house where none lives
   C. a house without door and lock
   D. a house near the forest

PASSAGE-7

Once Govind intended to go on pilgrimage with his family. He asked Mirind to accompany. But for his trade's reason, he did not go with him. So Govind thought it safe to leave the box of his jewellery with him, as it was dangerous to leave it in a lone house or take it on the journey. So he went to him with the box. He took him to a lonely place under a tree and handed it over to him. He told Mirind, "Keep it safe with you. I shall return from the journey after six month then I shall take it back from you." Mirind said, "Don't worry, I shall keep it as safe as own."

PASSAGE-8

Zahir-ud-din Babar was the first Mughal emperor of India. A descendent of Timur on father's side and Changez Khan on his mother's side, Babar was a brave warrior. After defeating Ibrahim Lodhi in the First Battle of Panipat in 1526 he entered Delhi and soon gained control over Agra. After many more battles with Rajputs he extended his empire over Punjab, Uttar Pradesh and north Bihar. He died at a young age of 48 years in 1530 at his capital Agra without getting much time to consolidate his victories.

1. Zahir-ud-din Babar was the first
   A. Muslim ruler of India
   B. Mughal ruler of India
   C. Afghan ruler of India
   D. Turk ruler of India

2. Babar was born in the years
   A. 1480   B. 1482
   C. 1492   D. 1962

3. Babar first occupied
   A. Punjab   B. Agra
   C. Delhi   D. Panipat

4. Babar was a brave warrior. Here brave warrior means
   A. courageous soldier
   B. a kind hearted soldier
   C. a clever fighter
   D. a victorious general

5. Babar extended his empire over Punjab and Uttar Pradesh after many more battles with the
   A. Afghans   B. Rajputs
   C. Mughals   D. Lodhies

PASSAGE-9

Our National Flag is tricolour. It has three equal horizontal strips. The strip at the top is saffron, in the middle is white and at the bottom is green. The ratio of width to length of the flag is 2 : 3. In the centre of the white strip is a wheel in navy blue. The wheel represents the *chakra*. Its design is similar to the wheel which appears on the abacus of the Sarnath Lion Capital of Ashoka. Its diameter approximates to the width of the white strip. The wheel has 24 spokes. It was adopted by Constituent Assembly on July 22, 1947. We love our national flag. We respect it. We are ready to sacrifice our life to protect its honour. It represents the nation. So it is a symbol of national honour.

1. In our national flag the wheel is located in the centre of
   A. saffron strip   B. white strip
   C. green strip   D. blue strip

2. In our national flag which of the strips is at the bottom in our national flag
   A. blue   C. saffron
   B. white   D. green

3. Why do we love our national flag?
   A. Because it is tricolour
   B. Because it has three strips
   C. Because it has a wheel at the centre
   D. Because it is a symbol of national honour

4. Our national flag was approved by
   A. President
   B. Lok Sabha
   C. Parliament
   D. Constituent Assembly

5. The diameter approximates to the width of the white strip. Here the word 'approximates' means
   A. is more or less equal
   B. is exactly equal
   C. is not equal
   D. is related

PASSAGE-10

Distance in large cities are long. All the people do not have their own means of transport. They have to depend upon the state or private buses. The number of bus users is very large. Every bus stop is, therefore, crowded. The number of buses is not adequate. Thus people suffer the torture of long wait at the bus stop. Some bus stops are quite orderly. People form queues and get into the buses turn by turn. However, often this order is forgotten and confusion spreads when the bus comes and the law of jungle prevails.

1. Why are the bus stops crowded?
   A. Because they are small is size
   B. Because the number of passengers is very large
   C. Because they are situated at some busy centre
   D. Because people do not form queues

2. Long wait at the bus stop is the result of
   A. over-crowding in the buses
   B. late running of buses
   C. shortage of buses
   D. slow speed of buses

3. Some bus stops are quite orderly where
   A. there is no crowd
   B. the number of buses is adequate

C. people do not have to wait for long

D. people form queues and enter the buses one by one

4. Most of the people who travel by buses are

A. non-working

B. do not have their own vehicles

C. have to go a long distance

D. live in large cities

5. What happens when people do not have their own transport?

A. They have to wait for a bus at a bus stop

B. They have to depend upon the state or private buses

C. They have to travel long distances

D. They form queues and get into buses one by one

PASSAGE-11

A certain king once fell ill and doctors said that only a sudden fright would restore his health but the king was not a man for anyone to play tricks on, except his fool. One day, when the fool was with him in his boat he cleverly pushed the king into water but he was rescued and put to bed. The fright, the bath and bed cured the diseased king, but he was so angry with the fool that he turned him out of the country.

1. What did the doctor say about the king?

A. Only a sudden fright would restore the king's health

B. Only fool would cure the king

C. Only a boat trick could cure the king

D. The king had suffered a sudden fright

2. He cleverly pushed the king into water but *he* was rescued and put to bed. In this sentence *he* refers to

A. the king   B. the fool

C. the doctor   D. the river

3. When the fool pushed the king into water they were

A. in the palace   B. in the bed

C. in the garden   D. in a boat

4. Who played the trick on the king?

A. The doctor   B. The boatman

C. The fool   D. The fright

5. The fool who cured the king was

A. rewarded

B. thrown into water

C. turned out of the country

D. put into jail

ANSWERS

Passage 1.	1	2	3	4	5
	D	C	B	A	C
Passage 2.	1	2	3	4	5
	B	C	D	B	B
Passage 3.	1	2	3	4	5
	D	D	C	B	D
Passage 4.	1	2	3	4	5
	B	C	C	C	C
Passage 5.	1	2	3	4	5
	D	A	B	B	A
Passage 6.	1	2	3	4	5
	A	C	D	B	A
Passage 7.	1	2	3	4	5
	C	A	B	D	B
Passage 8.	1	2	3	4	5
	B	B	C	A	B
Passage 9.	1	2	3	4	5
	B	D	D	D	A
Passage 10.	1	2	3	4	5
	B	C	D	B	B
Passage 11.	1	2	3	4	5
	A	A	D	C	C

2. English Grammar

Part of speech	Definition or Function	Examples
Noun	Name of a person, place, animal, quality or thing	Ram, boy, dog pen, sun, Delhi, truth, honesty
Pronoun	Used in place of a noun	I, you, he she, they
Articles & Determiners	Points out indefinite and definite nouns	a, an, the, few, some
Adjective	Describes a noun or pronoun	big, honest, wooden valuable, quiet, deep, soft, narrow
Adverb	Describes a verb, an adjective or another adverb	silently, widely, softly, quietly, very, carefully
Verb	Tells about action or state of something or someone	is, am, was, have, do, like, walk, work, make, throw, tell
Conjuction	Joins words, clauses or sentences	and, but, when, yet, while, else
Preposition	Links a noun or pronoun to another word	at, to, after, on for, under, over, with
Interjection	Expresses sudden feelings or emotions	Ah!, Alas!, oh!, ouch!, hi!, well!, Hurrah!

NOUNS

A word which denotes a person, a thing, an animal or a place is said to be a noun.

There are two noun numbers in English — the *Singular* and the *Plural*.

Singular Numbers : A noun that denotes one person or one thing, is said to be in the Singular number. For example — book, pencil, bird, dog, hen etc. are in singular number.

Plural Number : A noun that denotes more than one person or one thing is said to be in plural number. For example — boys, pens, lions, girls, men etc. are in plural number.

REMEMBER

Singular	Plural
Cat	Cats
Book	Books
Pen	Pens
Room	Rooms
Tree	Trees
Bus	Buses
Bush	Bushes
Box	Boxes
Glass	Glasses
Dish	Dishes
Judge	Judges
Tax	Taxes
Watch	Watches
Calf	Calves
Thief	Thieves
Knife	Knives

Singular	Plural
Scarf	Scarves
Wife	Wives
Leaf	Leaves
Wolf	Wolves
Half	Halves
Monarch	Monarchs
Roof	Roofs
Hoof	Hoofs
Gulf	Gulfs
Staff	Staffs
Radio	Radios
Bamboo	Bamboos
Folio	Folios
Hero	Heroes
Volcano	Volcanoes
Mango	Mangoes
Potato	Potatoes
Photo	Photos
Piano	Pianos
Baby	Babies
Fly	Flies
Country	Countries
Lady	Ladies
Boy	Boys
Monkey	Monkeys
Ox	Oxen
Child	Children
Man	Men
Woman	Women
Tooth	Teeth
Axis	Axes
Basis	Bases
Foot	Feet
Goose	Geese
Englishman	Englishmen
Radius	Radii
Vertex	Vertices
Stimulus	Stimuli

1. Note the plurals of the following nouns:

Singular	Plural	Singular	Plural
copy	copies	cry	cries
baby	babies	duty	duties
body	bodies	country	countries
family	families	diary	diaries
fly	flies	fairy	fairies

city	cities	spy	spies
army	armies	storey	storeys
bay	bays	monkey	monkeys

2. The following nouns do not undergo any change in plural form, in general.

Singular	Plural	Singular	Plural
deer	deer	sheep	sheep
thousand	thousand	pair	pair
hundred	hundred	score	score
dozen	dozen	gross	gross

Note: We can write—

(a) thousands of men; (b) two pairs of shoes; (c) dozens of mangoes; (d) scores of people etc. But—

(a) two thousand rupees; (b) three hundred men; (c) five dozen eggs, etc.

3. The following nouns are usually used in plural forms. They take a plural verb after them—

eatables	fetters	surroundings
riches	alms	spectacles
trousers	pants	scissors
premises	thanks	annals
congratulations	goods	shorts
tongs	pains	arms
breeches	(for troubles)	

4. The following are the nouns which are plural in appearance but are usually used in singular number. They are followed by a singular verb—

news	politics	physics
mathematics	economics	ethics
politics	classics	gallows
statistics	athletics	innings
mechanics	summons	mumps

5. Collective nouns often used as plurals—

public	police	cattle
audience	clergy	folk
people	poultry	nation
elite	gentry	glitterati

6. The nouns that are usually used in singular forms—

advice	hair	rice
fuel	alphabet	machinery
offspring	issue	furniture
mischief	stationery	luggage
bedding	information	abuse

7. Material nouns are always used in singular number—

gold	copper	milk
water	silk	wool

Note: They may be used in plural with a different meaning.

copper coins (coppers), chains or fetters (irons), cans made of tin (tins).

GENDERS

The difference in sex is denoted by Gender in grammar. The various genders are as follows :

1. **Masculine Gender :** A noun that denotes a male is said to be of the masculine gender, as man, uncle, ox, boy etc.
2. **Feminine Gender :** A noun that denotes a female is said to be of feminine gender, as woman, aunt, princess, cow etc.
3. **Common Gender :** Nouns which denote both males and females are said to be of the common gender, as friend, cousin, person, parent, baby etc.
4. **Neuter Gender :** A noun that denotes the name of object without life is said to be of neuter gender, as file, table, pencil.

REMEMBER

Masculine	*Feminine*
Boy	Girl
Son	Daughter
Brother	Sister
Murderer	Murderess
Sorcerer	Sorceress
Son-in-law	Daughter-in-law
Father-in-law	Mother-in-law
Man-servant	Maid-servant
Land-lord	Land-lady
Bachelor	Maid
Gentleman	Lady
Monk	Nun
Earl	Countess
Lad	Lass
Sir	Madam
Duke	Dutchess
Emperor	Empress
Milk-man	Milk-maid
Pea-cock	Pea-hen

Masculine	*Feminine*
Step-father	Step-mother
Hero	Heroine
Viceroy	Vicerine
Mr.	Mrs.
Governor	Governess
Master	Mistress
Wizard	Witch
Heir	Heiress
Host	Hostess
Lion	Lioness
Mayor	Mayoress
Actor	Actress
Buck	Doe
Colt	Filly
Dog	Bitch
Horse	Mare
Count	Countess
Hunter	Huntress
Prince	Princess
Abbot	Abbess
God	Goddess
Author	Authoress
Ox	Cow
Widower	Widow
Grand-father	Grand-mother
He-goat	She-goat
Milk-man	Milk-woman
Bridegroom	Bride
Tiger	Tigress
Priest	Priestess
Poet	Poetess
Shepherd	Shepherdess
Nephew	Niece
Stag	Hind

PRONOUNS

The repetition of a noun in a sentence or a set of sentences is really boring. So, instead of repeating the noun, we can use a word (for that noun) called the pronoun.

"A pronoun is a word that we use instead of a noun".

Example:

This is *Sachin. He* plays cricket.

Note: *He* is the pronoun used in place of *Sachin.*

Kinds of Pronouns

1. **Personal pronouns :** A pronoun which is used instead of the name of a person is known as a 'Personal Pronoun'. A list of the 'Personal pronouns' is listed below :

   I, my, mine, me, we   (First Person)

   You, your, yours   (Second Person)

   He, his, him, she, her, hers, it,

   its, they, their, theirs, them   (Third Person)

2. **Demonstrative, Indefinite and Distributive Pronouns :**

   (a) Demonstrative Pronouns : Pronouns used to point out the objects to which they refer are called Demonstrative Pronouns.

   Examples :
   (i)   *This* is a present from my uncle.
   (ii) *These* are merely excuses.
   (iii) Bembay mangoes are better than *those* of Bangaluru.

   (b) Indefinite Pronouns : All pronouns which refer to persons or things in a general way and do not refer to any particular person or thing are called Indefinite Pronouns.

   Examples :
   (i)   *Somebody* has stolen my watch.
   (ii) *Few* escaped unhurt.
   (iii) Did you ask *anybody* to come?

   (c) Distributive Pronouns : Each, either, neither are called distributive pronouns because they refer to persons or things one at a time. For this reason they are always singular and followed by the verb in singular.

   Examples :
   (i)   *Each* of the men received a reward.
   (ii) *These* men received *each* a reward.
   (iii) *Either* of you can go.

3. **Relative Pronouns :** A relative pronoun refers or relates to some noun going before, which is called its Antecedent.

Examples :
(i)   I met Hari *who* used to live here.
(ii) I have found the pen *which* I had lost.
(iii) Here is the book *that* you lent me.

4. **Interrogative Pronouns :** These pronouns, are used for asking questions.

   Examples :
   (i)   *Whose* book is this?
   (ii) *What* will all the neighbours say?
   (iii) *Which* do you prefer, tea or coffee?

   Note : Interrogative pronouns can also be used in asking indirect questions. Consider the following examples :
   (i)   I asked *who* was speaking.
   (ii) Tell me *what* you have done.
   (iii) Say *which* you would like best.

Behaviour of the Pronouns

1. If three pronouns are used together in the same sentence they are arranged in the following order :

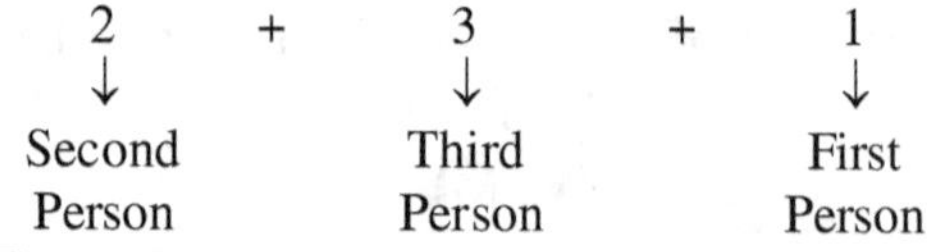

   Examples :
   I, you and he must help *that* poor man.
   (Incorrect)
   You, he and I must help *that* poor man.
   (Correct)

2. When two or more singular nouns are joined by and, the pronoun used for them should be plural.

   Examples :
   Mohan and Sohan are friends. *They* play football. *They* live at Lajpat Nagar.

3. But if these nouns joined by and refer to the same person or thing, the pronoun used should be singular.

   Examples :
   (i)   Delhi, the beautiful city and the capital of India, is famous for *its* historical monuments.
   (ii) The manager and owner of the firm expressed *his* views on the demands of the workers.

4. When two nouns are used with as well as, the pronoun agrees with the first subject.
   Examples :
   (a) Mohan as well as his friends is doing *his* work.
   (b) The students as well as their teachers are doing *their* work.

5. When two singular nouns joined by 'and' are preceded by *each* or *every,* the pronoun used must be singular and should agree in gender with the second noun.
   Examples :
   (a) Every man and every woman will do *her* best for the nation.
   (b) Each boy and each girl went to *her* house.

6. When two nouns are joined by using 'with', the pronoun agrees with the noun coming before 'with'.
   Examples :
   (a) The boy with *his* parents has gone to see a movie.
   (b) The children with *their* parents have gone to picnic.

7. When two different nouns are joined by either.......... or; neither .... nor, the pronoun is used according to the number and gender of the second noun.

Examples :
(a) Either your sister or you have done *your* work.
(b) Neither the students nor the teacher was in *his* class.

8. The pronoun coming after 'than' must be in the same case as that coming before 'than'.
   Examples :
   (a) She plays better than *me*. (Incorrect)
      She plays better than *I*. (Correct)
   (b) His elder brother is more intelligent than *him*. (Incorrect)
      His elder brother is more intelligent than *he*. (Correct)

9. 'Many a' always takes a singular pronoun and singular verb.
   Example :
   Many a soldier has met *his* death in the battle field.

10. 'Who', 'Whose', 'Whom' are used only for persons.
    Examples :
    (a) *Who* is knocking at the door?
    (b) *Whose* pen is this?
    (c) *What* do you want?

11. 'Which' is used for things.
    Example :
    Which game do you like?

MULTIPLE CHOICE QUESTIONS

Directions: *In the following questions choose the correct options to fill the blanks.*

1. The place was so dirty that ..... wished to run away from there.
   A. everybody   B. anybody
   C. few   D. some

2. ..... was there to help me.
   A. Somebody   B. Anything
   C. Anybody   D. Nobody

3. Is there .... to eat?
   A. some   B. something
   C. any   D. few

4. ..... of the students were making a great noise.
   A. Anyone   B. Somebody
   C. Many   D. Nobody

5. ..... of the students can solve this sum.
   A. Someone   B. Anybody
   C. Somebody   D. None

6. ...... of us should try our best to make India a heaven.
   A. Any   B. Somebody
   C. Anybody   D. All

7. ...... of us do not know the real meaning of our lives.
   A. Any   B. Something
   C. Several   D. Many

8. My .... black.
   A. hairs are   B. hair is
   C. hairs shall   D. hair will

9. She saw two .... on the last Sunday.
A. thiefs   B. theifs
C. thieves   D. theives

10. My sister is a ....
A. bacheloress   B. bachelor
C. unmaried   D. spinster

11. One is supposed to do ....
A. our duty   B. their duty
C. one's duty   D. his duty

12. Take anything .... you want.
A. that   B. which
C. than   D. then

13. I cannot tolerate ....
A. separated you
B. your separation
C. separation from you
D. you separated

14. He is .... faithful partner.
A. Yours   B. You
C. Your   D. Your's

15. Ajay is more smart than ....
A. her   B. hers
C. herself   D. she

16. Vivek works harder than ....
A. me   B. I
C. her   D. his

17. They should help ....
A. the poor people   B. the poor
C. the poor persons   D. the poor peoples

18. .... are mad.
A. All his sons   B. His all sons
C. Sons all his   D. All sons his

19. The poor fellow .... to fate.
A. resigned
B. resigned himself
C. resigned itself
D. resigned themselves

20. Nobody will help you but ....
A. I   B. me
C. ours   D. his

21. It is a good chance, You must avail ....
this opportunity.

A. of   B. yourself of
C. for   D. from

22. The person who is elected .... my relative.
A. is   B. he is
C. his   D. him

23. He made ....
A. yours mention   B. mention of you
C. mention for you   D. mention about you

24. .... I know, he is quite faithful.
A. As far as   B. So far as
C. So far this   D. So far so

25. It is a duty of a person to take .... for his
family.
A. pain   B. pains
C. pain-killers   D. pained

26. She does not love .... husband.
A. his   B. her
C. its   D. their

27. Let .... work together.
A. him and me   B. he and I
C. he and him   D. I and me

28. Copper, Silver and Gold ....
A. each will do   B. either will do
C. any one will do   D. any will do

29. Jessica and Roma are very irregular ....
habits.
A. in her   B. in their
C. in its   D. in every

30. One likes to enjoy .... who was a great
poet.
A. The sonnets of Shakespeare
B. Shakespeare's sonnets
C. Sonnets
D. Shakespeare

31. That is the boy .... everybody loves.
A. whom   B. who
C. that   D. whose

32. That is the girl .... won the first prize.
A. whom   B. who
C. whose   D. which

33. That is the man .... purse was lost.
A. who   B. whom
C. whose   D. their

ANSWERS

1	2	3	4	5	6	7	8	9	10
A	D	B	C	D	D	D	B	C	D
11	**12**	**13**	**14**	**15**	**16**	**17**	**18**	**19**	**20**
C	A	C	C	D	B	B	A	B	B
21	**22**	**23**	**24**	**25**	**26**	**27**	**28**	**29**	**30**
B	A	B	A	B	B	A	C	B	A
31	**32**	**33**							
A	B	C							

ARTICLES

The family of the articles has only three members. They are : A, An and The. However, they fall under two groups :

(a) Definite Article *(b)* Indefinite Article

'The' is known as definite article whereas 'a' and 'an' are known as indefinite articles.

Use of the Definite Article 'The'

'The' is used before

1. The superlative degree :
   He is the ablest man of the town.
   (ablest is a superlative degree)

2. The name of states, countries etc. having a descriptive name :
   (i) The J & K is a small state. (J & K is a descriptive name)
   (ii) He lives in the U.S.A. (U.S.A. is a descriptive name)
   (But the Delhi and the America are wrong because neither Delhi nor America is a descriptive name)

3. The names of the scriptures :
   The Gita is a holy book. (Gita is a scripture)

4. Name of newspapers :
   The Tribune is published from Chandigarh.

5. Name of rivers, canals, seas, oceans, bays, gulfs, groups of islands etc. :
   (i) The Ganga is a holy river.
   (ii) The Indian Ocean is the deepest ocean.
   (iii) The Persian Gulf is a narrow gulf.

6. The name of famous buildings :
   The Taj is one of the best buildings in India.

7. The names of nationals, sects and communities:
   (i) The English defeated the Germans in the World War.
   (ii) The rich should help the poor.
   (iii) The Hindus believe in the caste system.

8. Proper nouns used as common nouns :
   (i) Kalidas is the Shakespeare of India.
   (ii) Delhi is the London of India.

9. Famous historical events :
   The Industrial Revolution changed the face of England.

10. The directions and the celestial bodies:
    The sun rises in the east.

11. Titles :
    Akbar, the Great was loved by his subjects.

Do not use 'the'

1. Before languages :
   The English is an international language. (Incorrect)
   English is an international language. (Correct)

2. Before the names of games :
   The hockey is a popular game. (Incorrect)
   Hockey is a popular game. (Correct)

Use of the Indefinite Articles 'A' and 'An'

'A' is used before :

1. All singular common nouns beginning with a consonant :
   (i) A boy sings a song.

(ii) A black and a white cow were grazing in the field.

2. If a word begins with a vowel but gives the sound of a consonant, 'a' should be used before it :
 (i) He was helped in his work by a European.
 (ii) He is a one-eyed man.
 (iii) It is a useful work.

'An' is used as follows :

1. All singular common nouns beginning with a vowel (*i.e.*, a, e, i, o, u) :
 (i) He is an artist.
 (ii) He is an old man.
 (iii) I intend to buy an umbrella.

2. If a word starts with a consonant but gives the sound of a vowel, "an" should be used before it :
 (i) Brutus is an honourable man.
 (ii) He is an honour to his profession.
 (iii) He is an L.L.B.

(iv) He is an M.A.
(v) You will reach there in an hour.

Demonstratives, that, these and those

1. The demonstrative adjectives and pronouns are for objects nearby the speaker:
 this (singular) those (plural)
 and for objects far away from the speaker.
 That (singular) those (plural)

2. Demonstratives are the only adjectives that agree in number with their nouns.
 That hat is nice.
 Those hats are nice.

3. When there is the idea of selection, the pronoun "one" (or "ones") often follows the demonstrative.
 I want a book. I'll get this (one).
 If the demonstrative is followed by an adjective, "one"(or "ones") must be used.
 I want a book. I'll get this big one.

MULTIPLE CHOICE QUESTIONS

Directions: *In the following questions choose the correct options to fill the blanks.*

1. .... will have to be paid for this material.
 A. Half rupee
 B. Half a rupee
 C. A half rupee
 D. An half rupee

2. .... is taking keen interest in India.
 A. The USA
 B. USA
 C. An USA
 D. A USA

3. Only .... can save our country.
 A. the Hitler
 B. a Hitler
 C. Hitler
 D. an Hitler

4. I can run for ....
 A. hundred miles
 B. the hundred miles
 C. a hundred miles
 D. an hundred miles.

5. .... man-eater has been killed.
 A. The
 B. A
 C. An
 D. Either A or B

6. What .... fine idea!
 A. the
 B. an
 C. a
 D. No article

7. .... earth is moving around the sun.
 A. An
 B. A

 C. The
 D. No article

8. This is .... first example while I got.
 A. the
 B. a
 C. an
 D. No article

9. This is .... house which was built during earthquake.
 A. a
 B. an
 C. the
 D. No article

10. .... America is a rich country.
 A. The
 B. An
 C. A
 D. No article

11. .... U.S.A. is a developed country.
 A. A
 B. An
 C. The
 D. No article

12. .... Bible is a holy book.
 A. A
 B. The
 C. An
 D. No article

13. .... rich should help the poor.
 A. The
 B. A
 C. An
 D. No article

14. .... Gold is a costly metal.
 A. The
 B. A
 C. An
 D. No article

15. Kalidas is .... Shakespeare of India.
   A. a   B. an
   C. the   D. No article

16. I cannot do .... difficult work.
   A. a such   B. the such
   C. such the   D. such a

17. How foolish .... plan it is!
   A. a   B. an
   C. the   D. No article

18. An ink is .... useful article.
   A. an   B. a
   C. the   D. No article

19. There are .... husband and wife.
   A. a   B. an
   C. the   D. No article

20. He is learning .... French
   A. the   B. a
   C. an   D. No article

ANSWERS

1	2	3	4	5	6	7	8	9	10
B	A	B	C	D	C	C	A	C	D

11	12	13	14	15	16	17	18	19	20
C	B	A	D	C	D	A	B	D	D

ADJECTIVES & ADVERBS

An Adjective is a word which adds something to the meaning of a noun or a pronoun.

Mridula is an *intelligent* girl.

He has a *black* goat.

He is a *brilliant* student.

She is a *clever* girl.

It is a *beautiful* picture.

In the sentences given above, the words in italics are adjectives.

An Adverb is a word which qualifies the meaning of a Verb, an Adjective or another Adverb.

(*i*) He talks *slowly*.

(*ii*) He is a *very* good student.

(*iii*) He talks *very* slowly.

In sentence (*i*), *slowly* qualifies the verb *talks*.

In sentence (*ii*), *very* qualifies the adjective *good*.

In sentence (*iii*), *very* qualifies the adverb *slowly*.

Adjectives have three degrees of comparison :

1. **Positive Degree :** It expresses the common form of an adjective.

   Example :

   Ram is a *tall* boy.

   In the above sentence *tall* is an adjective and expresses the common form.

2. **Comparative Degree :** It expresses the more of the same form.

Example :

Ram is *taller* than Mahesh.

In the above sentence *taller* is an adjective that expresses the more of the common form of the adjective *tall*.

"When and How to Use" Comparative Degree?

(a) Comparative Degree is used when two persons or two groups of persons or things are compared.

   Examples :

   (a) He is *wiser* than his younger brother.

   (b) This glass is *cleaner* than the other.

(b) When two different qualities in the same person are compared, more is used instead of 'er' to form the comparative. The formula used in this case should be :

   More + Positive Degree

   She is *fairer* than polite.   (Incorrect)

   She is *more fair* than polite.   (Correct)

(c) When selection of one out of two persons or things is meant, the degree of comparison is followed by of and *the* is used before it.

   Example :

   Zia is abler of *the* two sisters.

(d) If two comparatives are used in the same sentence to impress upon an idea, both should be preceded by the definite article.

Examples :
   (i) The higher you go, the cooler it is.
   (ii) The more we get, the more we desire.

(e) When one person or thing is compared with another of the same kind, other is used after the comparative degree. In such sentences other is normally preceded by any or all.

Examples :
   (i) Kalidas is greater than any dramatist. (Incorrect)
   Kalidas is greater than any other dramatist. (Correct)
   (ii) Lead is heavier than all metals. (Incorrect)
   Lead is heavier than all other metals. (Correct)

(f) Senior, junior, superior, inferior, prior, anterior (earlier than) and posterior (later than) are always followed by 'to'.

Examples :
   (i) Ram is senior *to* Mohan by three years.
   (ii) That pen is inferior *to* that.
   (iii) He is junior *to* me in rank.
   (iv) This event was posterior *to* that.

Note: Never use *than* after the above mentioned adjectives.

Important Information

(a) 'Preferable' is also used as an adjective of the comparative degree. As such, it is always followed by *to* and not *a*.
   Death is preferable than dishonour. (Incorrect)
   Death is preferable *to* dishonour. (Correct)

(b) To intensify the Degree of comparison, we use *far* or *much* before the comparative.

Examples :
   (i) This book is *far* better than that.
   (ii) His performance was *much* better than Mohan's.

Warning : Always avoid the use of double comparatives.

Don't say : Ram is more cleverer than his younger brother.

Say: Ram is cleverer than his younger brother.

3. **Superlative Degree :** It expresses the most of the common form of an adjective.
   Example :
   He is the ablest man of the town.

How and when to use the Superlative Degree?

(a) The Superlative Degree is used when more than two persons or things are compared.

(b) The Superlative Degree is generally preceded by 'the' and followed by 'of' in most of the cases or otherwise.

(c) When an adjective of the superlative degree is preceded by a Possessive Adjective or a Noun in the Possessive case, 'the' should not be used before it.
   Example :
   Which is Kalidas' best play?
   It will be a blunder to use 'the' before the Superlative Degree in such cases.
   Don't say : Which is Kalidas' the best play.

(d) To intensify the degree of comparison, *by far* is used before the superlative degree.
   Example :
   India is *by far* the most beautiful country of the world.
   Note: Always avoid the use of double superlatives.
   Don't say : He is the most strongest boy in the class.
   Say : He is the strongest boy in the class.

Use of some Important Adjectives

1. (a) 'Some' is used as follows :
       (i) With countable nouns where it means— a little, a small quantity.
       (ii) In a question which shows some request.
   Examples :
       (i) There is some water in the bottle.
       (ii) Some of the students were absent yesterday.
       (iii) Will you have some milk?
       (iv) Will you buy some fruit for me?

  (b) 'Any' is used as follows :
       (i) In negative sentences.
       (ii) In interrogative sentences.

(iii) After 'Hardly', 'Scarcely' and 'Barely'.

(iv) After 'If'.

Examples :

(i) There is not any sugar in the pot.

(ii) We haven't any rice in the house.

(iii) I have hardly any money.

(iv) There are scarcely any plants in this field.

(v) If there is any danger, blow the whistle.

2. (a) **Older :** Older (and oldest) are used for persons animals and things. But 'Older' and 'Oldest' refer to the persons who do not belong to the same family.

Examples :

(i) Radha is older than Shyama.

(ii) John is the oldest member of the staff.

'Older' and 'Oldest' refer to the persons who do not belong to the same family.

(b) **Elder** (and **eldest**) are used in respect of the members of the same family like sons, daughters, brothers, sisters.

Examples :

(i) My elder sister is a lecturer.

(ii) Meenakshi is the eldest of the three sisters.

Note :

(i) 'Elder' is not followed by 'than'.

(ii) 'Elder' and 'Eldest' cannot be used for things.

3. (a) **'Few'** is negative and is the opposite of 'Many'. It means 'not many'.

(b) **'A few'** is positive and means 'some at least'. It is the opposite of 'None'.

(c) **'The few'** means 'minority' and suggests 'whether there is'.

Examples :

(i) We have few holidays in school.

(ii) Only a few boys will fail in the examination.

(iii) The few poems that he wrote are very popular.

4. (a) **Further** means 'something additional'.

(b) **Farther** means 'a greater distance'.

Examples :

(i) Further discussion will be held in the office of the principal.

(ii) Amritsar is farther from Delhi than Ambala.

5. (a) **Little** is negative. It means, 'not much', or 'hardly any'.

(b) **A little** is positive. It means 'some quantity'.

(c) **The little** denotes quantity. It means, 'not much but all that is, or whatever quantity there is'.

Examples :

(i) There is little hope of his success.

(ii) He knows a little of everything.

(iii) I have spent the little money I had.

(iv) The little knowledge of shoe-making proved very useful to me.

6. (a) **'Much'** expresses 'quantity'.

(b) **'Many'** expresses 'number'.

(c) **'Many a'**—'Singular noun' and 'Singular verb' are used with 'many a'.

Examples :

(i) There is not *much* water in the jug.

(ii) *Many* boys are absent today.

(iii) *Many* a battle has been fought on the soil of India.

7. (a) **'Less'** denotes 'in a small degree'.

(b) **'Fewer'** denotes 'number'.

Examples :

(i) He devotes less time to his studies.

(ii) There are no fewer than ten chairs in this room.

8. (a) **'Each'** is used for a single number of 'two persons' or 'things'.

(b) **'Every'** is used for a single number of 'many persons' or 'things'.

Examples :

(i) Each boy must take part in games.

(ii) There are only two poets. Each poet recited his poem.

(iii) Every man dies in this world.

(iv) Every man is expected to do his duty.

9. (a) **'Either'** means one of the two or both.

(b) **'Neither'** is negative of the either.

Examples :

(i) You may buy either of these two chairs.

(ii) Neither of them could speak on the stage.

10. (a) '**Later**' expresses 'late in time'.
    (b) '**Latter**' means 'second in position or order'.
    Examples :
        (i)   My father reached later than I expected.
        (ii) The latter position was better than the former.

Use of some Important Adverbs

1. (a) Also, too, enough:
        (i)   He taught English. Also, he edited the school magazine
        (ii) He is a writer and also he is a painter.
        (iii) He is too obstinate to listen to any reason.
        (iv) This is too difficult a piece for the junior students.
        (v)   Sarla was kind enough to help the poor.
        (vi) He is brave enough to help the truth.
        Note: 'Too' is used in a negative sense, but enough is used in a positive sense.
    (b) Fairly and rather: Both suggest the meaning 'moderately'. But, mainly 'fairly' is used with the words that denote a positive meaning and rather is used with the words that denote a negative meaning:
        (i)   Rita did fairly well in that competition, but her performance was rather poor in sports.
        (ii) Mona is fairly rich, but she is rather stingy.
        Note: 'Rather' can also be used in a positive sense.
        (i)   This is a rather interesting job.
        (ii) That boy is rather smart.
    (c) Hardly, barely, scarcely: These words mostly convey the negative suggestions and are almost similar.
        (i)   I have hardly any strength now.
        (ii) There was barely any supply to the township,
        (iii) There were scarcely a hundred guests present.
        Note: With slight variance in the meaning, the words given above convey the idea of 'very little', 'not enough', 'lack of quantity and number'.
    (d) Yet, Still: These adverbs can often be used to connect the sentence units:
        (i)   He has been defeated many times in the contest; still he wants to be a competitor.
        (ii) Mona was sick; yet she went on doing her work.
    (e) Alone:
        (i)   He alone (none else) is capable of handling that fire,
        (ii) He hunted all alone in the forest. (not in any company)

Special Note:
    (a) Apart from their conventional positions the adverbs might be used in different positions with different meanings and angles.
        (i)   He had only four books.
        (ii) John only contacted his friend in need.
        (iii) He greeted me only.
        (iv) Only he greeted me there.
    (b) Inversion: Some adverbs can be inverted *i.e.* placed in the beginning of the sentence and then be followed by an interrogative form. The most common of these adverb are: so, seldom, never, nowhere, under no circumstances, hardly, scarcely etc.
        (i)   So big was the bus that it could not enter the narrow lane.
        (ii) Hardly had he reached the station when he received the message.

MULTIPLE CHOICE QUESTIONS

Directions: *In the following questions choose the correct options to fill the blanks.*

1. The girl whom you met is the .... sister of Ravi.
    A. eldest   B. elder
    C. older   D. oldest

2. The historical place is ....
    A. seeing worth

B. worthy of seeing
C. worth seeing
D. worthy seeing

3. These flowers smell ....
   A. sweet   B. sweetly
   C. more sweetly   D. sweetest

4. .... aspirant cannot pass the entrance examination.
   A. Each   B. Every
   C. All   D. No

5. Harivansh Rai .... second Shakespeare.
   A. is a   B. is
   C. is the   D. is an

6. .... student in the class got prizes.
   A. Each and every   B. Every and each
   C. Every   D. Never

7. It is .... picture than the one we saw last Monday.
   A. interesting   B. much interesting
   C. more interesting   D. most interesting

8. She is clever ....
   A. that her mother is
   B. as her mother is
   C. to her mother is
   D. than her mother is

9. They will get ....
   A. Red, green and black paper
   B. Red, green black paper
   C. Red and green and black paper
   D. Red green black paper

10. Health is .... wealth.
   A. preferable to
   B. more preferable than
   C. more preferable to
   D. most preferable then

11. .... water that was in the jug evaporated.
   A. Little   B. The little
   C. Small   D. A small

12. He has not sung .... songs.
   A. much   B. most
   C. more   D. many

13. Srishti has searched .... office.
   A. whole the   B. the whole
   C. a whole   D. some whole

14. Premchand was .... best and ...... famous writer.
   A. a, the most   B. the, a most
   C. the, more   D. the, the most

15. William Shakespeare is famous as ....
   A. a poet and a dramatist
   B. a poet and dramatist
   C. the poet and the dramatist
   D. a poet and the dramatist

16. What does .... leader suggest?
   A. other   B. another
   C. others   D. anothers

17. He .... money.
   A. has few   B. have few
   C. has little   D. have little

18. The .... boys are rewarded.
   A. first two   B. two first
   C. firsts two   D. two's first

19. He is .... brave.
   A. stronger than
   B. stronger then
   C. more strong then
   D. more strong than

20. No sooner said ....
   A. so done   B. and done
   C. then done   D. but done

21. She returned .... than I had thought.
   A. quickly   B. more quicker
   C. more quickly   D. quicker

22. He is .... foolish person.
   A. rather the   B. a rather
   C. rather a   D. rather

23. This pen .... rupees.
   A. costs twenty
   B. twenty costs only
   C. costs only twenty
   D. only costs twenty

24. It is .... pride.
   A. nothing else but
   B. nothing else than
   C. else nothing than
   D. but

25. This tea is .... to drink.
   A. too hot   B. very hot
   C. enough hot   D. much hot

ANSWERS

1	2	3	4	5	6	7	8	9	10
A	C	A	B	A	C	C	C	A	A

11	12	13	14	15	16	17	18	19	20
B	D	B	D	B	B	C	A	D	C

21	22	23	24	25
C	C	C	A	A

DETERMINERS

Determiners are actually Adjectives. They are always followed by nouns.

Determiners are of the following kinds:

1. Demonstrative Determiners
   this, that, these, those

2. Possessive Determiners
   my, our, your, his, her, its, their

3. Quantitative Determiners
   some, any, much, enough, sufficient, whole, a little, the little, little, all, both

4. Numerical Determiners
   a few, some, few, the few, any, several, many, no, etc.

   One, two, three ...   (Cardinals)

   First, second, third ...   (Ordinals)

5. Distributive Determiners
   either, neither

6. Articles
   Indefinite: a, an

   Definite: the

MULTIPLE CHOICE QUESTIONS

Directions: *In the following questions choose the correct options to fill the blanks.*

1. Give me .... rice.
   A. some
   B. few
   C. a few
   D. any

2. .... sheep grazing on the slope of the hill had gone away.
   A. Any
   B. The few
   C. This
   D. Much

3. Have you got .... magazines to read?
   A. all
   B. much
   C. some
   D. little

4. I have .... money that I want to spend on shares.
   A. any
   B. much
   C. less
   D. some

5. There is .... owl on the branch of the tree.
   A. a
   B. the
   C. an
   D. some

6. My brother is .... MBA.
   A. a
   B. an
   C. the
   D. any

7. Have you got .... cheese?
   A. some
   B. many
   C. a few
   D. few

8. No, I have not got .... cheese.
   A. many
   B. few
   C. any
   D. some

9. There is only .... milk left in the bottle.
   A. enough
   B. few
   C. much
   D. a little

10. There is .... hope of his recovery.
    A. any
    B. little
    C. many
    D. few

11. .... dogs were barking at the strangers.
    A. Some
    B. Any
    C. Much
    D. Less

12. The girl bought her father .... juice.
   A. few   B. some
   C. any   D. many

13. You should take .... honey everyday.
   A. any   B. many
   C. a little   D. a few

14. .... boy was punished by the teacher.
   A. Either   B. All
   C. Any   D. Many

15. .... girl was asked to join the army.
   A. None   B. Neither
   C. All   D. Any

16. .... water in the jug has been drunk by Mohan.

   A. The little   B. The few
   C. A few   D. Few

17. I shall play .... piano at the party.
   A. some   B. any
   C. the   D. few

18. .... labourers were found dead in the mine.
   A. Any   B. Fewer
   C. Many   D. Less

19. Could I borrow .... umbrella?
   A. our   B. your
   C. yours   D. my

20. My brother is standing in the .... row.
   A. any   B. many
   C. some   D. first

ANSWERS

1	2	3	4	5	6	7	8	9	10
A	B	C	D	C	B	A	C	D	B

11	12	13	14	15	16	17	18	19	20
A	B	C	A	B	A	C	C	B	D

THE VERB

A Verb is a word that tells something about the action or state of or happenning to a person or thing.

A Verb tells the following:

1. What a person or thing does.
   Sachin goes to school daily.
   The bell *rang* loudly.
   Many birds fly in the sky.
   She *sang* a song.

2. What a person or thing is.
   India *is* the biggest democracy in the world.
   Ram Mehar *is* very rich.
   They *are* happy.

3. What is done to a person or thing.
   You *are liked* by all.
   Two thieves *were arrested.*
   Four students *were punished* by the teacher.

4. What happens to a person or thing.
   His maternal uncle *died* last week.
   Two ships *sank* yesterday.
   Leaves *turn* yellow in autumn.

5. What a person or thing has, had, and so on.
   I *have* a new car.
   He *had* a scooter last year.
   He *has* several cows and goats.

It goes without saying that a verb is the most important part of a sentence. No sentence is complete without a Verb.

Important Information

1. If two or more singular nouns are joined by 'and' the verb used will be plural.

   Example:
   (i) He and I were going to the market.
   (ii) Ram and Mohan are friends.

2. If two singular nouns joined by 'and' points out to the same thing or person, the verb used must be singular.

   Example:
   (i) Rice and curry is the favourite food of the Punjabis.
   (ii) The Collector and District Magistrate is away.

3. In case two subjects are joined by 'as well as' the verb agrees with the first subject.

   Example :
   (i) Kanta as well as her children is playing.
   (ii) Children as well as their mother are playing.

In the case of first sentence the verb (is) agrees with Kanta and in the case of second sentence the verb (are) agrees with the children.

4. 'Neither', 'Either', 'Every', 'Each', 'Everyone', and 'Many a' are followed by a singular verb.
   Example :
   (i) Either of the plans is to be adopted.
   (ii) Neither of the two brothers is sure to pass.
   (iii) Every student is expected to be obedient.
   (iv) Everyone of them desires this.
   (v) Many a person is drowned in the sea.

5. If two subjects are joined by 'Either .... or' / 'Neither .... nor', the verb agrees with the subject near to it.
   Example :
   (i) Either my brother or I am to do this work.
   (ii) Neither he nor they are prepared to do this work.

6. 'A great many' is always followed by a 'plural noun' and a 'plural verb'. For example :
   A great many students have been declared successful.

7. Similarly if two subjects are joined by 'with', 'together with', 'no less than', in addition to 'and not', etc. the verb agrees with the first subject.
   Example :
   (i) The boy with his parents has arrived.
   (ii) He, no less than I, is to blame.

8. Nouns, plural in form, but singular in meaning, take a singular verb.
   Example :
   This news was broadcast from television yesterday.

MULTIPLE CHOICE QUESTIONS

Directions: *In the following questions choose the correct options to fill the blanks.*

1. The bus with all its passengers .... lost.
   A. were   B. was
   C. are   D. would

2. You as well as I .... responsible for this work.
   A. am   B. are
   C. was   D. is

3. Raghava like all his companions .... a spoiled child.
   A. are   B. were
   C. is   D. will be

4. Pen and ink .... required for me.
   A. are   B. were
   C. is   D. has required

5. Every girl and every boy .... attended the seminar.
   A. have   B. has
   C. is   D. are

6. Not only she but all her sisters ...... been married.
   A. has   B. have
   C. is   D. are

7. There .... nothing but miseries in life.
   A. is   B. are
   C. were   D. will be

8. Neither prose nor poem .... given.
   A. were   B. was
   C. has   D. have

9. Either he or I .... wrong.
   A. is   B. are
   C. am   D. were

10. Either Sulekha or Rekha .... coming here.
    A. are   B. is
    C. were   D. have

11. .... the child or his parents to blame?
    A. Is   B. Are
    C. Were   D. Has

12. You and I .... neighbours.
    A. am   B. are
    C. was   D. has

13. The house with all its belongings ..... sold away.
    A. were   B. are
    C. was   D. must

14. Either water or juice .... required.
    A. is   B. are
    C. were   D. has

15. There were not as many tables as .... required.
    A. was   B. were
    C. is   D. are

16. They each .... a book.
- A. have
- B. are
- C. has
- D. is

17. He and I .... class friends.
- A. is
- B. am
- C. was
- D. are

18. She as well as I .... guilty.
- A. is
- B. are
- C. am
- D. must be

19. Purushottam .... not read more on this chapter.
- A. needs
- B. has been need
- C. need
- D. had been need

20. He came .... to his aunt.
- A. run
- B. running
- C. to run
- D. in run

21. She dislikes .... meat.
- A. eat to
- B. to eat
- C. eating
- D. to eating

22. He likes ....
- A. sing to
- B. singing
- C. to sing
- D. to singing

23. We are ready .... the match.
- A. play to
- B. to playing
- C. playing
- D. to play

24. .... is injurious to health.
- A. Smoking
- B. To smoke
- C. To smoking
- D. Smoke to

25. He loves .... raw vegetables.
- A. eaten
- B. eating
- C. to eating
- D. eat to

26. He seemed .... finished his homework.
- A. have to
- B. to have
- C. having
- D. to having

ANSWERS

1	2	3	4	5	6	7	8	9	10
B	B	C	C	B	B	A	B	C	B
11	**12**	**13**	**14**	**15**	**16**	**17**	**18**	**19**	**20**
A	B	C	A	B	A	D	A	C	B
21	**22**	**23**	**24**	**25**	**26**				
C	B	D	A	B	B				

CONJUNCTIONS

A conjunction is a word which connects words, clauses or sentences.

Look at the following sentences.

  (i) He bought apples *and* mangoes.

  (ii) God made the country *and* man made the town.

  (iii) The door was open *but* there was no one in the house.

  (iv) He knows that I am here *and* that I want to see him.

In the sentence (i), *and* connects two words—*apples* and *mangoes*.

In the sentence (ii), *and* connects two sentences—*God made the country* and *man made the town*.

In the sentence (iii), *but* connects two sentences—*The door was open* and *there was no one in the house.*

In the sentence (iv), *and* connects two clauses—*that I am here* and *that I want to see him.*

The main coordinating conjunctions are:

and, but, for, or, nor, also, either ..... or, neither ..... nor.

There are some conjunctions which are used in pairs. They are:

either .... or, ... neither .... nor, both .... and, though .... yet, whether .... or, not only .... but also.

Example: *Either* take it *or* leave it.

It is *neither* useful *nor* ornamental.

They *both* like *and* respect me.

Though he is suffering from high fever, *yet* he does not cry.

He does not care *whether* you go *or* stay.

He is *not only* doltish, *but also* obstinate.

The conjunctions which are used in pairs in this way, are called correlative conjunctions, or merely correlatives.

Use of Important Conjunctions

1. **As soon as :** As soon as denotes simultaneous time.

   Example : As soon as he saw his enemy, he took to his heels.

2. **No sooner .... than :**
   (a) 'No sooner' is always followed by 'than'.
   (b) Please remember that 'No sooner' is always followed by do/does/did. As such only first form of the verb should be used after the subject.

   Example :

   No sooner did he see his enemy than he took to his heels.

3. **Hardly :** Hardly is followed by when.
   Examples :
   (i) Hardly had I left the house when it started raining.
   (ii) We had hardly come into the room when his father began chastising him.
   Note :
   A. Hardly is never followed by than.
   B. 'Scarcely' can also be used in the sense and manner of 'Hardly'.

4. **Lest :** Lest is used in the sense of so that .... not. It is always followed by should. Lest is negative in sense. Hence 'not' should never be used with it.
   Example :
   Work hard lest you should fail.
   Note : 'Lest' is always followed by 'should' and not 'may'.

5. **Unless :** Unless expresses condition. It is also used in the negative sense. Use of 'not' is not allowed with unless because unless is already in the negative sense.
   Example :
   Unless you labour hard you will not pass.

6. **Until :** 'Until' expresses time. It means 'till not'.
   Example :
   Wait here until I return.
   Note : Until is in the negative sense. So 'not' should not be used with it. Example :
   Wait here until I do not return.   (Incorrect)
   Wait here until I return.   (Correct)

7. **As well as :** When two subjects are joined by 'as well as', the verb always agrees with the first subject.
   Examples :
   (i) The teacher as well as students is playing.
   (ii) Students as well as the teacher are playing.
   Note : 'Both' and 'as well as' cannot be used together in the same sentence.
   Examples :
   Both Sita as well as Kanta are beautiful.
                                          (Incorrect)
   Sita as well as Kanta is beautiful.   (Correct)
   Both Sita and Kanta are beautiful. (Correct)

8. **As if :** 'As if' is used in the sense of pretension. While using 'as if' in a sentence, we should see that even the third person singular subject gets 'were'.
   Example :
   He talks as if he were mad.

9. **Till :** Till expresses time. Till is always used in the affirmative.
   Example :
   We did not come back till sunset.

10. **Rather than :** 'Rather than' is used in the sense of 'preference'. 'Rather' is always followed by 'than'.
    Example :
    I would rather die than submit.

11. **As long as/so long as :** Both express time during which an action or event takes place.
    Example :
    As long as there is life, there is hope.

12. **However :** It is both a subordinate and co-ordinate clause.
    Examples :
    (a) Mala worked hard, she however, failed.
    (b) However hard he may work, he cannot pass.

13. **Such as :** 'Such as' gives us the sense of 'like'. Such is always followed by 'as'.
    Example :
    Life is such a puzzle as cannot be solved.

MULTIPLE CHOICE QUESTIONS

Directions: *In the following questions choose the correct options to fill the blanks.*

1. Neither he .... his friend is good.
   A. or B. and
   C. but D. nor

2. The officer asked the peon .... why he was late.
   A. that B. if
   C. but D. No word needed

3. Both Ajay .... Vijay are intelligent.
   A. or B. nor
   C. and D. No word needed

4. No Sooner did the thief see the public .... he ran away.
   A. then B. and
   C. but D. than

5. Abhinav .... his brothers was going to Mumbai.
   A. but B. yet
   C. No word needed D. together with

6. He behaves .... he were the captain of the team.
   A. as if B. as
   C. No word needed D. that

7. Either Rupali .... Sonali is going to attend the meeting.
   A. and B. but
   C. nor D. or

8. Neither Nirmal .... Ashwinee is going to listen the speech.
   A. and B. but
   C. nor D. or

9. Ravi .... Prakash are going to Kolkata.
   A. or B. nor
   C. but D. and

10. Rice .... curry is my usual breakfast.
    A. and B. but
    C. then D. than

11. Hardly had he left .... his brother came.
    A. then B. than
    C. when D. that

12. I would rather have a copy .... a book.
    A. then B. than
    C. when D. that

13. He is no other .... my friend.
    A. then B. than
    C. when D. but

14. He saw a snake ....he awoke.
    A. then B. when
    C. than D. No word needed

15. Ten years have passed .... my grandmother died.
    A. since B. when
    C. then D. than

16. She is .... good .... bad.
    A. either, not B. neither, or
    C. neither, nor D. neither, than

17. The cellphone is both cheap .... best.
    A. than B. and
    C. then D. or

18. No sooner did the rogue see the police .... he disappeared.
    A. then B. than
    C. so D. because

19. Srishti will go .... Sanju goes.
    A. if B. than
    C. then D. although

20. She is wise .... timid.
    A. and B. yet
    C. but D. however

21. Make hay .... the sun shines.
    A. though B. while
    C. after D. before

22. He is so weak .... he cannot walk.
    A. but B. that
    C. then D. so

23. Although he is rich, ... he is unhappy.
    A. but B. yet
    C. so D. still

24. Wait here .... I come back.
    A. till B. until
    C. before D. after

25. He is my friend .... I shall help him.
A. so
B. hence
C. that is why
D. therefore

26. He must go away .... he will be beaten.
A. otherwise
B. and
C. or
D. else

27. God loves good men .... good men love God.
A. and
B. or
C. that
D. those

28. He was late .... he was not punished.
A. but
B. yet
C. still
D. therefore

29. Walk slowly ...., you may fall.
A. and
B. or
C. so
D. otherwise

30. Work hard, ... you will fail.
A. and
B. or
C. otherwise
D. else

ANSWERS

1	2	3	4	5	6	7	8	9	10
D	D	C	D	D	A	D	C	D	A

11	12	13	14	15	16	17	18	19	20
C	B	B	B	A	C	B	B	A	C

21	22	23	24	25	26	27	28	29	30
B	B	B	A	B	C	A	C	D	D

PREPOSITIONS

A *Preposition* is a word which is placed before a noun or a pronoun to show its relation to some other word in the sentence.

1. I saw a goat *in* the field.
2. I am fond *of* hot coffee.

In sentence 1, the word *in* shows the relation between two things—*goat* and *field*.

In sentence 2, the word *of* shows the relation between the attribute expressed by the adjective *found* and *tea*.

The words *in* and *of* are here used as prepositions.

The noun or pronoun which is used with a preposition is called its object. The noun or pronoun is in the objective case. It is governed by the preposition. Now it is absolutely clear that in sentence 1, the noun *field* is in the objective case. The word *field* is governed by the preposition *in*.

A preposition may have two or more objects.

The road runs over *hill* and *plain*.

Here, the words *hill* and *plain* are used as objects.

Use of Important Prepositions

1. Among, Between

'**Among**' is used for more than two persons or things; '**Between**' is used only for two.

Examples :

(i) Distribute these sweets *among* the poor students of the class.
(ii) Distribute these books *between* Ram and Shyam.

2. Among, In

'**Among**' is used before collective plural nouns. '**In**' is used before collective singular nouns.

Examples :

(i) I found him standing *among* the crowd.
(ii) I saw him in the crowd.

3. Beside, Besides

'**Beside**' means 'by the side of'. '**Besides**' means 'in addition to'.

Examples :

(i) The daughter was sitting *beside* her mother.
(ii) *Besides* his relatives, he invited his friends also.

4. In, Within

'**In**' means at the expiry of a period of time in future, '**Within**' means before the expiry of a period of time in any tense.

Examples :
(i)   She will return *in* a week.
(ii) I shall finish my work *within* a weak.

5. On, Upon
   'On' is used for things at rest; **'Upon'** is used for things in motion.
   Examples :
   (i)   He is sitting *on* the floor.
   (ii) The dog sprang *upon* the table.

6. By, With
   'By' denotes the agent or doer, **'With'** denotes the instrument with which anything is done.
   Examples :
   (i)   The bird was killed *by* the hunter with an arrow.
   (ii) He beat the dog *with* a stick.
   (iii) I shall reach here *by* five o'clock.

7. After, In
   'After' means at the end of a period of time in the past. **'In'** means at the end of a period of time in future.
   Examples :
   (i)   I shall return your book *in* a week.
   (ii) He returned the book *after* a week.

8. For, From, Since
   'For' is used before a noun denoting a period of time with all the tenses. **'From'** is used before a noun or phrase denoting a point of time, it is used in all the tenses. **'Since'** is used before a noun or phrase denoting some point of time and is always produced by a verb in the perfect continuous tense or third form of a verb.
   Examples :
   (i)   We have been playing cards *for* two hours.
   (ii) She stayed with her uncle *from* the 15th of March to the 15th of May.
   (iii) I have been reading this book *since* morning.

9. Above, Over
   'Above' means 'higher from', **Over** is used in the following four senses :
   (i)   In the sense of 'above' :
         At noon, the sun is *over* our heads.

(ii) In the sense of 'beyond' :
      I cannot get *over* my disappointment.
(iii) In the sense of 'Superiority' :
      God *over* all blesses for ever more.
(iv) In the sense of 'Conclusion' :
      It is all *over* with me.

10. At, Towards
   'At' denotes the idea of aim, **'Towards'** denotes the idea of destination.
   Examples :
   (i)   He threw the stone *at* the cat.
   (ii) He went *towards* the house.

11. At, In, On
   'At' is used as follows :
   (i)   'At' is used with small towns and villages.
         Examples :
         (a) He was born *at* Sonepat.
         (b) He lives *at* village Bangra. (Bangra is a village)
   (ii) 'At' is used before a noun denoting a definite point of time.
         Example :
         He called on me *at* 9 p.m. yesterday.
         'In' is used as follows :
   (iii) 'In' is used with the names of big cities, provinces and countries.
         Examples :
         (a) His father lives *in* England.
         (b) His younger brother lives *in* Calcutta.
   (iv) 'In' is used before the names of months and years.
         Example :
         His elder sister was born *in* 1972 *in* the month of May.
         'On' is used with dates and names of days.
         Examples :
         (a) I joined college *on* the 26th April.
         (b) He will leave for Kolkata *on* Wednesday next.

Important Information

1. 'In' is also used in the following phrases :
   In the morning; In the evening, In winter, In summer.

2. **'In'** also denotes a place inside anything.
   He travelled *in* a crowded bus.
3. **'At'** is used in the following phrases :
   At home, *At* the station, *At* work, *At* play.

12. **Below, Beneath**
    Below means 'of lower level in position, dignity and expectation' etc. *Beneath* means 'under'.
    Examples :
    (i) It is *below* my dignity to talk to her.
    (ii) They rested *beneath* the shade of a tree.

13. **In, Into, To**
    'In' expresses Rest or Motion inside anything. **'Into'** expresses Motion towards the inside of anything or change from one medium to another. **'To'** denotes motion from one place to another.
    Examples :
    (i) The boys are *in* the room.
    (ii) Translate this passage from English *into* Hindi.

(iii) Every morning he goes *to* the temple.

14. **Till, By, Of, Off**
    - 'Till' means upto or not earlier than.
    - 'By' means not later than.
    - 'Of' shows cause, source, separation, quality, contents, possession, apposition, point of reference, space in time etc.
    - 'Off' shows separation at a near distance, and detached condition.

Consider the following examples:
(i) I shall work *till* 5 a.m.
(ii) Madhu died *of* cancer.
(iii) The nib *of* the pen is made *of* gold.
(iv) He presented me a bottle *of* perfume.
(v) Our principal is a man *of* principle.
(vi) He lived in the house *of* his friend.
(vii) *By* this time tomorrow, I'll have finished my job.
(viii) My house is *off* the road.
(ix) The book fell *off* the table.

MULTIPLE CHOICE QUESTIONS

Directions: *Tick the correct preposition for the blank in each of the following sentences.*

1. He applied ...... the manager.
   A. for
   B. to
   C. with
   D. by
2. Trust ...... God and do the right.
   A. in
   B. for
   C. to
   D. with
3. She is worthy ...... a prize.
   A. with
   B. for
   C. to
   D. of
4. Mr. Gomes has no taste ...... music.
   A. of
   B. for
   C. with
   D. to
5. You are hard ...... hearing.
   A. at
   B. of
   C. with
   D. for
6. He is sure ...... his success
   A. for
   B. with
   C. on
   D. of

7. Preeti was warned ...... the danger ahead.
   A. for
   B. at
   C. of
   D. about
8. I am thankful ...... you for a good advice.
   A. for
   B. with
   C. to
   D. of
9. Deepak would not surrender ...... the police.
   A. with
   B. to
   C. for
   D. on
10. The small plant in your lawn is very sensitive ...... touch.
    A. on
    B. with
    C. to
    D. about
11. Divya was sure to succeed ..... the examination.
    A. for
    B. in
    C. to
    D. with
12. Geeta was jealous ...... Ravina's beauty.
    A. to
    B. with
    C. for
    D. of

13. He was ignorant ..... what was happening there.
    A. for   B. of
    C. to   D. with

14. Your pen is inferior ...... mine.
    A. than   B. with
    C. from   D. to

15. Reenu is no match ...... Meenu.
    A. to   B. for
    C. with   D. upon

16. It is necessary ...... you to apply for this job.
    A. on   B. with
    C. for   D. to

17. Be loyal ...... your country.
    A. for   B. to
    C. on   D. with

18. Mukesh is junior ...... me.
    A. than   B. to
    C. from   D. of

19. Deepika was innocent ...... the crime.
    A. of   B. with
    C. from   D. to

20. I am desirous.... joining the Indian cricket team.
    A. for   B. of
    C. to   D. on

ANSWERS

1	2	3	4	5	6	7	8	9	10
B	A	D	B	B	D	D	D	B	D

11	12	13	14	15	16	17	18	19	20
B	D	B	D	B	D	B	B	A	B

SYNONYMS

A synonym is a word which conveys a meaning similar to the given word.

REMEMBER

Words	Synonyms
Add	Increase
Adequate	Enough
Adjust	Adapt
All	Aggregate
Allow	Permit
Abode	Dwelling
Apt	Proper
Assess	Appraise
Accuse	Calumniate
Abashed	Timid
Annoy	Displease
Ample	Enough, Sufficient
Amplify	Increase
Apathetic	Unenthusiastic
Accost	Address
Authentic	True

Words	Synonyms
Adjust	Fit
Approve	Assent, Allow, Accept
Adapt	Conform
Adversary	Opponent, Rival, Competitor
Beat	Whack
Benign	Kind
Breeze	Zephyr
Baffle	Puzzle
Booty	Spoil
Beauty	Charm
Beast	Animal
Bandit	Robber
Blaze	Shine
Bond	Tie
Bend	Twist
Bate	Diminish
Beg	Plead
Barbaric	Wild, Savage
Bashful	Shy, Reserved

Words	Synonyms	Words	Synonyms
Begin	Start	Dwell	Live, Dilate
Blend	Mix, Mingle	Declare	Pronounce
Bizarre	Funny	Drunk	Flushed
Below	Under	Deficient	Lacking
Bedevil	Confuse	Damn	Condemn, Curse
Bemoan	Lament	Decrease	Diminish
Babble	Nonsense	Destruction	Devastation
Blame	Fault	Efficient	Competent
Behaviour	Demeanour	Ethnic	Racial
Call	Accost	Enthral	Enslave
Copy	Imitate	Earnest	Serious
Close	Shut	Envious	Jealous
Caress	Love	Ending	Final
Camp	Stay	Egg	Incite
Connect	Attach	Extempore	At once
Cut	Injure, Curtail	Extensive	Far-ranging
Cling	Stick	Extra	Surplus
Conical	Funny	Existence	Life
Convey	Carry	Exceed	Overstep
Conspicuous	Prominent	Enormous	Vast
Cheerful	Happy, Pleasant	Excessive	Superfluous
Curtail	Decrease	Free	Unhindered
Cheerless	Sad, Dejected	Frigid	Cold
Curious	Strange	Feed	Cater
Circumstance	Factor, Situation, Condition	Fame	Reputation
Competent	Capable	Frame	Make
Congruent	Overlapping	First	Initial
Cope	Deal, Endure	Frighten	Terrorise, Intimidate
Confident	Sure	Fervent	Fervid
Complex	Intricate	Fall	Decline
Cajole	Coax, Flatter	Feeble	Frail
Cunning	Crafty	Fickle	Changeable
Delectable	Joyful, Delightful	Finish	Conclude
Devilish	Diabolical	Fraud	Deception
Delicate	Soft	Forgiving	Placable
Devil	Fiend	Grow	Develop
Delay	Postpone	Greed	Avidity
Dislike	Repugnance	Greet	Welcome
Destroy	Ruin	Grave	Serious
		Group	Constellation

Words	Synonyms
Given	Bestowed
Gratitude	Thankfulness
Have	Possess
Hire	Rent
Hit	Strike
Handsome	Beautiful
Hinder	Prevent
Heap	Pile
Hope	Expect
Hard	Harsh
Help	Aid
Hymn	Song
Henpecked	Enslaved
Hoodwink	Mystify, Cheat
Humble	Polite, Urbane, Modest
Harass	Vex, Trouble
Impart	Instil
Intact	Untouched
Instal	Establish
Indict	Impeach
Imitate	Ape
Instigate	Incite
Initiate	Start, Introduce
Inimical	Unfriendly
Insufferable	Intolerable
Impartiality	Justice
Jolly	Merry
Joyful	Delectable
Join	Conjoin
Kind	Benign
Kill	Murder
Kindred	Similar
Kinship	Relationship
Keen	Sharp
Knowledge	Scholarship
Lazy	Slothful
Large	Substantial, Gargantuan
Listless	Careless, Lackadaisical
Lax	Loose
Little	Small
Lifelike	Realistic

Words	Synonyms
Lofty	High
Lenient	Soft, Gentle
Lacking	Deficient, Wanting
Lessen	Decrease
Middleclass	Bourgeois
Mitigate	Lessen, Abate
Modesty	Humility, Lowliness
Mix	Mingle, Blend
Mixture	Mingling
Mixed	Assorted
Modify	Decrease
Mean	Imply
Multifarious	Varied
Miscarry	Abort
Note	Notice
Noble	Stately
Native	Indigenous
Needful	Necessary
Notify	Declare
Nervous	Shaky, Tremulous, Timid
Natural	Spontaneous
Near	Close
Normal	Natural
Offend	Displease
Oppress	Persecute, Tyrannize
Opponent	Adversary
Obstruct	Hinder, Check
Offence	Fault
Offender	Villain
Overstep	Exceed
Overlapping	Congruent
Occult	Mystic
Profane	Unholy
Patience	Forbearance
Pornographic	Obscene
Plenitude	Abundance
Prominent	Important
Prodigal	Spender
Procrastinate	Postpone
Promote	Develop, Honour
Persecute	Tyrannise

Words	*Synonyms*
Profess	Claim
Pliant	Flexible
Plebian	Common
Polished	Sophisticated
Quake	Shake
Quit	Leave
Queer	Eccentric
Quell	Suppress
Quantify	Allot
Reply	Answer
Relinquish	Retire
Read	Peruse
Relation	Reference
Render	Do
Remainder	Residuals
Repeat	Reiterate
Repentant	Contrite
Retaliative	Retaliatory
Rumour	Hearsay
Reveal	Divulge
Ritualistic	Ceremonious
Soft	Delicate
Sort	Kind, Choose, Select
Selfish	Egoistic
Sensual	Earthly
Suppress	Quell, Check
Stimulate	Provoke
Tasteless	Insipid
Travel	Journey
True	Authentic, Faithful, Truthful
Turbulence	Turmoil
Tragedy	Calamity
Tasteful	Tasty, Delicious
Touching	Painful
Thankful	Grateful
Tremendous	Great, Huge
Tough	Strong
Terminate	Conclude, End
Theory	Doctrine
Tell	Relate
Tremble	Shake, Shiver
Urge	Spur

Words	*Synonyms*
Unbeaten	Unsubdued
Use	Utilize, Practise
Underhand	Unfair, Undue
Unfair	Unjust
Unravel	Reveal, Divulge
Unimportant	Common
Unconcerned	Apathetic
Unimitated	Inimitable
Unfortunate	Unlucky
Understand	Perceive, Comprehend
Vain	Proud, Haughty, Conceited, Shameless
Vale	Valley, Dale, Dell
Vice	Fault
Virtue	Quality
Veracity	Reality
Value	Price, Prize
Vex	Tease
Vibrate	Quiver, Shake
Violent	Excessive
Vivid	Clear, Lucid
Victory	Triumph
Vulgar	Indecent
Virtuous	Honest
Variegated	Varied, Multifarious
Well	Good
Yell	Cry, Shout
Yonder	There
Yearn	Wish, Desire
Yoke	Slavery
Zest	Earnestness, Enthusiasm
Zealous	Earnest

ANTONYMS

A antonym is a word which conveys a meaning opposite to the given word.

REMEMBER

Words	*Antonyms*
Abhor	Love
Abnormal	Normal
Able	Unable
Acceptable	Unacceptable
Adequate	Inadequate
Amusing	Boring

Words	Antonyms
Angry	Calm
Apex	Bottom
Attract	Repel
Bad	Good
Barren	Fertile
Beautiful	Ugly
Bitter	Sweet
Brave	Cowardly
Brief	Lengthy
Bright	Dull
Calm	Violent
Careful	Careless
Clear	Vague, Cloudy
Cold	Hot
Cruel	Kind
Dear	Cheap
Deep	Shallow
Difficult	Easy
Direct	Indirect
Dishonest	Honest
Disobey	Obey
Encourage	Discourage
Enormous	Tiny
Excellent	Bad
Expensive	Cheap
Eat	Fast
Fair	Unfair
Fake	Authentic
False	True
Famous	Notorious
Fool	Genius
Generous	Miserly
Genius	Fool
Genuine	Unauthentic
Gigantic	Tiny
Glad	Depressed
Good	Bad
Great	Little
Happy	Sad
Hard	Soft
Hate	Love
Honest	Dishonest
Idle	Busy
Immoral	Moral
Include	Exclude
Incorrect	Correct
Intelligent	Unintelligent
Kind	Cruel
Like	Dislike
Long	Short
Lucid	Vague
Major	Minor
Naive	Experienced
Nadir	Apex
Neat	Clumsy
Obedient	Disobedient
Obscure	Clear
Oppose	Support
Optimistic	Pessimistic
Out	In
Patience	Impatience
Peaceful	Belligerent
Pious	Impious
Polite	Impolite
Potent	Impotent
Prominent	Unimportant
Proper	Improper
Pure	Impure
Quick	Slow
Quiet	Disturbance
Real	False, Unreal
Reject	Select, Choose
Reliable	Unreliable
Respect	Disrespect
Right	Wrong
Robust	Feeble, Weak
Sad	Happy

Words	Antonyms	Words	Antonyms
Secret	Open	Strong	Weak
Sensible	Insensible	Big	Small
Severe	Mild	Easy	Difficult
Sharp	Blunt	Fast	Slow
Simple	Complex	High	Low
Sociable	Unsociable	Catchy	Unattractive
Tall	Short	Ugly	Handsome, Beautiful, Tidy
Tidy	Untidy		
Uncanny	Canny	Tasty	Insipid
Violent	Calm	Sonorous	Harsh
Vivid	Vague		

MULTIPLE CHOICE QUESTIONS

Directions (Qs. 1 to 20): *In the following questions choose the word which best expresses the meaning of the given word.*

1. ABSURD
   - A. Foolish
   - B. Simple
   - C. Courageous
   - D. Silly

2. ABANDON
   - A. Lose
   - B. Profit
   - C. Vacate
   - D. Foil

3. CAJOLE
   - A. Pause
   - B. Lenient
   - C. Blast
   - D. Lure

4. COMBAT
   - A. Fight
   - B. Conflict
   - C. Shoot
   - D. Quarrel

5. LAMENT
   - A. Condone
   - B. Console
   - C. Complain
   - D. Contribution

6. DEBACLE
   - A. Disgrace
   - B. Defeat
   - C. Collapse
   - D. Decline

7. SHIVER
   - A. Fear
   - B. Tremble
   - C. Shake
   - D. Ache

8. TORTURE
   - A. Terror
   - B. Harassment
   - C. Torment
   - D. Tranquility

9. LAUDABLE
   - A. Lovable
   - B. Commendable
   - C. Profitable
   - D. Oblivious

10. FIXED
    - A. Sterile
    - B. Static
    - C. Stubborn
    - D. Parennial

11. QUEER
    - A. Unfamiliar
    - B. Cute
    - C. Curious
    - D. Strange

12. SUFFICIENT
    - A. Fit
    - B. Proper
    - C. Adequate
    - D. Vast

13. GLOSS
    - A. Brightness
    - B. Soothing
    - C. Rubbing
    - D. Miracle

14. LONGING
    - A. Prune
    - B. Apathy
    - C. Curtail
    - D. Craving

15. JEER
    - A. Applaud
    - B. Magnanimity
    - C. Avoid
    - D. Scoff

16. ZENITH
    - A. Minimum
    - B. Nadir
    - C. Plant
    - D. Peak

17. GARB
    - A. Distort
    - B. Dress
    - C. Trivial
    - D. Rage

18. ABHOR
- A. Rude
- B. Reconcile
- C. Crave
- D. Detest

19. YIELD
- A. Shum
- B. Incisive
- C. Retain
- D. Surrender

20. YOKE
- A. Twist
- B. Release
- C. Link
- D. Extra

Directions (Qs. 21 to 38): *In the following questions choose the word which best expresses the opposite of the given word.*

21. TRAGIC
- A. Dramatic
- B. Strong
- C. Gentle
- D. Comic

22. ORAL
- A. Verbal
- B. Sane
- C. Minor
- D. Written

23. ADMIRE
- A. Hate
- B. Unlike
- C. Dislike
- D. Enough

24. VIOLENT
- A. Gentle
- B. Savage
- C. Haughty
- D. Decline

25. ADVERSITY
- A. Windfall
- B. Inprosperity
- C. Prosperity
- D. Slave

26. GENUINE
- A. Spurious
- B. Obscure
- C. Countless
- D. Apathetic

27. GRUDGE
- A. Essence
- B. Guile
- C. Goodwill
- D. Ill-will

28. STIFF
- A. Soft
- B. Courteous
- C. Lively
- D. Flexible

29. VANITY
- A. Conceit
- B. Pride
- C. Ostentious
- D. Humility

30. FRONT
- A. Upper
- B. Unusual
- C. Back
- D. Rear

31. ATTRACT
- A. Lured
- B. Longing
- C. Repel
- D. Disguise

32. COMFORT
- A. Discomfort
- B. Discontent
- C. Uncomfort
- D. Miscomfort

33. WELCOME
- A. Repel
- B. Accept
- C. Resist
- D. Fight

34. TACTFUL
- A. Naive
- B. Loose
- C. Strict
- D. Uncivilized

35. DUTIFUL
- A. Harmful
- B. Watchful
- C. Forgetful
- D. Remiss

36. RIGID
- A. Flux
- B. Adoptable
- C. Yielding
- D. Adaptable

37. RARE
- A. Petty
- B. Poor
- C. Small
- D. Common

38. ZEAL
- A. Despair
- B. Calmness
- C. Passiveness
- D. Indifference

ANSWERS

1	2	3	4	5	6	7	8	9	10
D	C	D	A	C	C	B	C	B	B

11	12	13	14	15	16	17	18	19	20
D	C	A	D	D	D	B	D	D	C

21	22	23	24	25	26	27	28	29	30
D	D	C	A	C	A	C	D	D	D

31	32	33	34	35	36	37	38
C	A	C	A	D	D	D	D

3. Sentence Completion

It is such an exercise which starts with the primary schools and continues in the highest level of competitive examinations. One must practise it regularly to score well.

Directions (Qs. 1 to 15): *Pick out the most effective word(s) from the given words to fill in the blanks to make the sentence meaningfully complete.*

1. The student ...... that book from the library to study at home.
   A. issued
   B. borrowed
   C. hired
   D. lent

2. I wish I ...... a king.
   A. was
   B. am
   C. should be
   D. were

3. He ...... to listen to my arguments and walked away.
   A. denied
   B. disliked
   C. objected
   D. refused

4. The flow of blood was so ...... that the patient died.
   A. intense
   B. adequate
   C. profuse
   D. extensive

5. When I met her yesterday, it was the first time I ...... her since Christmas.
   A. saw
   B. have seen
   C. had seen
   D. have been seing

6. Can you pay ...... all these articles?
   A. for
   B. of
   C. off
   D. out

7. I ...... you to be at the party this evening.
   A. expect
   B. hope
   C. look forward to
   D. desire

8. ...... being a handicapped person, he is very cooperative and self-reliant.
   A. Because
   B. Although
   C. Since
   D. Despite

9. The child broke ...... from his mother and ran towards the painting.
   A. away
   B. after
   C. down
   D. with

10. With his ...... income, he finds it difficult to live a comfortable life.
    A. brief
    B. sufficient
    C. meagre
    D. huge

11. He could ...... a lot of money in such a short time by using his intelligence and working hard.
    A. spend
    B. spoil
    C. exchange
    D. accumulate

12. Though the brothers are twins, they look ......
    A. alike
    B. handsome
    C. indifferent
    D. different

13. Unfavourable weather conditions can ..... illness.
    A. cure
    B. detect
    C. treat
    D. enhance

14. No sooner did the bell ring, ... the actor started singing.
    A. when
    B. than
    C. after
    D. before

15. If I ...... realised it, I would not have acted on his advice.
    A. was
    B. had
    C. were
    D. have

Directions (Qs. 16 to 25): *In each question, an incomplete statement (Stem) followed by four fillers* *is given. Pick out the best one which can complete the incomplete stem correctly and meaningfully.*

16. Unless you work harder you will fail, means .....
 A. if you fail you will work harder.
 B. you must at least plan well than you will not fail.
 C. hardly you will fail if you do not desire so.
 D. if you do not put more efforts, then you will fail.

17. Even if it rains I shall come, means .....
 A. if I come it will not rain.
 B. if it rains I shall not come.
 C. I will certainly come whether it rains or not.
 D. whenever there is rain I shall come.

18. Dinesh is as stupid as he is lazy means .....
 A. Dinesh is stupid because he is lazy.
 B. Dinesh is lazy because he is stupid.
 C. Dinesh is either stupid or lazy.
 D. Dinesh is equally stupid and lazy.

19. He is so lazy that he .....
 A. cannot depend on others for getting his work done.
 B. cannot delay the schedule of completing the work.
 C. can seldom complete his work on time.
 D. dislike to postpone the work that he undertakes to do.

20. He always stammers in public meetings, but his today's speech .....
 A. was fairly audible to everyone present in the hall.
 B. was not received satisfactorily.
 C. could not be understood properly.
 D. was free from that defect.

21. In order to raise the company's profit, the employees .....
 A. demanded two additional increments.
 B. decided to go on paid holidays.
 C. requested the management to implement new welfare schemes.
 D. offered to work overtime without any compensation.

22. Although, he is reputed for making very candid statements, ...
 A. his today's speech was not fairly audible.
 B. his promises had always been realistic.
 C. his speech was very interesting.
 D. his today's statements were very ambiguous.

23. I felt somewhat more relaxed .....
 A. but tense as compared to earlier.
 B. and tense as compared to earlier.
 C. as there was already no tension at all.
 D. and tension-free as compared to earlier.

24. With great efforts his son succeeded in convincing him not to donate his entire wealth to an orphanage .....
 A. and lead the life of a wealthy merchant.
 B. but to a home for the forsaken children.
 C. and make an orphan of himself.
 D. as the orphanage needed a lot of donations.

25. Even though it is a very large house, ...
 A. there is a lot of space available in it for children.
 B. there is hardly any space available for children.
 C. there is no dearth of space for children.
 D. the servants take a long time to clean it.

ANSWERS

1	2	3	4	5	6	7	8	9	10
B	D	D	C	C	A	A	D	A	C

11	12	13	14	15	16	17	18	19	20
D	D	D	B	B	D	C	D	C	D

21	22	23	24	25
D	D	D	C	B

4. <u>Spotting Errors</u>

The most common errors in English are of spellings, grammar and usage of words. By regular practice, the errors can be easily spotted and minimised.

MULTIPLE CHOICE QUESTIONS

Directions: *In the following questions some of the sentences have errors and some are correct. Find out which part of a sentence has an error, the number of that part is your answer. If a sentence is free from errors, then your answer is D i.e., No error.*

1. (A) Either Ram or/(B) you is responsible/(C) for this action./(D) No error.

2. (A) The student flatly denied/(B) that he had copied/(C) in the examination hall./(D) No error.

3. (A) By the time you arrive tomorrow/(B) I have finished/(C) my work./(D) No error.

4. (A) The captain with the members of his team/(B) are returning/(C) after a fortnight./(D) No error.

5. (A) After returning from/(B) an all-India tour/(C) I had to describe about it./(D) No error.

6. (A) The teacher asked his students/(B) if they had gone through/(C) either of the three chapters included in the prescribed text./(D) No error.

7. (A) Do you know/(B) how old were you/(C) when you came here?/(D) No error.

8. (A) Beware of/(B) a fair-weather friend/(C) who is neither a friend in need nor a friend indeed./(D) No error.

9. (A) Copernicus proved/(B) that Earth/(C) moves round the Sun./(D) No error.

10. (A) The property/(B) was divided/(C) among the two brothers./(D) No error.

11. (A) I am quite certain/(B) that the lady is not only greedy/(C) but miserly./(D) No error.

12. (A) The brilliant success in the examination/(B) as well as his record in sports/(C) deserves high praise./(D) No error.

13. (A) I cannot find/(B) where has he gone/(C) though I have tried may best./(D) No error.

14. (A) If I was/(B) the Prime Minister of India/(C) I would work wonders/(D) No error.

15. (A) If it weren't/(B) for you,/(C) I wouldn't be alive today./(D) No error.

16. (A) He looked like a lion/(B) baulked from/(C) its prey./(D) No error.

17. (A) Widespread flooding/(B) is affecting/(C) large areas of the villages./(D) No error.

18. (A) If we really set to/(B) we can get the whole house/(C) cleaned in an afternoon./(D) No error.

19. (A) It's arrogant for you/(B) to assume you'll/(C)win every time./(D) No error.

20. (A) The two books are the same/(B) except for the fact that this/(C) has an answer in the back./(D) No error.

21. (A) Your husband doesn't/(B) believe that you are older/(C) than I./(D) No error.

22. (A) I could not/(B) answer to/(C) the question./(D) No error.

23. (A) Two years passed/(B) since/(C) my cousin died./(D) No error.

24. (A) I am learning English/(B) for ten years/(C) without much effect./(D) No error.

25. (A) Ramesh has agreed/(B) to marry with the girl/(C) of his parent's choice./ (D) No error.

26. (A) When he was arriving./(B) the party was/(C) in full swing./(D) No error.

27. (A) The most studious boy/(B) in the class/(C) was made as the captain./(D) No error.

28. (A) I am participating/(B) in the two-miles race/(C) tomorrow morning./(D) No error.

29. (A) When the boy committed a mistake/(B) the teacher made him to do/(C) the sum again./(D) No error.

30. (A) Whenever a person lost anything/(B) the poor folk around/(C) are suspected./(D) No error.

ANSWERS

1	2	3	4	5	6	7	8	9	10
B	D	B	B	C	C	D	D	B	C

11	12	13	14	15	16	17	18	19	20
C	D	B	A	C	C	C	A	A	C

21	22	23	24	25	26	27	28	29	30
C	B	A	A	B	A	C	B	B	A

EXPLANATORY ANSWERS

1. Replace 'is' by 'are'.

2. No error.

3. Replace 'have' by 'would have'.

4. Replace 'are' by 'is'.

5. Replace 'had to describe' by 'described'.

6. Replace 'either' by 'any'.

7. No error.

8. No error.

9. Omit 'that'.

10. Replace 'among' by 'between'.

11. Add 'also'.

12. No error.

13. Replace 'has he' by 'he has'.

14. Replace 'was' by 'were'.

15. Replace 'wouldn't be' by 'would not have been'.

16. Replace 'its' by 'his'.

17. Replace 'areas' by 'area'.

18. Replace 'set to' by 'set on'.

19. Replace 'for' by 'of'.

20. Replace 'in' by 'on'.

21. Replace 'I' by 'me'.

22. Omit 'to'.

23. Replace 'passed' by 'have passed'.

24. Replace 'am' by 'have been'.

25. Omit 'with'.

26. Replace 'was arriving' by 'arrived'.

27. Omit 'as'.

28. Replace 'in' by 'at'.

29. Omit 'to'.

30. Replace 'lost' by 'loses'.

5. <u>One Word Substitution</u>

There are many single words in English language which can be perfectly used for a number of words. These words help in expressing ideas in a short and correct manner for the right occasion. Such words not only increase the vocabulary but also enable you to economise in the use of words to a great extent.

Multiple Word Expression	*Substitution*
One who always looks towards the bright side of things	Optimist
One who always looks towards the dark side of things	Pessimist
The time when one develops from a child into an adult	Adolescence
The process of growing more plants in order to form a forest.	Afforestation
The science which deals with farming	Agriculture
From some other country or place etc.	Alien
A term, etc. giving more than one meaning	Ambiguous
A vehicle which is used to carry sick persons	Ambulance
An animal which can live both in water and on land	Amphibian
A lawless situation when there is no government	Anarchy
Belonging to the history of thousands of years old	Ancient
Once a year	Annual
A very old object but still valuable	Antique
Words of opposite meanings	Antonyms
Words of similar meanings	Synonyms
Signatures of a famous person	Autograph
A government led by one person with absolute authority	Autocracy
A written work of one's own life history	Autobiography
A person who has never been married	Bachelor
A person usually having no hair on his head	Bald
A place where one can deposit money and get interest	Bank
A person who cuts our hair	Barber
A building/group of buildings where soldiers live	Barracks
A person who makes buns and biscuits	Baker
A person who lives by asking people for food and money without doing any useful job	Beggar
The crime of having married to two persons at the same time	Bigamy
The branch of science which deals with the study of plants	Botany
Able to speak two languages	Bilingual

Multiple Word Expression	Substitution
Able to speak more than two languages	Polyglot
The branch of science which deals with the living organisms	Biology
A powerful snow storm	Blizzard
A great successful book or movie	Blockbuster
A short news on the radio or TV	Bulletin
A system in which the most important works are organised by the government officials	Bureaucracy
A person who has no vision in his eyes	Blind
A page or a series of pages on which the information of days, weeks, months, etc. is given	Calendar
A person who eats human flesh	Cannibal
A complete list of items often arranged alphabetically	Catalogue
A sudden disaster	Catastrophe
A period of 100 years	Century
A branch of science which deals with chemicals	Chemistry
A printed leaf usually issued by banks that we sign to carry certain financial deal	Cheque
A person who makes or mends shoes	Cobbler
A group of people who has been chosen by others to make decisions on their own	Committee
A building in which nuns live	Convent
An animal which feeds on other animals	Carnivorous
A person who does criticism	Critic
A person who cannot hear	Deaf
A condition in which one loses a lot of water from one's body because of vomiting, etc.	Dehydration
A system of government in which the people cast their votes to elect their leaders	Democracy
The study of skin problems	Dermatology
A long piece of land covered with sand	Desert
The art of managing relationships between countries	Diplomacy
A piece of information about the words in a book form	Dictionary
A piece of information about the telephone numbers of the people in a book from	Directory
A person in charge of a newspapers, magazine etc.	Editor
A person who thinks he is better than the others	Egoist
To leave your country and settle in some other country	Emigrate
A book or series of books giving almost all knowledge about an area or some persons etc.	Encyclopaedia
Study of insects	Entomology
Time when day and night are of the same duration	Equinox
To sell things out of the country	Export
To purchase things from some other country	Import
A plant or animal no longer in existence	Extinct
A situation when there is a shortage of food for a long period of time	Famine
An amount of money that we pay for some action or services	Fee
Related to women	Feminine
An animal strong and aggressive	Ferocious

Multiple Word Expression	*Substitution*
A piece of land where plants grow easily from the soil that is favourable to them	Fertile
A work of literature having some imaginary events	Fiction
A large amount of water covering certain area	Flood
A person who sells flowers	Florist
A religious ceremony for burying or cremating a dead person	Funeral
A substance which kills fungus	Fungicide
A person studying or having studied the diseases and the related things of female reproductory system	Gynaecologist
The murder of the person of the same group race or country	Genocide
A substance which kills germs	Germicide
A situation in which many people die because of fire during war	Holocaust
The act of killing a person deliberately	Homicide
A word having the pronunciation as the other one does but it differs in meaning	Homophone
A word having the same spelling as the other one does but it is pronounced in some other way	Homonym
A person who is attracted towards the person of the same sex	Homosexual
Go across and parallel to the ground	Horizontal
A substance which kills the insects	Insecticide
That cannot be corrected	Incorrigible
That cannot be defeated	Invincible
That cannot be eaten	Inedible
That cannot be seen	Invisible
A place in a school or college where books are kept for the benefit of students, teachers etc.	Library
A place in a school or college where scientific experiments are performed	Laboratory
An official who is a judge in the lowest court	Magistrate
A piece of music or a book before it is printed	Manuscript
Related to men	Masculine
One who believes in the existence of God	A theist
One who does not believe in the existence of good	An atheist
That can be believed	Credible
That cannot be believed	Incredible
That which dissolves in a solvent	Soluble
That which does not dissolves in a solvent	Insoluble
Hard writing that can be read	Legible
Hard writing that cannot be read	Illegible
A person who does jobs beneficial to mankind	Philanthropist
A person who goes on foot	Pedestrian
A person who fights for his own country	Patriot
An act of killing oneself	Suicide
A woman whose husband is dead	Widow
A man whose wife is dead	Widower
A person who eats vegetarian and non-vegetarian diets	Omnivorous

Multiple Word Expression	*Substitution*
Something which is everywhere at the same time	Omnipresent
One who knows everything	Omniscient
A child who does not have parents	Orphan
An award etc. given after the death of the person	Posthumous
The place where animals are kept for amusement and to increase the knowledge of the public	Zoo
The science which deals with the study of animals	Zoology

MULTIPLE CHOICE QUESTIONS

Directions: *In questions given below, out of the four alternatives, choose the one which can be substituted for the given words/sentences.*

1. Something that relates to everyone in the world
   A. General
   B. Common
   C. Usual
   D. Universal

2. An expression of mild disapproval
   A. Warning
   B. Denigration
   C. Impertinence
   D. Reproof

3. One who is not easily pleased by anything
   A. Maiden
   B. Medieval
   C. Precarious
   D. Fastidious

4. Murder of a king
   A. Infanticide
   B. Matricide
   C. Genocide
   D. Regicide

5. A remedy for all diseases
   A. Stoic
   B. Marvel
   C. Panacea
   D. Recompense

6. A dramatic performance
   A. Mask
   B. Mosque
   C. Masque
   D. Mascot

7. Study of birds
   A. Orology
   B. Optology
   C. Ophthalmology
   D. Ornithology

8. Ready to believe
   A. Credulous
   B. Credible
   C. Creditable
   D. Incredible

9. Incapable of being seen through
   A. Ductile
   B. Opaque
   C. Obsolete
   D. Potable

10. One who eats everything
    A. Omnivorous
    B. Omniscient
    C. Irresistible
    D. Insolvent

11. A place where bees are kept is called
    A. An apiary
    B. A mole
    C. A hive
    D. A sanctuary

12. One who cannot be corrected
    A. Incurable
    B. Incorrigible
    C. Hardened
    D. Invulnerable

13. One who is in charge of a museum
    A. Curator
    B. Supervisor
    C. Caretaker
    D. Warden

14. Continuing fight between parties, families, clans, etc.
    A. Enmity
    B. Feud
    C. Quarrel
    D. Skirmish

15. A voice loud enough to be heard
    A. Audible
    B. Applaudable
    C. Laudable
    D. Oral

16. A paper written by hand
    A. Handicraft
    B. Manuscript
    C. Handiwork
    D. Thesis

17. Habitually silent or talking little
    A. Serville
    B. Unequivocal
    C. Taciturn
    D. Synoptic

18. To slap with a flat object
    A. Chop
    B. Hew
    C. Gnaw
    D. Swat

19. A person who speaks many languages
    A. Linguist
    B. Monolingual
    C. Polyglot
    D. Bilingual

20. A light sailing-boat built specially for racing
    A. Canoe
    B. Yacht
    C. Frigate
    D. Dinghy

21. A fixed orbit in space in relation to earth
    A. Geological
    B. Geo-synchronous
    C. Geo-centric
    D. Geo-stationary

22. A style in which a writer makes a display of his knowledge
    A. Pedantic   B. Verbose
    C. Pompous   D. Ornate

23. A religious discourse
    A. Preach   B. Stanza
    C. Sanctorum   D. Sermon

24. A place that provides refuge
    A. Asylum   B. Sanatorium
    C. Shelter   D. Orphanage

25. Detailed plan of a journey
    A. Travelogue   B. Travelkit
    C. Schedule   D. Itinerary

26. A person who insists on something
    A. Disciplinarian B. Stickler
    C. Instantaneous   D. Boaster

27. A drawing on transparent paper
    A. Red print   B. Blue print
    C. Negative   D. Transparency

28. One who believes that all things and events in life are predetermined is a
    A. Fatalist   B. Puritan
    C. Egoist   D. Tyrant

29. A school boy who cuts classes frequently is a
    A. Defeatist   B. Sycophant
    C. Truant   D. Martinet

30. The act of violating the sanctity of the church is
    A. Blasphemy   B. Heresy
    C. Sacrilege   D. Desecration

31. A place where monks live as a secluded community
    A. Cathedral   B. Diocese
    C. Convent   D. Monastery

32. One who is fond of fighting
    A. Bellicose   B. Aggressive
    C. Belligerent   D. Militant

33. Tending to move away from the centre or axis
    A. Centrifugal   B. Centripetal
    C. Axiomatic   D. Awry

34. Words inscribed on tomb
    A. Epitome   B. Epistle
    C. Epilogue   D. Epitaph

35. Leave or remove from a place considered dangerous
    A. Evade   B. Evacuate
    C. Avoid   D. Exterminate

36. Original inhabitants of a country
    A. Abroge   B. Aborger
    C. Aborgory   D. Aborigins

37. Government by the officials
    A. Theocracy   B. Plutocracy
    C. Bureaucracy   D. Democracy

38. Incapable of being exhausted
    A. Inexhaustible   B. Inaexhaustible
    C. Exhaustable   D. Non-tired

39. A person of good understanding, knowledge and reasoning power
    A. Expert   B. Intellectual
    C. Snob   D. Literate

40. One absorbed in his own thoughts and feelings rather than in things outside
    A. Scholar   B. Recluse
    C. Introvert   D. Intellectual

ANSWERS

1	2	3	4	5	6	7	8	9	10
D	D	D	D	C	C	D	A	B	A

11	12	13	14	15	16	17	18	19	20
A	B	A	B	A	B	C	D	A	B

21	22	23	24	25	26	27	28	29	30
D	A	D	A	D	B	D	A	C	C

31	32	33	34	35	36	37	38	39	40
D	A	A	D	B	B	C	A	B	C

6. Spelling Errors

There are thousands of words in English language. It is difficult to remember the spellings and meanings of all at once. Try to learn as many as you can. Use a dictionary regularly.

Directions: *Find the correctly spelt words.*

1. A. Damage
    B. Dammage
    C. Damaige
    D. Dammege

2. A. Efficiant
    B. Effecient
    C. Efficient
    D. Eficient

3. A. Schedule
    B. Schdule
    C. Schedale
    D. Schedeule

4. A. Occurad
    B. Occurred
    C. Ocurred
    D. Occured

5. A. Grieff
    B. Grief
    C. Grieef
    D. Grrief

6. A. Guarantee
    B. Garuntee
    C. Guaruntee
    D. Gaurantee

7. A. Meddicine
    B. Medicine
    C. Medicene
    D. Medicinne

8. A. Benefeted
    B. Benefitted
    C. Benifited
    D. Benefited

9. A. Acommodation
    B. Acomodation
    C. Accomodation
    D. Accommodation

10. A. Querrelsome
    B. Quarrelsame
    C. Quarrelsome
    D. Querralsome

11. A. Sympathetic
    B. Smypathetic
    C. Sympothetic
    D. Sympethetic

12. A. Prograssive
    B. Progressive
    C. Progresive
    D. Prograsive

13. A. Uncivilized
    B. Uncevilized
    C. Uncivillized
    D. Uncevelized

14. A. Extravagant
    B. Extreragent
    C. Extreregant
    D. Extravegent

15. A. Missunderstood
    B. Miesunderstood
    C. Misunderstood
    D. Misunderstod

16. A. Belligerent
    B. Beligirent
    C. Belligarant
    D. Belligerrent

17. A. Astonished
    B. Astronished
    C. Astoneshed
    D. Asstonished

18. A. Sincerely
    B. Sencerely
    C. Sincerelly
    D. Sincerrely

19. A. Rigourous
    B. Rigerous
    C. Rigorous
    D. Regerous

20. A. Satellite
    B. Sattellite
    C. Satelite
    D. Sattelite

21. A. Pesanger
    B. Passenger
    C. Pessenger
    D. Pasanger

22. A. Humurous
    B. Humorous
    C. Humoreus
    D. Humorrous

23. A. Exeggerate
    B. Exaggerate
    C. Exadgerate
    D. Exagerate

24. A. Fariegn
    B. Forein
    C. Foriegn
    D. Foreign

25. A. Excesive
    B. Excessive
    C. Exccessive
    D. Exccesive

26. A. Forcaust
    B. Forcast
    C. Forecast
    D. Forecaste

27. A. Paralleted
    B. Paralelled
    C. Parralleled
    D. Parallelled

28. A. Ocasion   B. Occassion
    C. Occasion   D. Ocassion

29. A. Boquet   B. Bouquet
    C. Bouquete   D. Bouquette

30. A. Chettering   B. Chaterring
    C. Chattering   D. Chatering

31. A. Discourage   B. Disscourage
    C. Discourege   D. Discaurage

32. A. Curageous   B. Courageous
    C. Courrageous   D. Couregeous

33. A. Abandon   B. Abanddon
    C. Abendon   D. Abbandon

34. A. Embarassment
    B. Emberrassement
    C. Embarrassment
    D. Embbaresment

35. A. Eccintric   B. Eccentrie
    C. Eccentric   D. Eccintrie

36. A. Occasional   B. Occassional
    C. Occesional   D. Occessional

37. A. Querrel   B. Querral
    C. Quarrel   D. Quarel

38. A. Contrebution   B. Contribution
    C. Contributtion   D. Conterbution

39. A. Desgrace   B. Disgrece
    C. Disgrice   D. Disgrace

40. A. Harassment   B. Herassment
    C. Harasment   D. Harassmient

41. A. Imaginative   B. Imeginative
    C. Imagenative   D. Imaginetive

42. A. Suficient   B. Suficiant
    C. Sufficient   D. Sufficiant

43. A. Adequate   B. Edequate
    C. Adaquete   D. Edaquete

44. A. Exparienced   B. Experianced
    C. Experienced   D. Experrienced

45. A. Flatering   B. Fletering
    C. Flattering   D. Fletaring

46. A. Cuttiveted   B. Culltrivated
    C. Cultivated   D. Caltivated

47. A. Praiceworthy   B. Peiseworthy
    C. Praiseworthy   D. Praisaworthy

48. A. Profesional   B. Professionel
    C. Professional   D. Profissional

49. A. Ameteur   B. Amateur
    C. Amataur   D. Amateor

50. A. Unfevourable   B. Unfevaurable
    C. Unfavourable   D. Unfivourable

ANSWERS

1	2	3	4	5	6	7	8	9	10
A	C	A	B	B	A	B	B	D	C

11	12	13	14	15	16	17	18	19	20
A	B	A	A	C	A	A	A	C	A

21	22	23	24	25	26	27	28	29	30
B	B	B	D	B	C	A	C	B	C

31	32	33	34	35	36	37	38	39	40
A	B	A	C	C	A	C	B	D	A

41	42	43	44	45	46	47	48	49	50
A	C	A	C	A	C	C	C	B	C

GENERAL AWARENESS

NATIONAL SYMBOLS

NATIONAL EMBLEM

State emblem of India is an adaptation from the Sarnath Lion Capital of Ashoka. It was adopted by the Government of India on January 26, 1950. In the adapted form, only three lions are visible, the fourth being hidden from the view. The wheel (Dharma Chakra) appears in relief in the centre of the abacus with a bull on the right and a horse on the left.

The bell-shaped lotus has been omitted. The words "Satyameva Jayate" meaning "Truth alone triumphs" are inscribed below the Emblem in Devanagari script.

NATIONAL FLAG

The National Flag of India is a horizontal tricolour of deep saffron (Kesari), white and dark green in equal proportion. In the centre of the white band there is a wheel in navy blue colour. It has 24 spokes. The ratio of the length and the breadth of the flag is 3 : 2. Its design was adopted by the Constituent Assembly of India on July 22, 1947.

NATIONAL ANTHEM

Rabindranath Tagore's song 'Jana-gana-mana' was adopted by the Constituent Assembly as the National Anthem of India on January 24, 1950.

Jana-gan-mana-adhinayaka jaya he, Bharata-bhagya-vidhata
Punjab-Sindh-Gujarat-Maratha-Dravida-Utkala-Banga
Vindhya-Himachala-Yamuna-Ganga Uchhala-jaladhi-taranga.
Tava subha name jage, Tava subha asisa mange, Gahe tava jaya gatha,
Jana-gana-mangala-dayak, jaya he Bharata bhagya vidhata,
Jaya he, jaya he, jaya he, Jaya jaya jaya, jaya he.

NATIONAL SONG

Bankim Chandra Chatterji's 'Vande Mataram' which was a source of inspiration to the people in their struggle for freedom, has been adopted as National Song. It has an equal status with the National Anthem.

Vande Mataram
Sujalam, suphalam, malayaja-shitalam,
Shasya shyamalam, Mataram
Shubhrajyotsna,pulkita yaminim,
Phulla kusumita drumadalashobhinim,
Subhasinim sumadhura—bhashinim,
Sukhadam, Varadam, Mataram.

National Bird and Animal of India: Peacock and Tiger; **National Aquatic Animal:** Dolphin; **National Flower:** Lotus; **National Game:** Hockey; **National Calendar:** It was adopted on March 22, 1957. It has 365 days in the year and the first month of the year is Chaitra.

NATIONAL CALENDAR

It is based on the Saka era with Chaitra as its first month and a normal year of 365 days. It was adopted from March 22, 1957. Dates of the national calendar have a permanent correspondence with dates of Gregorian calendar as Chaitra I falls on March 22 in a normal year and March 21 in a leap year. In official communications, both Saka and Gregorian calendar dates are written. Months of the national calendar are Chaitra, Vaishakha, Jaishtha, Ashada, Shravan, Bhadra, Ashvina, Kartika, Margashirsha, Pausha, Magha and Phalguna.

NATIONAL ANIMAL

The magnificent tiger — Panthera tigris (Linnaeus) is the national animal of India. Tiger is found in several parts of the country and is known for its grace, strength, agility and enormous power. 'Project Tiger' was launched in 1973 to check their dwindling population in India.

NATIONAL BIRD

The Indian Peacock — Pavo Christatus (Linnaeus) is the national bird of India. It is a colourful, swan-sized bird with a fan-shaped crest of feathers on its head and a long-slander neck. The male species is more colourful with blue breast and a spectacular bronze-green train of around 200 elongated feathers.

National Flower—Lotus

National Tree—Banyan

National Fruit—Mango

National Currency—Rupee '₹'

(One Rupee = 100 Paise)

National Aquatic Animal—Dolphin

BOOKS AND AUTHORS

Name of Book	Author
Ain-e-Akbari	Abul Fazal
Anand Math	Bankim Chandra Chatterjee
An Unknown Indian	Nirad C. Chaudhuri
Arthshastra	Kautilya
Coolie	Mulk Raj Anand
Das Kapital	Karl Marx
Discovery of India	Jawaharlal Nehru
Eternal India	Mrs. Indira Gandhi
Godan	Prem Chand
Gitanjali	Rabindranath Tagore
Gora	Rabindranath Tagore
Geet Govinda	Jayadeva
Harsha Charit	Bana Bhatta
Hindu View of Life	Dr. S. Radhakrishnan
India Wins Freedom	Maulana Abul Kalam Azad
Jobs of Millions	V.V. Giri
Jungle Book	Rudyard Kipling
Kamayani	Jai Shankar Prasad
Kadambari	Bana Bhatta
Life Divine	Sri Aurobindo
Last days of Netaji	G.D. Khosla
Les Miserables	Victor Hugo
Mahabharat	Veda Vyas
Macbeth	William Shakespeare
Mein Kempf	Hitler
Meghduta	Kalidas
Mother (Maa)	Maxim Gorky
Mother India	Katherine Mayo
My Experiments with Truth	Mahatma Gandhi
My Presidential Years	R. Venkataraman
Neeti Shatak	Bhartrihari
Nehru and His Vision	Dr. K.R. Narayanan
Old Man and the Sea	Ernest Hemingway
One World	Wendell Wilkie
Panchtantra	Vishnu Sharma
Paradise Lost	John Milton
Ramayana	Valmiki (in Sanskrit)
Raghuvansham	Kalidas
Rajtarangini	Kalhan
Ram Charit Manas	Tulsi Das
Abhijnan Shakuntalam	Kalidas
Satanic Verses	Salman Rushdie
Saket	Maithili Sharan Gupta
Speed Post	Shobha De
The God of Small Things	Arundhati Roy
Treasure Island	R.L. Stevenson
Twelfth Night	William Shakespeare
Train to Pakistan	Khuswant Singh
Uttara Ram Charitra	Bhava Bhuti
Vanity Fair	W.M. Thackeray
War and Peace	Leo Tolstoy
Wealth of Nations	Adam Smith
Wake up India	Annie Besant

INVENTIONS AND DISCOVERIES

Geographical Discoveries

Discovery	Discoverer
America	Columbus
Brazil	Cabral
North Pole	Robert Peary
Everest (Conquered)	Tabie Junko
Planetary Motion	Kepler
Hawaiian Islands	Captain Cook
South Pole	Amundsen
Solar System	Copernicus

Chemistry and Physics

Discovery	Discoverer
Atom Bomb	Otto Hahn
Atomic Theory	Dalton
Atomic Numbers	Moseley
Cosmic Rays	R.S. Millikan
Dynamite	Alfred Nobel
Electrons Theory	Bohr
Electricity (current)	Volta
Electric Telegraphy (Code)	S. Morse

Discovery	Discoverer
Gravitation	Newton
Gas Light	Murdock
Oxygen	J. Priestly
Photography	L. Daguerre
Printing for the blind	Louis Braille
Radium	Madame Curie
Telegraph	Samuel Morse
Television	J.L. Baird
Telephone	Graham Bell
Wireless	G. Marconi
X-rays	W.K. Roentgen

Mechanical

Discovery	Discoverer
Aeroplane	Wright Brothers
Bicycle	Macmillan
Computer	Charles Babbage
Dynamo	Michal Faraday
Diesel Engine	Rudolf Diesel
Engine (Railway)	Stephenson
Fountain Pen	Waterman
Gramophone	Edison
Locomotive Power of Steam	James Watt
Helicopter	Brequet
Life Boat	Henry Greathead

Discovery	Discoverer
Microscope	Z. Jansen
Printing Press	Gutenberg
Revolver	Colt
Sewing Machine	Elias Howe
Thermometer	Fahrenheit
Transistor	W. Shockley
Typewriter	Sholes
Telescope	Hans Lippershey
Tank (Military)	Swinton

Medical

Discovery	Discoverer
Antiseptic Surgery	Lord Joseph Lister
Bacteria	Leeuwenhock
Circulation of Blood	William Harvey
Homoeopathy (Discovered)	Hahnemann
Insulin	F. Banting
Penicillin	Alexander Flemming
Malaria Parasite	Dr. Ronald Ross
Stethoscope	Laennec
Vitamins	Funk
Anti-Rabies Treatment	Pasteur

General

Discovery	Discoverer
Nylon	Carouthers
Science of Geometry	Euclids

WORLD'S GEOGRAPHICAL SURNAMES

● City of Sky-scrapers—New York ● City of Seven Hills—Rome ● City of Dreaming Spires—Oxford ● City of Golden Gate—San Francisco ● City of Magnificent Buildings—Washington D.C. ● City of Eternal Springs—Quito (S. America) ● China's Sorrow—Hwang Ho ● Cockpit of Europe—Belgium ● Dark Continent—Africa ● Emerald Isle—Ireland ● Eternal City—Rome ● Empire City—New York ● Forbidden City—Lhasa (Tibet) ● Garden City—Chicago ● Gate of Tears—Strait of Bab-el-Mandeb ● Gift of the Nile—Egypt ● Granite City—Aberdeen (Scotland) ● Hermit Kingdom—Korea ● Herring Pond—Atlantic Ocean ● Holy Land—Jerusalem ● Island Continent—Australia ● Islands of Cloves—Zanzibar ● Isle of Pearls—Bahrein (Persian Gulf) ● Key to the Mediterranean—Gibralter ● Land of Cakes—Scotland ● Land of Golden Fleece—Australia ● Land of Maple Leaf—Canada ● Land of Morning Calm—Korea ● Land of Midnight Sun—Norway ● Land of the Thousand Lakes—Finland ● Land of the Thunderbolt—Bhutan ● Land of White Elephant—Thailand ● Land of Thousand Elephants—Laos ● Land of Rising Sun—Japan ● Loneliest Island—Tristan De Gunha (Mid-Atlantic) ● Manchester of Japan—Osaka ● Pillars of Hercules—Strait of Gibraltar ● Pearl of the Antilles—Cuba ● Playground of Europe—Switzerland ● Quaker City—Philadelphia ● Queen of the Adriatic—Venice ● Roof of the World—The Pamirs, Central Asia ● Sugar bowl of the world—Cuba ● Venice of the North—Stockholm ● Windy City—Chicago ● Whiteman's grave—Guinea Coast of Africa ● Yellow River—Huang Ho (China) ● Sickman of Europe—Turkey

CAPITALS AND CURRENCIES OF COUNTRIES

Country	Capital	Currency	Country	Capital	Currency
Afghanistan	Kabul	Afghani	Indonesia	Jakarta	Rupiah
Algeria	Algiers	Dinar	Iran	Teheran	Rial
Angola	Luanda	New Kwanza	Iraq	Baghdad	Dinar
Argentina	Buenos Aires	Peso	Ireland	Dublin	Euro
Armenia	Yeravan	Dram	Israel	Jerusalem	Shekel
Australia	Canberra	Dollar	Italy	Rome	Euro
Austria	Vienna	Euro	Jamaica	Kingston	Dollar
Azerbaijan	Baku	Monat	Japan	Tokyo	Yen
Bahrain	Manama	Dinar	Jordan	Amman	Dinar
Bangladesh	Dhaka	Taka	Kazakhstan	Akmola	Tenge
Barbados	Bridgetown	Dollar	Kenya	Nairobi	Shilling
Belgium	Brussels	Euro	Korea (S)	Seoul	Won
Bhutan	Thimphu	Ngultrum*	Korea (N)	Pyongyang	Won
Bolivia	La paz	Boliviano	Kyrgyzstan	Bishkek	Som
Brazil	Brasilia	Cruzeiro	Kuwait	Kuwait City	Dinar
Bulgaria	Sofia	Lev	Laos	Vientiane	Kip
Byelorussia	Minsk	Zaichik	Latvia	Riga	Lat
Cambodia	Phnom-Penh	Riel	Lebanon	Beirut	Pound
Canada	Ottawa	Dollar	Libya	Tripoli	Dinar
Chile	Santiago	Peso	Lithuania	Vilnius	Litas
China	Beijing	Yuan	Malaysia	Kuala Lumpur	Ringgit
Colombia	Bogota	Peso	Maldives	Male	Rufiyya
Congo	Brazzaville	Franc	Mauritius	Port Louis	Rupee
Croatia	Zagreb	Kuna	Moldavia	Chisinau	Leu
Cuba	Havana	Peso	Mexico	Mexico City	Peso
Cyprus	Nicosia	Euro	Morocco	Rabat	Dirham
Czech Republic	Prague	Crown	Mozambique	Maputo	Metical
Denmark	Copenhagen	Krone	Myanmar	Yangon	Kyat
Egypt	Cairo	Pound	(Burma)	(Rangoon)	
Estonia	Tallinn	Kroon	Nepal	Kathmandu	Rupee
Ethiopia	Addis Ababa	Birr	Netherlands	Amsterdam	Euro
Fiji	Suva	Dollar	New Zealand	Wellington	Dollar
Finland	Helsinki	Euro	Nigeria	Abuja	Naira
France	Paris	Euro	Norway	Oslo	Krone
Georgia	Tbilisi	Lari	Oman	Muscat	Rial
Germany	Berlin	Euro	Pakistan	Islamabad	Rupee
Ghana	Accra	Cedi	Philippines	Manila	Peso
Greece	Athens	Euro	Poland	Warsaw	Zloty
Guatemala	Guatemala City	Quetzal	Portugal	Lisbon	Euro
Hong Kong	Victoria	Dollar	Qatar	Doha	Riyal
Hungary	Budapest	Forints	Romania	Bucharest	Leu
Iceland	Reykjavik	Krona	Russia	Moscow	Ruble
India	New Delhi	Rupee	Saudi Arabia	Riyadh	Rial

Country	Capital	Currency	Country	Capital	Currency
Slovakia	Bratislava	Euro	Turkey	Ankara	Lira
Spain	Madrid	Euro	Turkmania	Ashikabad	Manat
Sri Lanka	Colombo	Rupee	Uganda	Kampala	Shilling
Sudan	Khartoum	Dinar	Ukraine	Kiev	Hyrvna
Sweden	Stockholm	Krona	United Arab	Abu Dhabi	Dirham
Switzerland	Berne	Swiss Francs	Emirates		
Syria	Damascus	Pound	U.K.	London	Pound
South Africa	Capetown	Rand			Sterling
	(Legislative)		U.S.A.	Washington	Dollar
	Pretoria		Uzbekistan	Tashkent	Som
	(Administrative)		Vietnam	Hanoi	Dong
Tajikistan	Dushanbe	Somoni	Yemen	Sana'a	Rial/Dinar
Taiwan	Taipei	Dollar	Zimbabwe	Harare	Dollar
Tanzania	Dodoma	Shilling	Congo (Zaire)	Kinshasa	Zaire
Thailand	Bangkok	Baht	Zambia	Lusaka	Kwacha

INDIAN CITIES AND THEIR RIVERS

City	State	River	City	State	River
Agra	U.P.	Yamuna	Kanpur	Uttar Pradesh	Ganga
Ahmedabad	Gujarat	Sabarmati	Ludhiana	Punjab	Sutlej
Allahabad	U.P.	Confluence of the Ganga, Yamuna, and invisible Saraswati	Lucknow	Uttar Pradesh	Gomati
			Nasik	Maharashtra	Godavari
			Patna	Bihar	Ganga
			Srinagar	J & K	Jhelum
Alwaye	Kerala	Periyar	Surat	Gujarat	Tapti
Kolkata	West Bengal	Hooghly	Tiruchirapally	Tamil Nadu	Kaveri
Cuttack	Odisha	Mahanadi	Ujjain	Madhya Pradesh	Shipra
Delhi	Delhi	Yamuna	Vijayawada	Andhra Pradesh	Krishna
Haridwar	Uttarakhand	Ganga	Varanasi	Uttar Pradesh	Ganga

WONDERS OF THE WORLD

Seven Wonders of the Ancient World: (1) the Pyramids of Egypt, built in approximately 2700 BC; (2) the Hanging Gardens at Babylon; (3) the temple of Artemis at Emphesus; (4) the statue of Zeus at Olympia; (5) the tomb of Mausolus at Halicarnassus, built in nearly 350 BC; (6) the Colossus of Rhodes, built in nearly 280 BC; (7) the Pharos Lighthouse at Alexandria.

Seven Wonders of the Medieval World: (1) the Colosseum of Rome; (2) the Great Wall of China; (3) the Porcelain Tower of Nanking; (4) the Mosque at St. Sophia (Constantinople); (5) Stonehenge; (6) the Catacombs of Rome; (7) the Leaning Tower of Pisa.

Seven New Wonders of the World: (1) Taj Mahal of Agra (India); (2) Pyramid at Chichen Itza (Mexico); (3) Machu Picchu (Peru); (4) Statue of Christ The Redeemer (Brazil); (5) Great Wall of China; (6) Roman Colosseum, Italy; (7) Ruins of Petra, Jordan.

STATES OF INDIA (CAPITALS, PRINCIPAL LANGUAGES)

States Principal Languages	Capitals	States Principal Languages	Capitals
■ Andhra Pradesh *Telgu and Urdu*	Hyderabad	■ Meghalaya *Khashi, Jayantia and Garo*	Shillong
■ Arunachal Pradesh *Monpa, Adi, Nissi etc.*	Itanagar	■ Manipur *Manipuri*	Imphal
■ Assam *Assamese and Bengali*	Dispur	■ Mizoram *Mizo and English*	Aizawl
■ Bihar *Hindi and Maithili*	Patna	■ Nagaland *Naga, Assamese and English*	Kohima
■ Chattishgarh *Hindi*	Raipur	■ Odisha *Odiya*	Bhubaneshwar
■ Goa *Konkani*	Panaji	■ Punjab *Punjabi*	Chandigarh
■ Gujarat *Gujarati*	GandhiNagar	■ Rajasthan *Hindi, Rajasthani*	Jaipur
■ Haryana *Hindi*	Chandigarh	■ Sikkim *Sikkimese and Gorkhali*	Gangtok
■ Himachal Pradesh *Hindi and Pahari*	Shimla	■ Tamil Nadu *Tamil*	Chennai
■ Jammu & Kashmir *Kashmiri, Dongri, Urdu, Ladakhi, Dardi and Pahari*	Srinagar	■ Tripura *Bengali, Tripuri and Manipuri*	Agartala
■ Jharkhand *Hindi*	Ranchi	■ Uttar Pradesh *Hindi*	Lucknow
■ Kerala *Malyalam*	Thiruvananthpuram	■ Uttarakhand *Hindi*	Dehradun
■ Karnataka *Kannada*	Bengluru	■ West Bengal *Bengali*	Kolkata
■ Madhya Pradesh *Hindi*	Bhopal	■ Telangana *Telgu and Urdu*	Hyderabad
■ Maharashtra *Marathi*	Mumbai		

Union Territories Principal Languages	Capitals	Union Territories Principal Languages	Capitals
■ Andaman and Nicobar Islands *Hindi, Nicobarese, Bengali, Malayalam, Tamil, Telugu*	Port Blair	■ Daman and Diu *Gujarati*	Daman
■ Chandigarh *Hindi, Punjabi, English*	Chandigarh	■ Delhi *(Hindi, Punjabi)*	Delhi
		■ Lakshadweep *Malayalam*	Kavaratti
■ Dadar and Nagar Haveli *Gujarati, Hindi*	Silvasa	■ Puducherry *Tamil, Telugu, Malayalam, English and French*	Puducherry

HIGH COURTS IN INDIA

Name	Year	Territorial Jurisdiction	Seat
Allahabad	1866	Uttar Pradesh	Allahabad (Bench at Lucknow)
Andhra Pradesh	1954	Andhra Pradesh / Telangana	Hyderabad
Bombay	1862	Maharashtra, Goa, Dadar & Nagar Haveli and Daman & Diu	Mumbai (Benches at Nagpur, Panaji and Aurangabad)
Calcutta	1862	West Bengal and Andaman & Nicobar	Kolkata (Circuit Bench at Port Blair)
Chhattisgarh	2000	Chhattisgarh	Bilaspur
Delhi	1966	Delhi	Delhi
Guwahati	1948	Assam, Nagaland, Mizoram and Arunachal Pradesh	Guwahati (Benches at Kohima, Aizawl and Itanagar)
Gujarat	1960	Gujarat	Ahmedabad
Himachal Pradesh	1971	Himachal Pradesh	Shimla
Jammu & Kashmir	1928	Jammu & Kashmir	Srinagar and Jammu
Jharkhand	2000	Jharkhand	Ranchi
Karnataka	1884	Karnataka	Bengaluru (Circuit Benches at Dharwar and Gulbarga)
Kerala	1958	Kerala & Lakshadweep	Ernakulam
Madhya Pradesh	1956	Madhya Pradesh	Jabalpur (Benches at Gwalior and Indore)
Madras	1862	Tamil Nadu & Puducherry	Chennai (Bench at Madurai)
Orissa	1948	Odisha	Cuttack
Patna	1916	Bihar	Patna
Punjab and Haryana	1966	Punjab, Haryana and Chandigarh	Chandigarh
Rajasthan	1949	Rajasthan	Jodhpur (Bench at Jaipur)
Sikkim	1975	Sikkim	Gangtok
Uttarakhand	2000	Uttarakhand	Nainital
Tripura	2013	Tripura	Agartala
Meghalaya	2013	Meghalaya	Shillong
Manipur	2013	Manipur	Imphal

HILL STATION

Station		State
1.	Almora, Mussoorie Nainital	: Uttarakhand
2.	Cherrapunji (Shillong), Khasi Hills (Shillong)	: Meghalaya
3.	Ooty, Kodaikanal Yereaud	: Tamil Nadu
4.	Dalhousie, Kassauli	: Himachal Pradesh
5.	Darjeeling	: West Bengal
6.	Gulmarg, Srinagar	: Kashmir
7.	Mahabaleshwar	: Maharashtra
8.	Mt. Abu	: Rajasthan
9.	Panchmarhi	: Madhya Pradesh
10.	Ranchi	: Jharkhand

NATIONAL PARKS

1.	Corbett National Park	:	Nainital, Uttarakhand
2.	Dudhwa National Park	:	Lakhimpur Kheri, Uttar Pradesh
3.	Kaziranga National Park	:	Jorhat, Assam
4.	Kanha National Park	:	Jabalpur, Bhedaghat
5.	Gir National Park	:	Rajkot, Junagarh, Gujarat
6.	Guindy National Park	:	Guindy, Chennai, Tamil Nadu
7.	Nagairhole National Park	:	Coorg, Karnataka
8.	Bandipur National Park	:	Mysore, Karnataka

NATIONAL WILDLIFE SANCTUARIES

1.	Dachigam Wildlife Sanctuary	:	Srinagar, Jammu and Kashmir
2.	Sariska	:	Alwar, Rajasthan
3.	Hazaribagh Wildlife Sanctuary	:	Hazaribagh, Jharkhand
4.	Tiger Project	:	Sawai Madhopur, Rajasthan
5.	Mudhumali Wildlife Sanctuary	:	Mudhumalia, Nilgiri, Tamil Nadu
6.	Periyar Wildlife Sanctuary	:	Idukki, Kottayam, Kerala

HOLY PLACES IN INDIA

1.	Amarnath	Kashmir
2.	Ayodhya	Uttar Pradesh
3.	Badrinath	Uttarakhand
4.	Dwarka	Gujarat
5.	Haridwar	Uttarakhand
6.	Kancheepuram	Tamil Nadu
7.	Kedarnath	Uttarakhand
8.	Mathura	Uttar Pradesh
9.	Puri	Odisha
10.	Rameswaram	Tamil Nadu
11.	Tirupati	Andhra Pradesh
12.	Ujjain	Madhya Pradesh
13.	Varanasi	Uttar Pradesh
14.	Bodh Gaya	Bihar

SPORTS

Terms Associated With Sports :

Cricket : Ashes, Bye, Bodyline, Bowling, Break, Cover-point, Creases, Chinaman, Chucker, Drive, Duck, Follow on, Googly, Hit-Wicket, Hat-trick, Leg-before-wicket, Leg break, Leg-bye, Maiden over, No ball, Night-watchman, Runner, Run-out, Stumped, Silly-point, Slip.

Football : Handball, Corner kick, Dribble, Free Kick, Hat-trick, Off-side, Penalty Kick, Try, Throw in, Wembley.

Hockey : Bully, Carry, Corner kick, Corner, Penalty stroke, Off-side, Penalty, Roll in scoop, Sticks, Sudden death, Striking circle, Short Corner, Scoop, Tie-breaker, Under-cutting, Hat-trick.

Tennis : Backhand drive, Deuce, Fault, Half-volley, Net, Let, Volley, Smash, Service.

Billiards : Break, Cannons, Cue, Pot, Jigger, Scratch, In Bauk, In, Off.

Bridge : Dummy, Finesse, Grand-slam, Little Slam, Revoke, Ruff slam, Trump, Tricks, Vulnerable.

Volley Ball : Booster, Love, Service, Volley, Smasher.

Badminton : Smash, Drop, Let.

Chess : Check, Checkmate, Gambit, State-mate.

Golf : Bogy, Caddie, Hole, Links, Stymie, Tee, Put.

Polo : Chukker, Mallet, Bunder.

Baseball : Bunting, Diamond, Pitcher, Put-out, Strike, Home.

Boxing : Knockout, Punch, Upper-cut, Jab, Hook.

FAMOUS TROPHIES

Agha Khan Cup	Hockey
Beighton Cup	Hockey
Corbillion Cup	World Table Tennis (Women)
Davis Cup	Lawn Tennis
Duleep Trophy	Cricket
Durand Cup	Football
Ezra Cup	Polo
I.F.A. Shield	Football
Irani Cup	Cricket (India)
Jayalaxmi Cup	Table Tennis (Women)
Lady Rattan Tata Trophy	Hockey (Women)
Nehru Cup	Hockey (India)
Obaidullah Cup	Hockey
Ranji Trophy	Cricket (India)
Rangaswamy Cup	Hockey (India)
Rovers Cup	Football (India)
Santosh Trophy	Football (India)
Subroto Cup	Football
Thomas Cup	Badminton
Uber Cup	Badminton (Women)
Wellington Trophy	Rowing (India)

BIGGEST, LARGEST, TALLEST OF THE WORLD

Airport, *Largest*—King Fahd International Airport, Dammon (Saudi Arabia); *Tallest*—Giraffe (Average height 6.09 m); *Largest and Heaviest*—Blue Whale (190 tonnes)

Longest recorded Animal—Boot lace Worm (55 m); *Fastest*—Cheetah (Approximately 100 km/hr)

Bay, *With max. shore line*—Hudson Bay (Canada: 12268 km); *With maximum area*—Bay of Bengal (India: 217 million hc)

Bridge, *Highest*—Sidu River Bridge (China 1627 ft); *Road (longest)*—Gandhi Setu across the river Ganga at Patna (India : 5.5 km); *Railway/Road (longest)*—Seto-Ohashi Bridge (Japan)

Continent, *biggest*—Asia (31,845,872 km^2); *Smallest*—Australia Mainland (Area 76,17,930 km^2)

Dam, *Largest (concrete)*—Grand Coulee Dam (1272 m on Columbia River (Washington State, USA); *Highest*—Jinping-I (305 m)

Desert, *Largest*—Sahara (N. Africa; maximum length 5,150 km EW; maximum width 3,200 km NS)

Dome, *Largest*—Singapore National Stadium (310 m)

Fish, *Largest fresh water*—Plabeuk (China, Laos and Thailand); *Most abundant*—Bristle mouth; *Most venomous*—Stone Fish (Indo-Pacific Waters)

Fountain, *Tallest*—King Fahd's Fountain (Jeddah, Saudi Arabia)

Gulf, *Largest*—Gulf of Mexico (1,544,000 sq. km)

Island, *Biggest*—Greenland (now known as Kalaatdlit Nunaat---2,175,000 sq km)

Lake, *Largest*—Caspian Sea (Azerbaijan, Russia, Iran border: 37.18 lakh km^2); *Deepest*—Baikal (Siberia); *Largest (fresh water)*—Superior Lake (USA---Canada border: 82,350 km^2)

Mountain, *Highest peak*—Mt. Everest (8848 m; Nepal); *Highest range*—Himalayas, Asia (upto 4200 m); *Greatest mountain range*—Himalaya-Karakoram (96 out of 109 peaks over 7315 m are here)

Museum, *Largest*—American Museum of Natural History, New York

Ocean, *Largest and Deepest*—The Pacific (Area: 166,240,000 km^2; Depth: 10,924 m)

Platform, *Longest (rail)*—Gorakhpur (Uttar Pradesh; India, 1355.4 m. long)

Port, *Largest*—Port of New York and New Jersey (USA); *Busiest*—Rotterdam (Netherlands)

Railway Station, *Largest*—Grand Central Terminal (New York City; 19 hc); *Highest*—Condor (Bolivia; 4786 m)

Rivers, *Longest*—(i) Nile (6650 km) (ii) Amazon (6437 km)

Sea, *Largest*—South China Sea (2,974,600 sq. km); *Largest (inland)*—Mediterranean

Star, *Brightest*—Sirius A (also called Dog Star)

Telescope, *Largest (radio)*—Five Hundred meter Apertune Spherical Telescope (FAST), China.; *Largest (solar)*—Kitt Peak National Observatory, (Arizona; USA); *Largest refractor*—At Yerkes observatory (Wisconsin; USA; 18.9 m)

Temple, *Largest*—Angkor Vat (Cambodia: 402 acres)

Train, *Fastest*—Japan's magnetically levitated (magler) train (Speed over 500 km/hr)

Tunnel, *Longest (railway)*—Gotthard Base Rail Tunnel (Switzerland; 57.1 km); *Largest (road)*—Laerdal, Norway (24.51 km)

Volcano, *Greatest concentration in*—Indonesia; *Highest (extinct)*—Cerro Aconcagua (6960 m; Andes);

Zoo, *Largest*—Etosha Reserve (Namibia; area 10 million hc approx.).

FIRST IN INDIA

Governor General of Independent India — Lord Mountbatten

Commander-in-chief of free India — General Roy Bucher

Cosmonaut — Sq. Ldr. Rakesh Sharma

Field Marshal — S.H.F.J. Manekshaw

Indian Governor General of Indian Union — C. Rajagopalachari

Indian I.C.S. Officer — Satyendra Nath Tagore

Indian to swim across English Channel — Mihir Sen

Indian Women to swim across English Channel — Miss Arti Saha

Man to climb Mount Everest — Tenzing Norgay

Man to climb Mount Everest without Oxygen — Phu Dorjee

Man to climb Mount Everest twice — Nwang Gombu

Nobel Prize Winner — Rabindra Nath Tagore

President of Indian National Congress — W.C. Banerjee

President of Indian Republic — Dr. Rajendra Prasad

Talkie Film — Alam Ara (1931)

Test Tube Baby (Documented) — Indira

Viceroy of India — Lord Canning

Woman Minister of Indian Union — Rajkumari Amrit Kaur

Woman Governor — Mrs. Sarojini Naidu

Woman President of Indian National Congress — Dr. Annie Besant

Woman Prime Minister — Mrs. Indira Gandhi

Woman Speaker of a State Assembly — Mrs. Shanno Devi

Prime Minister of India — Pt. Jawaharlal Nehru

Muslim President of Indian Union — Dr. Zakir Hussain

Speaker of Lok Sabha — G.V. Mavlankar

Women to Climb Mount Everest — Bachhendri Pal

Woman Judge in Supreme Court — Mrs. Meera Sahib Fatima Biwi

Women Chief Justice of a High Court — Smt. Leela Seth

The First Indian Weightlifter to Win bronze medal in Olympics — Karnam Malleshwari (Sydney, in 2000)

World Chess Champion — Vishwanathan Anand
India's First Woman Merchant Navy Officer
                        — Sonali Banerjee
The First Woman Air Vice-Marshal
                        — P. Bandopadhyaya
The First Indian to be appointed as
United Nations Civilian Police Advisor
                        — Ms. Kiran Bedi
The First Women to be appointed Deputy
Governor of Reserve Bank of India — K.J. Udeshi
The First Indian Lady to win a medal in
World Athletic Championship
                        — Anju Bobby George
The First Sikh Prime Minister of India
                        — Dr. Manmohan Singh

IMPORTANT DAYS

15th January	—	Army Day
26th January	—	Republic Day
30th January	—	Leprosy Eradication Day/ Martyr's Day
28th February	—	National Science Day
8th march	—	International Women's Day
15th March	—	World Consumer's Day
21st March	—	World Disabled Day
5th April	—	National Marine Day
7th April	—	World Health Day
18th April	—	World Heritage Day
22nd April	—	International Earth Day
Ist May	—	Worker's Day
3rd May	—	International Sun Day
21st May	—	Anti-Terrorism Day
24th May	—	Commonwealth Day
31st May	—	World No Tobacco Day
5th June	—	World Environment Day
21st June	—	World Yoga Day
26th June	—	International Day against Drug Abuse
11th July	—	World Population Day
27th July	—	World Diabetes Day
15th August	—	Independence Day
24th August	—	Sanskrit Day
5th September	—	Teacher's Day
8th September	—	World Literacy Day
29th September	—	World Tourism Day
1st October	—	World Elder's Day
6th October	—	World Animal Day
8th October	—	Air Force Day
10th October	—	National Solidarity Day
16th October	—	World Food Day
24th October	—	U.N. Day
14th November	—	Children's Day
19th November	—	National Integration Day
26th November	—	Law Day
1st December	—	World AIDS Day
4th December	—	Navy Day
7th December	—	Flag Day
10th December	—	Human Rights Day

PARLIAMENTS OF IMPORTANT COUNTRIES

Afghanistan	—	Shora
Britain	—	Parliament House of Commons, House of Lords
Denmark	—	Folketing
The Netherlands	—	States General
India	—	Sansad
Israel	—	Knesset
Iran	—	Majlis
Ireland	—	Airetann
Iceland	—	Althing
Japan	—	Diet
Norway	—	Storting
Russia	—	Supreme Soviet
Spain	—	Cortes
Sweden	—	Riksdag
U.S.A.	—	Congress Senate
Germany	—	Bundestag

MINERAL RESOURCES OF THE WORLD

Mineral	Largest Producers		
Petroleum	Saudi Arabia, USA	Venezuela	Russia
Mica	India	China	U.S.A.
Manganese	Russia	India	Ghana
Silver	Mexico	U.S.A.	Peru
Gold	South Africa	Australia	Canada
Aluminium	USA	Canada	Russia
Iron Ore	China	Russia	U.K.
Coal	China	U.K.	Germany

WORLD'S LARGEST PRODUCERS

Articles	Producers	Articles	Producers
Carpets	Iran	Cheese	USA
Cocoa	Ghana	Coffee	Brazil
Copper	Chile	Cotton	China
Diamonds	Zaire	Jute	India
Rice	China	Rubber	Thailand
Silk	Japan	Steel	China
Sugar	India	Tea	India
Tin	Malaysia	Wheat	China
Wool	Australia		

TEN LARGEST COUNTRIES BY AREAS

Rank by Area	Country	Area (sq. km.)
1.	Russia	17,075,400
2.	Canada	9,976,139
3.	China	9,561,000
4.	U.S.A.	9,363,123
5.	Brazil	8,511,965
6.	Australia	7,686,848
7.	India	3,287,263
8.	Argentina	2,776,889
9.	Kazakhstan	2,724,900
10.	Algeria	2,381,741

PRESIDENT OF INDIA

1. Dr. Rajendra Prasad – Jan. 26, 1950 to May 13, 1962
2. Dr. S. Radhakrishnan – May 13, 1962 to May 13, 1967
3. Dr. Zakir Hussain – May 13, 1967 to May 3, 1969
4. V.V. Giri (Acting) – May 3, 1969 to July 20, 1969
5. Justice M. Hidayatullah (Acting) – July 20, 1969 to Aug. 24, 1969
6. V.V. Giri – Aug. 24, 1969 to Aug. 24, 1974
7. Fakharuddin Ali Ahmad – Aug. 24, 1974 to Feb. 11, 1977
8. B.D. Jatti (Acting) – Feb. 11, 1977 to July 25, 1977
9. Neelam Sanjiva Reddy – July 25, 1977 to July 25, 1982
10. Gyani Zail Singh – July 25, 1982 to July 25, 1987
11. R. Venkatraman – July 25, 1987 to July 25, 1992
12. Dr. Shankar Dayal Sharma – July 25, 1992 to July 25, 1997
13. Dr. K.R. Narayanan – July 25, 1997 to July 25, 2002
14. Dr. A.P.J. Abdul Kalam – July 25, 2002 to July 25, 2007
15. Pratibha Devi Singh Patil – July 25, 2007 to July 25, 2012
16. Pranab Mukherjee – July 25, 2012 to July 25, 2017)
17. Ram Nath Kovind – July 25, 2017 – till date)

VICE-PRESIDENT OF INDIA

1. Dr. S. Radhakrishnan — 1952 - 1962
2. Dr. Zakir Hussain — 1962 - 1967
3. V.V. Giri — 1967 - 1969
4. G.S. Pathak — 1969 - 1974
5. B.D. Jatti — 1974 - 1979
6. Mohamad Hidayatullah — 1979 - 1984
7. R. Venkatraman — 1984 - 1987
8. Dr. S.D. Sharma — 1987 - 1992
9. K.R. Naraynan — 1992 - 1997
10. Krishna Kant — 1997 - 2002
11. Bhairon Singh Shekhawat — 2002 - 2007
12. Md. Hamid Ansari — 2007 - 2017
13. M. Venkaiah Naidu — 2017 - till date

PRIME MINISTERS OF INDIA

No.	Name	Term
1.	Jawaharlal Nehru	Aug. 15, 1947 — May 27, 1964
2.	Guljari Lal Nanda (Acting)	May 27, 1964 — June 9, 1964
3.	Lal Bahadur Shastri	June 9, 1964 — Jan. 11, 1966
4.	Guljari Lal Nanda (Acting)	Jan. 11, 1966 — Jan. 24, 1966
5.	Indira Gandhi	Jan. 24, 1966 — March 24, 1977
6.	Morarji Desai	March 24, 1977 — July 28, 1979
7.	Ch. Charan Singh	July 28, 1979 — Jan. 14, 1980
8.	Indira Gandhi	Jan. 14, 1980 — Oct. 31, 1984
9.	Rajiv Gandhi	Oct. 31, 1984 — Dec. 2, 1989
10.	V.P. Singh	Dec. 2, 1989 — Nov. 9, 1990
11.	Chandra Shekhar	Nov. 10, 1990 — June 21, 1991
12.	P.V. Narsimha Rao	June 21, 1991 — May 15, 1996
13.	A. B. Vajpayee	May 16, 1996 — May 31, 1996
14.	H.D. Deve Gowda	June 1, 1996 — April 20, 1997
15.	I.K. Gujaral	April 21, 1997 — March 19, 1998
16.	A.B. Vajpayee	March 19, 1998 — April 17, 1999
		April 17, 1999 — Oct. 12, 1999 (Caretaker)
17.	A.B. Vajpayee	Oct. 13, 1999 — May 22, 2004
18.	Dr. Manmohan Singh	May 22, 2004 — May 26, 2014
19.	Narendra Modi	May 26, 2014 — till date.

THE SOLAR SYSTEM: SOME FACTS

Number of Planets: 8—Mercury, Venus, Earth, Mars, Jupiter, Saturn, Uranus and Neptune.

Largest most

Massive planet .... Jupiter

Brightest planet .... Venus

Brightest star .... Sirius

Fastest orbiting planet .... Mercury

Longest (Synodic) day .... Mercury

Most moons Jupiter-67

Planet with largest moon .... Jupiter

Greatest average density .... Jupiter

Tallest mountain .... Earth

Strongest magnetic fields .... Jupiter

Most circular orbit .... Venus

Shortest (synodic) day .... Jupiter

Hottest planet .... Venus

No moons .... Mercury, Venus

Planet with moon with most eccentric orbit .... Neptune

Lowest average density .... Saturn

Deepest Oceans .... Jupiter

Greatest amount of liquid on the surface .... Earth

THE EARTH: FACTS AND DATA

Composition of the Earth: Aluminium (0.4%), Sulphur (2.7%), Silicon (13%), Oxygen (28%), Calcium (1.2%), Nickel (2.7%), Magnesium (17%), Iron (35%)

Surface area	: 510100500 sq km	Type of water	: 97% salt, 3% fresh
Land Surface (29.1%)	: 148950800 sq km	Total area of water	: 382672000 sq km
Ocean Surface (70.9%)	: 361149700 sq km	Equatorial diameter	: 12753 km

Equatorial Circumference	: 40066 km	Earth's orbit speed (around sun)	: 107320 kmph
Polar Circumference	: 39992 km	Period of Revolution	
Polar diameter	: 12710 km	(round the sun)	: 365 days 5 hrs
Equatorial radius	: 6376 km		48 min. 45.51
Polar radius	: 6335 km		seconds
Mass (estimated weight)	: 594×10^{19} metric tons	Time of Rotation (on its axis)	: 23 hrs 56 min 4.09 seconds
		Inclination of the axis	
Mean distance from the Sun	: 149407000 km	(to the plane of the ecliptic)	: 23°27'

PRINCIPAL MOUNTAIN PEAKS OF THE WORLD

Mountains	Height in Metres	Range	Date of First Ascent
1. Mount Everest	8,848	Himalayas	May 29, 1953
2. K-2 (Godwin Austen)	8,611	Karakoram	July 31, 1954
3. Kanchenjunga	8,597	Himalayas	May 25, 1955
4. Lhotse	8,511	Himalayas	May 18, 1956
5. Makalu I	8,481	Himalayas	May 15, 1955
6. Dhaulagiri I	8,167	Himalayas	May 13, 1960
7. Mansalu I	8,156	Himalayas	May 9, 1956
8. Chollyo	8,153	Himalayas	Oct. 19, 1954
9. Nanga Parbat	8,124	Himalayas	July 3, 1953
10. Annapurna I	8,091	Himalayas	June 3, 1950
11. Gasherbrum I	8,068	Karakoram	July 5, 1958
12. Broad Peak I	8,047	Karakoram	June 9, 1957
13. Gasherbrum II	8,034	Karakoram	July 7, 1956
14. Shisha Pangma (Gosainthan)	8,014	Himalayas	May 2, 1964
15. Gasherbrum III	7,952	Karakoram	Aug. 11, 1975

POPULAR NICK NAMES OF SOME FAMOUS PERSONALITIES

Andhra Kesari	T. Prakasam	Lal, Bal, Pal	Lala Lajpat Rai, Bal Gangadhar Tilak, Bipin Chandra Pal
Anna	C.N. Anna Durai		
Bang Bandhu	Sheikh Mujibur Rehman	Little Corporal	Napoleon Bonaparte
Bapu	Mahatma Gandhi	Lokmanya	Bal Gangadhar Tilak
Bard of Avon	William Shakespeare	Mahamana	Pt. Madan Mohan Malaviya
Chachaji	Jawaharlal Nehru	Maid of Orleans	Joan of Arc
Desh Bandhu	C.R. Das	Maiden Queen	Queen Elizabeth I
Frontier Gandhi	Khan Abdul Gaffar Khan	Missile Man	A.P.J. Abdul Kalam
Fuhrer	Adolf Hitler	Man of Destiny	Napoleon Bonaparte
G.B.S.	George Bernard Shaw	Netaji	Subhash Chandra Bose
Grand Old Man of India	Dadabhai Naoroji	Nightingale of India	Sarojini Naidu
Grand Old Man of Britain	Gladstone	Panditji	Jawaharlal Nehru
Guru Dev	Rabindra Nath Tagore	Punjab Kesari	Lala Lajpat Rai
Guruji	M.S. Golwalkar	Shastriji	Lal Bahadur Shastri
Iron Man of India	Sardar Patel	Uncle Ho	Ho Chi Minh
Lok Nayak	Jayaprakash Narayan	Wizard of the North	Walter Scott
Lady with the Lamp	Florence Nightingale		

FAMOUS INTERNATIONAL ORGANISATIONS, HEADQUARTERS AND YEAR OF ESTABLISHMENT

International Organisations	Headquarters	Year of Establishment
United Nations Organisations (U.N.O.)	New York	1945
International Monetary Fund (I.M.F.)	Washington	1945
World Health Organisation (W.H.O.)	Geneva	1948
Food & Agricultural Organisation (FAO)	Rome	1943
International Labour Organisation (ILO)	Geneva	1919
UNESCO	Paris	1946
International Court of Justice	The Hague	—
Universal Postal Union (UPU)	Berne	1874
International Civil Aviation Organisation (ICAO)	Montreal	1947
UNIDO	Vienna	1967
International Atomic Energy Agency (IAEA)	Vienna	1957
International Finance Corporation (IFC)	Washington	1956
United Nations Development Programme (UNDP)	New York	—
UNICEF	New York	1946
International Maritime Organisation (IMO)	London	1948
World Meteorological Organisation (WMO)	Geneva	1951
International Telecommunication Union (ITU)	Geneva	1947
Arab League	Tunis	1945
Commonwealth of Nations	London	1931
World Trade Organisation (WTO)	Geneva	1995
International Development Association (IDA)	Washington D.C.	1960
International Bank for Reconstruction and Development (IBRD)	Washington D.C.	1946
World Intellectual Property Organisation (WIPO)	Geneva	1967
Organisation of Islamic Conference (OIC)	Mecca (Saudi Arabia)	1971
European Economic Community (EEC)	Geneva	1957
Red Cross	Geneva	1863
Interpol	Paris	1923
Asian Development Bank (ADB)	Manila	1966
North Atlantic Treaty Organisation (NATO)	Brussels	1949
Association of South East Asian Nations (ASEAN)	Jakarta	1967

BHARAT RATNA AWARD WINNERS

#	Name	Year
1.	Dr. S. Radhakrishnan	1954
2.	C. Rajagopalachari	1954
3.	Dr. C.V. Raman	1954
4.	Dr. Bhagwan Das	1955
5.	Dr. M. Visvesvaraya	1955
6.	Jawaharlal Nehru	1955
7.	Govind Ballabh Pant	1957
8.	Dr. D.K. Karve	1958
9.	Dr. Bidhan Chandra Roy	1961
10.	Purushottam Das Tandon	1961
11.	Dr. Rajendra Prasad	1962
12.	Dr. Zakir Hussain	1963
13.	Dr. Pandurang Vaman Kane	1963
14.	Lal Bahadur Shastri*	1966
15.	Indira Gandhi	1971
16.	V.V. Giri	1975
17.	K. Kamraj*	1976
18.	Mother Teresa	1980
19.	Acharya Vinoba Bhave*	1983
20.	Khan Abdul Ghaffar Khan	1987
21.	M.G. Ramachandran*	1988
22.	Dr. B.R. Ambedkar*	1990
23.	Dr. Nelson R. Mandela	1990
24.	Rajiv Gandhi*	1991
25.	Sardar Vallabhbhai Patel*	1991
26.	Morarji R. Desai	1991
27.	Maulana Abdul Kalam Azad*	1992
28.	Jehangir Ratanji Dadabhai Tata	1992
29.	Satyajit Roy	1992
30.	Gulzari Lal Nanda	1997
31.	Mrs. Aruna Asaf Ali*	1997
32.	Dr. A.P.J. Abdul Kalam	1998
33.	M.S. Subbalakshmi	1998
34.	C. Subramaniam	1998
35.	Jaya Prakash Narayan*	1999
36.	Prof. Amartya Sen	1999
37.	Pt. Ravi Shankar	1999
38.	Gopinath Bardoloi	1999
39.	Lata Mangeshkar	2001
40.	Bismillah Khan	2001
41.	Bhimsen Joshi	2008
**		
42.	C.N.R. Rao	2014
43.	Sachin Tendulkar	2014
44.	Madan Mohan Malaviya	2015
45.	Atal Bihari Vajpayee	2015

* Posthumous   ** The award has not been given from 2002 to 2007 and 2009 to 2012.

ART AND CULTURE

☞ Classical Dances

Dance	State	Famous Artists
Bharat Natyam	Tamil Nadu	Yamini Krishnamurthy, Rukmini Devi Arundale, Swapna Sundari, Sonal Mansingh, Vaijanti Mala, Mrinalini Sarabhai, Chandralekha, Indrani, Ram Gopal, Bal Saraswati
Kathakali	Kerala	Gopinath, K.K. Nayar, Kunju-Kurup, T.K. Chandu
Kuchipudi	Andhra Pradesh/ Telangana	Sapna Sundari, Raja Reddy, Shobha Nayar, Radha Reddy, Vedantam Satyanarayan, Vimpanti Chinna Satyam.
Kathak	North India	Birju Maharaj, Gopi Krishna, Shambhu Maharaj, Sitara Devi, Vishnu Sharma, Durga Lal, Shobhana Narayan
Odissi	Odisha	Kelucharan Mahapatra, Indrani Rehman, Madhavi Mudgal, Pratima Bedi, Samyukta Panigrahi, Sonal Mansingh, Debudas
Manipuri	Manipur	Uday Shankar, Bipin Singh, Suryamukhi, Darohra Jhaveri

☞ Famous Folk Dances

State	Folk Dance	State	Folk Dance
Andhra Pradesh/ Telangana	Dandari, Banjara	Kerala	Mohini Attam, Padayuni
Assam	Bihu, Keli Gopal, Sataria	Madhya Pradesh	Lota Nritya, Jawara
Bihar	Chhau, Magahi, Durga dance	Maharashtra	Tamasha, Dahi Handi, Gof, Deepak Dindi
W. Bengal	Kirtan, Kalatri, Asweabadh, Brita, Kalidance	Manipur	Dhol Cholam
Chhattisgarh	Saila, Karama, Bhagoria	Meghalaya	Nongakarem
Gujarat	Garba, Rasalila, Tippani, Dandia,	Nagaland	Bamboo dance
		Odisha	Chhau, Maya Shabari, Dalachai
Haryana	Damyal, Lahoor	Punjab	Gidda, Bhangra, Panihari
Himachal Pradesh	Dussehra dance, Hikat, Notio	Rajasthan	Thumar, Kathaputali, Tera Tali
		Tamil Nadu	Terukalathu, Kabalatam, Kargam, Pulivesham
Jammu & Kashmir	Dumhal	Tripura	Hazagiri
Jharkhand	Jhau, Ghumakudia, Jadur, Sarhul, Soharai, Karama, Vaima, Loojhari, Jat-Jatin, Vidayat	Uttar Pradesh	Rasalila, Nautanki, Thali, Dhurang, Jhumela, Huraka, Bol.
		Uttarakhand	Kajari, Karan
Karnataka	Yakshagan, Dolu Kunitha	Goa	Dhode Modini

MUSIC

Main Schools of Classical Music

- There are two main schools of classical music, namely, the Hindustani and the Carnatic. The Hindustani school of classical music is in vogue in north-western India, eastern India and northern parts of the South India.

Musical Instruments

- *They are:* Tabla, Mridangam, Pakhawaj, Chandai, Dholak, Veena, Sitar, Sarod, Gootuvadhyam, Sarangi, Flute, Nadaswaram, Shehnai, Shringi and Turahi.

FAMOUS INTERNATIONAL AIR SERVICES

Air Service	Name of Country	Air Service	Name of Country
Air India	India	Lufthansa Airlines	Germany
British Overseas Airways Corporation	Britain	Iraqi Airways	Iraq
		National Airlines	Iran
Trans World Airlines	America	Quantas Airlines	Australia
Russian Airlines	Russia	Hong-Kong Airlines	Hong-Kong
Japan Airlines	Japan	Egypt Airlines	Egypt
Pakistan International Airlines	Pakistan	Slovak Airlines	Slovakia
Malaysia Airlines	Malaysia	S.I.A.	Singapore
Royal Nepal Airlines	Nepal	Garuda Airways	Indonesia
Swiss Airways	Switzerland	Bangladesh Viman Sewa	Bangladesh
Air France	France	Air Lanka	Sri Lanka
Kuwait Airways	Kuwait	Elitalia Airlines	Italy
Pan American World Airways	America	Air Canada	Canada
K.L.M. Royal Airlines	The Netherlands (Holland)		

FAMOUS RELIGIONS, FOUNDERS, HOLY BOOKS & PLACES OF WORSHIP

Religion	Founder	Holy Books	Place of Worship
Hinduism	Hinduism has no one Founder. (This religion is based upon the religion of original Aryan Settlers)	Ramayan, Vedas, Puranas and Geeta	Temple
Sikh	Guru Nanak Dev	Guru Grantha Sahib	Gurdwara
Christianity	Jesus Christ	Bible	Church
Islam	Prophet Mohammed	Koran (Quran)	Mosque
Parsi	Zoroaster	Zend Avesta	Fire Temple
Jainism	Adinath Rishavdev	Jain Granth	Jain Temple
Buddhism	Gautam Buddha	Tripitaka	Buddha Temple
Jew	Moosa	Torah	Synagogue

INTELLIGENCE AGENCIES OF SOME PROMINENT COUNTRIES

Country	Intelligence Agency	Country	Intelligence Agency
India	Research & Analysis Wing (RAW), Intelligence Bureau (I.B.), Central Bureau of Investigation (C.B.I.)	Russia	K.G.B. (Komitel Gosudars-tvennoy Bezopasnosty) (Committee for State Security)
Pakistan	Inter Service Intelligence (I.S.I.)	Canada	Security Intelligence Service
U.S.A.	Central Intelligence Agency, Federal Bureau of Investigation	S. Africa	Bureau of State Security
		Iran	Sabak
Britain	Military Intelligence (M.I.)-5 and 6, Special Branch, Ultra, Joint Intelligence Organisation	Iraq	Al-Mukhabarat
		Australia	Australian Security and Intelligence Organisation
Israel	Mosad	France	S.D.E.C.E.
Egypt	Mukhabarat	Spain	C.E.S.I.D.
Japan	Nicho	Cuba	D.G.I.

SOME PROMINENT RACES OF THE WORLD

Races	Country	Races	Country	Races	Country	Races	Country
Veddas	Sri Lanka	Pygmy	Congo Basin	Eskimo	Canada, Tundra Region	Bushman	Kalahari Desert
Somaid	West Siberia	Bantu	Central and South Africa	Lapps	European Tundra	Red Indian	North America
Masai	East Africa		South Africa				
Muree	New Zealand	Tartars	Siberia				
Yakoot	Russian Tundra	Baddu	Arab's Desert	Hausa	Nigeria		
Papuans	New Guyana	Semang	Malaysia	Kirghiz	Steppes (Russia)		

FAMOUS STRAITS OF THE WORLD

Strait	Between	Country
Malacca Strait	Andaman Sea and South China Sea	Indonesia
Palk Strait	Mannar and Bay of Bengal	India-Sri Lanka
Magellan Strait	Pacific and South Atlantic Ocean	Chile
Dover Strait	English Channel and North Sea	England-France
Berring Strait	Berring Sea and Chukasi Sea	Alaska-Russia
Sugaroo Strait	Japan Sea and Pacific Ocean	Japan
Sunda Strait	Java and Indian Ocean	Indonesia
Gibralter Strait	Mediterranean Sea and Atlantic Ocean	Spain
Harmuj Strait	Persia and Bay of Oman	Oman-Iran
Hudson Strait	Bay of Hudson and Atlantic Ocean	Canada

FAMOUS NEWSPAPERS OF THE WORLD

Newspaper	Place of Publishing	Language	Newspaper	Place of Publishing	Language
Daily News	New York (America)	English	Hindu, Hindustan, Times of India, Tribune, Statesman, Indian Express, Economic Times	India	English
Guardian	London (Britain)	English			
Pravada	Moscow (Russia)	Russian			
Al-Ahram	Cairo (Egypt)	Arabic			
Merdeca	Jakarta (Indonesia)	Indonesian			
Times	London (Britain)	English	Hindustan, Nav Bharat Times, Dainik Bhaskar, Dainik Jagaran, Punjab Kesari	India	Hindi
People's Daily	Beijing (China)	Chinese			
New Statesman	Britain	English			
Daily Mirror	Britain	English			

IMPORTANT BOUNDARY LINES

Boundary Line	Countries	Boundary Line	Countries
Durand Line	Pakistan and Afghanistan	17th Parallel	The line which defined the boundary between North Vietnam and South Vietnam before the two were united.
Hindenberg Line	Germany-Poland		
Maginot Line	France and Germany		
Mannerhein Line	Russia-Finland		
Mc Mahon Line	India-China		
Order Niesse Line	Germany-Poland		
Radcliff Line	India-Pakistan	38th Parallel	North Korea and South Korea
Seigfrid Line	Germany-France		
24th Parallel	India-Pakistan	49th Parallel	U.S.A. and Canada

SIGNALS/SIGNS AND MEANING

Signal/Sign	Meaning	Signal/Sign	Meaning
Red Triangle	Family Planning	White Flag	Treaty or Surrender
Red Cross	Medical Help	Yellow Flag	Vehicles with patients
Red Light	Danger, 'Stop' for the		of contagious diseases
	movement of vehicles	Two Bones across	Danger of electricity
Green Light	Go	with a Skull	
Olive Branch	Peace	Half mast flown Flag	National mourning
White Pigeon or Dove	Peace	Lotus and culture	Sign of civilization
Black Strip on Arm	(i) Opposition	Wheel (Chakra)	Sign of Progress
	(ii) Sorrow	A blind folded	
Black Flag	Opposition	woman with	
Red Flag	(i) Danger	scale in hand	Sign of Justice
	(ii) Revolution	Reversed flown	National calamity flag

NATIONAL EMBLEMS OF IMPORTANT COUNTRIES

Country	National Emblem	Country	National Emblem
America	Golden Rod	New Zealand	Kiwi, Fern Southern Cross
Australia	Kangaroo	Norway	Lion
Ireland	Shamrock	Nepal	Kukri
Italy	White Lily	Pakistan	Crescent
Israel	Candelabrum	Poland	Eagle
Iran	Rose	France	Lily
Canada	White Lily	Belgium	Lion
Great Britain	Rose	Bangladesh	Water Lily
Chile	Candor and Huemul	Mongolia	The Soyombo
Germany	Corn Flower	Russia	Double headed eagle
Japan	Chrysanthemum	Lebanon	Cedar Tree
Zimbabwe	Zimbabwe Bird	Sudan	Secretary Bird
Denmark	Beach	Syria	Eagle
Turkey	Crescent and Star	India	Lioned Capital
The Netherlands	Lion		

THE CONTINENTS OF THE WORLD

Name	Area (In sq. km.)	Population (2017) (In million)	Per cent of the world's population
Asia	4,40,30,000	4,504	59.66
Africa	2,97,85,000	1,256	16.64
Europe	1,04,98,000	742	9.83
North America	2,42,55,000	582	7.71
South America	1,77,98,000	424	5.62
Australia	76,87,120	40.69	0.54
Antarctica	1,33,38,500	NA	NA

COMPUTER

The computer is the system of that electronic device through which various informations are processed on the basis of a definite set of instructions called program and mathematical (numerical) and non-mathematical both types of informations are processed.

The first mechanical computer was composed or fabricated by Blaise Pascal in 1642 and it is called Pascalene. But in 1833, Charles Babbage first time conceived an automatic calculator or computer. Charles Babbage is called the father of modern computer. Herman made an electronic tabulating machine based on punch cards which operates automatically.

In 1937, first mechanical computer mark-I was fabricated by Howard Akeen. The most outstanding contribution in the development of modern computer goes to John Wan Newmaan who brought the 2nd revolution in the area of computer in 1951. He discovered EDVAC (Electronic Discrete Variable Automatic Computer) and utilised the stored program and the binary number system in the computer.

FUNCTIONS OF COMPUTER

1. Collection and composition (input) of datas;
2. Storage of datas.
3. Processing of datas.
4. Retrieval or output of the proccessed informations and datas.

UNITS OF COMPUTER

1. Input unit.
2. Central processing unit–CPU.
3. External Memory unit.
4. Output unit.

The CPU of the computer is called brain of the computer and sometimes CPU is also called Micro Processor of the computer. The data is entered through the input unit in the computer and through the central processing unit with the help of External Memory Unit datas are arranged and processed. Ultimately by the output unit these datas or informations are issued or released.

PARTS OF COMPUTER

- **Monitor :** The monitor of the computer is like a television in which the picture appears in the form of doted points on the screen and these are called pixels.
- **Hard Disc and Floppy Disc :** The Hard Disc is the permanent disc in the computers while the Floppy Disc is the disc utilised when datas or informations are to be transferred from one computer to another.
- **Mouse :** The mouse of the computer is like the remote control of TV through which computer is directly regulated or controlled without utilising the key-board.
- **Printer :** The printer is a device which prints any documents or processed informations of the computer.

SOME HIGH LEVEL LANGUAGES

1. **FORTRAN :** This language was developed for solving the mathematical formulae very quickly and conveniently.
2. **COBOL :** This language was developed for the commerical purposes. For the processing of this language a group of sentences is selected called paragraph and all paragraphs composed are called a section, while all sections composed are called a division.
3. **BASIC :** In basic a definite part of the prescribed instruction is only inserted in the computer.
4. **ALGOL :** This was basically fabricated and designed for the complex algebraic calculations.
5. **PASCAL :** It is an amplified and modified form of ALGOL.
6. **COMAL :** This computer language is used for the students of secondary level.
7. **LOGO :** This language is used for children and kids for drawing Graphic line diagrams.
8. **PROLOG :** This language is developed in 1973 in France and this language is used for Artificial Intelligence which is capable and equivalent to the logical program.

9. FORTH : This language was invented by Charles Mure which is frequently used in all types of the works in the computer.

COMPUTER VIRUS

The computer virus is an electronic code which is used to abolish or erradicate the inclusive informations or programs of the computer. Some important computer viruses are Micheleanjalo, Dork Avangor, kilo, filip, Macmug, Scores, Casecade, Jeruslem, Date crime, Coloumbs crime, Internet virus, Pachcom, Pach EXE, COM-EXE, Marizuana, C-brain, bloody, Chenge Mungu and Desi etc.

COMPUTER NETWORKING

There are two types of networkings which are usually occur—Local Area Networking (LAN) and Wide Area Networking (WAN). By LAN all the computers of the same buildings are connected like the computers of university premises, computers of offices etc.

By WAN all the comptuers of a large area are connected like the computers of all the offices of a city or town etc. In India a very large computer network namely INDONET has been installing through which all the main towns and cities has to be interlinked.

COMPUTER TERMINOLOGY

- **Bit :** The bit is a unit of measurement of the electronic data. One bit is either 0 or 1 but not both. On composing 8 bits, 1 byte is formed.
- **Bug :** The Bug is the error in the computer program or system and its eradication is called Debug.
- **Byte :** Total eight bits compose a byte. Thus 8 bits = 1 byte.
- **CD-ROM :** A CD like of music CD in which data can be stored substantially called CD-ROM. In a CD with comparison to floppy extremely more datas can be stored but one problem in it is that one time recorded data can not be deleted or modified.
- **Chip :** It is a thin slice on which by a special mechanism a circuit is designed which is normally made from Silicon.
- **Memory System :** The place where computer data and program are temporarily kept is called Memory system. Usually memory is implied from RAM.
- **Modem :** The device which converts digital signals into analogue signals and vice-versa is called Modem.

- **RAM :** It is Random Access Memory (a place) where datas to be processed are kept temporarily and it is unstable memory.
- **ROM :** It is Read Only Memory and it is stable or Non-valatile memory which doesn't ended after power off.
- **Scanner :** It is a device through which graphic image is transformed to digital image and the scanners are of usually two types one desktop and another hand operating.

PROGRAMING

Computers perform phenomenal feats of calculation, but they do not do so in a complicated way. They actually carry out very simple operations, such as addition and subtraction. They achieve their fantastic computing power by carrying out these operations at incredible speed.

The programme, or set of instructions for operating the computer, is therefore written as a sequence of very simple steps. (See box below) Several computer languages have been developed for different applications, including BASIC, COBOL, FORTRAN and PASCAL. Writing programmes is very skilled and time-consuming work. But for most typical computer applications ready-written programmes are available, called "packages".

☞ **How A Programme Works**

Without a programme to tell it what to do and how to do it, a computer is unable to function. If, for example, you wanted to know how many times the word 'the' appears in this paragraph, or in the whole book, it would not be enough merely to put the text into a computer and then ask it how many times the word appears. For the computer to accomplish the calculations it has to be told what to do in simple steps. The instructions might be:

1. Scan the text until a space followed by 'T' or 't' is found.
2. If the next letter is not 'h', go back to step 1.
3. If the letter is 'h', is the next letter 'e'?
4. If not, go back to step 1. If it is, go to step 5.
5. If 'e' is followed by a space, add 1 to the total.
6. Go back to step 1.

A full computer programme for this operation would need to be broken down into even more simple steps, but a series of such programmes could enable a computer to analyse any amount of text in great detail.

DEFENCE

The Supreme Command of the Armed Forces is vested in the hands of the President of the Country. The responsibility for national defence, however, rests with the Cabinet. All important questions having a bearing on defence are decided by the Cabinet Committee on Political Affairs, which is presided over by the Prime Minister. The Defence Minister is responsible to Parliament for all matters concerning the Defence Services. All the administrative and operational control of Armed Forces are exercised by the Ministry of Defence. The three services – Army, Navy and Air Force function through their respective service headquarters headed by the chief of Staff.

COMMISSIONED RANKS IN DEFENCE SERVICES

Army	Navy	Air Force
General	Admiral	Air Chief Marshal
Lieutenant-General	Vice-Admiral	Air Marshal
Major-General	Rear-Admiral	Air Vice-Marshal
Brigadier	Commodor	Air Commodor
Colonel	Captain	Group Captain
Lieutenant-Colonel	Commander	Wing Commander
Major	Lt.Commander	Squadron Leader
Captain	Lieutenant	Flight Lieutenant
Lieutenant	Sub-Lieutenant	Flying Officer

INTERNAL SECURITY ORGANISATIONS OF INDIA

S. No	Name of Organisation	Year of Creation	Headquarters
1.	Assam Rifles (A.R.)	1835	Shillong
2.	Central Reserve Police Force (C.R.P.F.)	1939	New Delhi
3.	National Cadet Corps (N.C.C.)	1948	New Delhi
4.	Territorial Army	1948	In different States
5.	Indo-Tibetan Border Police	1962	New Delhi
6.	Home Guard	1962	In different States
7.	Coast Guard	1978	New Delhi
8.	Border Security Force (B.S.F.)	1965	New Delhi
9.	Central Industrial Security Force (C.I.S.F.)	1969	New Delhi
10.	National Security Guard	1984	New Delhi
11.	Police	—	In different States

COMMANDER-IN-CHIEFS OF INDIA

1. General Roy Bucher — Jan. 1, 1948 — Jan. 14, 1949
2. General K. M. Kariappa — Jan. 15, 1949 — Jan. 14, 1953
3. General Maharaj Rajendra Sinhji — Jan. 15, 1953 — March 31, 1955
4. First Marshal of the Indian Air Force Arjan Singh

FIRST CHIEFS OF STAFF OF INDIAN FORCES

1. General Maharaj Rajendra Sinhji (Army Staff) — April 1, 1955 — May 14, 1955
2. Vice Admiral R.D. Katari (Naval Staff) — April 22, 1958 — June 4, 1962
3. Air Marshal Sri Thomas Elmherst (Air Staff) — Aug. 15, 1947 — Feb. 21, 1950

ARMY INSTITUTES

1. Sainik Schools upto +2 Level — 18 places in India
2. Rashtriya Indian Military College (prepare for entrance to N.D.A) — Dehradun
3. National Defence Academy (three services) — Khadakwasla, Pune
4. Indian Military Academy (Army) — Dehradun
5. Officers Training Academy (3 services) Short Courses — Chennai
6. National Defence College — New Delhi
7. The College of Combat — Mhow
8. The College of Military Engineering — Kirkee
9. Military College of Telecommunication Engineering — Mhow
10. The armoured Corps Centre and School — Ahmed Nagar
11. The School Artillery — Deolali
12. The Infantry School — Mhow and Belgaum
13. College of Material Management — Jabalpur

AIR FORCE INSTITUTIONS

Air Force Academy	Hyderabad
Helicopter Training School	Hakimpet
Flying Instructors School	Tambaram, Chennai
The College of Air Warfare	Secunderabad
Air Force Administrative College	Coimbatore
Air Force Technical College	Jalahalli

DEFENCE PRODUCTION UNITS

1. Bharat Dynamites Ltd. — Hyderabad
2. Praga Tools — Hyderabad
3. Mishra Dattu Nigam — Hyderabad
4. Bharat Electronics Ltd. — Bangalore
5. Bharath Earthmovers Ltd. — Bangalore
6. Heavy Vehicles Ltd. — Avadi, Chennai
7. Garden Reach Ship Builders and Engineers Ltd. — Kolkata
8. Mazagaon Dock — Mumbai
9. Goa Shipyard — Marmugao
10. Hindustan Shipyard Ltd. — Vishakhapatnam
11. Hindustan Aeronautics Ltd. — Bangalore, Hyderabad, Nasik, Koraput, Kanpur, Lucknow

☞ Indian Army Commands

Command	HQ Location	Command	HQ Location
Eastern Command	Kolkata	Western Command	Chandigarh
Northern Command	Udhampur	Southern Command	Pune
Central Command	Lucknow	Training Command	Shimla
South-Western Command	Jaipur		

☞ Indian Air Force Commands

Command	HQ Location	Command	HQ Location
Western Air Command	New Delhi	South-Western Air Command	Gandhinagar
Central Air Command	Allahabad	Eastern Air Command	Shillong
Southern Air Command	Thiruvananthapuram	Training Command	Bengaluru

☞ Indian Navy Commands

Command	HQ Location	Command	HQ Location
Eastern Naval Command	Vishakhapatnam	Western Naval Command	Mumbai
Southern Naval Command	Cochin		

☞ Missile and Other Weapons

Name	Class	Range	Name	Class	Range
✱ Agni I	SRBM	850 km	✱ Brahmos	Supersonic Cruise Missile	290 km
✱ Agni II	MRBM	2500 km			
✱ Agni III	IRBM	3500 km-5500 km	✱ Brahmos 2	Hypersonic Cruise Missile	290 km
✱ Agni IV *or* Agni II Prime	IRBM	4000 km			
			✱ Prithvi I	SRBM	150 km
			✱ Prithvi III	SRBM	350 km
✱ Agni V	ICBM	5000 km-6000 km	✱ Sagarika	SLBM	700 km-2200 km
✱ Agni VI	ICBM	8000 km-10000 km	✱ Shaurya	TBM	700 km-2200 km
✱ Agni 3SL	ICBM	5200 km-11600 km	✱ Astra	Air to Air Missile	80 km-100 km
✱ Dhanush	SRBM	350 km			
✱ Nirbhay	Subsonic Cruise Missile	1000 km	✱ Barak-I	SRSAM	12 km
			✱ Barak-8	SRSAM	90 km

MULTIPLE CHOICE QUESTIONS

1. Match List-I with List-II and select the correct answer from the codes given below the lists:
   List-I
   (*a*) Napoleon Bonaparte
   (*b*) Jean Jacques Rousseau
   (*c*) Croce
   (*d*) Madame Roland
   List-II
   1. 'A history is contemporary history'
   2. 'Liberty what crimes are committed in thy name'
   3. 'Man is born free but everywhere he is in chains.'
   4. 'I am the Child of Revolution'
   Codes :

	(a)	(b)	(c)	(d)
A.	1	2	3	4
B.	4	3	1	2
C.	3	4	2	1
D.	3	4	1	2

2. Abraham Lincon was elected the President of United States in:
   A. 1862 B. 1860
   C. 1875 D. 1855

3. Who was known as the 'Prince of Humanists'?
   A. Francisco Petrarch B. Dante
   C. Boccacio D. Erasmus

4. D-Day is the day when:
   A. Germany declared war on Britain
   B. US dropped the atom bomb on Hiroshima.
   C. Allied Troops landed in Normandy
   D. Germany surrendered to the allies

5. Whose teachings inspired the French Revolution?
   A. Locke
   B. Rousseau
   C. Hegel
   D. Plato

6. At a time when empires in Europe were crumbling before the might of Napoleon which one of the following Governor-Generals kept the British flag flying high in India?
   A. Warren Hastings B. Lord Cornwallis
   C. Lord Wellesley D. Lord Hastings

7. Which one of the following statements regarding Fascism in Italy is *not* true?
   A. The Fascists came to power as a result of popular uprising
   B. In 1926, all political parties except Mussolini's party were banned
   C. The Fascists suppressed the Socialist movement
   D. The Fascists were hostile to the Communists

8. The fall of Czar Nicholas-II is known as:
   A. Bloody Sunday
   B. Bolshevik Revolution
   C. February Revolution
   D. October Revolution

9. Industrial Revolution took place first in:
   A. France B. Germany
   C. United Kingdom D. Japan

10. The British Prime Minister at the outbreak of World War II was :
    A. Churchill B. Baldwin
    C. Attlee D. Chemberlain

11. The 'Great Depression' (1929) economic crisis was met by adopting the policy of
    A. Stimulus B. Marshall Plan
    C. New Deal D. Open Door

12. The slogan "No taxation without representation" was raised during the:
    A. American War of Independence
    B. Russian Revolution
    C. French Revolution
    D. Indian Freedom struggle

13. In the nineteenth century the people of Europe started moving from the villages to the cities due to the impact of :
A. Epidemics
B. War
C. Industrialisation
D. Population explosion in villages

14. The important cause of the Civil War in America was:
A. Abolition of slavery
B. Quest for freedom
C. Industrialisation
D. Rebellion by the native Americans

15. Industrial Revolution could not have come about without:
A. Merchant capitalism
B. The Enclosure Movement
C. The services of the proletariat class
D. An agricultural revolution

16. Consider the following statements :
The French Revolution came about mainly due to the :
1. Extreme poverty of the people
2. Impact of the works of great writers
3. Cruelty of the rulers
4. Impact of impulsive reaction
Which of the above statements are correct?
A. 1, 2 and 4   B. 2 and 3
C. 1, 3 and 4   D. 1, 2, 3 and 4

17. Asia's oldest and largest Buddhist monastery is situated in :
A. Tawang (Arunachal Pardesh)
B. Lhasa (Tibet)
C. Trincomallee (Sri Lanka)
D. Ulan Bator (Mongolia)

18. Who was the main architect of the Russian Revolution?
A. Karl Marx   B. Lenin
C. Stalin   D. Tolstoy

19. V.I. Lenin is associated with :
A. Russian Revolution of 1917
B. Chinese Revolution of 1949
C. German Revolution
D. French Revolution of 1789

20. Which one of the following statements is *not* correct?
A. Voltaire believed in Natural Religion
B. Rousseau wrote *Social Contract*
C. Montesquieu authored *The Spirit of Laws*
D. Necker believed in 'General Will'

21. 6th April, 1930 is well known in the history of India because this date is associated with...........
A. Dandi March by Mahatma Gandhi
B. Quit India Movement
C. Partition of Bengal
D. Partition of India

22. Which ruler enforced the system of 'Price Control' in India?
A. Mohammad Tughlak
B. Razia Begum
C. Alauddin Khilji
D. Sher Shah Suri

23. The concept of 'Din-e-Elahi' was founded by which king?
A. Dara Shikoh   B. Akbar
C. Sher Shah Suri   D. Shahjahan

24. Who are supposed to be the earliest inhabitants of India? Where did they come from?
A. Aryans from Central Asia
B. Dravidians from Mediterranean
C. Negroids from Africa
D. Bhils and the Santhals from West Asia

25. The one chief characteristic of temple architecture of the Gupta Age was :
A. Absence of dome
B. Huge size
C. Beautiful carvings
D. absence of a covered courtyard for the gathering of worshippers

26. The Rigveda consists of :
A. 1000 hymns   B. 2028 hymns
C. 1028 hymns   D. 1038 hymns

27. The central point in Ashoka's dharma was :
A. royalty to kings
B. peace and non-violence
C. respect to elders
D. religious tolerance

28. The social evil which was conspicuously absent during ancient India was :
A. *Sati*-System
B. *Devadasi*-System
C. Polygamy
D. *Purdah*-System

29. Which, among the following, can be accepted as a novelty introduced by Mughal emperors to their buildings?
A. Domes
B. Minarets
C. Arches
D. Attached gardens

30. The first ruler of India who defeated Muhammud of Ghur was :
A. Mularaja II of Gujarat
B. Prithviraja Chauhan of Delhi
C. Jayachand of Kannauj
D. Parmaldeva of Bundelkhand

31. What important event happened in India in 1911?
A. Bengal was partitioned
B. Non-Cooperation movement was launched
C. India's capital was shifted from Calcutta to Delhi
D. Mahatma Gandhi presided over the Congress session

32. The first phase of the Congress Party (1885-1905) was characterized by its efforts to secure:
A. limited independence
B. complete freedom
C. Indianization of services
D. constitutional reforms

33. The Muslim League demanded a separate homeland for the Indian Muslims openly for the first time at its annual session held in Lahore in the year :
A. 1931 A.D.
B. 1936 A.D.
C. 1940 A.D.
D. 1941 A.D.

34. Under whose governorship did the East India Company secure the Diwani Rights in Bengal, Bihar and Odisha from Emperor Shah Alam?
A. Lord Cornwallis
B. Lord William Bentinck
C. Lord Clive
D. Lord Wellesley

35. The Simon Commission was generally boycotted by the Indian political parties. What was the reason for this general non-cooperation?
A. the Commission aimed at dividing the people
B. it was an 'all white' Commission
C. it came after the Jallianwala Bagh carnage
D. it was an eye wash

36. Aligarh Muslim University was founded by :
A. Dr. Saifuddin Kitchlu
B. Mohammad Ali Jinnah
C. Sir Syed Ahmed Khan
D. Maulana Mohammad Ali

37. Ibn Batutah was an African traveller visiting India during the time of :
A. Alivardi Khan
B. Ala-ud-din Khalji
C. Iltutmish
D. Mohammad-bin-Tughlaq

38. The battle of Wandiawash was fought in :
A. 1726
B. 1760
C. 1818
D. 1857

39. The abolition of *Sati* by government regulation was at the time of :
A. Warren Hastings
B. Lord Wellesley
C. Lord Bentinck
D. Lord Ahmerst

40. Pick out the wrong combination :
A. Dilwara Temple : Mt. Abu
B. Pashupati Temple : Kathmandu
C. Padmanabh Temple : Bangalore
D. Minakshi Temple : Madurai

41. Match the following:
(a) Chanhudaro
(b) Kalibangan
(c) Lothal
(d) Surkotada
1. Alleged discovery of the skeleton of horse.
2. Bead making.
3. Traces of a dock and ship on seal.
4. Evidence of ploughing the fields.
The Correct code is :

	(a)	*(b)*	*(c)*	*(d)*
A.	2	4	3	1
B.	2	1	3	4
C.	1	2	3	4
D.	2	1	4	3

42. Match the Harappan settlements with the banks of rivers on which they were located :

(a) Harappa	1. Ravi
(b) Mohenjodaro	2. Indus
(c) Ropar	3. Sutlej
(d) Kalibangan	4. Ghaggar
(e) Lothal	5. Bhogava

Codes :

	(a)	(b)	(c)	(d)	(e)
A.	1	2	3	4	5
B.	1	2	3	5	4
C.	2	1	3	5	4
D.	2	1	4	3	5

43. The Goddess 'Kannagi' whose many temples were erected during the 'Sangam Age' was the goddess of :

    A. Chastity   B. Love
    C. Prowess   D. Wisdom

44. The Jain goal of life is to attain deliverance from the fetters of mudane existence, the way to which lies through three jewels. Which one of the following was not included among the 'three jewels' of Jainism?

    A. Right faith   B. Right action
    C. Right knowledge   D. Right conduct

45. The most striking feature of the Ashokan pillar is polish. Name the Ashokan pillar which is considered to be the most graceful of all Ashokan pillars.

    A. Sarnath
    B. Rampurva
    C. Laurya-Nandangarh
    D. Rummindei

46. Which are the correct statements?

1. The land grants, started in Satavahana period, paved the way for feudal developments in India.
2. Silk and spices were the Chief Indian export articles of Indo-Roman trade.
3. The Guptas issued the largest number of gold coins in ancient India.
4. The first memorial of a 'SATI' dated 510 A.D. is found at Eran in Madhya Pradesh.

    A. 1 and 2   B. 1, 3, and 4
    C. 1 and 4   D. 1, 2, 3 and 4

47. Who among the following patronised the 'Gandhara' (Indo-Greek style) School of Art?

    A. Ashoka, the Great
    B. Harsha Vardhana
    C. Kanishka
    D. Chandragupta Vikramaditya

48. The Sultanate of Delhi had five ruling dynasties. The dynasty having longest and shortest period were :

    A. Ilbari and Khalji
    B. Tughlaq and Khalji
    C. Tughlaq and Sayyid
    D. Ilbari and Lodis

49. Which one of the following events took place at the last during reign of Muhammad-bin-Tughlaq?

    A. Introduction of token currency
    B. Increase of land-revenue in Doab
    C. Transfer of Capital from Delhi to Devagiri.
    D. Conquest of Khurasan and Iraq

50. The most learned medieval Muslim ruler who was well versed in various branches of learning including astronomy, mathematics and medicine was :

    A. Jalaluddin Khilji
    B. Sikander Lodi
    C. Ghiyasuddin Tughlaq
    D. Muhammad-bin-Tughlaq

51. The 'Sufis' had 12 silsilas. They propounded the idea of Union with God through:

    A. Love   B. Rituals
    C. Fasts   D. Prayers

52. Match the following:

(a) Peshwa	1. Foreign affairs
(b) Panditrao	2. Audit and accounts
(c) Amatya	3. Providing grants to scholars
(d) Sumant	4. General supervision
	5. Military affairs

Select the correct code :

	(a)	(b)	(c)	(d)
A.	2	3	4	5
B.	4	1	2	3
C.	4	3	2	1
D.	3	1	4	2

53. The Regulating Act of 1773 can be regarded as the first measure to :
A. assert the right of British Parliament to legislate for India
B. separate the legislature from the executive
C. separate the judiciary from the executive
D. centralise law-making

54. What was the exact constitutional status of the Indian Republic on 26th January, 1950?
A. A Democratic Republic
B. A Sovereign, Democratic Republic
C. A Sovereign, Secular, Democratic Republic
D. A Sovereign, Socialist, Secular, Democratic Republic

55. When the British obtained the grant of Diwani of Bengal, Bihar and Odisha they acquired the right to :
A. maintain law and order in these territories
B. administer civil justice and collect revenue in these territories
C. collect revenue and establish revenue administration in these territories
D. militarily defend these territories

56. Which of the following were responsible for the growth of nationalism in India during the British rule?
1. Economic exploitation of India.
2. Impact of western education.
3. Role of the Press.
Select the correct answer using the codes given below :
Codes:
A. 1, 2 and 3   B. 1 and 2
C. 2 and 3   D. 1 and 3

57. Which one of the following nationalist leaders has been described as being radical in politics but conservative on social issues?
A. G.K. Gokhale
B. B.G. Tilak
C. Lala Lajpat Rai
D. Madan Mohan Malviya

58. Provincial Autonomy in British India was envisaged by the :
A. Act of 1909   B. Act of 1919
C. Act of 1935   D. Act of 1947

59. Dyarchy means :
A. double government
B. a government in which the centre is very powerful
C. a government based on division of power between centre and provinces
D. None of the above

60. The Indian National Congress observed 'Independence Day' for the first time on 26th January in :
A. 1920   B. 1925
C. 1930   D. 1947

61. ....is situated near the banks of Sabarmati River
A. Bhavnagar   B. Aurangabad
C. Ahmedabad   D. Rajkot

62. Sericulture is:
A. science of the various kinds of serum
B. artificial rearing of fish
C. art of silkworm breeding
D. study of various cultures of a community

63. The most abundant constituents of earth's crust are:
A. Igneous rocks
B. Sedimentary rocks
C. Metamorphic rocks
D. Granite

64. Indian Standard Time is based on:
A. 80°E longitude   B. 82½°E longitude
C. 110°E longitude   D. 25°E longitude

65. Tides in the oceans are caused by :
A. Gravitational pull of the moon on the earth's surface including sea water
B. Gravitational pull of the sun on the earth's surface only and not on the sea water
C. Gravitational pull of the moon and the sun on the earth's surface including the sea water
D. None of these

66. Nagarjunasagar Project is situated on the river:
A. Tungabhadra
B. Cauvery
C. Krishna
D. Godavari

67. The difference between the Indian Standard Time and the Greenwich Mean Time is:
A. $-3\frac{1}{2}$ hours   B. $+3\frac{1}{2}$ hours
C. $-5\frac{1}{2}$ hours   D. $+5\frac{1}{2}$ hours

68. Which of the following dams is not on Narmada river?
A. Indira-Sagar Project
B. Maheshwar Hydel Power Project
C. Jobat Project
D. Koyna Power Project

69. Which of the following statements is **not true** about the availability of water on the earth, the crisis for which is going to increase in the years to come?
A. About 97.5 per cent of the total volume of water available on the earth is salty
B. 80 per cent of the water available to us for use comes in bursts as monsoons
C. About 2.5 per cent of the total water available on the earth is polluted water and cannot be used for human activities
D. Possibility is that some big glaciers will melt in the coming ten-fifteen years and sea level will rise by 3-4 metres all over the earth

70. Which of the following is **not** a cash crop?
A. Jute   B. Paddy
C. Cashewnut   D. Sugarcane

71. Through which States does Cauvery River flow?
A. Gujarat, M.P., Tamil Nadu
B. Karnataka, Kerala, Tamil Nadu
C. Karnataka, Kerala, Andhra Pradesh
D. M.P., Maharashtra, Tamil Nadu

72. Indian Standard Time is the local time of $82\frac{1}{2}°E$ which passes through :
A. Guntur   B. Delhi
C. Allahabad   D. Kolkata

73. The 17th parallel defines the boundary between:
A. North and South Korea
B. USA and Canada
C. North and South Vietnam
D. China and Russia

74. During the period of south-west monsoon, Tamil Nadu remains dry because:
A. the winds do not reach this area
B. there are no mountains in this area
C. it lies in the rain shadow area
D. the temperature is too high to let the winds cool down

75. Which country does top in producing cocoa?
A. Ghana   B. Brazil
C. Ivory Coast   D. Nigeria

76. The biggest reserves of thorium are in :
A. India   B. China
C. The Soviet Union   D. U.S.A.

77. The Girnar Hills are situated in which of the following states?
A. Gujarat   B. Karnataka
C. Madhya Pradesh   D. Maharashtra

78. During December 22nd the sun is vertically over:
A. Tropic of Cancer
B. Tropic of Capricorn
C. The Equator
D. None of the above

79. Photosphere is described as the :
A. Lower layer of atmosphere
B. Visible surface of the sun from which radiation emanates
C. Wavelength of solar spectrum
D. None of the above

80. Broadly, there are three layers of the earth of the crust, the mantle and the core. The crust forms what percentage of the volume of the earth?
A. 0.5%   B. 2.5%
C. 7.5%   D. 12.5%

81. The grassland of Argentina is known as :
A. Pampas   B. Campos
C. Savanna   D. None of the above

82. Different seasons are formed because :
A. Sun is moving around the earth
B. of revolution of the earth around the Sun on its orbit
C. of rotation of the earth around its axis
D. All of the above

83. Eskers and Drumlins are features formed by:
A. underground water
B. running water
C. the action of wind
D. glacial action

84. Match List-I and List-II and select the correct answer using the codes given below the Lists :

	List-I		**List-II**
	(Rivers)		*(Towns)*
(a)	Ghaghara	1.	Lucknow
(b)	Brahmaputra	2.	Hoshangabad
(c)	Narmada	3.	Ahmedabad
(d)	Sabarmati	4.	Guwahati
		5.	Ayodhya

	(a)	(b)	(c)	(d)
A.	4	5	1	2
B.	5	4	2	3
C.	5	4	3	1
D.	3	5	2	1

85. Which of the statements as regards the consequences of the movement of the earth is not correct?
A. Revolution of the earth is the cause of the change of seasons.
B. Rotation of the earth is the cause of days and nights.
C. Rotation of the earth causes variation in the duration of days and nights.
D. Rotation of the earth effects the movement of winds and ocean currents.

86. The world is divided into :
A. 12 time zones
B. 20 time zones
C. 24 time zones
D. 36 time zones

87. The 'Kiel' canal links the :
A. Pacific and Atlantic Oceans
B. Mediterranean Sea and Red Sea
C. Mediterranean Sea and Black Sea
D. North Sea and Baltic Sea

88. Match the following :

	List-I		**List-II**
(a)	Himadri	1.	Outer Himalayas
(b)	Shivalik	2.	Inner Himalayas
(c)	Himanchal	3.	Middle Himalayas
(d)	Sahyadri	4.	Western Ghats

Codes:

	(a)	(b)	(c)	(d)
A.	1	2	3	4
B.	4	2	3	1
C.	2	1	3	4
D.	1	2	3	4

89. The term 'Regur' refers to:
A. Laterite soils
B. Black Cotton soils
C. Red Soils
D. Deltaic Alluvial Soils

90. Location of sugar industry in India is shifting from north to south because of:
A. cheap labour
B. expanding regional market
C. cheap and abundant supply of power
D. high yield and high sugar content in sugarcane

91. Consider the following statements :
1. Ozone is found mostly in the Stratosphere.
2. Ozone layer lies 55-75 km above the surface of the earth.
3. Ozone absorbs ultraviolet radiation from the Sun.
4. Ozone layer has no significance for life on the earth.

Which of the above statements are correct?
A. 1 and 3   B. 2 and 4
C. 2 and 3   D. 1 and 4

92. Match List-I with List-II and select the correct answer using the codes given below the Lists :

	List-I		**List-II**
	(Crops)		*(Producer)*
(a)	Banana	1.	Colombia
(b)	Cocoa	2.	Ghana
(c)	Coffee	3.	Jamaica
(d)	Tea	4.	Kenya

Codes :

	(a)	(b)	(c)	(d)
A.	2	3	1	4
B.	3	2	1	4
C.	3	2	4	1
D.	2	3	4	1

93. Darjeeling and Dharamsala would be the right places to visit if one wanted to get a clear view respectively of :
    A. Kanchanjunga and Dhauladhar ranges
    B. Nandadevi and Dhauladhar ranges
    C. Kanchanjunga and Nandadevi ranges
    D. Nandadevi and Nanga Parvat

94. Atmosphere exists because:
    A. The Gravitational force of the Earth
    B. Revolution of the Earth
    C. Rotation of the Earth
    D. Weight of the gases of atmosphere

95. Victoria lake is located in the continent:
    A. Africa
    B. Asia
    C. North America
    D. South America

96. The famous Lagoon Lake of India is :
    A. Dal Lake   B. Chilka Lake
    C. Pulicat Lake   D. Mansarover

97. Where are most of the earth's active volcanoes concentrated?
    A. Indian Ocean   B. Pacific Ocean
    C. Aral Sea   D. Atlantic Ocean

98. Through which of the following states does the river Chambal flow?
    A. U.P., M.P., Rajasthan
    B. M.P., Gujarat, U.P.
    C. Rajasthan, M.P., Bihar
    D. Gujarat, M.P., U.P.

99. Which country is called the sugar bowl of the world?
    A. Cuba   B. India
    C. Argentina   D. USA

100. The area covered by forest in India is about:
    A. 46%   B. 33%
    C. 23%   D. 21%

101. A closed economy is the one which :
    A. does not permit emigration or immigration
    B. permits emigration but no immigration
    C. engages in no foreign trade
    D. engages in no foreign and domestic trade or transit

102. In a developed economy the major share of employment originates in the :
    A. primary sector   B. tertiary sector
    C. secondary sector   D. any of the above

103. The Economic and Social Commission for Asia and Pacific (ESCAP) is located at :
    A. Bangkok   B. Kuala Lumpur
    C. Manila   D. Singapore

104. Commercial vehicles are not produced by which of the following companies in India?
    A. TELCO   B. Ashok Leyland
    C. DCM Daewoo   D. Birla Yamaha

105. In India, the Public Sector is most dominant in:
    A. transport
    B. steel production
    C. commercial banking
    D. organised term-lending financial institutions

106. The main argument advanced in favour of small scale and cottage industries in India is that:
    A. cost of production is low
    B. they require small capital investment
    C. they advance the goal of equitable distribution of wealth
    D. they generate a large volume of employment

107. The most serious economic problems of India are:
    A. Poverty and unemployment
    B. Stagnation, not poverty
    C. Unemployment, not poverty
    D. Underdevelopment, not poverty

108. Which of the following is not one of the three central problems of an economy?
    A. What to produce
    B. How to produce
    C. When to produce
    D. For whom to produce

109. If saving exceeds investment, the national income will:
    A. fall   B. rise
    C. fluctuate   D. remain constant

110. In which of the following industries in India are the maximum number of workers employed?
A. Sugar
B. Jute
C. Textiles
D. Iron and Steel

111. Terrace Cultivation is practiced mostly:
A. in urban areas
B. on slopes of mountains
C. on tops of hills
D. in undulating tracts

112. Which of the following is a Selective Credit Control method?
A. Bank Rate
B. RBI directives
C. Cash Reserve Ratio
D. Open market operations

113. Which of the following taxes is not shared by the Central Government with the States?
A. Union excise duties
B. Customs duty
C. Income tax
D. Estate duty

114. ICICI is the name of a:
A. Financial Institution
B. Chemical Industry
C. Cotton Industry
D. Chamber of Commerce and Industry

115. Structural Unemployment arises due to
A. Deflationary conditions
B. Heavy industry bias
C. Shortage of raw material
D. Inadequate productive capacity

116. Which of the following is the largest single source of the government's earning from tax revenue?
A. Excise duties
B. Customs duties
C. Corporation tax
D. Income tax

117. The largest public sector bank in India is:
A. Central Bank of India
B. Punjab National Bank
C. State Bank of India
D. Indian Overseas Bank

118. Which of the following statements best explains the term contraband goods?
A. Goods produced only for exports
B. Goods produced in joint sector only
C. Goods for the trading of which licence is not required
D. Goods that are forbidden, from export, import or even possession, by law

119. Price in the market is fixed by:
A. Stock exchange rates
B. The demand and supply ruling in the market at a particular time
C. The Finance Minister
D. None of the above

120. Devaluation of currency helps to promote:
A. National Income
B. Savings
C. Imports at lower cost
D. Exports

121. Balanced economic growth can be achieved only if:
A. All the sectors of economy grow at the same rate
B. Population growth is arrested
C. All the inter dependent sectors grow in harmony
D. Basic and heavy industries are assigned highest priority

122. Which one of the following contributes most to the National Income in India?
A. Agricultural Sector
B. Industrial Sector
C. Foreign Trade Sector
D. Tertiary Sector

123. 'MODVAT' stands for:
A. Ad Valorem tax on output
B. Deduction of cost of inputs from the value of output
C. Reduction in import duties
D. Imposition of tax on professions

124. Largest revenue in India is obtained from:
A. Excise duties
B. Corporation tax
C. Income tax
D. None of the above

125. The term 'devaluation' means:
A. Reducing the value of a currency in terms of another currency
B. Increasing the value of a currency
C. Revising the value of a currency
D. None of the above

126. Per capita net availability of pulses has shown a tendency of:
A. Increase over time
B. Decrease over time
C. Constant over time
D. First increase then decrease

127. National Income is the same as:
A. Net national product at market price
B. Net domestic product at market price
C. Net national product at factor cost
D. Net domestic product at factor cost

128. Which one of the following is not an example of indirect tax?
A. Sales tax   B. Excise duty
C. Customs duty   D. Expenditure tax

129. The major aim of devaluation is to:
A. encourage imports
B. encourage exports
C. encourage both exports and imports
D. discourage both exports and imports

130. Structural unemployment arises due to:
A. deflationary conditions
B. heavy industry bias
C. shortage of raw materials
D. inadequate productive capacity

131. When was the Family Planning Programme officially started in India?
A. 1950   B. 1952
C. 1956   D. 1962

132. When was the Reserve Bank of India nationalised?
A. 1947   B. 1949
C. 1950   D. 1951

133. Which of the following is *not* a feature of the Indian economy?
A. High rate of population growth
B. Disguised unemployment
C. Lowest rate of adult literacy
D. High rate of exports

134. The 'Relative Deprivation' approach for measuring poverty has been adopted by:
A. developing countries
B. developed countries
C. under-developed countries
D. None of the above

135. One of the main factors that led to rapid expansion of Indian exports is:
A. Imposition of import duties
B. Liberalisation of the economy
C. Recession in other countries
D. Diversification of exports

136. Sustainable economic development means an increase in the rate of growth of real:
A. total and per capita product
B. total and per capita product and level of literacy rate
C. total and per capita product and life expectancy at birth
D. total and per capita product, taking into account the cost of degradation of the quality of environment in this process

137. Functional unemployment occurs when:
A. unemployed have no qualification for job
B. people frequently change their job
C. people were thrown out from job due to recession
D. None of these

138. Which among the following does **not** have a 'free trade zone'?
A. Kandla   B. Mumbai
C. Visakhapatnam   D. Thiruvanantpuram

139. Sun Belt of USA is important for which one of the following industries?
A. Cotton textile
B. Petrochemicals
C. Hi-tech electronics
D. Food Processing

140. Commercial banking system in India is
A. unit banking   B. branch banking
C. mixed banking   D. None of the above

141. Who gives recognition to political parties in India?
A. Parliament

B. President
C. Supreme Court
D. Election Commission

142. The Quorum of the Legislative Council is :
A. one-fourth of its total membership
B. one-third of its membership
C. one-tenth of its membership
D. 25

143. The Indian Constitution is:
A. federal
B. unitary
C. a happy mixture of the federal and unitary
D. federal in normal times and unitary in times of emergency

144. Universal adult franchise implies a right to vote to all:
A. adult residents of the State
B. adult male citizens of the State
C. residents of the State
D. adult citizens of the State

145. When a resolution prefering a charge against the President has been passed by a specified majority in the House, it is sent to the other House for investigation. If, as a result of such an investigation, a resolution is passed through a specified majority by the other House, declaring that the charge has been sustained, the President shall leave his office. The specified special majority must not be less than :
A. two-third of the members present and voting
B. one-third of the members present and voting
C. three-fourth of the members present and voting and two-third of the total membership
D. two-third of the total membership

146. Which one of the following judicial powers of the President of India has been *wrongly* listed?
A. he appoints the Chief Justice and other judges of the Supreme Court
B. he can remove the judges of the Supreme Court on grounds of misconduct

C. he can consult the Supreme Court on any question of law or fact which is of public importance
D. he can grant pardon, reprieves and respites to persons punished under Union Law

147. The Vice-president of India can be removed from his office before the expiry of his term if :
A. the Rajya Sabha passes a resolution by a majority of its members and the Lok Sabha agrees with the resolution
B. if the Supreme Court of India recommends his removal
C. the President so desires
D. None of the above

148. The Chief Justice of a High Court in India is appointed by the :
A. Governor of the State
B. Prime Minister of India
C. Chief Justice of the Supreme Court
D. President of India

149. Which of the following statements is constitutionally not true about the passing of the Union Budgets, Railway Budgets and Finance Bill in India?
1. Under the law, Finance Bill should be adopted by both the Houses of the Parliament within 45 days of its introduction.
2. If the Finance Bill is not adopted within specified period, the government loses its authority to levy the taxes proposed in the budgets.
3. In the absence of full budget, a vote-on-account gives the power to the government to spend.
4. Government cannot raise revenues without a proper approval of the Finance Bill
A. Only 2   B. Only 3
C. Only 4   D. Only 1, 2 and 3

150. Normally, on whose advice the President's Rule is imposed in a State?
A. Chief Minister
B. Legislative Assembly
C. Governor
D. Chief Justice of High Court

151. Which Article of the Indian Constitution deals with Amendment procedure?
A. Article 368   B. Article 358
C. Article 367   D. All of these

152. Government is the agency through which the will of :
A. the state is expressed
B. the people is expressed
C. the head of the state is expressed
D. the majority is expressed

153. In a unitary system of government :
A. The centre is all powerful
B. The centre is weaker than the states
C. The centre and states stand at par
D. The states and centre are supreme in their respective spheres

154. In Cabinet System of Government the real executive authority rests with :
A. The Council of Ministers
B. The Prime Minister
C. The Constitution
D. The Parliament

155. The Head of the State under a parliamentary government:
A. is an elected representative
B. is a hereditary person
C. is a nominated person
D. may be any one of the above

156. In the event of a ministerial proposal being defeated on the floor of the legislature, under the parliamentary system :
A. the government waits for a general no-confidence motion
B. the minister concerned is taken to task by the Prime Minister
C. the minister is forced to resign
D. the whole Council of Ministers resign

157. The "due process of law" is an essential characteristic of the judicial system of:
A. UK   B. France
C. USA   D. India

158. Under the Constitution it is :
A. obligatory for the President to accept the advice of the Council of Ministers but is not obliged to follow it
B. obligatory for the President to accept the advice of the Council of Ministers
C. not obligatory for the President to seek or accept the advice of the Council of Ministers
D. obligatory for the President to seek the advice of the Council of Ministers if his own party is in power

159. Which one of the following statements is correct?
A. the Presiding Officer of Rajya Sabha is elected every year
B. the Presiding Officer of Rajya Sabha is elected for a term of two years at a time
C. the Presiding Officer of Rajya Sabha is elected for a term of six years
D. the Vice-President of India is the ex-officio Presiding Officer of Rajya Sabha

160. The introduction of "no confidence" motion in the Lok Sabha requires the support of at least:
A. 50 members   B. 70 members
C. 60 members   D. 80 members

161. The High Court comes under :
A. State List   B. Union List
C. Concurrent List   D. None of the above

162. Which one of the following has been wrongly listed as a Fundamental Duty of the Indian citizens?
A. to develop scientific temper, humanism and spirit of inquiry and reform
B. to work for raising the prestige of the country in the international sphere
C. to protect and improve the natural environment
D. to strive towards excellence in all spheres of individual and collective activity

163. Which one of the following is not a Fundamental Duty as outlined in Article 51A of the Constitution?
A. to abide by the Constitution and respect its ideals
B. to defend the country and render national service when called upon to do so

C. to work for the moral upliftment of the weaker sections of society
D. to preserve the rich heritage

164. The main characteristics of the Directive Principles of State Policy given in the Indian Constitution are :
A. not enforceable by any court
B. fundamental in the governance of the country
C. 'Like instruments, instructions, political manifesto and a code of moral precepts which have to guide governors of the country'
D. no law can be passed, which is opposed to these principles

165. Of the following which are true?
A. In a State, the Legislative Council is dominant with regard to non-financial bills and the Legislative Assembly with regard to financial (money) bills
B. Vidhan Parishad can virtually block legisla-tion even if the same is passed by the Vidhan Sabha
C. In case of a tie between the two Houses, the Governor is duty-bound to call a joint session of the two Houses to have the issue settled on a majority verdict
D. If a Bill is twice approved by the Vidhan Sabha, it becomes law even if rejected by the Vidhan Parishad

166. Which one of the following types of emergency can be declared by the President?
A. Emergency due to threat of war and external aggresion
B. Emergency due to break-down of constitutional machinery in a State
C. Financial emergency on account of threat to the financial credit of India
D. all the three emergencies

167. The chairman of which of the following parliamentary committees is invariably from the members of ruling party?
A. Committee on public undertakings
B. Public accounts committee
C. Estimates committee
D. Committee on delegated legislation

168. Which of the following is not a formally prescribed device available to the members of parliament?
A. Question hour
B. Zero hour
C. Half-an-hour discussion
D. Short duration discussion

169. Which of the following is not a tool of executive control over public administration?
A. Power of appointment and removal
B. Line agencies
C. Appeal to public opinion
D. Civil services code

170. If the Speaker of the State Legislative Assembly decides to resign, he should submit his resignation to the:
A. Judges of the High Court
B. Deputy Speaker
C. Chief Minister
D. Finance Minister

171. The Constitution of India provides for the nomination of two members of Lok Sabha by the President to represent:
A. the Parsis
B. men of eminence
C. the business community
D. the Anglo-Indian community

172. India is a Federal State because of:
A. dual judiciary
B. dual citizenship prevalent here
C. share of power between the Centre and the States
D. rigid Constitution

173. Residuary Subjects are those subjects which are:
A. contained in the State list
B. contained in the Union list
C. contained in the Concurrent list
D. not covered by any of the three lists

174. Which of the following writs can be issued, by the Supreme Court, to enforce Fundamental Rights?
A. Writ of Habeas Corpus
B. Writ of Mandamus
C. Writ of Quo Warranto
D. All of these

175. When the offices of both the President and the Vice-President of India are vacant, who will discharge their functions?
A. Prime Minister
B. Home Minister
C. Chief Justice of India
D. The Speaker

176. The Supreme Court tenders advice to the President of India on a matter of law or fact:
A. on its own
B. only when such advice is sought
C. only if the matter relates to some basic issue
D. only if the issue poses a threat to the unity and integrity of the country

177. Six months shall **not** intervene between two sessions of the Indian Parliament because :
A. it is the customary practice
B. it is the British convention followed in India
C. it is an obligation under the Constitution of India
D. None of the above

178. The States of the Indian Union can be recognised or their boundaries altered by:
A. the Union Parliament by a simple majority in the ordinary process of legislation
B. two-thirds majority of both the Houses of Parliament
C. two-thirds majority of both the Houses of Parliament and the consent of the legislatures of concerned States
D. an executive order of the Union government with the consent of the concerned State governments

179. The Basic Feature theory of the Constitution of India was propounded by the Supreme Court in the case of :
A. Minerva Mills Vs. Union of India
B. Golaknath Vs. State of Punjab
C. Maneka Gandhi Vs. Union of India
D. Keshavananda Vs. State of Kerala

180. Which one of the following writs is issued by a court in case of illegal detention of a person?
A. Habeas corpus   B. Mandamus
C. Certiorari   D. Quo-warranto

181. Name the instrument with the help of which a sailor in a submarine can see the objects on the surface of the sea.
A. Telescope   B. Periscope
C. Gycroscope   D. Stereoscope

182. 'HEMOPHILLIA' is the disease of ....
A. liver   B. blood
C. brain   D. bones

183. Vitamin A is abundantly found in ....
A. Brinjal   B. Tomato
C. Carrot   D. Cabbage

184. .... is not soluble in water.
A. Vitamin A   B. Vitamin B
C. Vitamin C   D. None of these

185. The blood vessels with the smallest diameter are called ....
A. capillaries   B. arterioles
C. venules   D. lymphatics

186. Out of the following .... has the greatest elasticity.
A. steel   B. rubber
C. aluminium   D. annealed copper

187. Cooking gas is a mixture of which of the following two gases?
A. Carbon Dioxide and Oxygen
B. Butane and Propane
C. Carbon Monoxide and Carbon Dioxide
D. Methane and Ethylene

188. The substance most commonly used as a food preservative is:
A. sodium carbonate B. tartaric acid
C. acetic acid   D. benzoic acid

189. Normally, the substances that fight against diseases in human systems are known as:
A. dioxyribonucleic acids
B. carbohydrates
C. enzymes
D. antibodies

190. The SI unit of temperature is ....
A. Kelvin   B. Celsius
C. Fahrenheit   D. None of the above

191. One of the common fungal diseases of man is :
A. plague   B. ringworm
C. cholera   D. typhoid

192. A clear sky is blue because:
A. red light is scattered more than blue
B. ultraviolet light has been absorbed
C. blue light is scattered more than red
D. blue light has been absorbed

193. Jenner introduced the method of making people immune to :
A. small pox   B. rabies
C. cholera   D. polio

194. The largest cell in the human body is :
A. Nerve cell   B. Live cell
C. Muscle cell   D. Kidney cell

195. What is the device that steps up or steps down the voltage?
A. Dynamo   B. Conductor
C. Inductor   D. Transformer

196. The protein deficiency disease is known as :
A. Kwashiorker   B. Cirrhosis
C. Eczema   D. Clycoses

197. Iron deficiency causes :
A. rickets   B. anaemia
C. cirrhosis   D. goitre

198. Blood group of an individual is controlled by :
A. Haemoglobin   B. Shape of RBC
C. Shape of WBC   D. Genes

199. In a normal man the amount of blood pumped out by the heart per minute is about :
A. 1 litre   B. 3 litres
C. 4 litres   D. 5 litres

200. Red/green colour blindness in man is known as :
A. Protanopia
B. Deutetanopia
C. Both A and B above
D. Marfan's syndrome

201. The blue colour of the water in the sea is due to :
A. Reflection of the blue light by the impurities in sea water
B. Reflection of the blue sky by sea water and scattering of blue light by water molecules
C. Absorption of other colours by water molecules
D. None of the above

202. The image formed on the retina of the eye is:
A. upright and real
B. larger than the object
C. small and inverted
D. enlarged and real

203. Unit of loudness of sound is:
A. bel   B. decibel
C. phon   D. none of these

204. Oil rises up the wick in a lamp :
A. because oil is volatile
B. due to the capillary action phenomenon
C. due to the surface tension phenomenon
D. because oil is very light

205. The 'stones' formed in human kidney consist mostly of :
A. calcium oxalate
B. sodium acetate
C. magnesium sulphate
D. calcium

206. We hear the sound later, while the light is seen earlier:
A. because light's speed is more than that of sound
B. because lights travel in a straight direction while sound in a zigzag direction
C. because sound's frequency is lower than light
D. All of the above

207. Which part of an eye is transplanted?
A. Cornea   B. Retina
C. Iris   D. Sciera

208. The Universal donor group of blood is:
A. O   B. A
C. B   D. AB

209. The green colour of the leaf is due to :
A. Presence of Chloroplast
B. Presence of Chromium
C. Presence of Nicoplast
D. Presence of excess of oxygen

210. Voice of a child is more shrill than that of an elderly person because:
A. the pitch of the child's voice is higher than that of the person
B. the pitch is lower
C. the child is more energetic
D. None of the above

ANSWERS

1	2	3	4	5	6	7	8	9	10
B	C	D	C	B	C	A	C	C	D

11	12	13	14	15	16	17	18	19	20
C	A	C	A	A	D	A	B	A	D

21	22	23	24	25	26	27	28	29	30
A	C	B	C	D	C	B	D	D	B

31	32	33	34	35	36	37	38	39	40
C	D	C	C	B	C	D	B	C	C

41	42	43	44	45	46	47	48	49	50
A	A	A	B	C	D	C	B	B	D

51	52	53	54	55	56	57	58	59	60
A	C	A	B	B	A	B	C	A	C

61	62	63	64	65	66	67	68	69	70
C	C	B	B	C	C	D	D	D	B

71	72	73	74	75	76	77	78	79	80
B	C	C	C	A	A	A	B	B	A

81	82	83	84	85	86	87	88	89	90
A	B	D	B	C	C	D	C	B	D

91	92	93	94	95	96	97	98	99	100
A	B	A	A	A	B	B	A	A	D

101	102	103	104	105	106	107	108	109	110
C	B	A	D	D	D	A	C	D	C

111	112	113	114	115	116	117	118	119	120
B	B	B	A	D	A	C	D	B	D

121	122	123	124	125	126	127	128	129	130
C	A	A	B	A	D	C	D	B	D

131	132	133	134	135	136	137	138	139	140
B	B	D	A	B	D	B	D	D	C

141	142	143	144	145	146	147	148	149	150
D	C	D	D	D	B	A	D	C	C

151	152	153	154	155	156	157	158	159	160
A	B	A	A	A	D	C	B	D	A

161	162	163	164	165	166	167	168	169	170
B	B	C	B	D	D	C	B	B	B

171	172	173	174	175	176	177	178	179	180
D	C	D	D	C	B	C	A	D	A

181	182	183	184	185	186	187	188	189	190
B	B	C	A	A	A	B	D	D	A

191	192	193	194	195	196	197	198	199	200
B	C	A	A	D	A	B	D	D	A

201	202	203	204	205	206	207	208	209	210
B	B	B	B	A	A	A	A	A	A

1802